2008 EDITION

The NATIONAL CONSUMER LAW CENTER

GUIDE TO

SURVIVING DEBT

2008 EDITION

The NATIONAL CONSUMER LAW CENTER

GUIDE TO

SURVIVING DEBT

From

THE NATIONAL CONSUMER LAW CENTER

America's Consumer Law Experts

Principal Author

Deanne Loonin

For reprint permissions or ordering information, contact
Publications, NCLC, 77 Summer Street, 10th Floor, Boston MA 02110,
(617) 542-9595, Fax (617) 542-8028, E-mail: publications@nclc.org

Library of Congress Control No. 2008920742
ISBN-13: 978-1-60248-027-8
ISBN-10: 1-60248-027-3

This project was originally supported by AT&T Universal Card Services
Partners in Credit Education, the Public Welfare Foundation,
the National Consumer Law Center, the AFL-CIO,
the United Auto Workers, and others.

10 9 8 7 6 5 4 3 2 1

This book is intended to provide accurate and authoritative information in regard to the subject matter covered. This book cannot substitute for the independent judgment and skills of a competent attorney or other professional. Non-attorneys are cautioned against using these materials in conducting litigation without advice or assistance from an attorney or other professional. Non-attorneys are also cautioned against engaging in conduct which might be considered the unauthorized practice of law.

Printed in Canada
Cover design and illustration by Lightbourne, copyright © 2008.

CONTENTS

Contents

About the Author

The National Consumer Law Center (NCLC) is the nation's expert on the rights of consumer borrowers. Since 1969, NCLC has been at the forefront in representing low income consumers before the courts, government agencies, Congress, and state legislatures.

NCLC has appeared before the United States Supreme Court and numerous federal and state courts and has successfully presented many of the most important cases affecting consumer borrowers. NCLC provides consultation and assistance to legal services, private, and government attorneys in all fifty states.

NCLC publishes a nationally acclaimed series of manuals on all major aspects of consumer credit and sales. (See Bibliography for a complete list of NCLC publications.) NCLC also conducts state and national training sessions on the rights of consumer borrowers for attorneys, paralegals, and other counselors.

This book draws on the expertise of numerous present and former NCLC attorneys, each averaging about twenty years of consumer law specialization. Deanne Loonin is the principal author for this edition. John Rao and Deanne Loonin were the principal authors of the 2005 and 2006 editions. Gary Klein was a principal author for 1996, 1999, and 2002 editions; Jon Sheldon was the principal author of the 1992 edition; and Odette Williamson was a principal author of the 2002 edition.

Deanne Loonin is a staff attorney at National Consumer Law Center, focusing on consumer credit issues as well as student loan, credit counseling and credit discrimination issues. Ms. Loonin previously worked at Bet Tzedek Legal Services in Los Angeles.

Acknowledgments

The *NCLC Guide to Surviving Debt* is the culmination of years of work and numerous contributions from experts in the field. Along the way we have received generous support form the AFL-CIO, the United Auto Workers, the Public Welfare Foundation, various church groups, and particularly NCEE/ AT&T Consumer Credit Education Fund. The views in this book are NCLC's and should not be construed as those of any other entity contributing to the development of the *NCLC Guide to Surviving Debt.*

Numerous individuals contributed to the writing and final production of this volume and prior editions. Although Deanne Loonin was the principal author of this edition, the volume is truly a collaborative effort by NCLC staff. NCLC staff and consultants contributing to this edition include: Carolyn Carter, Elizabeth De Armond, Charlie Harak, John Rao, Elizabeth Renuart, Jon Sheldon, Geoff Walsh, and Chi Chi Wu. Thanks also to Christina Cook.

Special thanks to Gary Klein, whose authorship of the 1996, 1999, and 2002 editions and extensive advice on the 1992 edition are central to this volume. Thanks also to Jon Sheldon for authoring the 1992 edition, Odette Williamson for co-authoring the 2002 edition, and John Rao for co-authoring the 2005 and 2006 editions. We would like to thank current and former NCLC attorneys and other experts in the field for their assistance in this project through five prior editions: Nancy Brockway, Mark Budnitz, Carolyn Carter, Roger Colton, Elizabeth De Armond, Charles Delbaum, Richard Du Bois, Charlie Harak, Deborah Harris, Robert Hobbs, Elizabeth Imholz, Kathleen Keest, Richard McManus, Willard Ogburn, Jerry Oppenheim, Rita Gordon Pereira, John Rao, Susan Reif, Elizabeth Renuart, Elizabeth Ryan, Margot Saunders, Henry Sommer, Olivia Wein, Odette Williamson, and Chi Chi Wu.

Special thanks to Denise Lisio for editing the book, helpful recommendations, production work, and extraordinary patience with the authors; to Katherine Hunt and Nathan Day for providing editorial and production assistance; to Shirlron Williams for providing editorial assistance; and to Mary McLean for indexing this edition. Julie Gallagher designed and typeset this edition; Donna Wong provided advice on style; and Lightbourne designed the cover.

Introduction:
How to Use This Book

GETTING STARTED

If you are having debt problems, you may feel overwhelmed and powerless. During periods of financial hardship, you may not have the resources to pay pressing debts, to meet family needs, and to get legal help. You may feel helpless to fight debt collectors pressing you for payment or threatening to seize your home, car, or other possessions.

In writing this book, we hope to help you make the best choices possible despite difficult financial circumstances. We will help you decide whether there are debts you can ignore for a period of time while you get back on your feet. When you cannot ignore a particular debt without serious consequences, this book sets out helpful options to deal with these problems, both in the short term and the long run.

This book also explains your *rights as a consumer.* Many federal and state laws are designed to help people facing financial problems. These include protections against abusive debt collectors, relief from unfair business practices, limits on wage garnishments and seizures of property, and the right to eliminate many obligations in bankruptcy. This book attempts both to explain these rights and to tell you when and how to use them.

HOW THIS BOOK IS ORGANIZED

The process of dealing with financial problems is mostly about making the best available choices. This book is organized into seven parts, each part dealing with different types of choices you may face. Each part of the book is further divided into chapters which cover more specific issues.

Part I (Understanding Your Options, Chapters 1–3) covers the different choices you will face when you cannot keep current on your debts. Chapters One and Two help you evaluate your budget and choose which debts to pay first. The goal is to put you in a position to deal with your most pressing problems first and to have as much money as possible available to meet those needs. Chapter Three will help you understand your credit report. Reviewing your credit report is a very useful strategy to find out more about your overall financial situation. You will also learn about the main factors that affect your credit report and credit score and what, if anything, you can do about it.

Part II (Making Sensible Choices, Chapters 4–7) focuses on strategies, both good and bad, to repay debts. Chapter Four provides information about whether you are likely to benefit from credit counseling services and if so, how to find a good credit counseling agency. This chapter also discusses certain "debt relief" companies that are likely to cause you greater problems. Examples of the services they might offer include debt settlement and debt termination. Chapter Five offers advice about credit cards and understanding your credit card rights. Chapters Six and Seven first warn you about a number of choices you may be tempted to make that are likely to make your financial problems even worse. These chapters also review strategies that are more likely to be helpful, such as selling off assets in some circumstances or borrowing money at reasonable rates. Chapter Six focuses on home equity and home refinancing loans while Chapter Seven covers a number of different strategies to raise money that do not involve borrowing against your home.

Part III (Debt Collection and Collection Lawsuits, Chapters 8–9) are very important chapters to help you understand the possible consequences when you cannot pay back your unsecured debts. Chapter Eight focuses on strategies for responding to debt collectors who are pressuring you to pay your unsecured debts. Chapter Nine includes specific information about collection lawsuits, including how likely you are to face lawsuits when you are delinquent on your unsecured debts, how to respond to lawsuits, and how to analyze whether a lawsuit is likely to hurt you. This chapter also reviews defenses to debt collection that may arise in special circumstances, such as when you are a member of the military or when you owe medical debts.

Part IV (Home Foreclosures, Chapters 10–13) deals in depth with one of the most severe consequences of financial distress—the potential loss of your home. If you have put up your home as collateral on a loan, that lender can seize your home if you fall behind on your payments. Part IV provides key information about your mortgage and mortgage payments, the foreclosure process, what steps you can take to avoid foreclosure, and what you should do if foreclosure cannot be avoided. If you are a homeowner, this part of the book will be extremely useful for you as you decide how to get out of financial trouble.

Part V (Student Loan and Federal Income Tax Collection, Evictions, Utility Shut-Offs, Repossessions, and Other Threats to Property, Chapters 14–18) covers strategies, both in the short term and the long term, to deal with other debts that can threaten your property. Each chapter covers a different type of debt problem that may lead to the immediate loss of property or essential services, such as evictions, utility terminations, student loans, or car repossessions. The basic lesson of each chapter is that there are many things you can do for almost every common consumer debt.

Part VI (Your Bankruptcy Rights, Chapter 19) provides a brief overview of your bankruptcy options, which may be particularly useful in dealing with your long-term financial difficulties. Bankruptcy is your most basic protection against unmanageable debt. The information in Part VI is intended to help you understand when bankruptcy relief makes sense. This chapter is important for any consumer in financial trouble and should at least be skimmed by all readers.

Part VII (Getting Back on Your Feet, Chapter 20) offers advice to help you rebuild your credit once your financial problems are under control. After you have addressed your current problems, you can begin to take steps to reestablish yourself for the future.

Glossary and Bibliography. A helpful glossary of terms appears at the back of the book. The terms used by lenders and debt collectors can vary. We have attempted to give you basic definitions of relevant terms.

Finally, you may decide you need more information about a particular topic than we have included in this book. A bibliography at the back of the book suggests some sources—including books, periodicals and websites—for more information.

Budget Forms. Budget forms are provided at the back of the book with notes designed to help you fill them out. These forms are designed to help you get a clearer picture of what resources you have available to meet your family's financial needs. Consider using these forms as you read through Chapters One and Two.

Business and Tax Debts. This book does *not* address business-related debts. Although some of the issues related to enforcement of business debts are the same as those discussed here, major business debts often involve complicated issues. These can include the extent of your liability for debts of corporations and partnerships with which you have been affiliated, complicated tax issues, enforcement of personal guarantees, and special liabilities associated with employment relationships. We recommend that you consult a lawyer if you have significant business-related debts.

Income tax issues can also be very complicated. In this book, we do little more than alert you to the need to deal with those debts and to some issues in dealing with IRS income tax collection activity. We recommend that you consult a tax lawyer or an accountant if you have significant potential debts to the IRS or state taxing authorities.

OBTAINING PROFESSIONAL ASSISTANCE

This book outlines your rights and gives you basic information about enforcing them. In many cases, exercising your legal rights is difficult because the applicable law and court procedures are complicated. You may need a lawyer to help you.

An additional factor is that many consumer rights come from state law instead of federal law. These laws can vary substantially from state to state. You may need to get more information about the laws in your state. We have tried to point this out whenever possible.

Hiring a Lawyer. It can be difficult to get legal help when you do not have much money. A good place to start to find free or affordable legal help is your local legal services office. In most communities (or close by if you live in a rural area), there are organizations which provide free legal help to people whose incomes fall below certain amounts.

These organizations vary widely with regard to the type of cases they handle. They also have strict income limits, so they are forced to turn away many cases. However, it can't hurt to ask. If they can't help you, they generally will make a referral to the appropriate legal organization (often called "bar association"), sometimes for free help from a private lawyer. They also may have special pamphlets or other helpful information on your state's laws.

Many legal services programs are funded by the Legal Services Corporation (LSC). You can find out more about programs near you by looking up LSC's website, www.lsc.gov, or by calling 202-295-1500. To find out if there are legal services programs in your area that are not funded by LSC, you should check your local phone book or ask a local social services or consumer protection agency. Court clerks often have information about legal services programs as well. If you are an older consumer, you should also check with your local department on aging or senior center to find out whether there are special legal services programs for older persons in your area.

If you need to pay for a lawyer, it is important to get competent help. All lawyers, like all doctors and all accountants, are not the same. You should try to find someone who has expertise in consumer rights. A first step is to ask friends and relatives for referrals. If you cannot get a referral, try calling your state or county bar association. Most such organizations maintain a referral service that will give you names of lawyers who specialize in consumer problems. However, these referral services rarely screen for quality.

Another option is to do some research at your local law library and find out if anyone in your city or state has written on your particular legal problem. For consumer law problems, you should also look up the National Association of Consumer Advocates (NACA) list of members. NACA's list is divided by region and by area of practice. The members also rate their level of experience in different consumer areas. Contact NACA by calling 202-452-1989 or check out the NACA website at www.naca.net. Another helpful resource is The National Association of Consumer Bankruptcy Attorneys, which provides referral lists for local bankruptcy lawyers. You can find out more from their website, www.nacba.org or by calling 202-331-8005.

You should always have an opportunity to talk to a lawyer before you agree to pay for that lawyer's services. Make sure you have a clear idea of what the lawyer will do for you and what you will be charged. You should also feel comfortable with the lawyer. Has she told you what you can expect from your case? Has she agreed to communicate regularly with you?

You should know whether you are paying an hourly rate or if you are paying a flat fee for a particular service. If you pay a flat fee, you should be sure to get a written statement of what the fee covers. Some lawyers will agree to a contingency fee arrangement where the lawyer gets paid only if you win your case. The lawyer's payment is usually a percentage of the money you win in the case. If you decide to set up a contingency fee arrangement, make sure you get in writing exactly how the fee will be calculated. Contingency fees are not always a good idea, particularly if you have a very strong case.

After you have signed a "retainer" (a contract with the lawyer laying out the services to be provided and how much you will pay), you can later cancel if you are dissatisfied with the service you are getting. You will only have to pay for services you have already received. If you are entitled to a refund that you do not receive, consider making a complaint to the local disciplinary agency for attorneys.

Unfortunately, the cheapest lawyer will not necessarily be the best. Price should not be the only consideration when hiring a lawyer—although it is always a factor. Be sure to get someone whom you feel can help you with your specific problem. Lawyers should be willing to provide a free initial consultation. They should also be willing to explain the potential consequences of doing nothing about your delinquent debt.

Finally, you should be wary about lawyers that make advertising claims that are too good to be true. Some lawyers read published foreclosure notices or review court lists to find out who is being sued and then solicit these individuals. Some lawyers make outrageous claims in their advertisements. Although not all lawyers who advertise are untrustworthy, you should not take an advertisement at face value. Make sure you know what the lawyer will do for you and whether the advertised services meet your needs.

Getting Help from a Counselor. If you cannot afford a lawyer or feel you don't want one, another place to get help is from a nonprofit counselor. Many communities have both nonprofit "debt" or "credit" counselors and nonprofit "housing" counselors. If you have a housing related problem, a housing counselor is usually preferable. Many agencies offer both housing and credit counseling.

There have been many changes in the credit counseling world in recent years. On the positive side, many agencies are more efficient and better able to help their customers. Unfortunately, there have also been very serious abuses in the industry. There are credit counseling agencies that are rip-offs, in business first and foremost to make money, not to help consumers.

Despite the problems with the credit counseling industry, there are still good credit counselors out there. You will need to shop very carefully to find one of these legitimate agencies. Chapter Four provides tips to help you understand whether credit counseling is right for you and, if so, how to find a good agency.

NOTE TO COUNSELORS USING THIS BOOK

This book is a revision of a prior publication which was addressed directly to debt counselors. Although the book is now written directly to consumers, it is still very valuable to counselors. Most of your clients will need your help to exercise the basic rights and options and to understand the information discussed in this book.

Because you regularly see clients with financial problems, you will almost always have more expertise in addressing these problems than the particular individual who seeks your help. Although we encourage you to recommend this book to your clients, you can also use it to advise clients on specific issues. Your background as a counselor and your explanations will help to reinforce the information provided in this book.

We recognize that many of the strategies discussed in this book go beyond what you are accustomed to doing in the counseling process. Each counselor must make his or her own decision about how far to go in actively intervening in a clients' debt problems. You must make these decisions within the limits of what you are legally allowed to do. Most important, if you are not a lawyer or are not supervised by lawyer, you cannot engage in the unauthorized practice of law. But you can help a consumer with many financial problems and help figure out when it is most appropriate to refer them to a lawyer.

Within these boundaries, it is critical that you make every effort to discuss the full range of options with financially stressed consumers. This means, for example, if you work for an organization which helps consumers make payment agreements with their creditors, you should nevertheless explain that bankruptcy is an alternative to some payment agreements. Similarly, if you are accustomed to dealing with credit card issues, you should not recommend a strategy for dealing with credit cards which undermines a consumer's ability to deal with a mortgage, car, or utility payment.

NOTE TO LAWYERS USING THIS BOOK

For lawyers who do not specialize in consumer rights, this book is intended to be a useful introduction to strategies for dealing with debts. We have included a bibliography with references to treatises containing more detailed legal information.

The best source of information for lawyers on consumer claims related to credit and utility issues is the National Consumer Law Center's series of consumer law manuals. For more details, see the bibliography, visit our website at www.consumerlaw.org, call NCLC Publications at 617-542-9595, FAX 617-542-8028, or write: National Consumer Law Center, Publications Department, 77 Summer Street, 10th Floor, Boston, MA 02110-1006.

Lawyers who specialize in consumer credit problems may already own other NCLC publications. You should consider using the *NCLC Guide to Surviving Debt* to educate your clients, paralegals, law students, or others in your office. Bulk publication orders can be arranged at substantial discounts by contacting NCLC Publications at the phone number or address above.

SOME FINAL THOUGHTS

This book is not a consumer credit law treatise. Readers who want more information should refer to the bibliography and the sources mentioned in each chapter. As stated in an earlier disclaimer, the book is also not intended to substitute for the independent judgment and skills of a competent attorney or other professional. Please read the disclaimer on the reverse of the title page for related information.

The law often changes. In addition, state laws vary a great deal. You should always make sure that you have the most recent edition of this book, and that you get necessary information about issues described here as "state" law. If the law does change, consider getting additional help.

Finally, we are eager to have feedback on your use of this book. If you have other suggestions about how to deal with debts, experiences which are contrary to the advice given here, or other comments, please feel free to write to the authors at the National Consumer Law Center or to e-mail them at consumerlaw@nclc.org.

1

Choosing Which Debts to Pay First

FIRST STEPS TO DEALING WITH DEBT PROBLEMS

Most people in financial distress will first want to deal with the worst symptoms of a deteriorating financial situation. For example, if you are facing debt collector harassment, you should review Chapter Eight and learn about ways you can stop this harassment. You might also want to consider other measures such as negotiating with certain creditors to temporarily stop billing you.

You will need to move quickly to the next steps in the process—developing longer-term strategies to deal with debt problems. This includes figuring out which debts to repay, understanding the likely consequences if you cannot pay certain debts, and deciding whether to seek professional counseling advice or to file bankruptcy.

In order to get started with a longer-term strategy, you will need to take a look at your overall debt picture. This usually involves writing down your expenses and income and keeping track for a few months. Coming up with your budget or spending plan is discussed in Chapter Two.

Although figuring out your budget is very important, it doesn't do everything for you. It doesn't tell you which debts you should pay if you cannot afford to pay all of them. Or, if you have some extra money left over, your budget will not tell you how best to spend that money.

All of these issues are discussed in various chapters of this book. Chapter Two will help you develop a budget. Chapters Six and Seven cover strategies, both good and bad, if you decide you want to raise money or dig into your savings or assets to pay off your debts. Chapter Nine reviews the likely consequences you will face if you decide that you cannot afford to repay your lower priority, unsecured debts, including a discussion of what is likely to happen if you get sued. Chapters Ten through Thirteen review strategies to consider when you are behind on your mortgage debt, and Chapter Sixteen discusses car-related debt. Chapter Eighteen covers issues related to student loan and tax debts.

This chapter will help you sort out which debts are your highest priorities. This is a necessary process because once you determine that you can't afford to pay all of your bills, you will have to make hard choices about which to pay first. Following the advice in this chapter may make the difference between keeping or losing important property.

Unfortunately, there is no magic list of the order in which debts should be paid. Everyone's situation will be different. The information in this chapter should be used as a guide as you make these critical decisions.

DEBTS WITH COLLATERAL
ARE TOP PRIORITIES

Collateral is property that a creditor has the right to take if you do not pay a particular debt. The most common forms of collateral are your home in the case of a mortgage (or deed of trust) and your car in the case of most car loans.

A creditor may also have collateral in your household goods, business property, bank account, or even wages. Collateral can take many forms. When a creditor has taken collateral for your loan, it has a "lien" on your property.

Creditors who have collateral are usually referred to as "secured" creditors. They know that if you don't pay, they can take the collateral from you and sell it to get their money. Creditors without collateral are often referred to as "unsecured." It is usually hard for unsecured creditors to collect what they are owed unless you pay voluntarily.

Debts with collateral are almost always your highest priority debts. How important it is to repay your other debts, particularly in the short-term, depends a lot on your individual circumstances. You should carefully review Chapter Nine to understand the consequences you are most likely to face if you stop paying your lower priority debts. This will help guide your decision making as you choose which debts to repay and in what order.

Regardless, it is almost always going to be true that the creditor making the most noise is not necessarily your most important creditor. Creditors who yell the loudest often do so only because they have no better way to get their money.

UNSECURED VS. SECURED DEBTS

Keep in mind this list of common unsecured and secured debts as you set your debt priorities. Remember that secured debts have some type of collateral, such as your house, attached to them.

SECURED DEBTS:	Mortgages
	Car Loans
	Loans secured by household goods
UNSECURED DEBTS:	Credit and charge cards
	Legal or medical bills
	Loans from friends or relatives
	Department store and gasoline card charges (unless the card specifically says that it is a "secured credit card")

SIXTEEN RULES ABOUT WHICH DEBTS TO PAY FIRST

These sixteen rules about how to set debt priorities are followed by advice about what to do if you cannot pay all of your high-priority debts. Other chapters in this book provide much more detailed information about the consequences of not paying certain types of debts. The following list is a good place to start.

1. Always pay family necessities first. Usually this means food and unavoidable medical expenses if the medical provider requires pre-payment.

(Do *not* pay old medical bills first.) You may want to look at ways to keep these expenses to a minimum as discussed in Chapter Two.

2. Next pay your housing-related bills.

Keep up your mortgage or rent payments if at all possible. If you own your home, real estate taxes and insurance must also be paid unless they are included in the monthly mortgage payment. Similarly, any condo fees or manufactured home lot payments should be considered a high priority. Failure to pay these debts can lead to loss of your home.

If you are having very serious problems that require you to move to a cheaper residence, you might choose to stop paying the mortgage or rent. When you do so, you should not use that money to pay other debts, but rather save it as a fund to use for moving. Dealing with mortgage debts is discussed in more detail in Chapters Ten through Thirteen. Rent payments and dealing with landlords are discussed in Chapter Fourteen.

3. Pay the minimum required to keep essential utility service.

At the very least, you should pay the minimum payment necessary to avoid disconnection. Working hard to keep your house or apartment makes little sense if you cannot live there because you have no utilities. Options for dealing with utility payments and disconnections are discussed in Chapter Fifteen.

4. Pay car loans or leases next if you need to keep your car.

If you need your car to get to work or for other essential transportation, you should usually make your car loan or lease payments your next priority after food, housing costs, unavoidable medical expenses, and utilities. You may even want to pay for the car first if the car is necessary to keep your job.

If you do keep the car, stay up to date on your insurance payments as well. Otherwise the creditor may buy costly insurance for you at *your* expense that gives you *less* protection. And in most states it is illegal not to have automobile liability coverage.

If you can give up your car or one of your cars, you not only save on car payments, but also on gasoline, repairs, insurance, and automobile taxes. Car loan debts are discussed in Chapter Sixteen.

5. You must pay child support debts.

These debts will not go away and can result in very serious problems, including prison, for nonpayment.

4

6. Income tax debts are also high priority. You must pay any income taxes you owe that are not automatically deducted from your wages, and you certainly must file your federal income tax return even if you cannot afford to pay any balance due. The government has many collection rights that other creditors do not have, particularly if you do not file your tax return. Remember, though, if you have lost income due to a change of circumstances, your tax obligations will also be reduced. Pay only what is necessary. See Chapter Eighteen.

7. Loans without collateral are low priority. Most credit card debts, attorney, doctor, and hospital bills, other debts to professionals, open accounts with merchants, and similar debts are low priority. You have not pledged any collateral for these loans, and there is rarely anything that these creditors can do to hurt you in the short term.

8. Loans with only household goods as collateral are also low priority. Sometimes a creditor requires you to place some of your household goods as collateral on a loan. You should generally treat this loan the same as an unsecured debt—as a low priority. Creditors rarely seize household goods because they have little market value, it is hard to take them without involving the courts, and it is time-consuming and expensive to use the courts to seize them. These issues are discussed in more detail in Chapter Seventeen.

9. Do *not* move a debt up in priority because the creditor or collector threatens suit. Many threats to sue are not carried out. Even if the creditor does sue, it will take a while for the collector to be able to seize your property, and much of your property may be exempt from seizure. On the other hand, nonpayment of rent, mortgage, and car debts may result in immediate loss of your home or car. Debt collection lawsuits and threats to sue are discussed in Chapter Nine.

10. Find out whether you have good legal defenses to repayment. Some examples of legal defenses are that the goods you purchased were defective or that the creditor is asking for more money than it is entitled to. If you have a defense, you should obtain legal advice to determine whether your defense will succeed. In evaluating these options, remember that it is especially dangerous to withhold mortgage or rent payments without legal advice. However, for all debts, you should consider fighting back when you have a valid defense, as discussed in Chapter Nine.

11. Court judgments against you move debts up in priority, but often less than you think. After a collector obtains a court judgment, that debt often should move up in priority, because the creditor can enforce that judgment by asking the court to seize certain pieces of your property, wages, and bank accounts. How serious a threat this really is will depend on your state's law, the value of your property, and your income. It may be that all your property and wages are protected under state law. If this is the case, you are considered to be "collection proof." This means that your income and assets are fully protected from seizure. If you are collection proof, you do not really have to worry about the judgment unless your financial situation gets much better. If you are not collection proof, you will need to evaluate whether the consequences of not paying your debts are likely to be worse than the costs of paying them. You might also want to consider whether bankruptcy is a useful option for you. This is also a good time to obtain professional advice if you have not done so already.

12. Government student loans are medium-priority debts. Government student loans should generally be paid ahead of low-priority debts, but after top-priority debts. Most delinquent student loans are federal government loans. The law provides special collection remedies to the government that are not available to other creditors. These include seizure of your tax refunds, special wage garnishment rules, denial of new student loans and grants, and, in some cases, seizure of federal benefits such as Social Security. The law also provides special remedies for borrowers hoping to get out of default. These include reasonable and affordable payment plans, loan consolidation, and even cancellation in some circumstances. These extreme collection powers do not apply to private student loans. Private student loans should be treated more like other types of unsecured debt. These issues are discussed in Chapter Eighteen.

13. Debt collection efforts should *never* move up a debt's priority. Be polite to the collector, but make your own choices about which debts to pay based on what is best for your family. Debt collectors are unlikely to give you good advice. Debt collectors may be most aggressive when trying to get you to pay debts that you should actually pay last. You can stop debt collection contacts and you have legal remedies to deal with collection harassment. See Chapter Eight.

14. Threats to ruin your credit record should *never* move up a debt's priority.

Many collectors that threaten to report your delinquency to a credit bureau have already done so. If the creditor has not yet reported the status of your account to a credit bureau, it is unlikely that a collector hired by that creditor will do so. In fact, your mortgage lender, your car creditor, and other big creditors are *much* more likely to report your delinquency (without any threat) than is a debt collector who threatens you about your credit record. See Chapter Three.

15. Cosigned debts should be treated like your other debts.

You may have cosigned for someone else and put up *your* home or car as collateral. If the other cosigner on the loan is not keeping the debt current, you need to treat that loan as a high-priority debt. If you have *not* put up such collateral, treat cosigned debts as a lower priority. If others have cosigned for you and you are unable to pay the debt, you should tell your cosigners about your financial problems so that they can decide what to do.

16. Refinancing is rarely the answer.

You should always be careful about refinancing. It can be very expensive and it can give creditors more opportunities to seize your important assets. A short-term fix can lead to long-term problems. Some refinancing rules and techniques to avoid scams are discussed in Chapter Six.

IF YOU CAN'T PAY ALL YOUR HIGH-PRIORITY DEBTS

You may find that your financial situation is so bad that you cannot even maintain required payments on your high-priority debts. Your income, for example, may not be enough to pay the mortgage and the car loan.

One serious mistake that some people make in this situation is to pay smaller, low-priority debts if they cannot keep up with their high-priority debts—"If I can't pay my mortgage, at least I will keep up with my credit cards."

This is a bad idea. Almost any long-term plan for saving your home and your car will require that you start making payments again at some point.

In the short term, if you don't have enough money to make full payments, you can try to negotiate with the creditor to accept partial payments. If you are unsuccessful, save the money. You can use it later to make a down payment to get caught up or to cover the costs of moving to a new residence or buying a new car.

You should also avoid making desperate choices. Although it is hard to accept that you will lose a home or a car or other valuable property, the alternatives can sometimes be worse. For example, refinancing a low-rate mortgage with a high-rate mortgage may buy you a few months, but in the long term the situation is likely to be hopeless. You have a better chance of working out a solution with the existing lender than you do of avoiding foreclosure by taking out a loan with an aggressive finance company that makes high-rate loans. Some of the worst choices you can make in borrowing against your home are discussed in Chapter Six. Other good and bad strategies for raising money are discussed in Chapter Seven.

There are many strategies for dealing with debt problems discussed throughout this book. Occasionally, though, it is best to step back and accept the inevitable change which money problems sometimes require. You may be living in a home you can't afford or you may need to substitute a cheaper car to fit a new lifestyle.

Once that point is reached, you can do things which make the transition easier. These may include selling the property at a good retail price to avoid a low foreclosure sale price or giving up the property in exchange for a promise that the creditor will not make you pay any deficiency. See Chapter Ten for more information about deficiencies in foreclosure sales. Deficiencies from car repossession sales are discussed in Chapter Sixteen.

These choices are difficult and have to be made based on your individual evaluation of your long-term prospects. Once the choice is made, however, it is a good idea to stop making payments on that debt in favor of other pressing items. Continuing to pay a debt on property that you will lose in the long term anyway is expensive.

USING BANKRUPTCY TO GET A FRESH START

Since there are situations in which rights in bankruptcy can be lost by delay, you should consider bankruptcy as an option from the start of your "surviving debt" planning process.

When you file for bankruptcy, most of your *unsecured* debts will be "discharged." This means that your legal obligation to pay those debts will end even if you can't pay. On the other hand, despite your bankruptcy, a *secured* creditor usually will eventually be able to seize its collateral unless you make a plan to pay that debt. This difference in bankruptcy between unsecured and secured debts is another reason to make unsecured debts a lower priority.

Bankruptcy can also be used to get a creditor to back off of aggressive collection efforts. If a creditor refuses to give you some time to get things together or if a creditor refuses to accept small but affordable payments, filing bankruptcy can take care of the problem. Sometimes just telling a creditor that you are considering bankruptcy will make that creditor more reasonable.

Making a choice about whether to file bankruptcy can be difficult. There are complicated issues in this area that usually require legal assistance. Some basic information to help you make a good choice about bankruptcy is provided in Chapter Nineteen, but this is not a substitute for individualized legal advice.

FEELINGS OF OBLIGATION TO PARTICULAR CREDITORS

In deciding your priorities, you may feel that some creditors are more entitled to repayment than others. These feelings should rarely be a factor in deciding which debts to pay first. Giving up the family home to pay off a creditor for whom you have good feelings is too big a sacrifice. If a creditor is sympathetic or has done you favors in the past, they are more likely to be patient as you work out your financial problems.

A related issue comes up in small communities where there may only be one store or one doctor or one pharmacist with whom you can do business. You may not want to lose your ability to obtain services from that particular creditor and you may feel you have no choice other than to pay that debt first. This may be true, but only in limited situations.

You should not assume that a business or a doctor will cut you off from future service right away if you don't pay. Explain the situation and ask for understanding. Similarly, before assuming that you need to use a particular creditor, look around. There may be others in or near your community who are available in a pinch.

Almost everyone has financial problems at one time or another. You are not alone if you are experiencing these problems. You are also not alone if you continue to feel embarrassed, humiliated, or panicked about your situation. These feelings are common and can cause a lot of stress for you and your family. This pressure can cause quarrels, temporary separations, or even divorce. Some studies document increases in physical abuse associated with money problems. As you make the difficult choices associated with your financial problems, you should be aware of the emotional pressures which may build.

Mental health counseling, family therapy, and marriage counseling may be useful for managing the stress of financial problems. If you have health insurance, your policy may include free or low-cost mental health assistance. It can't hurt to ask your doctor. This type of assistance is also usually available from a variety of organizations on a sliding-scale fee basis or for free. Call a trusted local credit counseling agency or family services for a reference. You can also call and ask a therapist about low-cost or free mental health counseling options available in the community.

Whatever course you choose, it is important that you remain aware of the additional stress you may be feeling and that you try to deal with it in the healthiest possible way.

As you struggle to get past your financial difficulties, keep in mind that better days will come. With careful planning to minimize short-term hardship and with some patience, you can put yourself in the best possible position to get a fresh start and to recover good financial health.

2

Establishing a Budget Which Addresses Financial Problems

TOPICS COVERED IN THIS CHAPTER

- How to Develop an Income and Expense Budget
- Increasing Your Income and Lowering Your Expenses
- Medical and Dental Care
- Developing a Savings Plan

THE INCOME AND EXPENSE BUDGET

There are three primary reasons to set up a budget or spending plan as soon as you recognize that you are likely to be facing financial problems:

1. The budget will help you determine how much money you have to cover your necessities and how much is left over to pay your bills. This will help establish your range of choices on how to deal with your debts.

2. The budget will help guide your spending habits.

3. In some cases you will want to work with creditors that offer options for payment plans and modification of debts. These options will be particularly important if you wish to save your home and your car. Your ability to qualify for these programs will be based on your budget. If you have already done the work to develop a budget, you will have a sense of what you can afford to offer your creditors and you will be able to provide basic information that will make the process go more smoothly.

11

How to Set Up a Budget. Your budget is nothing more than a list of your anticipated income and a list of your expected expenses. This can be a much less formal process than it sounds. To help you create a budget, you will find sample budget charts in the *Appendix* at the back of this book, including notes on how to use them. The charts include many potential sources of income and common expenses. However, don't assume we have thought of everything. Your budget should be based on your personal experience.

These charts are helpful for some people, but may be intimidating for others. Regardless of how you get there, the main goal is for you to get an understanding of how much money you and your family bring in each month and how much you spend. It is important to write this down in a way that you can follow and keep track of.

We recommend that you make copies of the charts in the *Appendix*. You should use a new chart for each month. Keep these charts so that you can compare your income and spending in different months and see if you are making progress over time in cutting expenses and increasing income.

Once you have come up with a budget, you should try to live with it for a month or so to get a sense of whether it correctly reflects your actual income and expenses. Each month you should subtract your expenses from your income. You should not be surprised if you find that your expenses are more than your income. This is why you are having financial problems.

Income Budget. Your income budget should include all sources of income which you presently have. Employment income is a good place to start. If you are not working on salary, you should try to use the most realistic estimate of what you will earn. Overtime should be included if it is guaranteed, but it is a bad idea to budget based on hopes for extra work.

Your income budget should also include any additional money that you receive on a regular basis, including child support and alimony, trust payments, dividends, royalties, insurance, pensions and public benefits.

It is sometimes difficult to deal with expected future increases or decreases in your income. If you know of an expected change and that change is certain, you can use it in planning your budget. If you then share your budget charts with a creditor from whom you are seeking a modification of loan terms, the expected change should be fully explained. Most creditors will want documentation. If the change is very unlikely, it's best not to include it in your budget plan.

How to Include Your Savings and Other Assets in Your Income Budget. You will have to decide how to treat your savings and other assets in your budget plan. Ask yourself whether it makes sense to draw down money you have been saving for the future and then rebuild your savings plan after your financial problems are resolved. There are no easy answers to this question, and you will have to make a decision which is right for you.

Some people use a set amount of their savings each month in their monthly budget to meet essential expenses. This can be the right choice if you have good discipline and if the savings will make the difference between meeting your essential expenses and falling hopelessly behind. However, you should not fall into the trap of using your savings to finance an unrealistic lifestyle.

You should also think about whether you are better off spending your retirement money now or toughing it out so you have money when you retire. Should you take a little money out of your savings account each month to help balance your budget or should you take all your savings and pay it in one lump sum toward getting your mortgage current? Should you sell off stocks or other property to make ends meet? Later in this chapter, there is general information about developing a savings plan. Whether borrowing against your savings is a good idea is discussed in Chapter Seven.

How to Budget Lump Sums You Are Expecting but Have Not Received. Many people have money which they expect in the future but which is not yet in hand. Sometimes the expectation is no more than a possibility, while in other cases it is guaranteed. Examples include:

- Money or property which has been left to you by a deceased relative, but which is tied up in probate;
- Social Security or other public benefit lump sums;
- Money from a lawsuit which has not yet been heard in court or settled;
- Money for sale of property when the sale has not yet closed;
- Retirement funds or workers' compensation funds which are owed but unpaid;
- Money promised by a friend or relative to help you out in tough times; and
- Insurance money which has not yet been paid.

It is possible to include this money in your financial plan, but you need to be realistic about when the money may come and how much it will be.

If you are waiting for a lawyer to settle a lawsuit or an estate in probate, it may be a good idea to call to let the lawyer know about the nature and urgency of your financial difficulties. There may be things that can be done to speed up legal processes, although in some cases you will end up with a smaller recovery.

Some money is certain to come in on a particular date. For example, if your Social Security payments are due to start on a particular date, you can use this knowledge in making your financial plan. You may be able to supplement your income with savings for a few months while you wait for the permanent change to kick in. Similarly, if a lump sum is guaranteed, you can plan to use that lump sum in a way which will cure your defaults on urgent debts.

On the other hand, it can be a poor choice to count on money that is no more than a hope, either in timing or amount. Payments that are too uncertain should probably not enter into your plans at all.

When you prepare your income budget, you should carefully evaluate whether you are maximizing your income. A number of ideas to increase your income are discussed later in this chapter.

Expense Budget. Your expense budget should include all your expected monthly expenses, including food, housing costs, utilities, clothing, transportation, and medical expenses. It is often difficult to figure out exactly where all your money goes. A review of your check book and your credit card bills may serve as a reminder.

Figuring out the true cost in each expense category can also be difficult. Food expenses, for example, may consist of your costs at the grocery store and (most likely) a few trips to the convenience store for special needs each week, plus the costs of occasionally dining out. If you look at your grocery store bills alone, you may underestimate your food expenses. You should do your best to estimate the real total. Then, think about ways you can minimize unnecessary food expenses, for example, by regularly taking your lunch to work. You will find more information about cutting expenses later in this chapter.

When writing down your expenses, you should be sure to remember payments you are making on previously owed credit card charges. For example, you may have a balance of $5,000 on your Visa card. If you pay $100 each month to try to pay this down, you should list that amount as a credit card expense.

New charges should be listed in the appropriate "expense" category. For example, if you use your Visa to buy $200 worth of groceries, you should include this expense in the food category.

A critical point to keep in mind is that you should generally not include credit card and other unsecured debts in your expense budget unless you can afford to meet all your obligations. If you do not have enough income in your budget to pay all your bills, Chapter One discusses the best ways to make choices among your various debts. Credit card and other unsecured debts are usually low priorities. For reasons discussed throughout this book, you should always protect important property by making plans to prevent foreclosure or repossession before you worry about your credit rating and your ability to borrow again in the future.

You should also keep in mind that there may be costs to this strategy. The likely consequences of not paying your lower priority debts are discussed in Chapter Nine.

Always pay essential debts first. If any money is left,
you can decide which nonessential debts,
if any, to keep in your expense budget.

FINE TUNING YOUR BUDGET

Throughout the budgeting process, your goal should be to get as much money as possible on the income side and spend as little as possible on the expense side. The following sections will focus mainly on ideas for adjusting your budget to see if you can reduce expenses and increase income to come up with additional money to repay debts. There is also a separate section on medical and dental care.

In reading through these sections, particularly the section on increasing your income through the Earned Income Tax Credit and certain public benefit programs, keep in mind that the law on these issues often changes. We try to point out some programs that are likely to be available for the foreseeable future, but you will need to get more detailed information if you wish to pursue these options. This chapter only summarizes these various programs.

Ideas for places to go for more information are listed in this chapter and in the bibliography at the back of this book.

You should take advantage of these programs when they are available. Each program was created to help people with financial problems and there is no reason to be ashamed of using them. It is likely that you contributed financially to funding the programs either through tax payments or by payroll deductions.

You should also remember that most of the programs discussed here have appeal rights and procedures. If you are denied assistance which you think you are entitled to, consider filing an appeal. Professional help may be useful but is not required.

SOME OPTIONS FOR INCREASING YOUR INCOME

The Earned Income Tax Credit. The Earned Income Tax Credit is a frequently overlooked means of increasing your income if you are employed. If you have not qualified for this credit in the past, a change in your income or a lay-off may make you eligible during a year in which you have financial problems.

The amount of your tax credit is based on the amount of your income and the size of your family. If you are employed and your total income falls below a certain amount, you qualify for the credit even if you do not have to pay any taxes that year. You can get money back even if you pay little or no taxes. You can also get advance payments on your credit if your employer provides that option.

You should check with a tax professional to determine if you qualify. Obtaining the credit will require that you file the necessary tax returns.

Unemployment Compensation. You should always think about unemployment compensation when you have lost your job for any reason or when your hours have been significantly reduced. You should apply as quickly as possible after your employment is terminated or reduced.

Unemployment benefits are most commonly available after a lay-off. You may not be eligible for benefits if you have been fired for cause or if you voluntarily quit. However, in some cases, you may still qualify for benefits even if your employer told you that you were fired rather than laid off. Similarly, you may qualify in some circumstances even if you quit your job. In general, it can't hurt to apply, although if you were fired or if you quit, you may first want to learn more about your state's benefit program.

Some lawyers and other professionals specialize in this area. In addition, there are several books and pamphlets available which discuss unemployment compensation. Call the personnel office of your former company, the state labor department, or your state's unemployment office. If you are a union member, ask the union if it provides help with unemployment compensation applications. The National Employment Law Project (NELP) has a number of useful publications on unemployment compensation. They may be reached at 212-285-3025 or www.nelp.org.

Food Stamps. If you are experiencing severe financial problems, food stamps can supplement your monthly food budget. To qualify, your income must be below program limits which vary by family size. Emergency food stamps may be available in certain circumstances.

You apply for food stamps by filing an application form with any food stamp office. Often food stamp offices are located within public assistance offices in your community. You can call and have an application mailed to you or you can visit the office in person. Some states allow you to file on-line. More information about application procedures in different states can be found on the website of the U.S. Department of Agriculture, www.usda.gov.

Sometimes, the agency improperly denies a food stamps application because of confusion about eligibility requirements or because of arithmetic mistakes. Do not take a denied application as final. Consider making an appeal before the required time deadline expires.

Program requirements are subject to change. For more detailed information about the program, you may want to review program manuals, regulations, and pamphlets available from the public assistance office or seek help from an advocate who specializes in food stamps. For more information, contact the Food Research and Action Center at 202-986-2200, www.frac.org or the U.S. Department of Agriculture, www.usda.gov.

Other Food Programs. Other food-assistance programs may be available in your community. If your family includes a pregnant woman or a child under five, you should inquire about assistance from the Women, Infants and Children (WIC) program. Typically, WIC is administered by local public health departments and provides vouchers for supplemental foods important to the health of mothers and to the early development of their children. Eligibility for this program is based on family income and on whether the women, infants or children in the family are at nutritional risk. Public assistance offices or health departments can provide information about WIC.

Many unions, churches and community groups have community cupboards or food pantries that distribute food for home preparation. Churches and social service organizations such as the Salvation Army maintain cafeterias to which families can turn. These programs can be located by contacting local church offices, United Way offices, or other social service agencies. Many food banks are run by America's Second Harvest. For more information, call 800-771-2303 or visit their website at www.secondharvest.org.

Other Public Assistance Programs. All states administer some form of cash and other assistance to families with children through the Temporary Assistance for Needy Families (TANF) block grant program. States have great flexibility in setting eligibility requirements and benefit levels. A universal requirement is that the family includes a minor child or a pregnant woman.

Applications for this assistance can be made at a local public assistance office, sometimes called a department of public assistance, department of social services, or department of human services. As with other programs, you need to provide proof that you are eligible.

If you qualify for the program, the amount of your benefits will be based on your other income and family size as well as certain other factors in some states. Job training, work requirements, and time limits may also apply.

Some states have other emergency assistance or other public assistance programs. Many states also have local general assistance or general relief programs. Benefits and eligibility requirements vary tremendously among states, but the programs are usually available only to people who don't qualify for any other form of assistance and who have few or no resources.

Some general assistance programs are available only to certain groups, such as children or the disabled. Some programs provide benefits for only a limited number of months each year. Most programs require that employable people participate in a work or job search program. Local legal services offices can provide more information about these programs.

Utility and Phone Assistance Programs. Utilities often have special programs which allow you to reduce the charges for the service you receive. There are also special programs offering discounts on local telephone rates for low-income households. These plans are discussed in Chapter Fifteen.

Other Emergency Programs. Some states and communities have other emergency funds available to help with basic needs, such as food, shelter, medical care, clothing, or transportation. Often, these programs provide vouchers rather than direct cash.

Private social service groups and charitable and religious organizations sometimes have small funds available that provide limited grants or short-term loans to families lacking other available resources.

Public and private funds are often difficult to locate. Some are listed in the social services section of the phone book. In many communities, one agency serves as an information clearinghouse or referral service for various sources of assistance.

Disaster Relief. Federal, state, and local government agencies and private charities have programs available to help deal with damages suffered due to disasters. The Federal Emergency Management Agency (FEMA) is the main federal agency that is supposed to coordinate state and federal government disaster benefits. You may also be eligible for expedited or replacement food stamps or disaster-related unemployed benefits. In some cases, private creditors will agree to impose moratoriums on credit card payments or offer other relief for disaster victims. Time deadlines are often critical for these programs. You can get more information from your local legal services office or from FEMA's website www.fema.gov or by calling FEMA at 1-800-621-FEMA (3362) or 1-800-462-7585 (TTY).

Social Security and SSI Benefits Based on Age. If you are age 62 or over, you may be eligible for Social Security benefits. Sixty-two is the minimum retirement age. Retiring at 62, or at anytime before the full retirement age, will result in reduced benefits. The full retirement age has been 65 for many years. Beginning with people born in 1938 or later, that age limit will gradually increase until it reaches 67 for people born after 1959. The survivors of an insured worker may also be eligible for Social Security benefits upon the worker's death.

Social Security benefits are available only for those who have been employed a sufficient number of years in covered jobs, that is, jobs that provide contributions to the Social Security fund. Those aged 65 or over who are not eligible for Social Security may still be eligible for Supplemental Security Income (SSI). This is a federal program open to those whose income and assets are under established guidelines.

Sometimes, people who are eligible to receive Social Security benefits at age 62 postpone receipt of these benefits because they will be eligible for larger monthly payments at a later date. While this strategy may make sense when the family's financial resources are adequate, it is not usually a good choice in times of financial distress. More information about Social Security is available by calling 800-772-1213 or by visiting Social Security's website at www.ssa.gov.

Disability Benefits. You may also be eligible for Social Security or Supplemental Security Income (SSI) disability benefits. Disabilities take many forms. Illnesses, physical and mental limitations, extreme pain, and depression or anxiety all qualify as disabilities. To qualify, the impairment or combination of impairments has to have lasted, or be expected to last, a year or more and has to prevent you from engaging in substantial gainful activity in light of your age, education, and work experience.

Federal disability benefits are paid by the Social Security Administration. Social Security is a federally administered program, separate from the other public assistance programs discussed here. Applications are made at local Social Security offices.

If your past employment record does not qualify you for Social Security disability benefits, you can apply for SSI disability benefits. SSI is the federal Supplemental Security Income program for individuals whose income and assets fall below established guidelines.

Many applicants who are initially denied disability benefits succeed on appeal. Make sure to file an appeal at each stage and consider contacting a lawyer or other advocate who specializes in disability benefit cases.

Workers' Compensation. If you were seriously injured on the job, or if you suffer from serious job-related medical conditions, it is likely that you are entitled to workers' compensation benefits. These may include medical benefits and monthly income payments until you are able to go back to work. If you are a union member, the union may help you qualify. Otherwise, contact the workers' compensation board in your state directly. Your doctor's assistance in this process will be helpful. If you are having difficulties qualifying, you may wish to contact a lawyer specializing in workers' compensation cases.

Child Support. You may be owed current or back child support. If you cannot obtain an attorney to press your claim for child support, a state agency should help you to collect. Contact the local public assistance office to see which state agency assists families in the collection of child support and what type of assistance they can offer.

Other Family Support Issues. If a family relationship is terminated or terminating, you may be entitled to alimony, property distribution, debt payment assistance, or other remedies in addition to child support. These options should be explored with a lawyer or family counselor who understands your financial problems. The nature of your financial difficulties is relevant to the family court process, so you should be sure to explain where things stand to the person who assists you.

Other Ways to Increase Income. Other ways to increase the family income include taking a second job temporarily, increasing overtime, or collecting debts owed to you by others. Consider also whether you have space in your home which you can rent or whether you have a marketable skill which you are not using. If you have made a voluntary decision not to work, financial difficulties create an opportunity to reconsider. Any choice to return to the workforce in this circumstance must be weighed against the potential increased costs of child care, taxes, and other expense.

Education. Education and job skills training may help you get a higher paying job so that you can better meet your expenses. This is often a good idea, but unfortunately there are schools that will try to take advantage of your attempts to get a better education.

   If you find out that education is likely to lead to employment in a particular field, it is a good idea to shop around, check out community colleges which often offer the same courses as private trade schools at a much lower cost. Student loan borrowing should be kept to a minimum to avoid future problems. See Chapter Eighteen for more information about student loans.

SOME OPTIONS FOR REDUCING YOUR EXPENSES

You will find a lot of advice about how to cut expenses. Much of this advice is helpful, but not every idea will work for everyone. As you consider cutting your expenses, it is important, above all, that you understand what your choices are, how you could change your spending habits, and the consequences of your decisions. You should also understand that this is not going to be easy. Cutting expenses is hard work and takes a lot of commitment. Try to work together with your family to understand the situation and to figure out ways to make it better. As part of this commitment, you will need to think about putting away your credit cards, at least for a while. Consider keeping only one to use for emergencies.

Everyone's expense needs are different and it is impossible to list all of the ways you might consider economizing. This chapter presents a few possibilities that you should consider.

Regardless of your strategy, you should try to be realistic while also making a serious commitment to cut expenses. For example:

1. Many budget books will tell you to save money by spending less during the winter holidays. Most know that you will want to buy some gifts. The point is to understand how much you spend and to see if you can save money by spending less. For example, can you work out an agreement with your relatives that you will only buy gifts for the children, not for the adults, or that you will all limit the amount you spend on gifts to a certain amount?

2. Food is another good example. You probably don't realize how much you spend on food. When you add up your monthly food costs, be sure and count not only purchases at grocery stores, but also eating out.

   You can save money on food in all kinds of ways, including:
   - Use coupons to save money on products you would generally buy.
   - Shop at different stores to get the best prices.
   - Plan menus ahead of time instead of at the grocery store.
   - Try not to shop when you're hungry!
   - Shop without your kids if possible.
   - Buy cheaper store brands.
   - Eat at home whenever possible.
   - Pack a lunch for school or work rather than eating out.
   - Bring coffee to work or drink free coffee at your office if it's available.

Avoid Pressure-Related Shopping. Some consumers respond to financial pressures and anxiety by going shopping, buying items they really don't need, or overspending. Not only does this dig you deeper into debt, but some types of spending for unnecessary items or through cash advances on credit cards can also cause you problems if you later decide to file for bankruptcy. You may lose your right to erase those debts in bankruptcy if the creditor can prove that you ran up your credit cards knowing that you could not pay them back.

There are counseling groups in many communities that can help you address uncontrollable spending habits. A credit counselor can usually point you in the right direction.

Try to think about what influences your decision to shop and what to buy. Almost everyone is affected by the views of friends, family, neighbors, and others. Certainly advertising and marketing executives know how to play upon your emotions when trying to get you to buy something.

It is important to try to resist the urge to spend unnecessarily by pausing before you buy. Think about creating a "cooling off period" or "time out" before you spend.

However, there will be cases where you pay too much not because you are on a shopping spree but because you are unable to figure out the true cost of your purchases. It can be very difficult to understand these costs, particularly if you are using credit to buy something. There are entire industries, such as rent-to-own, that cater to people facing financial problems. Although it can be difficult to find affordable alternatives, you should at least understand the real costs of businesses such as rent-to-own (discussed below) and try to shop around for more affordable options.

Avoid Rent-to-Own. In a rent-to-own deal, you are supposedly renting property for a period of time until you qualify for ownership. It is marketed as a way for people who do not qualify for credit to have use of an item while it is being purchased.

There are two major problems with rent-to-own deals. First, items purchased in this way are very expensive, often costing you more than three times the cash price. For example:

THE HIGH COST OF RENTING TO OWN
You rent a 19-inch color TV ($300 value)
You pay $16 per week for 52 weeks $832
Value of property you bought $300
Interest you pay (254% on an annual basis) $532

On top of that, you may have purchased a *used* TV that is only worth $150.

The second problem with rent-to-own occurs when you can't keep up the payments. If you miss even one payment, the item can be repossessed. You will then lose the benefit of any payments you have made toward owning the property. The more you have paid, the more you have to lose if, at some point, you end up missing a payment. Many people have paid more than $1,000 for property worth less then $500 only to lose that property for missing one payment.

If you need to buy furniture, appliances, or electronic goods, and you can't immediately afford them, you should look at options besides rent-to-own. The best option may be to save money, if at all possible, and then to pay cash. Consider selling something you don't need to buy something you do. Also, don't assume that you will not qualify for more conventional credit. Stores may grant credit even to people with a bad credit record or they may have other ways for you to purchase at a reasonable rate of interest. Shop for the best possible cash price and the best possible interest rate. You should also check to see whether the store has a layaway policy that might work for you.

Saving Money by Opening a Bank Account. You can avoid the high cost of cashing checks and buying money orders by opening a bank checking account. It is important to shop around to make sure you find an account that won't end up costing you a lot of extra money.

In exploring the costs of different checking accounts, find out whether the bank offers any free checking and under what terms. For example, is there a minimum balance you must keep in the account at all times to get free checking? If not, how much is the monthly fee? Will you be charged per check?

You should also find out about the bank's check clearing policy. You should not assume that the money from a check you deposit will be immediately available to you. Many banks require that you wait a certain amount of time until a deposited check clears. Knowing how long it will take for your money to be available will help you avoid bounced checks.

It is especially important to find out about automated teller machine (ATM) fees. These may be charged not only by your own bank but also by the bank that owns the machine where you withdraw money. These are unnecessary charges you should avoid as much as possible.

You should also ask about other ways that the bank might charge you fees. For example, most banks charge large fees if you write a check with insufficient funds in your account ("bounced check" or "NSF" fees). Some charge you these fees for bounce loans. These are loans that many banks automatically charge you for when you overdraw your account at an ATM or with a debit card. (See Chapter Seven for more information about bounce loans.) You can try to avoid these problems by asking about the bank's overdraft protection and whether this will cost you extra.

If You Are Having Trouble Getting an Account. If you are turned down for a checking account by one bank, you should find out why. Some banks deny accounts to people who have bounced checks in the past. Many use systems such as ChexSystems to keep track of past problems you may have had with checking or savings accounts.

Ask if the bank pulled a credit report and made a decision on that basis. You are entitled to a free copy of your report within sixty days of a credit denial. (For information about how to order a credit report, see Chapter Three.) If you are denied an account due to past problems, you may be able to explain the situation and get the bank to change the decision. If the bank used a screening company such as ChexSystems, you might also consider calling that company to try to resolve the problem. ChexSystems, for example, includes information on its website about how to dispute items in your file and how to put explanations about previous problems in your file. Go to www.consumerdebit.com for information about consumer checking accounts.

You should also look into alternatives to bank checking accounts. For example, there are generally a number of banks in most areas which offer the "ETA." This is a special, low-cost account which is only provided to recipients of federal payments, which may be—but is not always—all electronic. Fees are limited on these accounts.

Even if your credit is such a problem that no bank will open a checking or savings account for you, you can almost always obtain an ETA so long as you receive regular payments from the federal government. To find an ETA provider, call 1-888-382-3311 toll-free or visit www.eta-find.gov.

Many banks also offer no- or low-cost electronic accounts as alternatives to checking and savings accounts.

SOME ADDITIONAL LITTLE-KNOWN WAYS TO CUT EXPENSES

This section lists twelve additional tips which are often overlooked by consumers. A combination of these savings can reduce your expense budget by several hundred dollars a month.

1. Real estate tax reductions. If you own a home, many communities have a variety of real estate tax abatements, deferrals, and hardship repayment plans. Most states have an abatement for older homeowners and many have a deferral process for people facing financial hardship. Less than half of those eligible take advantage of available real estate tax reductions.

2. Utility conservation measures. If you pay for your own utilities, you may be paying too much. Look into utility conservation assistance programs, many of which are offered free by utility companies. In addition, many books and pamphlets offer valuable tips. These can lower your utility costs by one-half to one-third. A variety of options to reduce your utility costs are discussed in Chapter Fifteen.

3. Reduce your telephone expenses. Look into your telephone calling plan, including your cell phone if you have one. You may want to change your local billing method or comparison-shop among competing companies for long-distance service. The types of calls you make and times you are likely to use the phone can greatly affect what type of calling plan works best for you. These issues are discussed in more detail in Chapter Fifteen.

4. Re-evaluate your homeowner's insurance needs. Many people pay more than necessary for their homeowner's insurance. If your property value has decreased, or if you are insuring for a value which includes the cost of the land your home is on, you are paying too much for homeowner's insurance. You also can consider eliminating unnecessary coverages or applying for special rate programs (such as reductions for using a smoke detector). Check with your agent; you may be able to cut your annual bill by hundreds of dollars.

5. Cancel unnecessary private mortgage insurance. Private mortgage insurance (PMI) is usually required if the down payment on the loan you used to purchase your house was less than 20% of the sale price. The insurance protects the lender if you default on the loan. Once you have more than 20% equity in your property, however, there is no longer any need for the PMI and it should be cancelled. A 1998 law requires automatic termination of your PMI policy when you first owe less than 78% of the original value of the property. This law applies to loans made after July 1, 1999. Certain high-risk loans and affordable housing program loans are exempt from this law. If your loan does not fall under this law and you have 20% equity in your home, you may still request that the lender cancel the PMI. The mortgage contract or the lender's policy may require cancellation of the PMI if you request it. Refinancing your loan is another way to avoid payment of PMI if you have sufficient equity. See Chapter Six for a discussion of refinancing.

6. Re-evaluate your other insurance needs. Look into your life insurance and other coverages with the help of a trustworthy insurance agent. It helps for the agent to understand the nature of your financial problems. You may consider dropping optional coverages until your financial problems are solved. You might also consider converting a whole life policy to a term life policy in order to save money. Some policies may be "capped" or may include an option for deferring payments for a temporary period. Your car insurance coverage is another area where it may be possible to save. Are all your coverages required in order to operate your car? Do you qualify for any savings plans?

7. School-related expenses. If you have children in private school, you may have to consider a change during a period when you are experiencing financial problems. Family counseling may help with these difficult transitions. If you feel your children must stay in private school, you may want to speak with a school official or a financial aid officer. Special assistance programs may be available for families having temporary financial difficulties.

8. Religious expenses and charitable contributions. If you are having financial problems and religious expenses are stretching your budget, consider talking to your priest, minister, rabbi, or imam. More often than not, special efforts will be made to help you through a tough financial time without affecting your membership or standing in the community.

9. Sliding scale community services. Many community-based social service programs offer assistance for free or on a sliding scale. Low-cost counseling on a variety of issues is widely available if you are persistent in looking for it. These programs are designed to help people in your situation in a confidential and effective way. You should not be embarrassed to get help.

10. Public transportation versus driving. Automobiles can be very expensive. Between car payments, gas, repairs, and insurance, an automobile in some communities can be as expensive as a home. If you can find a way to get by without a car temporarily or permanently, you may find that you save many hundreds of dollars a month. Similarly, if you have two cars, consider whether your family can manage with one.

11. Unnecessary payroll deductions. If your income has gone down, you may be having excessive amounts deducted from your pay for income taxes. Check with your employer or with an accountant if necessary.

Similarly, you may have agreed to a payroll deduction for any of a variety of reasons when things were going well. These might include savings plans, voluntary pension contributions, vacation clubs, credit union deductions, optional but inessential health coverages, charitable contributions, or voluntary wage assignments to creditors that you have decided are not a high priority. Check to see if these deductions can be temporarily reduced or eliminated.

12. Adult children living at home. You may feel a great deal of obligation to adult family members or friends who share your home with you. However, if that person has income, it is certainly fair to ask for a contribution to the household expenses. Alternatively, it may be time to politely ask that person to find somewhere else to live permanently or temporarily. If you continue to pay the expenses of people who can manage on their own, this may stretch your budget to the point that everyone loses their home.

MEDICAL AND DENTAL CARE

Paying for medical and dental care may be a significant problem when you are experiencing financial problems. This section provides advice on obtaining low-cost and free care.

Unpaid doctor and hospital bills should not prevent you from getting free or low-cost medical and dental care.

Keeping Your Health Insurance After Losing Your Job. Ordinary preventive medical care, particularly dental care, tends to be postponed during times of crisis. Nevertheless, families sometimes suddenly confront large, unplanned medical expenses and are caught with no medical insurance. Such nightmares can sometimes be prevented, particularly if you have just been laid off.

Within thirty days of being laid off (unless the union or employment contract provides different terms), you should receive a notice from your former employer's health insurance company stating that your insurance has been terminated. The notice should specify a time period during which you can convert to an individual policy without any lapse in coverage.

If you can afford to pay the premium to convert to an individual family policy, you should do so, particularly if someone in your family has an existing medical condition requiring care. Often the only way to avoid restrictions on coverage of a pre-existing condition is to maintain coverage with the existing insurer.

Medicaid. If it is not possible to maintain private health insurance coverage, consider applying for a state or federally-funded medical assistance program, known in many states as Medicaid. Eligibility for Medicaid varies from state to state but depends on available family income and resources. Sometimes, you can get Medicaid for your children even if you don't qualify.

If services are covered, Medicaid pays the physician, the pharmacist, and any other service provider directly. Many states have co-payment systems in which the Medicaid patient pays a small amount, usually only a few dollars, toward the service. Under current federal law, states must provide certain mandatory services, including hospital care and doctor's visits. If you are a low-income senior, Medicaid generally also covers long-term care such as nursing facilities.

As with other assistance programs, applications and information about medical assistance are available at local public assistance offices. If benefits are initially denied, remember to exercise your appeal rights. The National Health Law Program publishes an excellent resource on the Medicaid program. For more information, call (310) 204-6010 or check out their website at www.healthlaw.org.

Medicare. If you are elderly or disabled, make sure you are getting available Medicare benefits. If payment of a claim is denied, make sure you know why. If you have a reason to disagree, contact your local Medicare office and file available appeals.

A Medicare prescription drug program for seniors went into effect in 2006. This program is called Medicare Part D. It is a voluntary program that allows seniors to shop around for a prescription drug provider among a number of different private insurance companies. The program has been very confusing because of the many different drug prices and co-pay options. The stakes are high. Selecting a plan that is favorable for you could save you a lot of money on drug costs. It is important to shop around and call providers to find out about costs and about any restrictions on access to the prescriptions drugs that you need. There are also a number of programs that provide supplements to Part D coverage.

For more information, you can check out the federal government's website on Medicare at www.medicare.gov. Both the National Senior Citizens Law Center (202-289-6976; www.nsclc.org) and the Center for Medicare Advocacy (860-456-7790; www.medicareadvocacy.org) are excellent resources for more information about Medicare Part D and about Medicare generally.

State Children's Health Insurance Program (SCHIP) and Other State Programs. SCHIP gives states matching federal funds to provide health coverage to children in families with incomes that are slightly above Medicaid limits. Each state program has its own rules. Because SCHIP is not a permanent law like Medicaid, Congress must vote to renew it. You should check with your state health department to find out more information.

A few states, such as Massachusetts, have passed laws or are considering laws that require residents to buy health insurance or obtain insurance through state-sponsored plans for low-income residents.

Other Medical Care Options. For applicants not qualified for Medicaid or for state medical assistance, Catastrophic Medical Assistance is available in some states to assist with major medical expenses. When medical bills exceed a certain percentage of an applicant's household income, the balance of the bill above that percentage is reimbursed.

Some hospitals have an obligation to provide free care to certain patients under either state or federal law. And hospitals have an obligation under federal law to treat or stabilize medical emergencies. In a crisis, you should use the emergency room of your local hospital and worry about the bill later.

Local service clubs also sometimes have programs designed to meet particular needs. The best known is the Lions Club, which helps to purchase eyeglasses for children.

Medical Prescriptions. Several options are available for families unable to obtain prescription drugs through Medicaid. Any patient receiving a prescription should ask whether or not a less expensive generic drug can be substituted. Many states also have programs to assist seniors in paying for prescription drugs. As discussed above in the Medicare section, there is also a Medicare prescription drug program called Medicare Part D.

Doctors may have free sample supplies of medication available if you explain your hardship. Additionally, most drug companies run programs which provide free medication for those in need. Find out the name of the company which makes the drug you need and call telephone information for that company's "800" phone number. Call the company to ask whether there is a program for reduced cost or free supply of prescribed medication. Finally, hospitals run by the Department of Veterans Affairs generally provide medicine to veterans for a small fee.

Low-Cost Dental Care. Dental care often takes a back seat to more pressing financial obligations. However, there are several ways that families can obtain free emergency dental care or low-cost preventive care. First, some types of dental care are covered by health or dental insurance. Some dental coverage is included in Medicaid. Second, if neither insurance nor Medicaid is available, many community college dental hygiene programs and university dental schools provide free or very low-cost services as part of their teaching programs. Some hospitals have low-cost oral surgery clinics.

SAVING

A good way to prevent future financial problems is to put aside money each week, if possible in a bank savings account, so that you can avoid expensive borrowing later. Non-profit budget counselors can help you figure out how to allocate your resources so that there is something left over each month for savings.

Your employer might have a plan where you can automatically contribute a certain amount each month to a retirement plan. Chapter Seven has a more detailed discussion about when to dip into savings and retirement money. In general, you should try to avoid the temptation to use up retirement savings to get through temporary financial difficulties. This is particularly true if you are close to retirement age.

It is sometimes difficult to think about saving in a society that bombards you with advertisements and encourages you to spend, spend, spend. However, in making your budget, you should carefully consider whether you can set aside even a very small amount each week or month for savings as a cushion against future problems.

You might also look into a savings program such as America Saves to help you with a savings plan. For more information, see www.americasaves.org or call Consumer Federation of America at 202-387-6121.

Many credit card companies offer savings plans that are attached to your credit cards. Usually, the creditor rounds up your purchases to the nearest dollar and makes a contribution of that amount to a savings account. For example, if you buy something for $9.95, the creditor will round up to $10 and contribute 5 cents to your savings account. Be sure and read the fine print before signing up for one of these programs.

A problem with these programs is that the creditor contributes to your savings account only if you use your credit card. This may encourage some consumers to spend more in order to try to save more. This is not going to help you in the long run if you are spending beyond your budget. It is also not going to help you if you don't pay off your credit balance and end up paying a much higher interest rate on your credit card payments than the generally low interest rate on savings accounts.

3

What You Need to Know About Your Credit Report

TOPICS COVERED IN THIS CHAPTER

- What Is a Credit Report
- How to Get a Copy of Your Own Credit Report
- Understanding Credit Scores
- Coping with a Bad Credit Record, Including How to Correct Errors and Delete Old Information
- Problems with Credit Repair Agencies
- Rebuilding Your Credit Record
- How to Deal With Identity Theft

THE TRUTH ABOUT CREDIT REPORTS

It can be painful, but consumers with financial problems should try to learn the truth about their credit reports. This will help you understand what you can and cannot do to improve your credit record. Although you cannot hide all of your credit problems, you can take a few very simple steps to make sure that your credit report is accurate and that any information which might be helpful is included. These strategies are discussed in this chapter.

This chapter will also help you understand who is allowed to look at your report and how you can review your own report. It will explain what a bad credit report does and does not mean for you and how you should deal with it. It also covers several strategies to improve your credit.

What Is a Credit Report? Your credit report (also called credit history) is a record of how you have borrowed and repaid debts. Almost every adult American has a credit file with the three major national credit bureaus: Experian, Equifax, and TransUnion.

Your credit report is an up-to-date, reasonably objective description of the status of many of your credit accounts. It has basic personal information about you—Social Security number, birth date, current and former addresses, and employers. For many of your debts, the report will also list basic account information, including the date you opened the account, the type of account (such as real estate, revolving (credit card), or installment); whether the account is currently open or has been closed; the monthly payment; the maximum credit limit; the latest activity on the account; the current balance; and any amounts past due.

Each account includes a code that explains whether the account is current, thirty days past due, sixty days past due, or ninety days past due, or if the account involves a repossession, charge off, or other collection activity. The report should also list the addresses and telephone numbers of your creditors, which you can use to contact them to dispute any inaccurate information they placed in your report.

The report will list any accounts that have been turned over to a collection agency. In addition, a credit report will include certain information of public record, including any court judgments (and possibly even mere lawsuits) against you, garnishments, tax liens, foreclosures, and bankruptcies. Finally, the report should note any consumer statement you've provided concerning an unresolved dispute.

How Do Credit Bureaus Collect Information? Most major creditors subscribe to one or more credit bureaus. Subscribing to a credit bureau is a two way street—the creditor agrees to continuously supply the credit bureau with current account information on the creditor's customers in exchange for the right to find out information about other credit applicants. Usually, creditors supply information to credit bureaus by computer. Each month the creditor transmits information about the status of its consumer accounts to the credit bureau. The bureaus use this information to update each borrower's credit file automatically.

CREDIT INQUIRIES

There is a separate box on your credit report called "inquiries." These are the names of creditors and others, such as employers, who have requested a copy of your credit report during the past year or two. If you follow the instructions for ordering your report described in the next section, you will see the complete list of companies that reviewed your report and the dates of their inquiries as well as a notation for each time you requested your own report. The list you will see might be quite long. This is because it also includes creditors that looked at your report for promotional purposes. These creditors may have followed up and sent out one of those pre-approved credit card applications that many consumers receive on a weekly basis.

This long list of inquiries may seem alarming. And in fact, many creditors view too many inquiries as a bad sign. They believe, often wrongly, that a large number of inquiries indicate that you have made frequent requests for credit and were turned down. However, there's no need to panic if you see a long list on your report. This list will appear only on the report that goes to you. The report that goes to prospective creditors and employers lists only those creditors that have requested your report after you applied for credit, *not* those who requested your report for promotional purposes. Only the first type of inquiry will affect your credit score; credit scores and the factors that affect them are discussed below. You should investigate the names of any inquirers whom you do not know because unfamiliar inquiries may indicate that someone is fraudulently using your identity. As with inquiries, only the report that goes to you will note how many times you have ordered your own report.

REVIEWING YOUR CREDIT REPORT

Order Your Report. The first step in learning about your credit report is to order copies from the three main credit bureaus and read these reports carefully. This will allow you to see if the bad information you think is listed in the report is really there. This section tells you how to get a copy of your report. A later section discusses what you can do if you don't like what you see on your report.

Because there can be differences in the reports kept by each of the three major national credit bureaus, you should order your report from all three, either on-line, in writing, or by telephone. You are entitled to one free copy of your report every year from each of the three major bureaus, but you must order from the centralized request service, described below.

You may want to order your free credit report by phone or mail, and not on-line. If you order by phone or mail, you will receive a paper credit report that has more information and is easier to read than the electronic version. Also, if you order your credit report on-line, there may be a risk that you might waive your right to take the credit bureaus to court.

Free Annual Credit Reports. You can get your free credit reports from the centralized request service by:

- Going to www.annualcreditreport.com;
- Calling 877-322-8228; or
- Completing the Annual Credit Report Request Form and mailing it to:
  Annual Credit Report Request Service
  P.O. Box 105281
  Atlanta, GA 30348-5281.

You can download the form at www.ftc.gov/credit.

Do not contact the credit bureaus individually for your free annual report. They are only providing free annual credit reports through the centralized service listed above. Beware of other websites that claim to provide free credit reports! Some of these offers are not really free, but introductory teasers that convert to an expensive subscription service.

You can get all three reports at no cost when you go to the centralized service or just one at a time if you prefer. However you wish to do this, you can get just one free report from each agency in each twelve month period under these rules.

You need to provide your name, address, Social Security number, and date of birth. If you have moved in the last two years, you may have to provide your previous address. To maintain the security of your file, each credit bureau may ask you for some information that only you would know, like the amount of your monthly mortgage payment. Each bureau may ask you for different information.

Other Ways to Get a Free Credit Report. In addition to the free annual credit report you are entitled to receive under federal law, you should be able to get your report for free if you live in a state that allows its residents to get one free report each year. These states are Colorado, Georgia, Maryland, Massachusetts, New Jersey, and Vermont. These special state law rights should be in addition to the right to a free report that is available under federal law.

The credit bureaus are also required to give you a copy of your report for free if you have been denied credit within the past sixty days. Even if you haven't been denied credit, there are other situations in which you can get reports for free.

You can get one free report in any twelve-month period if you:

—Are unemployed and will be applying for a job within the next sixty days; or

—Are receiving public assistance; or

—You have reason to believe that the file at the credit bureau contains inaccurate information due to fraud.

In addition, credit bureaus must provide you with a free report if you have requested a fraud alert. Such alerts are discussed later in this chapter.

The current toll-free phone numbers and web addresses for ordering credit reports (other than free annual reports) are listed below. You can also order by mail; you should call or e-mail to get the current mailing addresses since they change frequently.

CREDIT BUREAU CONTACT INFORMATION

Experian's toll-free telephone number to order reports is 1-888-EXPERIAN (1-888-397-3742). You can also order on-line at www.experian.com.

Equifax's number is 1-800-685-1111. Reports can also be ordered on-line at www.equifax.com.

TransUnion Corporation's phone number is 800-916-8800. Reports can be ordered on-line at www.transunion.com.

Paying for a Credit Report. If you've already accessed your free annual report and the other special circumstances discussed above don't apply, credit bureaus can currently charge you no more than $10 per report. This is a maximum charge, not a required charge, and some states have passed laws limiting the amount credit bureaus can charge consumers for reports. You should check with your state consumer affairs department or legal services office to see what the limits are, if any, in your state.

Even though the maximum charge for a paid credit report is $10, the credit bureaus have developed various packages or services that cost much more. For example, the three major bureaus offer "three-in-one" reports that allow you to get all three reports at once, sometimes with a credit score, but you will probably pay $30 to $40 for these packages. The bureaus also offer "credit monitoring" services that cost $100 to $150 annually. The value of these expensive services is debatable, given the availability of free annual reports.

CREDIT SCORING

A credit score is a number which summarizes your credit history. The purpose of the score is to help lenders evaluate whether you are a risky borrower. Your score may differ depending on which credit bureau (Equifax, Experian, or TransUnion) is making a report. Credit scores can range from 350 to 900. Anything over about 750 is considered to be a very good score by most lenders.

CREDIT SCORING FACTORS

Each credit bureau and credit scoring company has a slightly different way of calculating credit scores. The biggest credit scoring company, Fair Isaac Corporation, has disclosed the factors it considers in generating credit scores. Fair Isaac's scores are called FICO scores. Most creditors and credit bureaus either use Fair Isaac's scoring system or have a system based on the Fair Isaac system. According to Fair Isaac, the factors that are considered in determining FICO scores are:

- Payment history (about 35% of the score).

- Amounts owed on credit accounts compared to available credit (about 30% of the score). High balances in comparison to your credit limits may indicate that you are over-extended.

- Length of credit history (about 15% of the score). In general, a longer credit history increases the score.

- New credit (about 10% of the score). You get more points in your score if you have an established credit history and don't have too many new accounts. Opening several accounts in a short period of time can indicate greater risk.

- Types of credit (about 10% of the score). Fair Isaac scoring systems look for a mix of different types of credit. However, this factor is usually not important if there is sufficient other information upon which to base your score.

More information is available on-line at www.myfico.com or by calling 1-800-319-4433.

Improving Your Credit Score. The best way to improve your score is to pay your bills on time and keep low balances. This is difficult to do when you are in financial trouble. The key factors disclosed with your score should help you identify what credit information is hurting your score the most, and you can focus on improving that area. The best strategy while you are still in trouble is to check your credit reports for errors or old information, as discussed in the next section, and then take no action on your credit score until you are financially stable again. At that point, you should follow the steps discussed at the end of this chapter on rebuilding credit. These same steps will also help improve your credit score.

In the meantime, you may also be able to explain a bad score to creditors. Although the creditor probably can do little to change your score with the credit bureau, it can override the score as an important factor in deciding to grant you credit. This flexibility makes it important that you explain in detail your reasons for problems on your credit record. For example, loss of a job due to an illness may explain an old default. If you have returned to work, the creditor may grant you a loan on good terms even if your credit score is low.

If a creditor does not respond well to your explanation, shop around. Other creditors may be more flexible.

Shopping for Credit and Your Score. You may also have heard that a large number of credit inquiries will lower your credit score. This is not always true. Some companies and credit bureaus take inquiries into account and some do not. However, even those companies that do count a large number of inquiries against you claim that this will have only a small impact on your score. Other factors are much more important.

You should not be afraid to shop for the best credit just because you are worried that too many inquiries will show up on your credit report or lower your credit score. Getting affordable credit and paying it off each month will outweigh any harm caused by too many inquiries.

Getting Your Score. Under federal law, the credit bureaus are required to provide consumers with their credit scores upon request. The credit score is not free, but the charge for the score will be set by the Federal Trade Commission. Mortgage lenders are also required to give you information about your credit score for free.

Perhaps nearly as important as the score itself are the factors that pulled a score down. Along with the score itself, the bureaus have to provide the top four factors that most affected the score. If the number of inquiries to a consumer's report pulled down the score, the bureau must disclose that too. This information is critical because knowing what goes into the score will help you figure out whether there is anything you can do to improve your score.

Despite these new consumer rights, the disclosure system is still far from perfect. For example, the scores sold by the credit bureaus to consumers may not be the same scores that they provide to lenders and creditors.

COPING WITH A
BAD CREDIT REPORT

Reviewing your credit report may have confirmed your worst fears. Although you cannot erase all of the bad information from the report, there are some simple steps you can take to make a bad situation better. The eight steps discussed in this section will help you cope with a bad credit report.

1. Correct any errors on your report. It is common to find that there is incorrect information in your credit file. You have the legal right to correct this information and should do so. Accurate damaging information is bad enough. You do not also need inaccurate damaging entries. You should send a written dispute to each credit bureau that has reported incorrect information. The credit bureau by law must investigate the entry and correct the mistakes. In most circumstances, the agency is required to get back to you with the results of the investigation within thirty days.

The creditor who first supplied the information to the bureau also has a duty to investigate your dispute and provide the bureau with the information necessary to make your report correct or complete.

Even after the entry is corrected, periodically check to make sure that this incorrect information has been deleted permanently. Inaccurate items have a habit of popping up again even after they are corrected. Making sure your credit report is accurate is also important for your credit score if the inaccurate information was used in calculating the score.

Do not assume that you are home free if you get a favorable response from credit bureau "A". You should follow-up by doing the following:

- Obtain another copy of your credit report with credit bureau "A" to confirm that the corrections were made.
- Check to see whether your reports at credit bureaus "B" and "C" contain the same error and if so, send the results of the investigation of credit bureau "A" to those agencies as well.
- Get another copy of the report from credit bureau "A" three to six months later to make sure that the bureau has not put the information back in.
- Consider requesting that all the credit bureaus notify past users of the corrections. The bureaus are required to do this only if you request it and only if you first file a statement of dispute with them. The correction can be sent only to users that you specifically designate

and, even then, only to users who received the report within the past six months (or two years if used for employment).

2. Clean up your file with the help of the creditor. As described above, filing a dispute with the credit bureau can delete unverified information that a particular debt was ever owed. However, this will not work if the creditor insists you owed the money and verifies that fact to the credit bureau. In that situation, you can try to obtain the creditor's help in deleting this information.

In trying to persuade the creditor that its information was inaccurate, you should supply whatever proof you have. If your proof is not enough to resolve the matter, you may have to agree to pay part or all of the debt, either immediately or in installments. If you agree to pay part or all of the debt, make sure to get the creditor's *written* agreement to delete the negative information. Simply paying off a debt will not remove the information from your credit report.

You may have a chance (particularly if you are persistent and talk to supervisors) to make an agreement with certain creditors for installment payments amounting to much less than the full amount owed. Other creditors, though, may refuse to change what they have already told a credit bureau. If you choose this strategy, keep in mind the rules from Chapter One about deciding which debts to pay first.

If a creditor does agree to delete information, it can contact the credit bureau to request the deletion. Second best, the creditor can agree not to verify its original information if asked by the credit bureau. Then, when you dispute the item, the information will not be verified on reinvestigation, and it will have to be deleted.

Be sure that any agreement with the creditor to remove historical information is clear and in writing. Otherwise, creditors may not actually follow through in deleting the information.

3. Use your federal rights to remove student loan defaults. If one of the more troubling delinquencies on your credit record is a student loan default, there are certain special steps you can take, as described in more detail in Chapter Eighteen. If you qualify for certain loan discharges described in that chapter, the fact that you were ever in default on the student loan is deleted from your credit record.

You can also consolidate or rehabilitate a defaulted student loan (as described in Chapter Eighteen), so that you are no longer delinquent. Rehabilitation will clear up the current and historical information on your credit record.

4. Clean up public record information. The most damaging information on your credit record is sometimes found from public records, such as arrests, convictions, judgments, foreclosures, tax takings, and liens. The best way to remove this information from your file is to do so at the source with the government agency supplying this information to the credit bureau, and then make sure the corrected information is updated in the credit bureau's files.

For example, you may be able to come to an agreement with a creditor to remove a default judgment against you in return for a promise to enter into a repayment plan. The court record will no longer indicate a default. You can then dispute the information in your file, and the credit bureau will have to remove the entry because it can no longer verify the accuracy of its entry of a default judgment.

5. Delete old information. Most bad information must be removed from your report after a certain number of years, as follows:

Seven Years.
- *Accounts sent for collection or charged off* may be reported from the date of the last activity on the account for up to seven years. The date of last activity is no later than 180 days from the delinquency itself.

  The seven-year clock does not start ticking again if the account is sold to another collection agency. However, some collection agencies will purposefully change the date of last activity to make the debt look less old, a practice called "re-aging." If you suspect re-aging, send a dispute to the credit bureau as well as the collection agency.
- *Lawsuits and judgments* may be reported from the date of the entry of the judgment for up to seven years or when the judgment expires.
- *Paid tax liens* from the date of the last activity for up to seven years.
- *Most criminal records* such as information about indictments or arrests may be reported for seven years.

Ten Years.
- *Bankruptcies* may be reported for no more than ten years. The clock starts ticking from the date you file.

Forever.

- *Records of criminal convictions* may be reported indefinitely.
- *Positive information* may be reported indefinitely. The limits discussed above apply only to bad information.

If you find old information on your report, you should follow the steps outlined above to request that the credit bureau investigate and delete the information.

6. Explain damaging items. It is often helpful to send a statement to the credit bureau explaining damaging items. Credit bureaus are required to accept these statements if they relate to why information in the report is inaccurate. They cannot charge to include this statement in your report.

The credit bureaus are not required to include in your file your explanation of why you were delinquent. However, they may agree to do so. For example, they may not have to include your letter explaining that you were sick or lost your job. But they must include a statement explaining that you were not delinquent because the creditor agreed to postpone payments until you could return to work from your illness.

These statements are limited to one hundred words if the bureau helps you write the summary. Otherwise, there is no word limit, but it is a good idea to keep the statement very short. If you request it, the bureau must give the statement or summary to anyone who received a copy of your report within the past six months (or two years if the report was given out for employment purposes).

Another approach that is often more effective is to explain the delinquency to the lender from whom you are applying for credit rather than to the credit bureau. Federal law requires that creditors at least consider your explanation. Similarly, Fannie Mae requires its mortgage lenders to review any letter you provide explaining your credit problems.

7. Avoid overreacting to threats to damage your credit rating. Creditors may threaten to report negative information to a credit bureau, but the threat is only meant to pressure you to pay. The reality is that they *automatically* report information about your account every month whether they threaten to do so or not. It is even more unlikely that a collection agency hired by a creditor will report information on you to a credit bureau just because you do not respond to the agency's collection attempts. Like creditors, they *automatically* report the fact that your account has been sent to a collection agency.

These threats are probably illegal under the federal Fair Debt Collection Practices Act (FDCPA). You can sue the collection agency under that statute and receive as much as $1,000 even if you are not injured by the threat. If a creditor itself is doing the threatening (not an independent agency hired by the creditor), then the FDCPA does not apply, but you may have other legal ways of challenging the creditor's conduct, as discussed in Chapter Eight.

8. Avoid credit repair agencies. Avoid companies that promise to fix your credit record for a fee. They usually call themselves credit repair, credit service, credit clinic, or similar names. These agencies usually cannot deliver what they promise. You can generally do a better job cleaning up your credit record at no cost, just by following the advice in this book. And in some cases, the credit repair strategies recommended by these companies may make matters worse for you or may even cause you other legal problems.

Recognizing the many problems with credit repair agencies, federal law and some state laws require most credit repair companies to give you certain information before you sign up. They are not allowed to provide any services until three days after you sign a written and dated contract, and they are not allowed to charge you in advance. You have the right to cancel the contract for any reason during this three-day period. The federal law (and many state laws) also makes it illegal for a credit repair agency to make false or misleading statements to credit bureaus. This includes statements that are intended to change the consumer's identification for the purpose of hiding bad information. You should contact a lawyer if you believe you have been ripped off by one of these companies. Remember, you can achieve the same or better results than credit repair agencies on your own.

BEWARE OF THESE COMMON CLAIMS MADE BY CREDIT REPAIR COMPANIES

"We can erase bad credit"
   The truth is that no one can erase bad credit information from your report *if it is accurate.*

"Only we can remove old or inaccurate information"
   The truth is that, if there are legitimate errors on your report or information that is old, you can correct the report yourself without paying a lot of money to one of these companies.

"The information on your report is accurate but we'll erase it anyway"
   The truth is that, if this means lying to the credit reporting agency, it is illegal.

Who Can See Your Credit Report. You may find that there are no mistakes or old information on your report. Your report may simply be bad because it reflects the fact that you are having financial difficulties. This is not easy to take but it may not be as bad as you think. Most importantly, there is a federal law that regulates who can and can't see your credit file. Not everyone is allowed to look at your report, and not everyone who is allowed to look at your report will do so.

Below is a list of who can see your report:

- **Creditors** can look at your report whenever you apply for credit, such as a mortgage, car loan, or credit cards.
- **Employers** can look at your report, but only under certain circumstances and only if you give them written authorization. Employers are allowed to look at your report to evaluate you for hiring, promotions, and other employment purposes. Employers are, more and more, using credit reports in making employment decisions.
- **Government agencies**, including those trying to collect child support, can look at your report. Those considering you for eligibility for public assistance may review your credit report as well. But their reason for doing this is not to see if you have unpaid bills, only to see if you have hidden income or assets.
- **Insurance companies** can look at your credit report. In many states, home and auto insurers now use specialized credit scores to decide whether to issue you a policy and how much to charge for it. Insurance companies may ask a reporting agency for information on your medical history and about any insurance claims you have filed.
- **Landlords** can look at your credit record when they are deciding whether to rent an apartment to you. Although your credit record can be important when you are leasing a residence, it is certainly more important when you take out a mortgage to buy a home. Larger landlords, landlords specializing in low-income housing, and larger-city landlords are most likely to pull your credit record. If a landlord turns down your rental application because of bad credit, you may still be able to rent the apartment if you can explain some of the problems. If the landlord doesn't accept your explanations, don't give up. You may have better luck with another landlord.

CHECKING FOR UNAUTHORIZED USERS

When reviewing your credit report, you should check to make sure that everyone who reviewed your report had authority to do so. Not everyone is allowed to request your report. Even creditors or merchants whom you contact cannot review your report unless you have made an offer to buy their product or otherwise applied for credit.

Car dealers, for example, are usually eager to look at your credit the minute you walk in the door. However, curiosity about your credit history is not a sufficient reason for the dealer to review your report. If a car dealer wants to look at your report while you are just shopping around, the dealer must either get your permission or you must indicate to the dealer that you are ready to enter into a credit transaction. To avoid the problem of too many inquiries on your report, do not give a car dealer (or anyone else) permission to review your report unless you are serious about a particular transaction.

When Is a Bad Credit Report Less Important? In some cases, your concerns about the impact of a negative credit rating are likely to be exaggerated. For example:

- *Utility service.* In many states, utility companies can request your credit report. The current trend is for these companies to use your credit score to determine whether to charge you a security deposit. However, there are special rules, discussed in Chapter Fifteen, that keep utility companies from denying you service in many cases even if your credit is bad. A critical precondition to obtaining utility service is that you do not owe that particular utility company any money.
- *Student loans and grants.* For most government student loans and grants, your credit record is irrelevant. There are a few exceptions. For example, parents applying for PLUS loans to help finance their children's education are required to pass a credit check. This is also required for graduate or professional student borrowers applying for the new student PLUS loans. Aside from these few exceptions, your credit report will only affect your ability to get new government loans and grants if you are in default on a prior student loan. This is not the case with private student loans. These lenders will usually check your credit or require a co-signor. Getting out of default and other student loan issues are explained in Chapter Eighteen.
- *Your credit report will not damage your friends, relations, and need not even affect your spouse.* Your credit report has no impact on the ability

of your friends, associates, or even family members to obtain credit or employment. A creditor is not allowed to look at your credit record if, for example, your spouse, child, or parent applies for credit and they are not relying on your income or assets in the credit application.

■ *Your credit report will not damage your reputation in the community.* No one can obtain your credit record for curiosity, gossip, or to determine your reputation. Your credit record can only be used to consider your application for insurance, credit, employment, and certain benefits and other business transactions. Federal law prohibits both credit bureaus and collection agencies from placing your name on a bad debt list that is circulated to the public.

Your credit record is just between you and creditors— your neighbors and friends should never see it.

■ *Your credit record cannot be used in divorce, child custody, immigration, and other legal proceedings.* Normally, no one can use your credit record in a divorce or in a proceeding to determine child custody or child support. Credit reports generally also cannot be used in other legal proceedings, such as immigration proceedings, applications for citizenship, or as a basis to deny your ability to register to vote.

REBUILDING CREDIT

The best way to rebuild credit is to get new credit and make timely payments. But be careful. You should not start trying to get new credit during times of financial difficulty simply to improve your credit report. This is likely to take your attention away from paying high-priority debts first. You are also likely to end up dealing with a lender advertising "easy credit" or "no credit history required." Many of these lenders are rip-offs, preying on consumers who fear that they cannot get traditional forms of credit. One of the most important steps you can take to cope with a bad credit history is to avoid getting deeper in debt during the bad times. Prioritize your debts, and then when you are ready, start following the strategies discussed in this section to rebuild credit.

1. Stabilize your situation. In the long run, the most important thing for you to do to reestablish a good credit rating is stabilize your employment, income, and debts. This will prevent new delinquencies from being reported. While your past delinquencies can stay on your record as long as seven years, creditors are likely to ignore older debt problems if your situation becomes stable and if you start paying your present obligations.

Once you get back on track, each year your older debt problems will have less of an impact on your ability to obtain credit. Seven years will come around sooner than you might think, and then there will be no record of those past problems at all.

If your financial problems are behind you, your credit record problems will not go away immediately. Be patient, your credit profile will improve over time. More information about getting back on your feet over the long haul is contained in Chapter Twenty.

2. Establish new credit accounts (with caution). You can improve your credit by getting new credit and paying it back on time. But be careful. Avoid causing yourself more problems by getting unaffordable high-rate credit. One way to avoid this trap is to wait until you are offered a credit card with reasonable terms. You may get credit card offers even though you have a negative credit history, but these offers may be for expensive subprime cards that offer little credit and charge high fees.

Credit cards advertised as helping with
"bad credit" can end up costing you a bundle
and make your credit history even worse.

Another approach is to get a secured credit card, offered by some banks and other creditors. These cards require that you keep a cash balance with the card issuer and draw down on this amount. You need to be very careful in selecting a secured card. For a detailed discussion of problems with secured cards as well as other tips on what types of credit card arrangements are likely to work best for you, see Chapter Five.

Finally, if you decide to get new credit, be sure that the creditor you use actually reports account information to a credit bureau. If not, your hard work to pay back the credit will not be reflected in your report.

3. Build credit in your own name. Particularly if you have been relying on your spouse's or partner's credit record, you may decide now to build credit in your own name. In general, only information about accounts in your name appear in your credit report. If you had a joint account with your spouse or partner (or anyone else), or if you were authorized to use that account, the credit bureau must include information about that account in both your report and the joint user's report. The bureau will also include information in your report about accounts that you co-signed even if your name is not the primary name on the account.

But individual accounts solely in your spouse's or partner's name will not be on your credit record, unless you were authorized to use the account. In many cases, it will be a relief to know that your credit report is yours alone. If your spouse or partner has bad credit, you do not have to worry that this information will ruin your credit. However, this may not be such good news if you are recently separated, divorced, or widowed and trying to establish credit in your own name. You may find that your spouse or partner had good credit. But you will get no benefit from his good credit if those accounts were in his or her name only.

Nevertheless, you can take certain steps to benefit from your spouse's good credit. If you are still married and your spouse is reliable, you should make sure that all joint accounts and accounts that you are obligated to pay appear on your credit report, too. If you are already divorced, separated, or widowed, you can still ask the creditor to consider any of your spouse's accounts that reflect on your creditworthiness. For example, if you and your spouse made payments on your spouse's accounts with joint checks, bring this to the creditors' attention. The creditor does not have to consider this information, but might do so.

To build credit in your own name, you should also follow the other steps listed in this section. Creditors must allow you to apply for an individual account if that's what you want. They cannot require that your spouse (or anyone else) co-sign as long as no jointly held or community property is involved and you can meet the creditor's standards on your own.

4. Explain damaging items. As discussed in an earlier section, it is often helpful to send a statement to the credit bureau explaining damaging items. Credit bureaus are required to accept these statements if they relate to why information in the report is inaccurate. They cannot charge to include this statement in your report.

Filing Bankruptcy May Actually Help You Rebuild Your Credit.

Filing bankruptcy sometimes actually improves your credit record. A bankruptcy discharge gets you off to a fresh start and should reduce your debt burden. It should also enhance the stability of your employment and income. Wage garnishments, continuous collection calls, car repossessions, telephone disconnections, and other consequences of an unaffordable debt burden are eliminated, and this should help you find and hold steady employment.

The resulting stability of your income and lowered debt burden may be more important to a potential creditor than the fact that certain older debts were discharged in bankruptcy. Another advantage of bankruptcy is that it should clear up the current account status of most entries in your file. The credit bureau will have to list the outstanding balance as "0" for each item. While the bankruptcy will be listed in your file and while the historical summary will list that certain debts had been delinquent at one time, the current account information should be much improved. This is a key part of any lender's review of a credit report and the deletion of numerous outstanding balances should be an improvement.

If you do file bankruptcy, you should check your credit report after your bankruptcy discharge. You should file a dispute with the credit bureaus if your discharged debts continue to be listed as having a balance owed.

The listing of a bankruptcy may mean that certain creditors will refuse to extend you credit or will offer credit only at higher rates. But other creditors look at the fact that you cannot file a second chapter 7 (straight) bankruptcy for another eight years and that fewer debts are now competing for your stream of income.

In addition, certain government agencies will not provide a government-backed mortgage if you have outstanding defaults, but will do so if you have discharged your debts in bankruptcy. Usually you will only have to wait a year or two after the bankruptcy to become eligible for the mortgage loan.

Bankruptcies stay on your credit record for ten years from the bankruptcy filing, while the underlying debts are usually only reported for seven years from the delinquency. This means that, if your delinquencies are five or six years old, bankruptcy may not be the best option to deal with the credit record issues. The debts will have to be deleted from credit reports within another year or two, while the bankruptcy will stay on your record for a full ten years from the date of the bankruptcy. For a more detailed discussion of bankruptcy, see Chapter Nineteen.

HOW TO OBTAIN A HOME MORTGAGE WITH A BLEMISHED CREDIT REPORT

Unfortunately, a bad credit report will make it more difficult to obtain a home mortgage at a reasonable rate, unless you can obtain a creditworthy cosigner.

Many conventional mortgages follow Fannie Mae or Freddie Mac guidelines. Under these guidelines, a foreclosure on your credit record will make it difficult to obtain a mortgage for about two to four years and will affect your ability to be considered a worthy borrower for seven years. You should try to establish at least a year of on-time mortgage payments and pretty close to on-time payments for your other loans before applying for a new mortgage. Furthermore, it is difficult to obtain a mortgage for at least two years after you receive a bankruptcy discharge.

VA, FHA, and RHS mortgages have looser guidelines than Fannie Mae or Freddie Mac. Even then, you should have no current defaults and a one- or two-year period since any bankruptcy discharge. You may also find other mortgage lenders with more flexible guidelines than those for Fannie Mae or Freddie Mac. Nevertheless, it is important to avoid con artists and unscrupulous lenders that charge outrageous interest rates for people with credit problems. As discussed throughout this book, desperate choices are likely to make your situation worse.

If you want to take out a home mortgage despite problems with your credit record, there are several steps you should take. First, obtain a copy of your own credit report and credit score from several of the major credit bureaus several months before you apply for the mortgage. (How to obtain copies of your own report was described earlier in this chapter.) In many home sales, time is of the essence, and you should already be dealing with your credit report problems before you apply for the mortgage.

Try to clean up the report as much as possible by notifying the credit bureaus of any inaccurate information and by establishing a good payment record on your current debts for a period of time. Paying down current balances is more important than addressing old ("charged-off") debts with creditors with whom you no longer do business.

There are some businesses that specialize in assisting consumers to raise their credit scores when applying for a mortgage, by helping them correct errors and getting their files "re-scored" quickly. These businesses can only help you with a referral from a mortgage lender or broker, so you should ask your lender or broker about re-scoring.

When the mortgage company questions an aspect of your credit record, try to explain any extenuating circumstances. You can also provide favorable information not present on your credit record, such as an excellent history of rent and utility payments.

Avoid any lender that solicits you, especially if they come to your door or call you at home.

Shop around for a mortgage company that says it can accept your credit history. Sometimes you may have to pay a slightly higher rate. For example, many lenders rate their applicants as A, B, C, or D, and then charge a slightly higher rate for each step in the scale. If you are offered a very high rate, don't assume that you can't find a better rate elsewhere. Find out your credit score—it may not be as bad as you think. Try to shop around. But definitely avoid extraordinarily high-rate lenders that prey on those in financial distress. They charge unaffordable interest rates as high as 13% to 30% (or higher) plus hidden fees, brokerage charges, and points. A good rule of thumb is to avoid any lender that solicits you, particularly door-to-door or over the telephone. Also be mindful of the rules about refinancing discussed in Chapter Six.

If a husband and wife are seeking a mortgage, and only one spouse has a bad credit record, you can apply in the name of the other spouse, relying exclusively on that spouse's income and assets. In that case, the creditor is not allowed to look at the other spouse's bad credit record. However, remember that any *joint debts* (debts owed by both spouses) will appear on both records no matter who had the primary responsibility to pay. This is true even after divorce and even if there is a court order requiring one spouse to pay.

IDENTITY THEFT

How Identity Theft Can Ruin Your Credit Record.
In some cases, you may have problems with your credit report even though you've paid all of your bills on time. Someone may have stolen your credit card or Social Security number and used it to obtain credit, destroying your credit history in the process. This section gives you advice if you are a victim of identity theft.

You may not even know you are a victim of identity theft until you try to get new credit or apply for a loan and are unexpectedly rejected. Identity theft is discovered an average of fourteen months after the crime has occurred.

Prevention is one of the most effective ways to avoid becoming a victim. Below are some tips on how to avoid identity theft:

- Place a "security freeze" on your credit history. A security freeze prevents your credit history from being shared with potential creditors. If your credit files are frozen, a thief will probably not be able to get credit in your name.

  A security freeze generally costs $10 to place with each credit bureau, for a total of $30. Some state cap the cost at a lower amount, or require freezes to be for free for identity theft victims.
- Do not carry your Social Security card with you. Keep it in a safe place at home or in a safety deposit box.
- Do not attach or write a personal identification number (PIN) or Social Security number on any card that you carry with you or anything you are going to throw away (such as an invoice or receipt).
- Shred any document that contains your credit card or Social Security number before throwing it away.
- Alert your credit card lender if you do not receive your statements. Someone may be stealing your mail.
- Do not give personal information or account numbers to anyone until you have confirmed the identity of the person requesting the information and verified that you need to provide this information.
- Frequently check your credit report to look for warning signs.
- Put passwords on your credit card, bank, and home accounts. Avoid using easily available information like your mother's maiden name or your birth date.

What to Do If You Are a Victim of Identity Theft. According to the Federal Trade Commission, the first four steps you should take if you believe you are the victim of identity theft are:

1. Contact the fraud department of a major credit bureau to place a fraud alert on your credit report. As soon as you make this initial report to a credit bureau and the bureau confirms your report, the other major credit bureaus will automatically be notified to place fraud alerts on your report as well. You should then automatically receive free copies of all three of your credit reports.

A fraud alert is a statement added to your report asking creditors to check with you before issuing credit. Furthermore, creditors must take steps to verify the identity of an applicant whose report contains such a fraud alert. Although this check doesn't always work, it is effective much of the time and is an important first step to take if you are a victim of identity theft.

The initial fraud alert lasts only ninety days. In order to get an extended alert, you will have to provide additional information, including an identity theft report. This is a copy of an official report filed with an appropriate federal, state, or local law enforcement agency.

In addition to the fraud alert, the credit bureaus are required to block the reporting of any information in a consumer's file that resulted from identity theft. Once a consumer provides the bureaus with proof of identity, an identity theft report, a list of theft-related information on the report, and a statement that the information does not relate to any transaction of the consumer, the bureaus must start blocking the identified information within four business days.

You should order copies of your credit reports from the three bureaus and review them to make sure no additional fraudulent accounts have been opened in your name or unauthorized changes made to your existing accounts. Also, look through the "inquiries" section and request that any inquiries that you did not initiate be deleted from your report. In a few months, order new copies of your reports to make sure that the corrections have been made.

2. Contact your creditors to find out about any accounts that have been tampered with or opened fraudulently. This includes credit card companies, phone companies, utilities, and others with whom you do business. Ask to speak with someone in the security or fraud department and follow up with a letter. You should immediately close any accounts that have been tampered with and open new ones with new PINS.

3. File a report with your local police or the police in the community where the identity theft took place. You will need this report in order to get an extended fraud alert in your credit file and to take advantage of some of the other identity theft protections. Unfortunately, some police departments will make it very difficult for you to file a report. A few states have passed special protections to require police departments to take these reports. If you have trouble with a police department, you should keep trying and be persistent. Be sure to give them as much documentation as possible to prove your case. If you can't get anywhere with the local police, try the state police, or the U.S. Postal Inspection Service if the mail was involved.

4. File a complaint with the Federal Trade Commission. The FTC cannot bring criminal cases but it can give you information about how to resolve problems. The FTC has a special Identity Theft Hotline (1-877-IDTHEFT), or you can file a complaint on-line at www.consumer.gov/idtheft.

There are other actions to consider as well. You may especially want to place a freeze on your credit file if you've been the victim of identity theft. Freezes are more powerful than fraud alerts.

If it appears that someone is using your Social Security number, for example, in applying for a job, call the Social Security office to see if your Social Security number was used fraudulently. They can verify the accuracy of earnings reported on your number. If you believe your mail was stolen, you should also contact the post office.

In addition, you can get more information from businesses that had transactions with an identity thief. These businesses must provide identity theft victims with information about transactions that occurred in their name. For example, an account application may have identifying information that can help track down the thief, such as the thief's true telephone number, address, or date of birth.

In some cases your identity may have been stolen by someone you know. These are usually the most emotional and difficult cases to resolve. If this happens to you, the bottom line is that you most likely have to report the theft in order to fully protect yourself. You may be able to work with the creditors to see if you can resolve the problem without notifying law enforcement, but this is difficult.

Federal credit reporting law provides special protections for active duty military. Consumers on active duty, including reservists serving anywhere other than their usual station, may place alerts on their credit file noting that they are on active duty. This should help prevent identity theft against soldiers who are stationed far away from their home addresses.

4

The Pros and Cons of Credit Counseling and Other "Debt Relief" Companies

TOPICS COVERED IN THIS CHAPTER

- Basic Facts About Credit Counseling
- Deciding Whether a Debt Management Plan Is a Good Idea
- Finding a Reputable Credit Counseling Agency
- Problems with Other "Debt Relief" Services Including Debt Settlement and Debt Elimination Companies

Seeking professional debt counseling assistance can be a good idea, but you should be very careful. It is extremely difficult to sort out the good credit counseling agencies from the bad. Many agencies are legitimate, but many are simply rip-offs. It is also important to understand that even good agencies won't be able to help you much if you're already too deep in financial trouble.

To make matters even more complicated, there are many other types of companies selling services that they advertise as more effective than credit counseling. This chapter includes information about the most common types of "debt relief" companies, including debt settlement and debt termination. The chapter will help you understand the differences between all of these companies and help you decide whether you are likely to benefit from their services.

CREDIT COUNSELING

Credit counselors used to be mainly small, community-based organizations. The quality of their services varied, but few marketed their services beyond their immediate community and few tried to pressure consumers into "buying" their products. This is no longer true. Credit counseling has grown into a big industry.

Today, there are a lot of very serious problems with the credit counseling industry. For example, nearly every credit counseling agency in the country has non-profit status. However, many are being investigated by the I.R.S. because of evidence that they operate like for-profit businesses rather than non-profits. This means that when an agency tells you it is "non-profit," you cannot assume that it is above board.

Federal and state enforcement agencies have caught up with many of the worst agencies, but there are still a lot of agencies that do not act in the best interests of consumers. It is largely up to you to figure out whether credit counseling services are likely to be useful for you and then to find a legitimate agency. This chapter includes information to help you through this process. It also includes basic information about the credit counseling requirement in the bankruptcy law. This issue is covered in greater detail in Chapter Nineteen.

What Is Credit Counseling? A legitimate credit counseling agency offers a range of services from basic budget counseling to educational courses about finances to debt repayment plans. Most agencies receive a lot of their funding from creditors through a process called Fair Share. Under the Fair Share process, creditors voluntarily return to the credit counseling agency a set percentage of the funds that are disbursed to them. For example, you might have a debt repayment plan where you pay $100 each month to the credit counseling agency for your Visa bill. If Visa's Fair Share to the agency is 5%, it will credit you with a $100 payment but will actually keep only $95. It will return the extra $5 to the credit counseling agency. Some creditors have stopped using the Fair Share system. Most of these creditors still provide funding to counseling agencies through different programs, such as grants for agencies that are considered "high performers."

Some agencies will tell you that they receive funding from creditors. Others will not. The important point to remember is that an agency is not necessarily bad just because it receives money from creditors. However, this arrangement does create the possibility of conflicts of interest. Agencies may, for example, be reluctant to advise you to consider bankruptcy even if is it in *your* best interests because it is not in the interests of creditors.

Most credit counselors also require consumers to pay fees directly to them. Some may have a sliding scale so that the lowest-income consumers pay less or even nothing at all. Beware of agencies that charge very high monthly and up-front or set-up fees. Some agencies will tell you that they don't charge anything, but will then pressure you to make a "voluntary" contribution. You should try to avoid these attempts to get you to pay a lot of money for counseling services. Be prepared to ask very specific questions about how much the agency will charge you for different types of services.

A very important point to keep in mind is that most credit counseling agencies help with credit card debt only. Some will also help you with other types of unsecured debt, such as medical bills, but most focus on credit card debt. If you are behind on secured debts such as mortgage or car loans, you should seek assistance elsewhere, possibly from a HUD approved housing counselor. In some cases, credit counseling agencies will have a separate housing counseling unit. Otherwise, if your main problem is your mortgage debt, you should look around for a local nonprofit housing counseling organization. The Department of Housing and Urban Development (HUD) maintains a database of HUD-approved counseling agencies. A list of those agencies can be obtained by calling HUD at 800-569-4287 or by visiting their website at www.hud.gov.

Debt Management Plans. A debt management plan is a service offered by most credit counseling agencies. Through a debt management plan (DMP), you send the credit counseling agency a monthly payment, which the agency then distributes to your creditors. In return, you are supposed to get a break, usually in the form of creditor agreements to waive fees and to lower interest rates. The creditor will often agree to "re-age" the account as well. Re-aging is a way of starting over again with your credit cards after you've been behind for a few months. A DMP also allows you to make only one payment to the agency rather than having to deal with multiple creditors on your own.

DMPs can be helpful for many consumers. For others, DMPs are a terrible idea. The problem is that many agencies will pressure you into a DMP whether it makes sense for you or not. A good agency will talk to you about whether a debt management plan is appropriate for you rather than assume that it is.

The challenge for you is to figure out BEFORE you go to a credit counselor whether a DMP will be right for you. The more prepared you are ahead of time, the less likely you will get into trouble.

Beware of an agency that tells you it has special connections with a particular creditor and can get you a better deal. Creditors generally offer the same types of terms through DMPs regardless of which agency they are dealing with.

A DMP may also have some effect on your credit report. Although some creditors disclose to credit reporting agencies whether a customer is participating in a debt management plan, this won't necessarily have a negative effect on your ability to get credit in the future. Fair, Isaac and Company, the developer of credit scoring software used by all major credit reporting agencies, has said that it does not negatively score a consumer's participation in a debt management plan. On the other hand, individual creditors that pull your entire credit report may consider your participation as a negative factor if you apply for credit after you enter the plan. In any case, if you are considering credit counseling because you are behind in paying your debts, your credit score has likely already been negatively affected. The situation varies significantly depending on your current credit situation. For more information about credit scores and credit reports, see Chapter Three.

A DMP is often sold as a way of avoiding bankruptcy. This may turn out to be true *if* a DMP is right for you. However, there are two very important points to keep in mind if you think that a DMP will keep you out of bankruptcy court:

1. Bankruptcy is not necessarily to be avoided at all costs. In many cases, bankruptcy may actually be the best choice for you. This is discussed in detail in Chapter Nineteen.

2. If you sign up for a DMP that you can't afford, you may end up in bankruptcy anyway.

Below are a few questions to ask to help you figure out whether a DMP is right for you.

1. Are you having trouble mainly with secured debts?
If you answered yes, a DMP is not likely to help you. There may be an exception to this general rule if you are only slightly behind on your secured debts. In that case, cutting your unsecured debts might free up extra money to help you pay your secured debts. Just remember that a DMP will not directly help you with your secured debt problems.

2. Do you have little or no money left over in your budget each month?
If you answered yes, a debt management plan is not right for you.

3. Are you still current on your credit cards? If so, a DMP is probably not a good idea. You might be able to improve your situation by taking a budget counseling class and sticking to a tight budget, or by asking your creditors to reduce the interest rate on your cards.

4. Are you able to pay your priority debts and still have some money left over each month? If so, a DMP may be helpful. However, be sure to factor in any fees you will have to pay to the agency. Priority debts are discussed in Chapter One.

5. Can you make a long-term commitment to making monthly payments? If you answered no, a DMP will not help you. The drop-out rates for these plans are very high and it is a particularly bad idea to start out thinking that you probably can't complete the plan. Ask the agency to explain to you how long it will take you to pay off your debts through a DMP. In some states, they are required to tell you this information.

6. Do you want to keep using all of your credit cards while on a DMP? If so, a DMP is not for you. Most agencies will require you to stop using any remaining credit cards. Some will allow you to keep one card for emergencies.

The bottom line is that a debt management plan is *never* a good idea if you do not have a significant amount of money left over each month to pay credit card debt. You still might want to go to a credit counselor just for counseling and educational courses. If you decide to seek help for these reasons, be sure to avoid getting lured into a debt management plan. If the agency pressures you to get involved in anything more than counseling and education, you should walk away.

You are only going to benefit from a debt management plan if you have enough money to pay the agency each month. Otherwise, there are alternatives that you should consider, including bankruptcy. Issues related to bankruptcy are discussed in Chapter Nineteen. The possible consequences of not paying your debts, including collection lawsuits, are covered in Chapter Nine. For more information about choosing which debts to pay first, see Chapter One.

FINDING A GOOD CREDIT COUNSELING AGENCY

Unfortunately, there are many agencies that are not acting in your best interests. At this point, you cannot assume that a particular affiliation means that an agency offers high-quality services. You also cannot assume that any particular promises are true. That doesn't mean stay away. It means go prepared. If you feel at all unsure about the answers you get from a particular agency, move on to another agency.

The ten tips below will help you find an honest agency.

1. Take the time to shop around. Making the wrong decision could cost you. You do not need to provide personal financial information in order to find out the basics about an agency. Ask friends and family for referrals. You might also ask a trusted social worker or your local legal services office or other charitable organization. Be careful about claims made in advertising. Many ads are exaggerated and some are even untrue. Call your local Better Business Bureau and the consumer protection office of your state Attorney General's office and rule out agencies that have been the subject of multiple complaints. Many states require agencies to register or get licenses in order to do business in those states. If you live in one of these states, you should check with the state licensing agency to find out whether there are complaints against the agency.

2. Consider visiting an agency in-person before signing up. Although it is sometimes embarrassing or inconvenient to talk face-to-face with counselors, it often leads to a more thorough and direct discussion of your finances than is possible by phone or Internet.

3. Look for a variety of services. Seek out an agency that will offer you a range of counseling options, not just enrollment in a debt management plan. The more options the agency offers, the more likely it will be able to meet your needs. Ask them if they offer budget counseling, savings, and debt management classes or other educational options. Ask them directly if they will tell you if you should consider options other than a DMP, such as bankruptcy or managing your own finances.

4. Check out all costs. Most agencies offer similar "deals" from creditors to cut your debt, but their fees can vary quite a bit. Find out what the agency charges to set up your account (get a specific dollar amount) and for a monthly fee. Ask them if any of the fees are voluntary, or if they offer lower fees for customers in serious financial hardship. Get a specific quote in writing.

5. Non-profit status or an affiliation with a particular trade group does not guarantee quality. Non-profit status does not guarantee affordable fees. Nearly all credit counseling agencies have non-profit status, including those that take advantage of consumers. Approval from the U.S. Trustee to provide bankruptcy counseling is also not a guaranty of quality.

6. Demand good customer service. The training and skill of agency employees can mean the difference between effective and shoddy credit counseling. It is hard to distinguish between the various employee training and certification programs, so ask a few specific questions. Find out if the employees you are dealing with have taken actual courses, not just a few weeks of training, in subjects like credit, budgeting, and savings. Make sure the employee spends a good deal of time carefully evaluating all of your debts, not just your credit card bills, and looks at your pay stubs and bills before recommending a counseling plan to you. Find out if the agency provides assistance after you enroll in a DMP, such as one-on-one counseling.

7. Ask about privacy. Make sure the agency does not sell or distribute any information about your account to others without your permission.

8. Find out about employee compensation. Ask employees directly if they are paid more if they sign you up for a debt management plan. Consider going elsewhere if they say yes or refuse to give an answer.

9. Get the specifics on credit concessions. Ask the agency if it will deal with all of your unsecured creditors, not just those that pay the agency a fee. Find out exactly how much lower your monthly credit card balance will be and how long it will take to pay off your bills. You should also ask about how credit counseling will affect your credit report or score.

10. Keep an eye on the agency after you sign up. If you sign up for a debt management plan, it is best not to stop paying your bills until the plan has been approved by your creditors. Make sure that the agency's payment schedule allows your debts to be paid before they are due each month. Call each of your creditors the first month to make sure they have been paid on time by the agency.

BANKRUPTCY AND CREDIT COUNSELING

You must receive budget and credit counseling from an approved credit counseling agency within 180 days before your bankruptcy case is filed. If you decide to go ahead with bankruptcy, you will need to file a certificate from the agency stating that you received counseling.

This is different than going to a credit counselor on your own because you must do this counseling in order to file for bankruptcy and because you must go to an agency that is approved by the United States Trustee Program for the jurisdiction where you are filing (consumers located in North Carolina or Alabama must use counseling agencies approved by the local Bankruptcy Administrator). You can check the United States Trustee Program's website for a list of approved agencies, at www.usdoj.gov/ust/. You can also ask the local bankruptcy court, or your bankruptcy attorney, for a list of approved agencies. Approved agencies are allowed to provide the counseling in-person, by telephone, or over the Internet.

If an agency advertises that it is approved by the United States Trustee, the advertisement must say that the approval is not an endorsement or assurance of quality services.

You have no choice but to use the approved list if you are going to counseling in order to file for bankruptcy. You may also want to consult this list if you are seeking help outside of bankruptcy, but do not assume that the list is a guaranty of good quality. Consumers should always follow the ten steps for finding a good credit counseling agency mentioned earlier in this chapter.

More information about this requirement is in Chapter Nineteen.

BEWARE OF OTHER DEBT RELIEF COMPANIES

There are a lot of companies trying to make money off of people in debt trouble. As with credit counselors, it is very hard to figure out what services many of these agencies are selling and whether the services are legitimate. Once again, you should approach these companies very cautiously. Ask a lot of questions before signing up and make sure you understand what the company is offering and whether these services are likely to help you.

These companies know that consumers in debt trouble often feel desperate. They make outrageous claims about supposedly magic solutions to debt problems. These claims are designed to pressure you to buy services that can be very expensive and will often get you even deeper in trouble. The truth is that the road to financial recovery usually takes time and is almost never easy. Try to keep this in mind as you sort through the claims of debt relief companies.

Debt Settlement. Unlike credit counseling agencies, most debt settlement and debt negotiation agencies are for-profit businesses. Negotiation and settlement services are different from debt management services mainly because the debt settlement agencies do not send regular monthly payments to creditors. Instead, these agencies generally maintain your funds in separate accounts, holding your money until the agency believes it can settle your debts for less than the full amount owed.

Here's how a typical debt settlement deal works. You go to the settlement agency because you are behind on credit card debt. In some cases, they will tell you to come back if you're not far enough behind on your debts. In some cases, they will offer to sell you services right away.

The agencies have different ways of doing business, but nearly all of them will require you to set money aside each month. Sometimes the settlement agency will set up an account for you. In other cases, they will ask you to show proof that you set up your own account. They will almost always figure out a way to take their fees directly from these accounts.

They will require you to deposit a certain amount of money in the account each month. This is intended to build up a fund that can later be used to try to settle your debts. In the meantime, you will not be making any payments on your debts. This means that you could be sued for collection or could be facing pressure from debt collectors to pay. Some debt settlement agencies will tell you about your right to be free from debt collection harassment, but most of their employees or "counselors" are not attorneys and cannot help you if you get into trouble that requires legal assistance. More information about responding to debt collectors can be found in Chapter Eight.

The companies usually claim that they will stay in contact with your creditors while you are depositing money into your account. They claim that they will monitor the account and will let you know when they think there is enough money to try to make a settlement. If they are able to work out a settlement with your creditor, they will almost always take a percentage of what you save as a fee. This fee is in addition to the fees that they charge you to start the service and the monthly fees they usually take from your account.

Trying to settle your debt may be a strategy that works for you. This option is discussed in Chapter Eight. The problem is that the debt settlement business model is rarely the best way to accomplish this. You are likely to end up paying very high fees, among other problems.

A debt settlement agency is also not likely to be of much help if you have a lot of debts. These agencies will generally try to settle your debts, if they do this at all, one at a time. If you have a lot of debts, this could be a very long process. In the meantime, you will not be paying all of your other creditors. This means that those creditors could sue you or keep trying to collect from you in other ways. And the interest is still growing on your debts. Also, even if one debt is settled, your credit report will still show that you are in default on your other debts.

If you have just one or maybe two debts and have the money to try to settle those debts, it is best to try negotiating on your own or finding an agency that is willing to help you without charging you high fees and without requiring you to pay them up-front.

Debt Termination or Elimination. "Debt termination" or "debt elimination" companies claim to be able to eliminate your debt usually through the use of specially prepared documents. The documents include fake financial papers that claim to eliminate your debt obligations. Some of the documents question the legitimacy of government agencies such as the Federal Reserve Board or even of U.S. currency itself. The documents have different titles, including "Declaration of Voidance," "Bond for Discharge of Debt," and "Redemption Certificate." Some claim to wipe out mortgage debt rather than credit card debt. In some cases, the agencies will send a series of letters to your creditors to try to get the creditor to set an arbitration hearing. The companies will claim that the bank will be unable to prove that you owe the money and so your debt can be cancelled.

The Federal Reserve Board and other federal agencies have announced that these schemes are complete frauds. Do not be fooled by their outrageous claims.

5

Credit Cards

Credit card debt generally should be considered low-priority debt. Yet, you may find that credit card obligations are your biggest headache due to collection calls, concern about future credit, or because you can afford to pay everything but unmanageable credit card debts. You are not alone—the average credit debt of all American households in 2004 was just over $8,000.

Contrary to popular myth, huge credit card bills are not mostly due to irresponsible overspending. Many consumers resort to credit cards to meet pressing family needs after losing a job or due to an emergency. Others find themselves hopelessly in credit card debt due to snowballing finance charges, late payment penalties, and other high fees.

PREVENTING OVER-EXTENSION ON CREDIT CARDS

There has been an enormous expansion of consumer credit card spending in recent years. A big part of this is due to lenders' increased marketing efforts.

Almost eight billion credit card offers are mailed to consumers each year. We see advertisements everywhere—on television, the Internet, at sporting events, in restaurants, and on college campuses.

These offers can be very enticing. Nearly every offer promises you some special benefit, such as a low rate or no annual fee. In some cases, the lenders lure you with frequent flyer miles, cash back, freebies such as T-shirts and mugs, or contributions to schools or favorite charities.

In the past, you rarely got new credit card offers if you had money problems. Lenders reviewed applications and chose not to offer credit if they considered you a bad risk. Times have changed. Many lenders now buy huge mailing lists and offer credit to everyone on the list without further evaluation. They offer credit cards to anyone with an adequate credit score, whether or not you can afford the credit or are already over-extended. Even consumers with a low credit score or bad credit history are offered high-cost "subprime" credit cards.

THINGS TO THINK ABOUT BEFORE YOU ACCEPT A NEW CARD

Avoiding credit cards completely may not be a practical solution. It is difficult to get by in our society without a credit card. You may need a credit card when you travel, for transacting business over the Internet, or to place orders by telephone.

Shopping around for credit cards is also tough. Lenders highlight low rates, but bury expensive fees, high penalty rates, and traps in the fine print. They reserve the right to change the terms of your account at any time, for any reason—or no reason at all. Here are some suggestions to keep in mind when reviewing credit card offers.

1. Avoid accepting too many offers. There is rarely a good reason to carry more than one or two credit cards. You should be very selective about choosing which cards are best for you. Too much credit can lead to bad decisions and unmanageable debts. Opening too many new credit card accounts can also lower your credit score.

2. Beware subprime credit cards. Instead of turning you down because of bad credit, some lenders will offer you subprime credit cards. These cards generally come with very high interest rates, expensive fees, and low credit limits. You may also be charged for unnecessary products such as "credit protection." Some lenders will actually issue cards called "fee-harvesters" with low credit limits, and then add so many fees that you can't charge any purchases to the card because you'll already be maxed out when you receive it!

Avoid credit cards advertised as helping with "bad credit." In addition to costing you a bundle, they may end up making your credit history even worse. Other lenders use subprime credit cards as a trick to revive old debts from other lenders. They offer you a new credit card, but then slap the old debt on the new account.

3. Watch out for bait & switch offers. Some credit card lenders will send you an offer advertising an attractive, low-interest credit card with a high limit, but include—in the fine print—the statement that the lender can substitute a less attractive, more expensive card if you don't qualify. The substituted card often has a higher interest rate, more expensive fees, and/or a lower credit limit.

4. Look carefully at the interest rate, but know that it can change at any time. You should always know the interest rate on your cards and try to find the lowest rate possible. It's often hard to do this, because the terms are so confusing and sometimes misleading. Credit card lenders usually have several interest rates for a credit card. They also constantly change their rates. Some important terms to understand are:

- **APR.** This is the interest rate expressed as an annual figure. Most cards have different APRs for purchases versus cash advances versus balance transfers and other types of transactions.
- **Variable rates.** Most credit cards use variable rates, which change with the rise or fall of a common index rate (an example of a variable rate might be "U.S. Prime Rate plus 5%"). If your rate is variable, you need to understand when and how it may change. Variable interest rates can be very confusing. And even "fixed" rates can be variable— your credit card lender usually has the right to change your interest rate with just a simple notice.
- **"Teaser" rates.** A teaser rate is an artificially low initial rate that lasts only for a limited time, such as six months or less. After that, the rate automatically goes up. If you build up a balance while a teaser rate is in effect, you'll end up repaying the debt at a much higher permanent rate.

- **Penalty rates.** Many credit card contracts, including those that advertise low permanent rates, provide in the small print that your interest rate increases if you make even a single late payment. Some lenders will increase your rate even if you are never late on their credit card, but are late with a payment to any other creditor or if your credit score drops too low. This is known as "universal default."

Penalty rates may be on top of late charges or other fees. If you are having financial problems, late charges and penalty interest rates will put you further into debt. Even if you are not having financial problems, these terms are important if you make a late payment by accident.

5. Fees, fees, fees. Other terms of credit may be just as important as interest rates. Credit card companies now impose a number of different fees—late fees, fees for exceeding a credit limit, annual fees, membership fees, cash advance fees, balance transfer fees, even fees for buying lottery tickets with a card—and keep raising these fees every year. These fees significantly increase the cost of a credit card, so that a card that appears cheaper with a low APR could end up being much more expensive.

6. Look for the grace period. Most credit cards offer a "grace period," the amount of time in which you can pay off purchases without incurring finance charges (cash advances usually don't have a grace period). Without a grace period, finance charges begin accruing immediately, and a low rate may actually be higher than it looks. If you intend to pay off the balance in full each month, the terms of the grace period are especially important. Many credit cards have reduced their grace period. They have also reduced the time between when they send a bill and when the payment is due, increasing the risk that you will go past the grace period and pay both interest charges and a late fee.

You also want to look out for early payment deadline times. For example, some companies have used times as early as 9 or 10 A.M. as the cutoff time for crediting payments received that day. Even if your payment is received later that same day, the company will consider it to be late and will charge you a late fee. For this reason, you should try to get your payments in as early as possible. If you are running very close to the deadline, you might consider paying, at least for that month, over the Internet or by phone, although you may have to pay a charge for paying by phone.

7. Always read both the disclosures and the credit contract. You will find disclosures about the terms of a credit card offer in a box, usually on the reverse side of or accompanying the credit card application. Review these carefully. If the disclosure box is on the reverse side of the application, make a copy. You should also read your credit contract, which comes with the card. If you do not understand these terms, call the lender for an explanation, or better yet, just say no.

8. If you take a credit card and discover terms you do not like: Cancel! You don't need to keep a credit card if you don't like the terms. Of course, if you have used the card, you will need to pay off the balance. You should also cancel the card if the lender changes the terms of your credit card and you don't like the new terms. Otherwise you will be stuck with the new (and probably unfavorable) terms.

Interest Rate Reduction for Members of the Military on Active Duty

While you are on active duty in the military, the interest rate on credit card debts that you incurred on your own or jointly with your spouse *before* you entered active duty must be reduced to 6%. This limit also includes any fees or other charges. Any interest above 6% that would normally be charged must be forgiven, not simply postponed. The lender must also reduce your regular payment amount to give you credit for the forgiven interest. This 6% limit applies to almost all types of debts that you incurred before going on active duty, not just credit card debts. For example, it also applies to mortgage loans, car loans, and some student loans.

To get your interest rate reduced, notify your creditors in writing that you are on active duty and that you want your interest rates reduced. You should also send them a copy of the orders calling you to active duty or extending your active duty. It is important to notify your creditors as soon as possible, but you must let them know no later than 180 days after your period of active duty ends.

In order to qualify for this protection, you must be a member of the Army, Navy, Marine Corps, Air Force, or Coast Guard or a commissioned officer of the Public Health Service or the National Oceanic and Atmospheric Administration. Members of the Reserves or National Guard who are called to active service also qualify. You can get more information on the website for the U.S. Army's Judge Advocate General's Corps at www.jagcnet.army.mil.

UNDERSTANDING ALTERNATIVE TYPES OF CREDIT CARDS

Secured vs. Unsecured Credit Cards. All things being equal, you should use an unsecured card rather than a secured card. Since interest rates on secured cards are typically just as high as those on unsecured cards, the choice in favor of an unsecured card should be clear. Whether secured or unsecured, you should avoid cards advertised as helping with "bad credit." The discussion below lists different types of secured cards to watch out for.

Credit Cards Secured by Your Purchases. Some credit card lenders claim to take collateral in items purchased with their card. If you have problems making payments, those lenders may threaten to repossess property bought with the card. In addition, this collateral may affect your rights if you later need to file bankruptcy. As discussed in Chapter Seventeen, most threats to repossess such personal property are not carried out because the expense of repossession outweighs the value of used property. Nevertheless, it is a good idea to use an unsecured card instead of a secured card whenever possible.

Credit Cards Secured by a Bank Account. Another type of secured credit card allows you a credit limit up to the amount you have on deposit in a particular bank account. If you can't make the payments, you lose the money in the account. These cards are usually marketed as a way to reestablish credit by showing that you have moved past financial problems and can make regular monthly payments on a credit card.

Some secured credit cards may be useful if you lack any credit history at all—for example, if you are a recent immigrant. However, it is preferable not to tie up your bank account.

Credit Cards Secured by Your Home. Some lenders offer credit cards in connection with a home equity line of credit. Each time you use the card, the balance is secured against your home. In many cases, home improvement contractors offer these cards as a way to pay for home improvements. Sometimes the initial amount advanced is as much as your credit limit.

Home secured credit cards are almost always a bad idea—the potential consequence of nonpayment is the loss of your family's shelter. Always beware of home improvement contractors offering credit. You will likely do better if you seek a more traditional home equity credit line from a bank at a lower interest rate. The pros and cons of refinancing are discussed in Chapter Six.

"Fake" Security Deposits. Some credit card offers will claim that they don't require a security deposit, but then "charge" a deposit to the card. These cards often come with low credit limits, so that the "deposit" eats up most of the credit line, leaving you with a virtually useless credit card that you still must pay fees for. You should try to avoid these types of "fake security" cards.

"Convenience" Checks. Another credit offer to avoid takes the form of a check mailed to your home, usually by your credit card company. When you cash the check, you not only accept a high interest rate, but also get stuck with a big balance on a new account right from the start. It is better to find a reasonable credit card offer and use the new card carefully.

CREDIT CARDS VS. DEBIT CARDS

Debit cards allow you to have money taken directly from your account to pay charges made with the card. Merchants accept debit cards, like credit cards, to pay for goods or services.

Although they often look the same, there are important differences between credit and debit cards. When you use a debit card, the money is immediately taken from your bank account. This is different than using a credit card, where you are getting money as a loan that you only have to pay back when the credit card bill comes.

Debit Cards with the VISA or MasterCard Brand. If you have a debit card with a VISA or MasterCard logo on it, sometimes when you swipe your card at a point-of-sale device (the card readers at the grocery store or gas station), you are given the option of using the card as "credit" or "debit." The credit option is confusing because really you are still using the card as a debit card. What this choice actually means for you is: do you want to use your debit card like an ATM card and enter your PIN (Personal Identification Number) for identification, or do you want to use your debit card like a credit card and sign your name on the receipt for identification? Either way, the money is taken out of your bank account within a short period of time.

Comparing Credit and Debit Cards. There are advantages and disadvantages to using a credit card versus a debit card. Using a debit card reduces the risk of running up a big unpaid balance on a credit card. However, be careful of overdrafts when using your debit card. Many banks allow their customers overdraw their accounts using their debit cards, then charging high overdraft fees up to $35 *per transaction*. It's possible to run up hundreds of dollars in fees in one day by overdrawing with your debit card.

With a credit card, you may prefer the flexibility of slower repayment with interest. You may need this flexibility if you are on a tight budget and want to make sure that your most pressing debts are paid first.

Your rights to dispute charges on debit cards (including debit cards with the MasterCard or VISA logo) are more limited than with credit cards. For example, if you purchased a vacuum cleaner from a nearby store with your credit card and it breaks during the first week of use and the merchant refuses to fix it, you may withhold payment for the charge for the vacuum on your credit card bill. (See discussion at the end of this chapter.) There are *no* similar rights available when you use your debit card.

Your responsibility for losses from a lost or stolen card is generally much greater for a debit card than for a credit card. Your responsibility for unauthorized credit card charges is limited to $50. Compare that to a debit card where you could be responsible for as much as $500 if you fail to notify the bank within two days from the time you found out the card was taken. There may be no limit to your liability if you fail to report an unauthorized transfer within sixty days of when the bank statement is mailed to you showing these changes.

In all of these cases, you will need to show that the losses resulted from an "unauthorized transfer." This may be an issue of dispute with the bank. For example, it is *not* considered an unauthorized transfer if the money is withdrawn by someone you know, to whom you had previously lent your card and provided with your PIN, even if this person took your card and used it without your permission a second time.

Both VISA and MasterCard have "zero liability" policies that limit your debit card losses in most situations. However, these policies do not apply when your debit card is used at an ATM or with some debit card transactions using a PIN.

Finally, the consequences of an unauthorized withdrawal from your bank account through your debit card may be worse than the consequences of an unauthorized charge on your credit card. Since the money to pay the debit comes directly out of your bank account, you may temporarily or permanently lose use of that money—effective immediately. Even if the money is later restored to your account, temporary loss of the money may mean that you cannot pay your bills or meet other pressing needs and may also cause your checks to bounce.

Stored Value Cards. Stored value cards are another type of card that can be used to make purchases or pay for items. The most familiar examples of stored value cards are gift cards, phone cards, and payroll cards. There are also stored value cards that work like debit cards to make purchases and withdraw cash, but are not linked to regular bank accounts. These cards are often called "prepaid debit cards" and carry a Mastercard or Visa logo. However, like Mastercard and Visa debit cards, these are NOT credit cards.

Whether a stored value card is a good idea depends on the details of the particular card program. The programs vary a lot in terms of the cost, convenience, and level of consumer protection. Here are a few issues to consider:

- **Financial Soundness**: You should avoid using a stored value card unless you know that the provider is in good financial shape. If you select a company that goes out of business, you could lose the money that is left on your card.
- **Consumer Protections**: Stored value cards that are not tied to an individual bank account may not give you the same protections that apply to bank debit cards, as discussed earlier in this chapter. If you choose to get a stored value card, you should ask if the issuer provides the same consumer protections as with bank debit cards. Don't rely just on the Visa or Mastercard "zero liability" policies—they don't cover losses from an ATM withdrawal or some PIN transactions.
- **Fees**: Try to avoid high fees and make sure that you get information about fees in writing before signing up. You especially want to avoid high monthly fees that will drain away the value in your card or "hidden" fees for services like getting an account statement or talking to a customer service representative.
- **ATM Access**: You should ask for a list of ATMs that will be available to you without an extra charge.
- **Overdraft Policy**: You do not want a stored value card if the card issuer allows you to overdraw even when they know that you don't have enough money on the card. The fees for overdrafts add up quickly.
- **Expiration Dates**: This problem is especially common with gift cards, which often contain hidden expiration dates or confusing information about when the card expires. If a card is reloadable, you also want to find out whether the expiration date starts over again.

AVOIDING CREDIT CARD PROBLEMS

Credit card debts can spiral out of control. Here are some ways to protect yourself from getting in over your head.

1. Do not use credit cards to finance an unaffordable lifestyle.
If you are constantly using your card without the ability to pay the resulting bill in full each month, consider whether you are using your cards to make an unreasonable budget plan work.

2. If you get into financial trouble, try to avoid making it worse by using credit cards to make ends meet. Finance charges and others fees will add to your debt burden. However, using a credit card in a period of financial difficulty is preferable to taking out a home equity loan and putting your home on the line.

3. Don't get hooked on minimum payments. Some credit card lenders have set their minimum payments to as low as 2% of the balance. Others have raised their minimum payments, sometimes to 4% of the balance due to pressure from federal banking agencies.

Even with slightly higher minimum payments, it will take you a long time to pay off credit card paying only the minimum.

Below are a few more examples of the time it takes to pay off credit cards when you pay only the minimum:

Balance	APR	Minimum Monthly Payment	Total Interest	Time To Pay
$4,500	12%	2%	$ 4,196	24 yrs, 1 mo.
$4,500	12%	4%	$ 1,455	10 yrs, 4 mos.
$4,500	18%	2%	$12,431	44 yrs, 4 mos.
$4,500	18%	4%	$ 2,615	12 yrs, 2 mos.

Also, lenders reserve the right to increase the minimum payment at their option. This means that you can budget for a $50 minimum payment only to find out that the new minimum payment of $100 applies.

4. Don't run up the balance in reliance on a temporary "teaser" interest rate. Money borrowed during a temporary rate period of 4% is likely to be paid back at a much higher permanent rate of 15% or more.

5. If you can afford to do so within your budget, make your credit card payments on time. Avoid late payment charges and penalty rates if you can do so without endangering your ability to keep up with higher priority debts. Bad problems get worse fast when you have a new higher interest rate and late charge to pay during a time of financial difficulty.

Most lenders will waive a late payment charge or default rates of interest only once. It is worth calling to ask for a waiver if you make a late payment accidentally or with a good excuse.

6. Avoid the special services, programs, and goods that credit card lenders offer to bill to their cards. Most of these special services—credit card fraud protection plans, credit record protection, travel clubs, life insurance, and other similar offers—are bad deals.

7. Beware of unsolicited increases by a credit card lender to your credit card limit. Some lenders increase your credit limit even when you have not asked for more credit. Do not assume that this means that the lender thinks you can afford more credit. Lenders generally increase the limit for consumers that they think will carry a bigger balance and pay more interest.

8. Don't max out. Charging your credit card up to your limit is risky behavior. It's easy to get socked with high over-limit fees. Plus, a credit card account close to its limit will cause a big drop in your credit score. This may even cause the lender to impose a penalty rate.

WHAT TO DO IF YOU GET BEHIND ON CREDIT CARD PAYMENTS

Unmanageable credit card debts can be the first sign of serious financial problems. If you have been scraping by and making minimum payments for several months, it is time to reevaluate your plan for managing debt. A number of other chapters will help you do this.

In general, credit card debt is low priority debt and you should avoid feeling pressured to keep up with a credit card at the risk of losing a home or car. Chapters One and Two include detailed information about choosing which debts to pay first and about establishing a budget.

Strategies to deal with creditors and debt collectors are covered in Chapter Eight. That chapter will help you deal with aggressive debt collectors. It also includes tips for negotiating with creditors or collectors. Particularly if you think you have some extra money to pay credit card debt, you should also consider contacting a credit counseling agency for help. Chapter Four provides information to help you choose a reputable agency.

Chapter Nine will help you evaluate the likelihood that a creditor or collector will sue you. There are many more threats of lawsuits than there are actual cases filed. Chapter Nine also discusses the possible consequences if you are sued. It is important to keep in mind that even if a case is filed, there may be little or nothing that the lender can do to hurt you.

CREDIT CARD DISPUTES

Most of us experience a problem with credit card bills at some point in our lives, such as a mysterious charge, double-billing, or mail-order merchandise that never arrived. Federal law protects credit card consumers in these situations. There are three separate protections you should know about.

Unauthorized Use of Your Card. The first credit card protection shields you against liability for unauthorized use of your credit card, that is, when someone steals, borrows, or otherwise uses your card or card number without permission. These problems have increased with identity theft (see Chapter Three) and as hackers have become more sophisticated in stealing credit card numbers from the computers of businesses.

Under the law, your liability for unauthorized use of your credit card is limited to $50. If someone steals your card, for example, your credit card lender can charge you a maximum of $50 no matter how much the thief has charged on your card.

The situation may be trickier in cases where someone you know used your card. In general, you should not be liable if you did not authorize this use. But if gave your card to your son, for example, you are liable for any charges he runs up even if you told him to use the card for emergencies only. If your son took your card without your knowledge, however, the law limits your liability in the same way as if your card was lost or stolen.

As soon as you know of any type of unauthorized use of your credit card, call the lender to make a report. If you call before unauthorized charges are incurred, you cannot be charged even $50, since the lender can take steps to cancel your card and send you a new one.

WATCH OUT FOR IDENTITY THEFT PROTECTION SCAMS

Federal law protects you when your card is lost or stolen. You cannot be charged more than $50 for unauthorized charges.

Unfortunately, an "identity theft protection" industry has developed to take advantage of those consumers who don't know this law. These companies exploit the growth and awareness of identity theft to either sell useless products or for marketing advantages. There is no reason to pay extra money for "identity theft protection" when federal law protects you.

If a charge unexpectedly appears on your bill for something you did not authorize, you can also use your right to dispute the charge, as discussed below. Some credit card lenders have been telling consumers they can only report unauthorized use by sending a written dispute within sixty days of receiving the bill with the unauthorized charge. *This is not true.* You can report unauthorized use over the telephone. You also are not required to do so within sixty days, although the sooner you report it, the better.

After you report an unauthorized charge, the credit card lender must conduct a "reasonable" investigation of your claim, unless it simply decides to take the charge off your account. A reasonable investigation might include analyzing the signature on the credit card slip, obtaining a copy of a police report, or comparing where a purchase was made versus where you live.

Billing Error Disputes. The second type of credit card protection involves disputes about your bill. These disputes may include a merchant overcharging you or charging you for products you never received. A law called the Fair Credit Billing Act forces lenders to follow specific "billing error" procedures to resolve the dispute. (As discussed above, this protection does not apply to debit cards.)

Under this law, you must raise a dispute *in writing* to your credit card company, usually by sending a letter. The letter must be sent within sixty (60) days of the first bill with the improper charges. The letter must include the following information:

- Your name and account number;
- The dollar amount you dispute; and
- A statement of the reason for your dispute.

You must send your letter of dispute to the address provided by the lender for this purpose. Information about this address and how to raise a dispute appears on the back of your credit card statement.

The law only permits you to raise certain types of disputes using the billing error procedures. Some examples of reasons for dispute are:

- I did not authorize this charge (remember—you can raise the issue of unauthorized use by sending a written billing error notice, but you can report unauthorized use over the telephone, too);
- I did not receive the goods I ordered;
- I returned the goods I ordered because they were defective but did not get a credit;
- The merchant sent me the wrong goods;
- The merchant did not complete the services I contracted for or performed them incompletely;
- The merchant billed me for an amount higher than I agreed to pay;
- I canceled the contract with the merchant or contractor before work was performed;
- Although I agreed to buy something from this merchant, I did not authorize them to bill my account.

You cannot raise a complaint about the quality of merchandise or services you bought with a credit card in the form of a billing dispute. However, you can withhold payment to your credit card lender for poor quality goods or services in many cases, which is the third type of credit card protection discussed below.

An example of a dispute letter appears below. If appropriate, send backup documentation such as a letter explaining the problem to the merchant.

Once you have raised a dispute, the credit card company must investigate and report back to you in writing within two complete billing cycles or within ninety days, whichever comes first. In some cases, the charge will be canceled. Interest associated with a successfully disputed debt must also be canceled.

When you raise a written dispute with a credit card lender about a charge, the lender is required to investigate. You do not need to pay the disputed portion of the bill during the investigation.

SAMPLE CREDIT CARD DISPUTE LETTER

January 15, 2007

Jane Consumer
101 Main Street
Anytown, USA 12345

Big Credit Card Co.   *[The actual address you need to use appears on the*
P.O. Box 666   *back of the credit card bill you are disputing in a*
Somewhere, DE 11111   *section called "Billing Rights Summary."]*

Dear Big Credit Card Co.:

My name is Jane Consumer. My account number is 123456789. I am disputing a charge on the bill you mailed on January 15, 2007. That bill includes a charge in the amount of $2,000.00 to Fix-It Garage. This amount is in error.

In September 2006 I took my car to Fix-It Garage to be repaired. They estimated that the work would cost $400. I told them not to do any work in excess of $400. When they called to say the repairs were completed, they told me that the bill was $2,000. I did not agree to pay this amount and they have charged my account without my authorization.

I have contacted Fix-It Garage by telephone, in person, and by the enclosed letter in order to try to resolve the dispute. They have not agreed to withdraw the charge.

Please investigate this dispute and provide me with a written statement of the outcome. Thank you for your time and attention to this matter.

Very truly yours,

Jane Consumer

Until the dispute is resolved, you do not need to pay the disputed portion of your bill. However, you must make a payment to cover any undisputed amount. The credit card company cannot report you as delinquent with respect to the disputed amount but may do so if part of your debt is undisputed and you do not make necessary payments.

If the credit card company does not resolve the dispute in your favor, it must send you a written explanation and give you any supporting documentation upon your request. It must allow you the grace period normally permitted for the charge (unless you made the dispute after the grace period).

Stopping Payment on Your Credit Card. The third important credit card dispute protection is the right to stop payment. Stopping payment is a very powerful tool that you can use when you are dissatisfied with something you bought with a credit card. You can use this strategy if you have a legitimate complaint about the quality of goods or services you bought with the card *and* you first make a good faith effort to resolve the problem with the merchant directly. (As discussed above, this protection does not apply to debit cards.)

There are a few other important limits to the stop payment right:

- The goods or services you bought must have cost more than $50; and
- You must have bought those goods or services in your home state or within 100 miles of your mailing address.

However, these last two limits do not apply if the credit card was issued by the seller (such as a department store card) or if the seller mailed you the advertisement for the goods or services you purchased. You still need to make a good faith effort to resolve the problem with the seller in these circumstances.

After you notify your credit card company that you are withholding payment, they cannot report the disputed amount as delinquent to a credit bureau until the dispute is settled or a court judgment is issued against you. The lender cannot treat the dispute as "settled" or take collection action against you unless it has completed a reasonable investigation of your claim.

How to Enforce Your Credit Card Dispute Rights. In many cases, a credit card dispute will be resolved after you contact the credit card company. However, if the company does not respond to your dispute or you are not satisfied with the results, there are steps you can take beyond raising your complaint to the company.

- **Complain to OCC.** Most credit card companies are national banks, which are regulated by a federal agency called the Office of the Comptroller of Currency. While the OCC's main mission is to protect the economic health of national banks, they do have a division that assists consumers. You can file a complaint with the OCC at the following address:

Office of the Comptroller of Currency
Customer Assistance Group
1301 McKinney Street
Suite 3450
Houston, TX 77010
FAX: 713-336-4301
You can also find out more about the OCC on-line at
www.helpwithmybank.gov or by calling 800-613-6743.
You should also send a copy of your complaint to your state
Attorney General.

- **Sue the company or take them to arbitration.** Federal law permits you to sue the credit card company if it does not follow the dispute procedures discussed above or takes some action forbidden by law (such as reporting a disputed amount as delinquent to a credit bureau). Your right to sue may be limited by a mandatory arbitration provision. Most credit card companies have slipped these provisions into their contracts (probably one of those bill stuffers with tiny print that few consumers read), which prevent you from suing a credit card company in court. Instead, you are required to use a private company to resolve your claim. Some consumers have successfully challenged arbitration provisions in their credit card contracts. If you are forced to use the arbitration process, make sure to have the company agree to pay the costs. Otherwise, arbitration is very expensive, with filing fees that usually cost $100–$200 and daily fees up to $1,000 per day. More information about credit card arbitration can be found in Chapter Nine.

- **Raising claims when sued.** If you do not pay the disputed amount, the company may sue you to recover it. You can always raise an unauthorized use claim, billing error dispute, or a claim over shoddy goods or services as a defense when you are sued.

6

Home Equity and Refinancing Loans

Your home is your most important asset. If you have equity in your home, you may feel tempted to take out a new loan or refinance an old loan to pay off other debts (for a definition of "equity," see the *Glossary*). We recommend that you be very careful when borrowing against the equity in your home. This is one of the riskiest steps you can take when you have financial problems. Many of these loans will hurt you more than they help.

The attraction of refinancing is that it seems to resolve your financial problems even though your income and your expenses do not change. The disadvantages are often hidden. Problems occur because of the complex math involved in the lending process, including hidden fees and costs, and because the new loan may give the lender ways to force payment and seize your property that were not available under the prior loan. There are even times when a refinancing deal is nothing more than a scam to steal your home or other property. Each potential refinancing deal must be reviewed carefully based on the principles discussed in this chapter.

WHAT IS REFINANCING?

Refinancing is a process in which you pay off one or more debts by borrowing new money from an existing lender or a new lender. Home equity loans that are used to pay off other debts may also be called consolidation loans. In other cases, the loans are new loans, usually in the form of a second mortgage on your home. Often, when you apply to borrow against your home, you will be refinancing a current mortgage, whether you realize it or not.

The differences between these loans are not always obvious. For example, you may start out thinking you are getting a second mortgage, but end up with a refinancing of your current mortgage instead. This is a common tactic, often used by unscrupulous lenders, to make money at your expense.

Below are some rules and warning signs to think about if you are considering borrowing against your home to pay off other debts.

TWELVE REFINANCING RULES

1. When in doubt, do not refinance or consolidate debts. Refinancing deals almost always come with significant costs. These costs will usually just make matters worse in the long term.

2. Do not let debt collectors pressure you into refinancing. Debt collectors may try to scare you into refinancing because they have no other way to get their money. Better ways to address debt collection problems are discussed in Chapter Eight.

3. Never (or almost never) refinance unsecured debt into secured debt. By trading in unsecured debt for a mortgage loan, you face loss of your home if you continue to have financial problems. Do not refinance unsecured debt, that is, most credit card debt, into secured debt even if this allows you to lower the interest rate you are paying. The interest rate on a mortgage loan may be lower, but these are usually at least twenty and more commonly thirty year loans. Paying at a lower rate for that long period of time will almost always cost you more than a higher rate on a shorter-term loan. Think of it this way: Would you ever want to pay off the pizza you bought for dinner with a credit card by stretching the payments out for thirty years? This is the result of adding your credit card debt to a mortgage loan. And if you don't cut up those credit cards and close those accounts, you may end up with both a bigger mortgage and a new round of credit card debt.

4. If you have an existing debt with a finance company or high-rate second mortgage lender, do not refinance that debt with the same lender. Ask the company to agree to lower payments on the existing loan, but do not allow the lender to refinance that loan, which may involve new closing costs and perhaps even a higher interest rate.

5. Do not turn your car loan into a second mortgage unless you would rather lose your home than your car. If you are in danger of losing your car, you may be tempted to pay off your car loan by taking out a second mortgage on your home. You may save your car temporarily this way, but you are putting your home in danger. Although repossession is bad, foreclosure is worse. This type of refinancing adds the car loan into the mortgage loan, turning a five year car loan into a thirty year mortgage. This greatly increases the amount of interest you pay.

6. Do not refinance low-interest debts with higher interest loans. You should always evaluate the interest rate on the new debt and look for a lower rate than on the old debts. You have already paid certain fees in the old loan, and you must make sure that a new lower rate is actually lower after both the old and new fees are accounted for. Furthermore, the "APR" (Annual Percentage Rate) of the new loan must be lower than the *interest rate* stated in the note of the old loan, or you will be losing money. The APR is the cost of credit as a yearly rate. It is often higher than the interest rate on your loan note because the APR takes into account both the interest plus certain fees that the lenders add to the cost of the loan.

The interest rate is not the only consideration when evaluating a loan. Other fees, charges, and expenses which are not considered interest may make a loan which looks cheaper into one which is actually more expensive. Later in this chapter you will find sample documents where you can compare an APR to an interest rate.

You should review the sample disclosures in this chapter to get a better sense of the information that lenders must give you.

7. Do not include your long-term first mortgage in a refinancing package. Do not let potential lenders pay off your first mortgage and give you a new mortgage equal to the first mortgage plus the new loan amount. The only exception is if the new mortgage is for the equivalent length of time and the APR is significantly *lower* than the interest rate on the old first mortgage—to offset prepayment penalties and fees and charges.

8. Be careful about variable rates. Variable-rate refinancing loans can be tricky. In any variable-rate transaction, the monthly payment can increase drastically when you can least afford it. Some loans have artificially low rates (and payments) during the first months or years, called "teaser rates." Other variable rate loans provide that the rate will only go up, never down. More information about adjustable rate mortgage loans can be found later in this chapter.

9. Do not refinance loans when you have valid legal reasons not to pay that debt. If you have a legal defense to repayment of a debt, such as lender fraud, you can raise that defense in court. If you refinance with a new lender, the defense may not be available against the new lender. If you need legal help to determine if you have a defense, you should get that help *before* entering the refinancing deal. The Introduction to this book contains advice to help you find a lawyer.

10. Be wary of claims that you will get a tax advantage from a debt consolidation loan. Many lenders offering bad refinancing deals talk about the benefit of the tax deductibility of mortgage interest. Make sure you understand how your personal tax situation will be affected. For example, if you do not itemize deductions, the tax deductibility of mortgages interest is worthless.

11. Avoid refinancing deals that are scams. Refinancing involves great potential for hidden costs, fees, and other unfair loan terms. Even some reputable lenders make unfair refinancing deals. When in doubt, get help in reviewing the loan papers *before* you sign anything. You can walk away from a bad deal even at the last minute. A lender that is unwilling to let you get outside help should not be trusted. Another way to avoid scams is never to let a contractor or salesperson arrange financing for you and be wary of mortgage brokers. Unfortunately, some brokers find you refinancing deals which involve big commissions for them rather than good loans for you. More information about refinancing scams can be found at the end of this chapter.

12. If your home is collateral in a refinancing deal, remember that you have three days to cancel. In most refinancings in which you give the lender a mortgage, federal law gives you the right to cancel for any reason for three business days from the date you sign the papers. If you wish to cancel, make sure you do so in writing before the deadline. The lender is required to give you a form for this purpose. You can, but need not, use the cancellation form provided by the lender. You may cancel the loan by sending a signed, dated letter indicating your desire to cancel the refinancing. You should keep a copy of this letter and be sure to send it by registered or certified mail. See Chapter Thirteen for more information about your right to cancel certain loan transactions.

DECIDING WHEN TO REFINANCE

Based upon the twelve rules described above, many refinancings and other home equity loans are bad deals that will make matters worse for you. This section goes into more detail about the factors you must consider before deciding to pay off debts by borrowing against your home. The rule of thumb is that, when in doubt, do *not* refinance even if you are behind on a debt.

Unsecured and Secured Debts. Most debts are called "unsecured." This means that a home, car, or other property is *not* collateral for the loan. Good examples of unsecured debt are hospital and doctors' bills, lawyers' bills, and most credit card debt. Utility debt is also unsecured. As described in Chapter One, unsecured debts are usually your lowest priority debts.

It is almost always a bad idea to refinance unsecured debt into secured debt, such as happens when you use a mortgage loan to refinance your debt. When you put up your home, car, or other property as collateral on a loan, this is a secured loan and the lender has a "security interest" in your property. This property is called "collateral." Secured debt will cause serious problems for you if you get behind in payments because the lender has the right to quickly seize the collateral.

Be sure to look at the loan documents and disclosure statements in any refinancing deal to see what property you are putting up as collateral. These documents will describe whether you are giving the lender a "security interest" in any of your property. You will notice this information in the sample Truth in Lending Disclosure Statement following this discussion.

Utility Bills. Utility debts should not be refinanced. While you do not want your heat or electricity shut off, there are many preferable ways to prevent a utility termination or to get service turned back on (see Chapter Fifteen) than to refinance your utility debt with a new lender.

Refinancing a utility debt can begin a downward spiral. If you are having trouble paying the utility bills, refinancing these low- or no-interest debts will not improve matters. Instead, you will have to pay *both* the old bills now refinanced with interest *and* your current monthly utility bills. It is particularly unwise to fold a utility debt into a home mortgage debt. Not only are you paying more in interest, but the risk in the event of default is much more serious. Even if you are facing shut-off, there are always better ways to deal with the back debt than to refinance.

Low-Cost vs. High-Cost Credit. Refinancings or loan consolidation often converts low-cost loans into high-cost loans. This makes things more unaffordable for you. Many of your existing bills charge you *no* interest or charge only minimal late charges. A mortgage loan you take out to purchase your home also usually has a relatively low-interest rate.

Refinanced loans, on the other hand, will often be higher-cost loans. Not only will the stated interest rate be high, but the lender will charge points, closing costs, insurance charges, maybe even broker fees or hidden charges. In addition, the loans you are paying off may include penalties for early payment (prepayment penalties).

One way of determining the real cost of the new loan is to look at the "disclosure statement" explaining all the terms for the new loan. The federal Truth in Lending Act requires that lenders provide this statement before you sign the loan papers. When you are buying a home, you should get an estimated Truth in Lending disclosures statement shortly after you apply for the loan. You should look at the APR (Annual Percentage Rate) of the new loan rather than just the amount of the monthly payments. The APR (the cost of credit to you on a yearly basis) is the most important number to use when shopping for a loan, whether it is for a car, home, or small loan.

The sample disclosures below will give you an idea of the information lenders must give you in a mortgage loan.

FIGURING OUT THE COST OF A LOAN

Lenders have many ways of making the monthly payments look low even when the loan is at a very high cost to you. For example, in some variable-rate loans, also called "adjustable rate mortgages" (ARMS), your monthly payments will climb after the first several months. See the sample ARM loan note. Monthly payments can also be artificially low if there is a large, lump-sum "balloon" payment at the end of the loan. If there is a balloon payment, it will be listed under "Your payment schedule will be:" in the Truth in Lending disclosure.

Truth In Lending Disclosure Statement

ANNUAL PERCENTAGE RATE	FINANCE CHARGE	Amount Financed	Total of Payments
The cost of your credit as a yearly rate.	The dollar amount the credit will cost you.	The amount of credit provided to you on your behalf.	The amount you will have paid after you have made all payments as scheduled.
12.107%	$163,806.74	$54,811.86	$218,618.60

You have the right to receive at this time an itemization of the Amount Financed.

[x] I want an itemization   ☐ I do not want an itemization

Your payment schedule will be:

Number of Payments	Amount of Payments	When Payments Are Due
36	456.72	12/1/2002
6	541.43	6/01/2005
6	586.40	6/01/2006
311	626.34	12/01/2006
1	617.96	01/01/2032

Variable Rate Feature: Your loan contains a variable rate feature. Disclosures about the variable rate feature have been provided to you earlier.

Insurance: You may obtain property insurance from anyone you want that is acceptable to TOP QUALITY.

Security: You are giving a security interest in:
    [x] the goods or property being purchased
    ☐ (brief description of other property)

Filing fees $30   **Non-filing insurance** $_____

Late Charge: If a payment is late, you will be charged $___/___% of the payment.

Prepayment: If you pay off early, you
    [x] may   ☐ will not   have to pay a penalty.
    ☐ may   [x] will not   be entitled to a refund of part of the finance charge.

See your contract documents for any additional information about nonpayment, default, any required repayment in full before the scheduled date, and prepayment refunds and penalties.

SAMPLE LOAN DOCUMENTS

HUD-1 Settlement Statement

D. Name & Address of Borrower:	E. Name & Address of Seller:	F. Name & Address of Lender:
Arturo and Maria Homeowner 123 Main Street Anytown, USA 00000		TOP QUALITY Mortgage 678 Money Way Anytown, USA 00000

G. Property Location	H. Settlement Agent:	
SAME AS ABOVE	Ed Smith, ESQ	
	Place of Settlement: 678 Money Way Anytown, USA 00000	I. Settlement Date: 10/27/02

J.	Summary of Borrower's Transaction		K.	Summary of Seller's Transaction	
100.	**Gross Amount Due From Borrower**		400.	**Gross Amount Due to Seller**	
101.	Contract sales price		401.	Contract sales price	
102.	Personal property		402.	Personal property	
103.	Settlement charges to borrower (line 1400)	13,813	403.		
104.			404.		
105.			405.		
Adjustments for items paid by seller in advance			**Adjustments for items paid by seller in advance**		
106.	City/town taxes to	410	406.	City/town taxes to	
107.	County taxes to		407.	County taxes to	
108.	Assessments to		408.	Assessments to	
109.	TOP QUALITY Acct. # 25240	50,046	409.		
110.			410.		
111.			411.		
112.			412.		
120.	**Gross Amount Due From Borrower**	64,269	420.	**Gross Amount Due To Seller**	
200.	**Amounts Paid By Or In Behalf of Borrower**		500.	**Reductions in Amount Due to Seller**	
201.	Deposit or earnest money		501.	Excess deposit (see instructions)	
202.	Principal amount of new loan(s)	65,000	502.	Settlement charges to seller (line 1400)	
203.	Existing loan(s) taken subject to		503.	Existing loan(s) taken subject to	
204.			504.	Payoff of first mortgage loan	
205.			505.	Payoff of second mortgage loan	
206.			506.		
207.			507.		
208.			508.		
209.			509.		
Adjustments for items unpaid by seller			**Adjustments for items unpaid by seller**		
210.	City/town taxes to		510.	City/town taxes to	
211.	County taxes to		511.	County taxes to	
212.	Assessments to		512.	Assessments to	
213.			513.		
214.			514.		
215.			515.		
216.			516.		
217.			517.		
218.			518.		
219.			519.		
220.	**Total Paid By/For Borrower**	65,000	520.	**Total Reduction Amount Due Seller**	
300.	**Cash at Settlement From/To Borrower**		600.	**Cash At Settlement To/From Seller**	
301.	Gross Amount due from borrower (line 120)	64,269	601.	Gross amount due to seller (line 420)	
302.	Less amounts paid by/ for borrower (line 220)	65,000	602.	Less reduction in amt. due seller (line 520)	( )
303.	Cash ☐ From ☒ To Borrower	731	603.	Cash ☐ To ☐ From Seller	

800.	**Items Payable In Connection With Loan**			
801.	Loan Origination Fee	3.25 %	2,112.50	
802.	Loan Discount	%		
803.	Appraisal Fee	to Top Quality		
804.	Credit Report	to Top Quality		
805.	Lender's Inspection Fee			
806.	Mortgage Insurance Application Fee	to		
807.	Loan processing fee to WE CAN		395	
808.	Br. Comp. (WE CAN)		5,000	
809.	(YSP)	(325)		
810.	Underwriting Fee to Top Quality		395	
811.	Tax service fee to Top Quality		81	
812.	Flood certification fee to Top Quality		17	
900.	**Items Required By Lender To Be Paid In Advance**			
901.	Interest from 10/27 to 11/1/04	@$13.63 /day	91.78	
902.	Mortgage Insurance Premium for	months to		
903.	Hazard Insurance Premium for	years to		
904.		years to		
1000.	**Reserves Deposited With Lender**			
1001.	Hazard insurance	months @$ per month		
1002.	Mortgage insurance	months @$ per month		
1003.	City property taxes	months @$ per month		
1004.	County property taxes	months @$ per month		
1005.	Annual assessments	months @$ per month		
1006.		months @$ per month		
1007.		months @$ per month		
1008.		months @$ per month		
1100.	**Title Charges**			
1101.	Settlement or closing fee	to Ed Smith	450	
1102.	Abstract title search	to		
1103.	Title examination	to Ed Smith		
1104.	Title insurance binder	to		
1105.	Document preparation	to WE CAN	295	
1106.	Notary fees	to		
1107.	Attorney's fees	to Ed Smith		
	(includes above items numbers:)			
1108.	Title insurance	to Title Abstract	295	
	(includes above items numbers:)			
1109.	Lender's coverage	$		
1110.	Owner's coverage	$		
1111.	Endorsement fee		95	
1112.	Express mail		45	
1113.	Courier fees		7.20	
1200.	**Government Recording and Transfer Charges**			
1201.	Recording fees:	Deed $; Mortgage $30 ; Releases $	30	
1202.	City/county tax/stamps:	Deed $; Mortgage $		
1203.	State tax/stamps:	Deed $; Mortgage $		
1204.				
1205.				
1300.	**Additional Settlement Charges**			
1301.	Survey	to		
1302.	Pest inspection	to		
1303.	Appraisal review to Top Quality		175	
1304.	Funding fee to Top Quality		175	
1305.	Administrative fee to WE CAN		795	
1306.	Delinquent county taxes		3,358.52	
1400.	Total Settlement Charges (enter on lines 103, Section J and 502, Section K)		13, 813	

LOAN NOTE

We the borrowers, Arturo and Maria Homeowner, of 123 Main Street, Anytown, USA, do hereby agree to repay TOP QUALITY Mortgage, Inc., or it transfers and assigns under the following provisions and terms,

Borrowers' Promise to Pay. In return for the loan we have received, we promise to repay $65,000 (the "principal amount"), plus interest to TOP QUALITY Mortgage Co. We understand that this note may be transferred at any time to another holder. If the loan is transferred, we agree to pay the new holder under this contract.

Interest. Interest will be charged on the principal amount until the loan is fully paid. We will pay interest at an initial yearly rate of 7.550%. The interest rate may vary during the loan terms as discussed below.

Interest rate and monthly payment changes.
(A) Change dates. The interest we will pay may change on the first day of June, 2005 and on that day every 6th month thereafter. Each date on which our interest rate could change is called a "Change Date."
(B) Index. Beginning with the first Change Date, our interest rate will be based on an "Index." The Index is the average of interbank offered rates for 6-month U.S. dollar-denominated deposits in the London market based on quotations of major banks, as published in the "Money Rates" section of the Western Edition of the Wall Street Journal. The most recent Index figure available as of the date 45 days before each Change Date is called the "Current Index."
(C) Calculation of Changes. Before each Change Date, the Note Holder will calculate our new interest rate by adding 5.25% to the Current Index. The Note Holder will then round the result of this addition to the nearest one-eighth of one percentage point (0.125%). Subject to the limits stated in Section (D) below, this rounded amount will be our new interest rate until the next Change Date. The Note Holder will then determine the amount of the monthly payment that would be sufficient to repay the unpaid principal that we are expected to owe at the Change Date in full on the Maturity Date at our new interest rate in substantially equal payments. The result of the calculation will be the new amount of our monthly payment.
(D) Limits on Interest Rate Changes. The interest rate we are required to pay at the first Change Date will not be greater than 9.55% or less than 7.55%. Thereafter, our interest rate will never be increased or decreased on any single Change Date by more than 1% from the rate of interest we have been paying for the preceding 6 months. Our interest rate will never be greater than 14.55% or less than 7.55%.
(E) Effective Date of Changes. Our new interest rate will become effective on each Change Date. We will pay the amount of our new monthly payment beginning on the first monthly payment date after the Change Date until the amount of my monthly payment changes again.
(F) Notice of Changes. The Note Holder will deliver or mail to us a notice of any changes in our interest rate and the amount of our monthly payment before the effective date of any change. The notice will include information required by law to be given us and the title and telephone number of a person who will answer any question we may have regarding the notice.

Payments. We will make our principal payment on the first of every month starting on December 1, 2002. The initial monthly payment shall be $456.72. All payments will be paid first to any charges due and owing on the account under the terms of this note, then to interest, then to reduce the principal amount. We will make payments on this account until the principal, interest and other charges due on this account are fully paid. If the note is not fully paid by January 1, 2032, the lender may declare the remaining principal, interest and other charges dues and owing full at that time.

Prepayment. If this loan is prepaid in whole or in part, we agree to pay a penalty of 5% of the principal balance due on the date of prepayment during the first five years of the term.

By signing below, the borrowers agree to all terms and covenants contained in this loan note.

Date

Similarly, some loans require monthly payments that are less than the monthly interest due so that the principal amount goes up even though you make your payments (this is called negative amortization). Other times, you will pay high closing costs and up-front fees but not realize this because they are deducted from your loan amount and financed as part of the loan principal. So, a loan advertised as a "no closing cost" loan may include hidden charges.

The monthly payment on most mortgage loans contains principal (P), interest (I), property taxes (T), and homeowner's hazard insurance (I), commonly abbreviated as "PITI." To make your new loan look affordable, a new mortgage lender may exclude the hazard insurance premiums and property taxes from your monthly payments. However, you will end up with unpaid home insurance premiums and property tax bills at some point each year. If so, the insurance and tax bills may be large sums (as opposed to being spread out over twelve months as part of your mortgage payment) which may trigger a financial crunch for you.

Some lenders will push a "consolidation" loan. They will tell you that it makes more sense for you to add your credit card debt to your mortgage loan because the interest rate on a credit card is much higher than on a mortgage loan. However, when you stretch credit card debt out for thirty years, the amount of interest you will pay is very large, even at a much lower interest rate. For example, paying off a credit card bill of $5,000 at 18% APR over five years requires a monthly payment of about $125. This high APR will generate $2,500 in interest. On the other hand, if you add the $5,000 to a $100,000 mortgage loan for a total principal of $105,000 at a 7% APR for a term of thirty years, the $5,000 creates additional interest of almost $7,000 and raises the monthly payment by about $30.

Here are some questions to ask when looking at the loan's disclosure statement. You should refer back to the sample disclosure statement and loan note above when going through these questions:

- *What is the Annual Percentage Rate or "APR?"* It represents the cost of the credit to you as a yearly rate. This will give you an idea of the size of both the interest rate *plus* many of the costs and fees on the loan included. If a lender tells you to ignore the APR and focus on the interest rate or monthly payment, walk away. Be sure you understand any variable-rate provisions, since this may later change the amount of your monthly payment.
- *What is "the finance charge" (the total cost of the credit over the life of the loan)?* This is how much you are paying the lender for use of its money over the term of the loan.

95

- *How much is the "amount financed?"* This is supposed to be the money the lender is giving you. Sometimes, much of the amount financed never goes to you or to pay off your obligations but, instead, goes to buy insurance or to pay various fees and charges. Request an "itemization of the amount financed" or a "good faith estimate," either of which should explain where your money is going and why. If these statements are different from what you expected, walk away from the loan. Most important, ask questions or seek professional help to review the paperwork if the loan terms are unclear to you.
- *Can you permanently afford the "payment schedule" for the loan?* The payment schedule shows not only the amount of your first payment, but also describes the ways that your monthly payments may change. Make sure all of the payments on the loan will be affordable. Do not rely on an oral promise to refinance when scheduled payments go up.

You can compare your answers to these questions about a new loan to those regarding your current debts as well as alternative loans.

Bank Loans vs. Finance Company Loans. In general, do *not* refinance a bank loan with a finance company loan. (In fact, try to avoid finance companies entirely, even if they appear to be related to a bank.) Finance companies tend to make loans at higher interest rates and may include unnecessary insurance, fees, and hidden charges. Some finance companies will even send you "live" checks in the mail to encourage you to borrow more money.

Many consumers think only finance companies will make loans to them and that banks will not make a loan because of a bad credit history. Do not make assumptions—ask a few banks. Also, beware of finance company loan "flipping." Many finance companies encourage frequent refinancings, each time making the loan more expensive to you and increasing the total amount you must repay. For this reason, some finance companies encourage you to refinance when you get behind on your payments rather than offer a repayment plan.

There may also be alternatives to banks and finance companies, such as credit unions, that can, in some cases, offer you better terms. These options are discussed later in this chapter.

Long-Term vs. Short-Term Credit. Always look at the length of a loan and whether there is a balloon payment (that is, a very large payment that is due as the last payment). You should not, for example, refinance a loan you are paying out over fifteen years with a loan you have to pay off in four years.

In particular, watch out if the monthly payments for the shorter loan are the same or lower than the longer-term loan. This almost always means the shorter-term loan has a large balloon at the end. You may not be able to pay the balloon payment when it comes due. You will be in a very weak position if you are later forced to refinance the balloon and will likely be stuck with whatever loan terms the lender wants to offer. If the lender will not refinance the balloon, and you cannot find another way to pay off the balloon, the lender may repossess seize any collateral in which you agreed to give a security interest, including your home.

Variable vs. Fixed Rates. You will be offered either a fixed- or variable-rate loan if you refinance. In a variable-rate loan, the interest rate you pay can go up or down during the life of the loan. The changes in the interest rate will cause your monthly payments to change. In contrast, the interest rate in a fixed-rate loan stays the same for the full term of your loan, as does your monthly payment.

Whether your variable-rate interest goes up or down will usually depend on whether other interest rates in the economy are going up or down. For example, your rate may be set at five percentage points above the current interest rate for one-year United States Treasury Bills. Your rate then changes in the same direction as the rate on one-year treasury bills.

You need to exercise care when refinancing from a fixed-rate to a variable-rate loan and sometimes vice versa, because it is difficult to compare loans of the two types. A good rule of thumb is never to refinance from a fixed rate into a variable rate, because of the risk of increased payments with variable-rate loans.

Occasionally, a variable-rate option is the right choice, but you must first make sure you know what you are doing. Getting help from an expert is good advice. Check the loan documents. The lender is required to tell you the maximum rate which could ever apply to your variable-rate loan. Make sure you can afford the loan even if the rate increases to the maximum. Ask the lender to tell you what your monthly payment would be if the interest rate reaches the maximum.

One other problem to watch out for in variable-rate loans is low "teaser rates." These are rates designed to be low for the first months of the loan but which often increase dramatically later. Pay less attention to the stated teaser rate than to the Annual Percentage Rate (APR) disclosed for the whole term of the loan. If you are not good at understanding interest rates, it is best to avoid teaser rates and variable-rate loans entirely. The more a particular lender pushes variable-rate loans as the only option, the stronger you should resist the deal.

Other variable rate loans are set up so that the interest rates only go up and never down. These loans are particularly dangerous for you if your income is fixed, such as Social Security or retirement pension income.

Some of the newer ARM loan products include hybrid, payment option, and interest-only ARMs. Hybrid ARMs often are advertised as 2/28 or 3/27 ARMs—the first number tells you how long the fixed interest-rate period will be, and the second number tells you the number of years the rates on the loan will be adjustable. Some 2/28 and 3/27 mortgages adjust every few months, not annually.

Payment option ARMs allows a number of different payment options each month, including very minimal payments. The minimum payment option can be less than the interest accruing on the loan, resulting in negative amortization. This means that your principal rises, rather than shrinks, when you make the minimum allowable payment. Once the principal increases to a certain level, the lender will recalculate your monthly payment and you will likely experience a dramatic increase in your monthly payment. This is often called "payment shock," that is, an unmanageable rise that will lead to default because the loan becomes unaffordable. When the principal increases, you also lose equity in your home, unless the fair market value also rises.

An interest-only (I-O) ARM allows you to pay only the interest for a specified number of years, typically between three and five years. This allows you to have smaller monthly payments for a period of time. After that, your monthly payment will increase, often a big jump because you must start paying back the principal as well as the interest each month. For some I-O loans, the interest rate adjusts during the I-O period as well.

For more detailed information about ARMs, the Federal Reserve Board published a booklet called *Consumer Handbook on Adjustable-Rate Mortgages* which you can read in English or Spanish at www.federalreserve.gov/pubs/arms/arms_english.htm#types.

Sticker Shock on a Five-Year Interest Only ARM	
Monthly payments on five-year IO, $350,000 loan:	
Initial interest rate: 5.75%	
Interest-only payment: $1,677	
Full payment after five years:	$2,202 ($525 higher)
Full payment after five years if interest rate rises to 7.75%:	$2,643 ($966 higher)

Beware of lenders trying to change the
loan terms at the last minute.
Whenever you have doubts about loan terms,
your best course is to walk away.

Another trick of unscrupulous lenders is to change a loan from a fixed rate to a variable rate at the last minute. This is a sure sign of a bad loan. If any term of the loan is changed at the last minute, do not sign the loan papers. You should either have a professional review the papers to make sure they don't include unfair terms or walk away from that lender entirely.

Points, Broker Fees and Other Up-Front Charges. When you refinance one or more loans into a new loan, you often have to pay points (one point equals 1% of the loan amount, for example, 1% of a $100,000 loan equals $1,000), closing costs, a broker's fee, or other up-front charges. Since you have already paid for any such charges on your old loans, these charges are an extra cost of the new loan. Even if the new loan's interest rate appears lower, these added charges may make the new loan more costly.

Make sure the "APR" (Annual Percentage Rate) on the new loan is lower than the *interest* rate stated on the old loan. The "interest rate" (as opposed to the APR) on the old loan will not reflect points, broker fees, closing costs, and other up-front fees. The APR is a measure of the total cost of a loan with all of these up-front costs factored in. For example:

COMPARING THE COSTS OF LOANS
Amount borrowed in new loan $25,000
Interest rate 10%
Origination Fee (3% of loan amount) $750
Broker fees $500
APR for new loan 12.23%
You should not use this loan to refinance an older loan which was at a 12% interest rate or lower. The origination fee of $750 and broker fee of $500 are additional costs of getting the new loan which are not included in the interest rate on the new loan. Factoring them in to the APR makes clear that the total cost of the new loan is actually higher than the rate you have been paying, even though the interest rate is lower.

Insurance and Other Extras. Consumer loans are frequently loaded up with a lot of extras. Just as some car dealers make their real profits selling expensive rustproofing and service contracts, so, too, lenders sell overpriced extras or tack on fees and charges to their loans in order to make money. Unless you have a special reason for wanting these extras, you should not purchase them. That sounds easy, but you often do not know what extras you are buying because lenders will try to trick you into buying unnecessary products.

One of the biggest problems is credit-life and credit-accident and health insurance or similar products called "debt cancellation" or "suspension" contracts. These policies or contracts are supposed to pay off your loan if you cannot do so or suspend your payments for a period of time. To sell this coverage to you, the lender will need you to initial a statement that you want this coverage. You should not do so. Only a small percentage of these insurance premiums or charges are ever paid out as losses to policyholders.

Additionally, these policies or contracts are often designed so that companies can deny coverage to you even when it appears that you have a valid claim. For example, the insurance may not cover many types of accidents that you would expect it to cover. Any benefits that are paid out are limited to the amount left on the loan, so you never actually receive much, if anything. You will always be better off buying insurance from other sources.

While you have the legal right to turn down credit insurance and many other extras, you are likely to be pressured to pay for certain other charges if you want a loan from a particular lender. Examples are property insurance on the collateral and title examination fees. However, you may be able to negotiate and lower the amount of these fees.

If the mandatory charges seem overpriced to you and the lender is unwilling to negotiate, shop around for another lender. You will find many differences between lenders as to closing costs and other charges. In addition, you should always factor in the cost of all extra charges when you are trying to decide whether you are saving or losing money by refinancing existing loans with a new loan.

Prepayment Penalties. When you pay off old loans through refinancing, there often are significant prepayment penalties on the existing debt. Prepayment penalties are costs the lender will charge you if you pay off a loan early. For example, on the sample loan note reprinted earlier in this chapter, see the paragraph titled "Prepayment" just above the consumer's signature line, indicating a 5% prepayment penalty. These penalties should be treated like extra charges on the *new* loan. Add them to the finance charge on the new loan and consider that they increase the interest rate on the new loan accordingly.

You will find it difficult to measure the size of these penalties, but they are usually there. Even if the lender does not have an explicit prepayment penalty, some states allow lenders to compute payoff figures to their own advantage. Additionally, if you purchased credit-related insurance on the old loan, that insurance will be canceled and you will receive less than a full rebate. (The lender may then try to sell a new insurance policy with the new loan.) If you have difficulty computing the prepayment penalties, assume that they exist and that they are a significant disadvantage to refinancing.

Borrowing More Than Your Home Is Worth. Some lenders offer to provide refinancing to consumers in amounts far more than their homes are worth. These loans are sometimes called "125%" loans, "high-LTV" loans, or "no-equity" loans. These loans can be quite large and very expensive. Some lenders provide misleading information about the tax consequences of such loans. They claim that you will be able to fully deduct interest charges in a way that the IRS may not allow.

Another example would be an adjustable rate mortgage where the principal rises due to negative amortization. When the monthly payments do not fully cover the interest earned for that period, the unpaid interest is added to the principal. When the principal rises, your equity decreases, unless the fair market value of your home also rises.

These loans can be very expensive and very risky. Mortgage lenders willing to lend you more than your home is worth typically charge rates about 5% higher than more traditional loans. In addition, your home will be at risk of foreclosure if you fail to pay the new higher loan amount. Finally, remember that taking a loan of this type will prevent you from building up equity in the home for a long time, if ever. The loan will make it very difficult to sell or refinance until you have paid the loan down below your property's market value. This can greatly reduce your flexibility if you need to move.

Sometimes, borrowing more than your home is worth occurs without you realizing it. This can happen if the appraiser inflates the market value of your home. Before taking out a mortgage loan, ask to see the appraisal. Compare the listed market value to the value that a friendly real estate agent estimates for you. You can also check the tax appraised value of the home. While the appraised value for tax purposes is usually lower than the market value, the appraised value should not be extraordinarily higher than the tax value. If so, this may be a warning sign of an inflated appraisal.

Consumer Defenses. You may have legal grounds not to pay a debt. These include, for example, that the goods were never delivered or that repair work was shoddy. Be aware that if you refinance such a loan with a different lender, you may lose the ability to raise these defenses against the new lender. The more removed a lender is from the original seller, the harder it is to raise defenses.

Backing Out of a Refinancing. If you change your mind about a refinancing deal in which your home is mortgaged, federal law allows you to cancel the loan within three business days of signing the loan papers. If you decide to cancel, you will need to fill out and mail in the cancellation form that the lender is required to provide you at the time you signed the contract. You may also cancel the deal by sending a signed and dated letter stating that you want to cancel the loan, instead of using the form provided by the lender. It is important that you send the lender either the cancellation form or your cancellation letter by the three-day deadline. You should mail the form or letter by certified or registered mail. If you do cancel the new loan by the deadline, you are responsible to pay the lender for any of the costs of the loan. These can include an appraisal fee, application charge, and many other closing costs. See Chapter Thirteen for more details.

Federal law also provides other grounds for canceling refinancings if your home is put up as security for up to three years for certain reasons. You will need a lawyer to review your paperwork and tell you whether you can cancel beyond the initial three days.

Any time you are considering refinancing, whether or not your home is collateral, you can always back out before the papers are signed. You should never feel embarrassed to walk away from a bad deal even if you are being pressured. Some lenders will threaten penalties or legal action if you do not sign papers which have already been prepared. These threats are false because you have no responsibility to pay if there is no binding agreement. There is no binding agreement until you sign the papers. There is no binding agreement if you cancel within three business days.

CREDIT DISCRIMINATION

If you are denied credit by banks and credit unions, or offered credit only at high rates, it is possible that you are being illegally discriminated against. There are a number of powerful federal laws and some state laws that can protect you from illegal discrimination.

Two main federal laws, the Equal Credit Opportunity Act (ECOA) and the Fair Housing Act (FHA) cover most credit discrimination situations. The ECOA prohibits discrimination in any part of a credit transaction, including applications for credit, credit evaluation, credit terms and even collection procedures.

To help you figure out if a lender is making a decision based on discrimination, the ECOA requires lenders to give you notice when they deny your credit application or change the terms. If they deny your credit application, they must give you a written explanation of the reasons for the denial.

Not all types of discrimination are illegal. The ECOA prohibits a lender from discriminating based on these factors:

- Race or color;
- National origin;
- Sex;
- Marital status;
- Religion;
- Age;
- Public Assistance Status.

The ECOA also prohibits lenders from discriminating against you for exercising your rights under consumer protection laws.

The federal Fair Housing Act (FHA) prohibits discrimination in residential real estate transactions. The law protects you from discrimination not only in the rental housing market but also in the home mortgage market. The FHA, like the ECOA, prohibits discrimination based on race, color, religion, national origin, and sex. In addition, the FHA covers discrimination based on familial status and disability. A few states have laws that prohibit credit discrimination on grounds other than those covered by the ECOA and FHA. For example, some states prohibit credit discrimination based on sexual orientation.

FINDING AFFORDABLE LOANS

This chapter sets out many different warning signs of unaffordable refinancing loans. But the reality is that there may be situations where borrowing against your home makes sense. This is especially true if you believe there will be serious consequences if you do not pay your other debts.

Finding the most affordable loan possible is easier said than done. In many cases, lenders use the term "alternative loans" as a secret code word for high-cost sub-prime or predatory loans.

It is very difficult for anyone to understand the true cost of a mortgage loan. Still, you should do your best to shop around. A first step is to review your credit report and credit score, as discussed in Chapter Three.

If you credit score is low (usually meaning that it is under 670), you should know that most lenders will consider you to be a riskier borrower and will probably charge you more. You can still shop around even if your credit score is low. Do not assume that the deal offered by a particular lender is the best you can do. Some studies have shown that up to one-third of all borrowers that end up with higher-cost loans actually qualified for lower-cost products.

Another strategy when you shop around is to find out anything you can about the lender. If you suspect there may be problems, check with you state's attorney general, banking commission, or consumer complaint hotline.

You should also review the cost estimates that lenders must give you no later than three days after applying for a mortgage loan. This is called a "good faith estimate" of settlement costs. The form the lenders use is often called a "HUD-1" form or "settlement statement." Be sure to ask for this information if you don't receive it after applying for a loan. This will help show the lender that you know about your rights and are taking a close look at what the lender is charging you. If you see anything that concerns you, you should seek help from a lawyer or trusted counselor.

You should examine all of the loan terms before you sign any papers. Do not look at the monthly payment as the only factor. The APR tells you the cost of the loan as a yearly rate. If loan terms are not favorable, shop around for another loan. You can always walk away from signing loan papers, even at the last minute. Definitely walk away if the lender tries to change the loan terms from what you had originally discussed. Remember also that, if you have to put up your primary residence as collateral for a refinancing, federal law allows you to cancel the loan *for any reason* up to three business days *after* signing the loan.

Avoiding these abusive services will save you money but won't necessarily help you get back on your feet. There are other options available in many communities where you can borrow money at reasonable rates. At the very least, you should not assume that one lender's evaluation of your credit history is the final word on the subject. Another lender may be able to give you a better deal.

Many credit unions have various types of lending programs with more flexible criteria than most banks. There are a number of different types of community development financial institutions (CDFIs), including community development loan funds, community development credit unions, community development venture capital funds, microenterprise development loan funds, and community development banks. You can find out more from the Coalition of Community Development Financial Institutions, 703-294-6970, www.cdfi.org.

One type of CDFI, Community Development Credit Unions (CDCUs) can be found in low- and moderate-income communities throughout the country. CDCUs provide a full range of credit and financial services to communities that are underserved by conventional financial institutions, including personal loans, mortgages, small business loans, savings clubs and accounts, check cashing, checking accounts and ATM access. To get a list of CDCUs in your area, contact the National Federation of Community Development Credit Unions, 212-809-1850 or visit www.natfed.org.

Just as with banks, you should shop around if you are considering borrowing with a credit union. Do not assume that you will automatically get a better deal just because an institution has "community" in its name or seems to be friendlier or more helpful.

Several non-profit organizations may offer "rescue funds" to help homeowners who received predatory loans refinance with better terms. ACORN Housing helps qualifying consumers obtain affordable mortgages or renegotiate their existing predatory mortgages. For more information on ACORN Housing visit http://acornhousing.org/index.php. The National Community Reinvestment Corporation (NCRC) administers the National Anti-Predatory Lending Consumer Rescue Fund, a program that provides mediation between eligible consumers and lenders to remove abusive terms from loans and to help secure refinancing of the loan whenever possible. For more information on NCRC's Consumer Rescue Fund visit www.fairlending.com. The Neighborhood Assistance Corporation of America (NACA) offers the Home Save program, providing consumers with subprime or predatory loans the chance to refinance their loans at below-market interest rates. For more information on NACA's Home Save program visit www.naca.com/buy_or_refi/130_refinance.pbl.

Another alternative product to consider, a reverse mortgage, is discussed below.

REVERSE MORTGAGES

The rules of reverse mortgages are different from those of traditional mortgages. In a traditional mortgage, the lender gives cash to the borrower and, in return, takes a mortgage. As the borrower repays, the amount of the debt decreases.

In a reverse mortgage, the lender gives the homeowner cash based on the value of the property without an immediate repayment obligation. In contrast to a traditional mortgage, the amount of the debt in a reverse mortgage increases over time.

For most reverse mortgages, you can draw down your home equity without having to repay that loan for quite some time. Some reverse mortgages have no repayment obligation as long as you remain in the property—no matter how long you stay. But the mortgage, including all interest and other charges, must be repaid when the last living borrower dies, sells the home, or permanently moves away.

In most reverse mortgages, the lender will look at your age (you must be at least 62 years old), the amount of equity you have in your home, and the prevailing interest rates in order to determine the amount it will lend you. You will then be able to receive your loan amount in one of the following ways:

- One large payment that is given to you in cash or is used to pay off other debt or both.
- Fixed monthly installments that will be paid to you for a set period of time. This is called a "term" plan.
- Fixed monthly installments (smaller ones) that will be paid to you for as long as you live in the home (this is usually called a "tenure" plan).
- As a line of credit to be drawn at your convenience. This may also be combined with a term or tenure plan.

A reverse mortgage may be a good way to get some money now based on the value of your house whether or not you are having financial problems. If you are interested, look for a bank or mortgage company in your community that offers this product. However, a good deal of caution is required for a number of reasons.

Most importantly, you can only borrow against your equity once. If you have taken a reverse mortgage and spent the money, you will not have the financial resource of home equity available again to you in the future. For example, if you use your home equity as a resource for a reverse mortgage or another loan at age 65, the equity will not be available to help pay for home health care later if you should need it.

Other potential drawbacks to a reverse mortgage include:

- The costs involved in getting a reverse mortgage can be very high. Some reverse mortgages include up-front fees as high as $5,000 or more. You should shop around for the loan product with the smallest total fees. A reverse mortgage will generally be most costly when you live in your home only a few years after taking out the loan.
- The amount of cash you get may not really meet your needs. For example, a 65-year-old with $50,000 in home equity may get as little as $100 per month on a term mortgage. (This calculation varies for different lenders and it depends on a variety of factors, including regional loan limits, interest rates, and the amount of the closing costs.) In addition, you keep title to your home and are still responsible for paying the property taxes, insurance, and for the general up-keep of the property.
- A reverse mortgage can affect your eligibility to receive certain government benefits such as SSI and Medicaid. (Social Security payments are not affected.) There may also be tax consequences to consider.
- Some shady lenders offer very unfair reverse mortgages or conventional mortgages that look like reverse mortgages. You should only work with a reputable lender in an established program. The lowest cost mortgages are offered by state and local governments. Some of these must be used for certain purposes such as home repairs. Generally the least expensive private sector reverse mortgage is the federally insured Home Equity Conversion Mortgage (HECM).
- A reverse mortgage makes it difficult to pass your home on to your heirs after your death; instead, the home usually will go to the lender when you move or if you die. This is not necessarily a bad decision if you need money now, but it is important to make the decision in full awareness of what it may mean for the future.

Reverse mortgages are not for everyone. You should work with a knowledgeable counselor if you are at all in doubt, especially since free counseling is an element of most reputable reverse mortgage programs. In fact, you must receive counseling from a HUD-approved agency before you can qualify for a reverse mortgage insured by the Federal Housing Administration (FHA). If you do take out a reverse mortgage, set up a plan to use the money wisely. You will not be able to tap into your home equity again.

You can receive free information about reverse mortgages by calling AARP at: 1-800-209-8085, toll-free or at www.aarp.org (click on "Money &

Work"). As of 2005, the Department of Housing and Urban Development also approved the National Foundation for Credit Counseling (1-866-698-6322) and Money Management International (1-877-908-2227) to provide HECM counseling by phone and face-to-face. More information about reverse mortgages is available from the Department of Housing and Urban Development, www.hud.gov or by calling 1-800-569-4287.

REFINANCING SCAMS

Tips to Avoid Refinancing Scams. Many unscrupulous companies prey on people in distress. Here are twelve tips to help you steer clear of frauds:

1. *Be wary of anyone who contacts you about refinancing or loan consolidation,* particularly if the solicitation does not come from an established financial institution in your community. Be skeptical of any solicitation from a finance company, even if the company has helped you out before. Well-known finance companies have engaged in serious fraud.

2. *Definitely avoid anyone who solicits loans via a "door-to-door" visit of your home.* It is very expensive to market anything door to door. The odds are that someone coming to the house to help bail you out of trouble is really aiming to get you deeper into it.

3. *When in doubt, check out the lender.* If you have any reason to suspect someone you are considering doing business with, check with your state's attorney general, banking commission, or consumer complaint hotline. You definitely want to know if there are complaints on file from other consumers. Check both the business name and the names of any individual you are dealing with because some individuals change their company names repeatedly to avoid becoming well-known in the community. If you do check on a business, remember that the absence of complaints does not necessarily mean that the business is reputable. You still need to keep in mind the other scam avoidance techniques discussed here.

4. *Never sign documents without knowing what is in them.* If you own a home, you should be especially wary, because odds are any deal to "help" you will involve a mortgage or other rights to your home.

5. *Avoid any offer where you sell your home with an option to buy it back.* This will always be the quickest way to lose your home and any equity

you have built up. Any sale of your home means that you no longer have the rights of an owner.

6. *Be careful of advertised schemes to save homes from foreclosure or of personal solicitations to help you avoid foreclosure.* "For-profit" foreclosure assistance has a very poor track record. Many financially strapped consumers pay money for short-term help or no help at all. Nonprofit counseling or bankruptcy assistance is usually a better alternative. However, as discussed in Chapter Four, not all non-profits can be trusted.

7. *If your regular banker or credit union cannot help you, odds are that lenders and brokers who advertise cannot get you a good deal either.* Most loan brokers and some lenders advertise themselves as offering help to people who are credit risks. These advertisements will usually get you involved with people who are known as "hard money lenders" and who will almost always make your situation worse. Brokers are often expensive to use. Many shop for loans which include big commissions for themselves, rather than the best terms for you.

8. *Beware of anyone who wants to consolidate all of your debts into one loan.* This *never* makes sense. The solicitation shows that the person suggesting the loan consolidation is not out to help you but to take advantage of you.

9. *Do not send an "application" or "processing" fee to a lender who advertises "Bad Credit, No Problem" and then asks you to call an 800 or 900 number or solicits you over the Internet.* This may just be a scam to make off with the fee. Any "900" number call will also cost you money that can be very difficult to get back.

10. *Do not refinance repeatedly with the same lender.* Encouragements to refinance regularly can only mean that the lender is looking to make a large profit at your expense by taking advantage of the hidden costs of frequent refinancing.

11. *Do not refinance to take advantage of offers of small amounts of cash or to get a gift.* These deals are almost always designed by lenders to be very costly to you. Cash or gifts are offered in order to convince you to make a deal which has no real financial advantages for you.

12. *If it is too good to be true, it is not true.*

Other Steps to Take If You Are Victimized by a Refinancing Scam.

It is much easier to avoid a refinancing scam than to get your money back. Do not expect a business that is ripping you off to easily agree to return money or to be responsive to your complaints. However, you should always take action if you are ripped off, both to try to get your money back and to help prevent the same thing from happening to other honest consumers.

Your first step should always be to ask for the return of any money you have lost in a refinancing scam. There is some hope that the lender will not want to alert law enforcement officials and will be willing to "buy off" one victim so that they can keep victimizing others. For this reason, threatening to go to a state attorney general's office or district attorney or the local press may help.

A second step is to not just threaten, but to actually complain to your attorney general, the state commission that oversees banks, and to your local better business bureau. Consumer complaint hotlines, the press, and neighborhood nonprofits can also be useful. You may find that other people have made similar complaints and that legal action is pending or can be brought. At a minimum, a complaint to a public official or complaint hotline will be on record and will help prevent others from being ripped-off. You should keep all paperwork and make records of all conversations with whomever you think is working a scam.

Your best course is usually to get help from an attorney who will represent your interests. Although some lawyers will not want to handle a consumer fraud issue, they may tell you if you have a good claim and may give you a referral to someone who does handle consumer law cases. You want to find an attorney who is willing to pursue your case aggressively. Please go to the *Introduction* to this book and the section there called *Obtaining Professional Assistance* for specific suggestions to help you find a lawyer.

Filing bankruptcy is another strategy. It will stop a scam company's attempt to foreclose your home. To be effective in the long run, however, your bankruptcy attorney must aggressively challenge the scam operator in the bankruptcy proceeding—something not all bankruptcy attorneys are prepared to do.

7

Raising Money to Repay Debts

Making Good Choices and Avoiding Choices That Could Get You into Trouble

---

TOPICS COVERED IN THIS CHAPTER

- Choices to Consider with Caution
- Choices That Could Get You into Trouble
- "Quick Money" Strategies to Avoid at All Costs

This chapter discusses strategies to help you raise money or use your existing assets or property to repay lower priority, unsecured debts. Information on holding on to your house or car by setting up a workout plan or negotiating with your creditors to repay debts over time can be found in Chapters Ten through Thirteen (mortgage issues) and Chapter Sixteen (car issues). For certain situations, you will want to use the strategies discussed in this chapter instead of deciding to stop paying your unsecured debts. This is particularly true if you are likely to face serious consequences by not paying. This chapter will help you sort out the different strategies and help you understand which are most likely to benefit you and which are most likely to get you into deeper trouble.

CHOICES TO CONSIDER WITH CAUTION

Borrowing from Friends and Relatives. Friends or relatives may be able to help you out, but be careful. In general, there is nothing wrong with accepting this help to get you through a tough period. Occasional problems arise, however, if you count on this help. Your friends and relatives may face their own financial difficulties and may withdraw their assistance—sometimes when you need it most. Debts can also cause problems between you and your friends or relatives.

Some creditors will push you to get a friend or relative to cosign on an account when you are facing financial problems. You should avoid this whenever possible. The person who cosigns will be on the hook with you. Your financial problems may become theirs as well if you cannot afford to pay.

Dipping into Savings. As discussed at the end of Chapter Two, setting aside even a very small amount each month as savings is extremely important. If you have done this and have some savings, you may be faced with the possibility of using some of your hard-earned savings to deal with current financial problems.

There are several things you should keep in mind about using savings when you are having financial problems. The most important point is that using your savings should be part of an overall plan, not your only plan.

Using savings or other assets to pay low priority debts is generally not a good idea. If your income does not meet basic expenses, your savings are a valuable resource which you should use only to protect important property or to pay for other necessities. You should not be pressured into using essential savings or your remaining assets to pay off your credit card bills or to get involved in a "get-rich-quick" scam.

You should also think carefully about spending your retirement money. You may be tempted to dip into your retirement savings to get you through temporary financial difficulties. The most important consideration is whether you will have time to rebuild these savings before you retire. You might also consider withdrawing money from a tax-deferred account such as an I.R.A. or 401(k). There are serious disadvantages to this option, including possible tax consequences. You should seek professional advice about these options.

Despite these warnings, in some cases it might make sense for you to dip into your savings or retirement to pay essential expenses. One difficult question you will face is how best to use your savings or the proceeds of an asset sale (discussed below) to help manage your financial problems. You should consider two choices.

Some people use a set amount of their savings each month in their monthly budget to meet essential expenses. This can be the right choice if you have good discipline and if the savings will make the difference between meeting your essential expenses and falling hopelessly behind. As discussed above, you should not fall into the trap of using your savings to finance an unrealistic lifestyle.

The other choice about savings or other assets is to spend them in a lump sum for a particular purpose, like paying down a mortgage default. This choice may be necessary in order to postpone a catastrophic loss of property to foreclosure or repossession. However, you should be careful not to make this choice unless you have a longer-term plan to get back on your feet. Paying many thousands of dollars on a mortgage to keep a home you cannot afford in the long term may be a waste of money.

In addition, if you plan to use savings on a mortgage or a car loan, you should probably avoid paying ahead. Use the savings to get caught up and then keep any extra money to make future payments as they come due. This will give you more flexibility for the future.

If you feel you must pay ahead, make sure to make clear to the creditor in writing that you are paying future payments rather than a lump sum toward the principal. (This will also help to make sure you are not being charged prepayment penalties.) Although it may be wise to pay down principal due on a debt in good financial times in order to reduce total interest payments, the opposite is true if you are having financial difficulties. A lump sum paid on the principal will not excuse you from future payments unless the loan is fully paid off. That is, even after you pay a lump sum as an advance on the principal, the next monthly or weekly payment will be due as scheduled. You will be in default if you do not pay it.

Selling Assets.   You might consider selling a major asset such as a car or house if you can no longer afford the payments. You will almost always do better selling the property yourself rather than hoping to get cash back from a foreclosure or repossession sale. Before you do this, make sure you have alternative housing or transportation. Otherwise, you could end up in even worse trouble.

Major assets are not the only possibilities. You might be able to raise money, particularly to help you in the short-term, by selling items you really

113

don't need such as old bicycles, furniture, or other household items. You might consider a yard sale or putting an ad in a local paper or on the Internet.

It may also be a good idea to sell assets which are easy to liquidate, like stocks and bonds, in order to give you more flexibility for meeting urgent financial needs. Sale of other nonessential valuable assets, like vacation homes and extra cars or even antique furniture and heirlooms, should be considered. It is sometimes better to make a difficult choice in order to raise cash rather than lose everything.

If there is an established market in which to sell certain of your assets, such as most stocks and bonds, you can delay selling this type of property until you need money urgently. For other types of property that are harder to sell, it is usually best to avoid panic sales at the last minute. Urgency will usually reduce the sale price.

CHOICES THAT COULD GET YOU INTO TROUBLE

Using Credit Cards to Borrow Money. Taking out new unsecured credit, such as adding to your credit card debt, is better than incurring new secured debts. Nevertheless, use of credit cards to balance your budget can make your situation worse. Credit card debt is high-interest debt with potential penalties for nonpayment. If you intend to make only the minimum payments each month on the bill, your debt will quickly compound—making it unlikely that you will ever get back on track. See Chapter Five for more about credit card use and costs.

Although credit card debt can usually be eliminated in bankruptcy, this may not be true if you run up big bills or take cash advances just before filing. Creditors have argued with some success that if you use a credit card at a time when you did not have the ability to repay, you have committed a fraud which prevents the debt from being eliminated in the bankruptcy process.

Borrowing Against Your Home. You may be tempted, as a way to make ends meet, to consolidate many small loans into one larger loan, to refinance your home mortgage, or to take other steps to turn old loans into new loans. Chapter Six evaluates refinancing as a strategy to deal with your financial problems. In general, it is a bad option when you are already facing financial problems. It is always a bad idea to refinance unsecured debt into secured debt and to trade low-interest rate credit for higher rate loans.

However, the reality is that there may be situations where borrowing against your home makes sense. This is especially true if you believe there will be serious consequences if you do not pay your other debts. If you do want to borrow against your home, you should shop around for the best deal. Do not assume that the rate or other terms quoted by one lender is the best you can do. You can find more information about borrowing against your home, including ideas to help you find the most affordable loan possible, in Chapter Six.

CHOICES TO AVOID

Below are "quick money" strategies that you should avoid at all costs. An entire industry of unscrupulous businesses exists to pressure you into making these mistakes. These businesses know that people in financial distress often make desperate or poorly informed choices. They also know that people who feel that their options are limited are likely to be willing to overpay for credit and other services.

Unfortunately, even reputable companies have gotten into businesses that take advantage of consumers in financial trouble. You cannot assume that because a company is well known or because it advertises on TV, it will give you a fair deal. Also be suspicious of companies that use names which are designed to create confusion about their identity, such as using the name "United States." Some companies use names very similar to legitimate organizations just to confuse you.

In the following list, we recommend avoiding a number of practices that may increase your financial problems. This is not a complete list of scams. New scams constantly arise and old ones change form. The main message is that services aimed at people with bad credit or other financial problems are often rip-offs. If they seem too good to be true, they probably are.

1. Bouncing checks. It may be tempting to write a check when you know that you have insufficient funds in your account to cover it. At best, you may hope to make a deposit before the check is cashed. At worst, you may be deliberately using the check as a way to make the creditor temporarily happy.

You should avoid this temptation. Bouncing checks is never the answer. You will be charged a hefty fee, often by both the bank and by the creditor each time the check is presented for payment. And creditors may present the check for payment a number of times. You could also face criminal prosecution for fraud. You may be able to defend yourself successfully if you are prosecuted, but it is far better not to have to deal with this problem at all.

Whenever you are in doubt, find out your balance with the bank before writing a check. Remember that your balance may seem higher than it really is because other checks you have written have not yet been deducted from your account. If you have a joint account, coordinate your check writing carefully with any other person who has power to write checks and make withdrawals.

2. Bounce loans. A growing number of banks and other financial institutions are offering a product called a "bounce loan" program that encourages consumers to overdraw their accounts. Banks that use these products let you overdraw at an ATM or when you use a debit card. The problem is that they won't tell you that you are taking out more money than you have in your account and that they are going to charge you fees.

Bounce loans may sound tempting but when you consider the fees, they don't look so good. Banks charge high penalty fees for each overdraft, ranging from $20 to $35 per overdraft. Some banks also charge a per day fee of $2 to $5 at some banks until the account is brought to a positive balance. With bounce loans, banks pay themselves back the amount of the overdraft and fees out of the next deposit. Bounce loans are astronomically expensive. A $100 overdraft with a $20 fee has an annual percentage rate (APR) of 520% if the overdraft lasts two weeks.

Some consumers have no idea they are getting a bounce loan. Yet in many ways these loans are even more dangerous than extraordinarily high-priced credit cards because you don't expect to be allowed to overdraw your accounts, especially at an ATM with a debit card.

3. Postdated checks. A postdated check is one dated later than the date on which the check was written, with the expectation that it will not be cashed until that later date. Usually this is done with the hope that there will be sufficient funds in the account by the time the check is cashed.

Never give a creditor a postdated check. Even if you believe that you will have the money in your account to pay the check by that date, you may be wrong because something unexpected could happen. In that case, you will bounce the check or you will not have the money for something else that is more important. Also keep in mind that creditors occasionally deposit checks before their due date, and banks will honor the check despite the date. Even though this may be improper, it does happen and can cause you substantial problems. Finally, if you give a postdated check and later change your mind about paying that debt, it may be difficult and expensive to stop payment on the check.

Collectors and creditors often encourage you to write postdated checks. They want your check in hand as a way to get their money. You should resist the urge to give in to this pressure. You can offer instead to deliver the check on the day you write it—a day on which you have sufficient funds in your account. This allows you to decide not to deliver the check if your priorities change or if you end up not having enough money in the account.

4. "Payday" lenders. Payday loans go by a variety of names, including "deferred presentment," "cash advances," "deferred deposits," or "check loans," but they all work in the same way. You, as the payday loan customer, write a check or sign an authorization for the lender to take money out of your account electronically. The amount on the check equals the amount borrowed plus a fee that is either a percentage of the full amount of the check or a flat dollar amount. The check (or debit agreement) is then held for up to a month, usually until the customer's next payday or receipt of a government check.

At the end of the agreed time period, you must either pay back the full amount of the check (more than what the lender gave you), allow the check to be cashed, or pay another fee to extend the loan.

The difference between the amount of your check and the amount of cash you get in return is interest or a loan fee that the lender is charging you. These types of short-term loans are always very expensive.

For example:

FIVE DAYS OF WORK FOR FOUR DAYS OF PAY? THE HIGH COST OF BORROWING AGAINST YOUR PAY CHECK	
You write a check dated in two weeks for	$256
You get back today	$200
Interest and charges	$56
The interest rate for a loan of two weeks is	730%

Compare this 730% interest rate loan to annual interest rates as low as 10%–15% that bank, credit unions, and finance companies charge. The $56 you spend on this short-term loan means that you will have that much less money in your monthly budget.

Some lenders making this type of loan will encourage you to keep refinancing over and over again. The loans are set up so that consumers will have problems paying them back by the due date. Full repayment is required within a short period of time with no option to make installment payments. Each time the consumer returns, the lender charges more interest and fees. This just makes a bad situation worse. These loans are marketed not only at check cashing stores and other locations but increasingly over the Internet as well.

Special Protections for Military Servicemembers

Some states have passed laws to help protect consumers from high-rate lenders, while there is very little regulation at the federal level. In 2006, however, Congress passed the Military Lending Act. Congress was concerned about reports of high-rate lenders setting up shop around military bases and targeting military personnel and decided to give special protections to military servicemembers. The most important protection is a 36% interest rate limit on certain types of credit.

The law applies to credit extended to an individual, who at the time she becomes obligated, is an active duty member of the military, including those on Active Guard and Reserve duty, or the servicemember's spouse, child, or dependent.

The types of consumer credit that are covered are payday, auto title, and refund anticipation loans. There are some restrictions on which of these three types of loans are covered.

If a credit transaction is covered, the following rules apply:

- The military APR may not exceed 36% (the definition of the military APR is broader than the APR definition in the Truth in Lending Act);
- The credit may not be secured with a check, access to a financial account, or military allotment;
- The military APR must be disclosed orally and in writing to the consumer;
- Mandatory arbitration clauses are banned;
- The credit may not be rolled over or renewed except on terms more favorable to the borrower; and
- Prepayment penalties are banned.

---

5. Selling or giving away a creditor's collateral.
You may have property that serves as collateral for a loan from one of your creditors. A common example is a car that serves as collateral for your car loan. It is a bad idea to give away or sell a creditor's collateral. This practice is usually called "conversion" of collateral.

If you have already lost, given away, or sold collateral, you may be prosecuted by a state official or sued by the creditor. There are many defenses to these types of suits. The most important defense is that your conduct was not intentional. In most cases, this means that you did not understand that the property was collateral or that you did know the consequences to the creditor of disposing of the property. In addition, most such prosecutions and lawsuits can be ended by payment of the value of the collateral either in installments or in a lump sum if you have it. Given overcrowding in most prisons and the technical nature of the supposed crime, jail time is rarely or never imposed. Still, this is not a risk worth taking.

6. Transferring property to protect it from creditors. If you are in debt and you have valuable property to protect from your creditors, it may occur to you to give it away to a friend or relative or to sell it for a small percentage of its real value to someone who will later return it. Some people believe that this will protect the property from judgment liens and other creditor collection.

There are many problems with these types of property transfers. When the transfer of some of your assets leaves you with insufficient assets to pay your debts, creditors can have the transfer canceled under your state's law covering "fraudulent transfers" or "fraudulent conveyances."

A transfer of this type may delay the inevitable because the creditor will have to bring a legal action in order to cancel the transfer. However, this extra time could cost you a lot of money later by increasing the amount you owe to a creditor, including attorney's fees and costs. You also may have to pay additional damages and you can lose your right to bankruptcy protection. In rare cases, you could be criminally prosecuted. It is also possible that the creditor will sue the person to whom you have transferred the property.

An improper transfer is different from exemption planning. Exemption planning is less likely to cause you problems. The idea of exemption planning is that you keep the total value of all of your property but trade one type of property that is not exempt from seizure under your state laws for another type that is. This type of planning is discussed in Chapter Nine.

7. Pawn shops and auto title pawn. Pawnbrokers take property from you in exchange for an amount of money that is always less than what the property is worth. If you cannot repay the loan, the pawn shop keeps the property. Usually pawnbrokers will only lend less than one-half of the value of your property so that they can be sure to get their money back if you don't pay. They also charge very high interest rates.

If you have valuable property you can live without, consider selling it in a more conventional way for its full value. When you get back on track, you can buy a replacement.

Another type of "pawn" that is legal in some states is called an "auto pawn" where you borrow money at very high interest rates (for example, 240% or 360%) and put up your car title as collateral for the loan. This is also a bad idea. An auto pawn is not as simple and hassle free as the title lenders advertise it to be. You can borrow money elsewhere at lower interest rates without endangering your car.

For example:

THE AUTO TITLE PAWN SCAM

Your car is worth $1,000.
You give up your car title ($1,000 value) for a $500 loan.
You pay weekly installments of $103.30 for 10 weeks. Your total payments are $1,033.
You pay $1,033
You receive $500
Interest and charges total $533
This is an interest rate of 830%.

---

8. Sale and lease back. Another way that some companies and individuals make money is to buy your property from you at a low price and then to lease that property back to you at a high rental rate. These deals are often targeted at people facing foreclosure or repossession. Some companies find potential customers by reading published foreclosure notices.

These businesses are rip-offs. Once you have sold your property to them, you no longer have the rights of an owner. You are likely to be overpaying in rent for something you formerly owned. You will have no certain way of getting it back. Additionally, there are many reported cases of fraud involving promises made in connection with these contracts. People have been talked into transferring title to property without getting anything in return.

There is a whole industry of lenders
preying on those in financial trouble,
overcharging them and taking unfair advantage.

---

9. "Hard money" lenders. A variety of companies advertise loans that are supposedly designed for people with bad credit or by promising no credit check. Other loan companies rely instead on a network of loan brokers to bring them business. These companies make money by lending to people in difficult financial situations on hard terms (usually meaning bad terms) including very high interest rates.

When you deal with such a lender, expect the lender to engage in some of the following shady practices:

- Misrepresenting the loan terms—a 10% loan will turn into a 20% loan at the time of closing;
- Making loans that the lender knows you cannot repay in order to seize valuable collateral such as your home or car;
- Charging unacceptably high interest rates;
- Refinancing debts that are better off left alone;
- Charging high hidden costs;
- Paying loan brokers, car dealers, and contractors incentives to mislead you about your credit options or to make inappropriate referrals;
- Hiding ties to loan brokers in order to charge you illegal commissions;
- Making loans on complicated terms in order to make an unaffordable loan look temporarily affordable; and
- Using high-pressure sales tactics designed to get you to agree to buy credit insurance or other unnecessary products.

Don't be suckered by hard-money lenders. They have many techniques designed to draw you into deals, only to make it almost impossible for you to back away. You should never agree to refinance a low-priority debt, as discussed in Chapter Six. Ways to avoid refinancing scams are discussed in more detail in that chapter.

10. Tax refund anticipation loans. Tax refund anticipation lenders advance you money in exchange for your expected tax refund. Most tax refund lending is now done by major depository banks and processed through local tax preparers. Most consumers hear about these loans through their tax preparers, although some preparers call them "advances," which does not sound like a loan. Do not be fooled.

The loan is for a very short period of time between when your return is filed with the government and when you would expect to get your tax refund.

The loans work like this. Customers are required to file their tax returns with the Internal Revenue Service (IRS) electronically. The customer pays a fee for the filing, usually ranging from $20 to $60. The electronic filing cuts the time it takes to get a tax refund, usually to two or three weeks. The refund lender pays the customer before then, but there's a catch. The loan amount does not equal the full amount of the refund. Instead, it is the refund amount *minus* the loan fee, *minus* the tax preparation fee, and *minus* the electronic filing fee. All of these fees add up to annual percentage rates of anywhere from 67% to 768% for a two-week loan.

There are also products called pay stub and holiday RALs. These are loans made prior to the tax filing season. Pay stub RALs are made in January using the year-end pay stub information. Holidays RALs are made during November and December. Both holiday and pay stub RALs are expected to be repaid from the consumer's tax refund. These products have their own set of risks. For example, pay stub RALs are based on estimated tax returns before the taxpayer receives final information from a W-2. The RAL could be even more expensive if the estimated tax return information is wrong.

Some companies may try to fool you about the annual interest rate by telling you the rate assuming that the company will not be repaid for two or three months. Since the company will actually get the money back in one month, the real interest rate is two or three times the rate you are told. The best advice is to avoid tax refund anticipation loans. Be patient and wait for your full refund if at all possible. If you file electronically with direct deposit, you can usually get your return in about ten days.

A great way to save money at tax time is to go to a Volunteer Income Tax Assistance (VITA) site. VITA sites provide free tax preparation to low- and moderate-income taxpayers. VITA sites are sponsored by the IRS and can be found in libraries, community centers, and other locations during tax time. For the nearest VITA site, call the IRS's general help line at 1-800-TAX-1040 or go to www.tax-coalition.org.

11. Get rich quick schemes. Many products and jobs are advertised with the promise that you will make a lot of money quickly. These are almost always scams.

For example, real estate investment seminars are sold with the promise that you can make a bundle by buying and selling investment property. The reality is that the only one making a bundle is the person selling you the seminar. When seminars of this type are offered for free, there will usually be an aggressive effort to sell you something which is very expensive or very profitable for the person giving the seminar.

A similar problem involves jobs which are offered with the promise of making quick financial returns. A common example is an advertisement with a bold heading such as **"Make up to $1,000 a week immediately—working at home."** The vast majority of these offers require payment of substantial "set up" or "one-time start-up" fees to a person or company that promises you a money-making plan in return. The company keeps these fees and you end up with no real way of making money.

Once again follow the rule: if it seems too good to be true, it probably is.

12. Telemarketing scams. Many products, services, investments, and loans are advertised over the telephone. Every consumer thinks that he or she recognizes telephone rip-off schemes; nevertheless, every year millions of people are victimized. Telemarketers use very sophisticated techniques to get consumers to sign up for things they don't need, products that don't work, services which are too expensive, or outright rip-offs. Elderly individuals, in particular, are often targeted for investment scams and other telemarketing abuses.

Most telemarketers are highly trained in aggressive sales techniques. For example, they may tell you that you have already won a prize, that you can participate in a sweepstakes, that they are only taking a survey, that they are offering a free product, or that they are selling something which has been endorsed by celebrities. Telemarketers are usually offered large commissions by their employers based on the number of sales they make—increasing their incentive to be aggressive on the phone or to deliberately mislead you.

For these reasons, it is a good idea to avoid buying anything over the phone. The best choice is not to waste time by listening to the sales pitch in the first place.

However, if you do listen or if you are interested, do not invite the telemarketer to call again or to come to your home. This will make you a target. Instead, ask that detailed follow-up information be sent in the mail before you agree to anything. Doing so will give you an opportunity to think clearly about whether you are being cheated and to see the terms of the offer in writing. Pressure to sign up right away without receiving detailed written information about what you are buying is always the sign of a scam.

STOPPING TELEMARKETING CALLS

You can save money by not buying products from telemarketers or signing up for sweepstakes or lotteries with these companies. To avoid being tempted by telemarketers, sign up for the Federal Trade Commission's "Do-Not-Call" registry. You may register on-line at www.donotcall.gov or by phone by calling 1-888-382-1222 (TTY 1-866-290-4236). You must call from the telephone number you wish to register. Registration with the FTC's do-not-call registry is free. If you register on-line you

---

must provide an e-mail address for confirmation. Once you have registered, your telephone number will remain on the registry for five years, or until it is disconnected or you delete it from the registry. After five years you can renew your registration. Your state may also maintain a "do-not-call" list. You can contact your state attorney general or state consumer protection program to learn if your state has such a list and how it may protect you.

Note: At the time this book was published, Congress was considering making the Do-Not-Call List permanent. You should check with the Federal Trade Commission and with your state consumer affairs department to find out whether you will have to renew your "membership" on the list.

13. The truth about the lottery and prize sweepstakes. People facing financial difficulties sometimes look to the lottery as a way to improve their financial situation. This is an expensive long shot at best. Spending substantial money on the lottery or other gambling can greatly compound your financial problems.

The lottery pays out only a percentage of the money it takes in. The percentage in some states is one-half or less. This means that, for every two dollars spent on lottery tickets, you are likely to win back only one.

Very few people win big prizes. The odds of winning a million dollars are worse than one in a million. While you are experiencing financial difficulties, it is best to reduce or eliminate your expenses on the lottery rather than looking at it as a way of solving your problems.

Similarly, most sweepstake offers, including those you receive by mail, are usually long shots meant to convince you that your odds of winning prizes are greater if you buy products you don't need, such as magazines. Others advertise prizes or "free" gifts as a come-on to get you interested in buying things you don't need.

8

Responding to Debt Collectors

DO NOT LET COLLECTORS PRESSURE YOU

It is important not to let debt collection harassment force you into making decisions that will hurt you later. Although this can be difficult when you are feeling pressured, it is important to make your own choices about which debts to pay based on what is best for you and your family.

Try to keep in mind that as bad as you may feel, you are not a deadbeat when circumstances outside your control prevent you from paying your debts. Believe it or not, the collector knows this even better than you. Creditors and collectors know from long experience that most people pay their bills and, when they do not, it is usually because of job loss, illness, divorce, or other unexpected events. Creditors take this risk of default into account when they set the interest rate—creditors make enough money from you and others in good times so that when you default, the creditor is covered.

Do not be fooled by collector statements to the contrary. Debt collectors are *instructed* to ignore your reasons for falling behind on your debts, to show no sympathy, and not to listen to reason.

You have no moral obligation to pay one debt before you pay another debt, particularly when the debt you do pay is more central to your family's survival. Creditors know this. They should not be rewarded for trying to pressure you to pay them off at the expense of another creditor or, more importantly, at the expense of your family.

COLLECTORS CANNOT LEGALLY DO MUCH TO HARM YOU

In order to fight back, it is important to know what a debt collector can and cannot legally do when you get behind on a particular debt. Most debts, such as almost all credit card obligations, doctor bills, small amounts owed merchants, and many small loans are "unsecured." This means you have not put up any collateral, such as the family home or car, to secure the loan's repayment. An *unsecured* creditor can legally do only the following three things:

1. Stop doing business with you. For example, a credit card issuer can cancel your card or a dentist to whom you owe money might refuse to let you continue as a patient. Usually, though, there are other merchants or professionals who will offer the same goods or services on a cash basis or even on credit. The threat of stopping business with you is greatest where a particular creditor has a monopoly in your community, such as the only doctor in a rural area. Utilities also usually have a monopoly, and dealing with utility bills involves special issues discussed in detail in Chapter Fifteen.

2. Report the default to a credit reporting agency. The fact that you are behind on your bills almost certainly will end up on your credit record. You cannot stop this, short of always being current on all of your bills. While this is unfortunate, you only make matters worse by paying a particular bill first just because that collector is threatening to ruin your credit record.

The reason you make matters worse is that the collection agency threatening to ruin your credit is almost always bluffing. If a creditor routinely reports delinquent debts to a credit bureau, the damage has most likely already been done. If the creditor does not normally report information to a credit bureau, they are not likely to start with you.

Many creditors never threaten to ruin your credit record. However, they automatically report to a credit bureau by computer every payment and delinquency *on a monthly basis.* So if you pay a creditor that threatens you rather than one that does not, you may end up with a problem on your credit record anyway. More information about your credit record can be found in Chapter Three.

3. Begin a lawsuit to collect the debt. This is the threat that may worry you the most, but the threat of a lawsuit may be much less serious than you imagine. These issues are discussed in detail in Chapter Nine and briefly below.

First, it is hard to predict whether a particular creditor will actually sue on a past-due debt. How aggressively a collection agency threatens suit is no indication whether the creditor will sue, even if the threat appears to come from an attorney.

Second, if the creditor does decide to sue you, you have a right to respond and raise any legitimate defenses. Do not let the creditor win by default. You do not have to hire an attorney to respond to the lawsuit. Often when a creditor sees that you will defend the action, it will stop pursuing the lawsuit.

Third, even if the creditor does pursue the lawsuit and eventually wins, the worst that can happen is that a court judgment will be entered against you. You will *not* automatically be in contempt of court for failure to pay the judgment. The judgment only gives the creditor the legal right to start the process of *trying* to take back your property, to garnish your wages, or to seek a court order requiring payment.

Chapter Nine will help you understand whether a collector's attempts to enforce a judgment are likely to harm you. As discussed in greater detail in Chapter Nine, if you are "collection proof," you have nothing to fear from even these special collection techniques. You are "collection proof" if all your assets and income are protected by law from a creditor trying to enforce a court judgment.

For these reasons, the threat of a court action on an unsecured debt is not nearly as real or dangerous as the threat of a landlord's eviction action, a bank's foreclosure on a mortgage, a car's repossession, or a utility's termination of gas or electricity service. These actions usually happen quickly with very little legal process and expense to the creditor.

Creditors who growl the loudest
should not drive you into the teeth
of a creditor with real bite.

EIGHT DIFFERENT WAYS TO STOP DEBT COLLECTION HARASSMENT

Because bill collectors have no bite behind their bark, they will bark very loudly, hoping to intimidate you. Do not let them. This section lists *eight different approaches* to stop debt harassment.

Keep in mind that the effectiveness of any of these approaches may depend on whether the creditor is doing its own collection (for example, the doctor's office is calling you up) or whether the creditor has hired a debt collection agency or attorney. You have more rights if you are dealing with a debt collection agency or an attorney.

The key federal law regulating debt collection, the Fair Debt Collection Practices Act (FDCPA), applies only to debt collection agencies and attorneys, and generally does *not* apply to creditors collecting their own debts. Nevertheless, most states have laws which regulate creditors collecting their own debts. In any case, the eight approaches listed here will often work with creditors collecting their own debt and not just with collection agencies.

1. Head off harassment before it happens. While you should pay your most important bills first, you should not totally ignore any of your bills, such as by tossing a series of warning letters in the trash. Instead, there are steps you can take short of payment which will make it clear to the creditor that you are not ignoring the bill.

It is to your advantage to try to deal with the problem before the creditor refers the debt to a collection agency. You should consider calling up the creditor to explain your situation. Promptly contacting the creditor is most important with hospitals, doctors, dentists, and similar creditors who would otherwise quickly turn a debt over to a collection agency. Although retailers, banks, and finance companies are more likely to have an in-house collection section, it still pays to try to avoid the transfer of the debt to that office.

If a certain bill is less important, explain to a creditor why you are not paying and when you propose to pay:

> *"I have to pay my rent and utility bills first. I just got laid off, but when I get a new job, I will do my best to meet my credit card debt. I understand that you will want to cancel my card and I will pay you when I can."*

You should try to make it clear that you cannot afford to pay the bill and will not pay a collection agency either. Do not over-promise, but be polite and honest. Make sure the creditor understands you will pay as soon as you can so that there is no need to go to the expense of hiring a collection agency.

The creditor then has a financial interest *not* to turn the matter over to a collector. Collection agencies usually charge the creditor a fee based on what they collect or sometimes a flat fee per debtor. The creditor can avoid paying these fees by sitting tight.

You may also have decided that you would like to try to work out a payment plan with the creditor. There are many ways to do this—you may want to negotiate with a creditor on your own, consider paying the creditor back through a debt management plan arranged by a credit counseling agency (see Chapter Four), or try to settle the debt by offering a lump sum. You can find some tips for negotiating on your own below at #4. These tips work well whether you are dealing with your own creditor or with a collection agency. But keep in mind that it is to your advantage to try to work out a plan with the creditor rather than with a collection agency. Creditors are generally more flexible than collection agencies. In addition, a collection agency may add the costs of collection to your debt.

2. The cease letter. Assuming you called the creditor or collector and didn't get anywhere, the simplest strategy to stop collection harassment is to write the collector a cease letter. Your rights will vary depending on whether you are dealing with your creditor or with a collection agency.

Federal law requires collection agencies to stop their collection efforts (sometimes referred to as dunning) after they receive a written request to stop. The federal law does not apply to creditors collecting their own debts, but even these creditors will often honor such requests.

You do not have to give any special explanation why the collector should cease contacts. Nevertheless, it is generally a good idea to explain why you cannot pay and your financial plans for the future. The letter might also describe prior abusive tactics of the collector's employees and any resulting distress this has caused you. It is very important to keep a copy of the written request and to send it by certified mail, return receipt requested. This will give you proof that the collector received your letter.

Here is an example of such a letter (delete references to billing errors, debt harassment, or any other statements that do not apply to you—a simple request to stop collection contacts is sufficient):

"CEASE" LETTER SAMPLE

Sam Consumer
10 Cherry Lane
Flint, MI 10886

January 1, 2007

NBC Collection Agency
1 Main Street
Flint, MI 10887

Dear Sir or Madam:

I am writing to request that you stop communications to me about my account number 000723 with Amy's Department Store, as required by the Fair Debt Collection Practices Act, 15 U.S.C. § 1692c(c). [*NOTE: Delete reference to the Fair Debt Collection Practices Act where the letter is to a creditor instead of to a collection agency.*]

I was laid off from work two months ago and cannot pay this bill at this time. I am enrolled in a training program which I will complete in March and hope to find work that will allow me to resume payments soon after that. Please also note that your letters mistakenly list the balance on the account as $245. My records indicate that the balance is less than that.

You should be aware that your employees have engaged in illegal collection practices. For example, I received a phone call at 6:30 A.M. from one of them last week. Later that day I was called by the same person at my training program which does not permit personal phone calls except for emergencies. My family and I were very upset by these tactics.

This letter is not meant in any way to be an acknowledgment that I owe this money. I will take care of this matter when I can. Your cooperation will be appreciated.

Very truly yours,

Sam Consumer

Even though it is against federal law, not all debt collectors will stop contacting you after they receive your letter. You should try not to let them get away with this. If necessary, send another letter and once again keep a copy. Let them know that you are aware that they are violating the federal law by continuing to contact you. You should also keep a careful record of any letters and phone calls you receive after sending the letter. This record may help you if you later decide to sue the debt collector.

You should also consider other options if the debt collector ignores your letter. In particular, you might think about contacting a lawyer to send a letter on your behalf (#3 below), complaining to a government agency about the collector's conduct (#6 below), or suing the debt collector (#8 below).

3. The lawyer's letter. You do not need a lawyer to send a cease letter. When your main goal is to get the bill collectors off your back, you can send a simple cease letter without the cost of legal assistance. However, if a cease letter does not stop collection calls, a letter from a lawyer usually will. In addition, the lawyer may be able to raise legal claims on your behalf for violations of the FDCPA.

Collection agencies must stop contacting a consumer known to be represented by a lawyer, as long as the lawyer responds to the collection agency's inquiries. Even though the FDCPA requirement does not apply to creditors collecting their own debts, these creditors will also usually honor requests from a lawyer. A collector's lawyer is generally bound by legal ethics not to contact debtors represented by a lawyer.

4. Negotiating work-out agreements. Probably the most common consumer strategy to deal with debt harassment, though not the best, is to work out a deal with the collector. Usually a consumer will try to figure out a way to make monthly payments to a creditor. Tips for negotiating payment plans are discussed below. Keep in mind that you can negotiate with creditors about other terms as well, including agreements to cancel a delinquency. This is sometimes called "re-aging" an account. Re-aging is a way of starting over again with your credit cards after you've been behind for a few months. It does not usually affect the total amount you owe, but the creditor will treat your debt as if it is current. You may also be able to persuade the creditor to restructure your payments or reduce the interest rate on future payments.

Regardless of the type of deal you try to negotiate, be careful about offering too much. As described in Chapter One, it is extremely important to prioritize

131

your debts. Even a small payment to an unsecured creditor is unwise if this prevents payment of your mortgage or rent. There are other, better ways to stop debt harassment.

Payment Plans. If you think you can make monthly payments, you should think about the best ways to negotiate with the creditor or collector. The tips below should be helpful whether you are dealing with a creditor or a collection agency, although a creditor is likely to be more flexible for the reasons discussed earlier in this chapter.

You should first think about whether you can offer a lump sum or whether you will have to make monthly payments. A lump sum will often be a better deal, but you may not be able to raise the money. Strategies for raising money to pay off debts are discussed in Chapter Seven.

Chapter Seven also reviews the choices that are most likely to get you into trouble. You should be very careful about making choices, such as payday loans, that may raise some money for you in the short-term, but will likely cause you more problems not too far down the road.

If you decide instead to negotiate a payment plan, it is critical to be sure that you pay enough each month to make a dent in your debt. An exception to this rule might arise if you are desperate to avoid collection efforts that might harm you. To get a better understanding of the possible consequences of a debt collection lawsuit, see Chapter Nine.

Paying down credit card debt through monthly payments is particularly difficult. This is because not all of your monthly payment will go toward the amount of your debt. For example, let's say you owe $1,000. If you pay $50, your debt will not be reduced to $950. Instead, most of the $50 will go toward paying just the interest on the loan. This is why it is almost impossible to get out of debt when you pay just the minimum payment on your credit card. For more information about credit card costs, see Chapter Five.

Negotiating Tips. In general, you may be surprised that you have some power in negotiating with a collector. Just knowing your rights in this situation can go a long way. Most important, you have the right not to be harassed or abused by debt collectors, as discussed in detail later in this chapter. Knowing that it is against the law for the collector to make false threats or to speak to someone else about your debt should help you avoid panicking and setting up an unreasonable or unaffordable plan.

Your ability to get an agreement depends on whether the creditor believes you will honor the agreement. Your chances are likely to decrease considerably if you have set up a payment plan with this creditor in the past and failed to keep making those payments. When negotiating with a creditor, you should also avoid over-promising. Be realistic about what you can pay and offer that amount. Remember that it will not help you much in the long-run if you can only pay a very small amount. If you're uncomfortable negotiating on your own, you might try to find a social worker, trusted friend, or relative to help you.

You might also think about going to a credit counselor for help in setting up a repayment plan. Chapter Four will help you decide whether you should seek help from a credit counselor and, if so, how to find a reputable agency.

One rule to keep in mind for any type of negotiation is to be sure and get any deal in writing. You should also try to negotiate to get the creditor to help you with your credit report.

5. Raise complaints about billing errors and other defenses.

Collection letters often contain errors, sometimes misstating the account number or the amount due, or billing the consumer instead of his or her insurance company. Occasionally, you may even receive collection letters aimed at someone with the same or a similar name. When a collection letter contains a mistake, write to request a correction. Collection agencies, by law, must inform you of your right to dispute the debt. They must do this the first time they communicate with you or within five days after first communicating with you about the debt. If you then dispute the debt in writing within the next thirty days, the collection agency must stop collection efforts while it investigates.

If the dispute involves a line of credit, a credit card, or an electronic transfer of money, you have the additional legal right under the federal Fair Credit Billing Act *to require* the creditor *to investigate* the bill. You must write a letter pointing out the mistake within sixty days of receipt of the disputed bill. Your rights to correct billing errors are periodically included with credit card statements. A sample letter for this purpose is contained in Chapter Five.

There are many other defenses to repayment you should also consider. These are discussed in Chapter Nine. You do not need to wait until you are sued to raise possible claims and defenses. In fact, it is usually best to raise all available complaints as early as possible in the debt collection process. Waiting too long may make you less believable later. You should mention your claims every time a creditor or collector contacts you about payment. If the creditor still pursues a lawsuit, raise the claims at that point as well.

If you believe you have claims against a creditor, it's a good idea to put those claims in writing and mail them to the creditor, collector, and any attorneys representing them. This is especially important if you believe that you have warranty or similar claims. Don't forget to keep a copy of anything you mail and send by certified mail, return receipt requested.

Collectors will often tell you to go talk to the original seller or to a prior creditor about any problems. Although the collector might not want to hear your complaints, you should tell the collector anyway. The key thing to remember is that it is always better to defend against the creditor or collector's attempt to collect a debt than to give the collector the money and then try to get it back from the original seller.

6. Complaining to a government agency. Another strategy is to write to government agencies responsible for enforcing laws that prohibit debt collection abuse, like the Federal Trade Commission or your state's attorney general's office. A government agency is not likely to investigate immediately unless it has other complaints against the same collector, a fact that probably cannot be known ahead of time. Even so, sending a copy of your letter to the collector often produces good results.

Your letter of complaint should be sent to the Federal Trade Commission's Consumer Response Center at Federal Trade Commission, CRC-240, Washington, D.C. 20580. You can also call the Commission toll-free at 1-877-FTC-HELP (382-4357) or file a complaint on-line at www.ftc.gov. Copies of the letter should also be sent to the consumer protection division within the state attorney general's office (usually in the state capitol), and also to any local office of consumer protection listed in the local telephone book or on the Internet. Addresses can be obtained from a local better business bureau or office of consumer affairs. An example of such a letter follows on the next page.

7. Bankruptcy. Filing your initial papers for personal bankruptcy instantly triggers the "automatic stay." This is a very powerful tool because it stops all collection activity against you, from collectors, creditors, or even government officials. No further collection activity can proceed unless a particular collector obtains permission from the bankruptcy court. The bankruptcy court will not grant this permission to collectors seeking to contact you about unsecured debts. For this reason, filing for bankruptcy can be a very effective means of stopping debt harassment. If you have filed other bankruptcy cases

SAMPLE COMPLAINT LETTER

Sam Consumer
10 Cherry Lane
Flint, MI 10886

January 25, 2007

Federal Trade Commission
Bureau of Consumer Protection
600 Pennsylvania Ave., N.W.
Washington, DC 20580

Dear Sir or Madam:

I am writing to complain of abusive debt collection tactics used by ABC Collection Agency, 1 Main Street, Flint, MI 10887. I request that you investigate this company.

I was laid off two months ago and have not been able to maintain all payments on all my bills. ABC began contacting me in December about my account with Amy's Department Store in Flint. ABC's abusive collection tactics have included:

1. Telephoning my sister asking her to lend me the balance when she does not have anything to do with this account.

2. Calling me repeatedly at 6:30 A.M. at home.

3. Using offensive language, such as calling me a "lousy deadbeat."

4. Writing that they would sue me if they did not receive payment in ten days. This was a month and a half ago, but all they have done since then is to call and to write. (A copy of that letter is enclosed.)

5. Continuing to contact me after I sent them a letter asking them to stop. (Enclosed is my letter to them and a later letter from them.)

6. Billing me for $245 when no more than $185 is owed on the account.

My family and I are doing our best to get back on our feet, and this abuse is very stressful. Your assistance will be appreciated.

Very truly yours,

Sam Consumer

cc: Attorney General's Office
Bureau of Consumer Protection
Lansing, MI

Flint Office of Consumer Affairs
Flint, MI

ABC Collection Agency
1 Main Street
Flint, MI 10887

that were dismissed within the previous twelve months, however, you may not get an automatic stay or it may only last for the first thirty days of your bankruptcy case. See Chapter Nineteen for more information about bankruptcy.

Nevertheless, as a general rule, a bankruptcy filing is not your best strategy where your only concern is debt harassment. Bankruptcy should be saved for when you have serious financial problems. Debt collection harassment can usually be stopped without having to resort to bankruptcy. In fact, be wary of any attorney offering to file bankruptcy for you where the only problem is debt harassment. More detailed information on bankruptcy can be found in Chapter Nineteen.

8. Sue the debt collector for illegal conduct. Federal and state fair debt laws provide consumers with strong protections from debt collection harassment. Debt collectors often break these rules because they know that in most cases they can get away with it. Most consumers either don't know about their rights or don't have the resources to fight back.

The rest of this chapter provides an introduction to fair debt and other laws that protect consumers from debt collection harassment. The remaining sections will also give you ideas on finding a lawyer to help you bring a lawsuit. Fighting back by suing debt collectors cannot only stop harassment against you and possibly get you a money recovery, but may also convince the debt collectors to stop harassing other consumers. You can also use the fair debt laws to make counterclaims against a creditor or collection agency that is suing you to collect money. More information on defending lawsuits and on counterclaims can be found in Chapter Nine.

ILLEGAL DEBT COLLECTION CONDUCT

This section lists many types of illegal debt collection harassment. This will help you to demand that the collector stop its harassment. If you suffered financial, physical, or even emotional harm from the illegal collection harassment, you might consider suing the collector. In a successful debt collection suit, you can recover all your damages, no matter how large they are. Even if you are not damaged by the illegal collection activity, you can also sue the collector for up to $1,000 plus all of your attorney fees.

The major law dealing with illegal debt collection conduct is the federal Fair Debt Collection Practices Act (known as the "FDCPA"). The protections provided by the FDCPA apply regardless of whether you want to pay the money back and regardless of whether you owe the money. The FDCPA applies only to debt collection agencies and attorneys, and generally does not apply to creditors collecting their own debts. However, most states have laws which regulate creditors collecting their own debts.

Debt collectors are required by law in all circumstances to respect your privacy and avoid using deceptive, abusive, or harassing collection tactics.

The FDCPA requires collection agencies to take certain actions, including:

- The collection agency must stop contacting you if you make a request in writing or if you dispute the debt in writing.
- The collection agency, in its initial communication or within five days of that communication, must send you a written notice. That notice must identify the debt and the creditor and explain your right to dispute the debt or to request the name and address of the original creditor, if it is different from the current one. If you raise a dispute, the collector must suspend collection efforts on the disputed portion of the debt until the collector responds to the request.
- Any lawsuit by a collector must usually be brought in the same county or other judicial district where you reside or signed the contract.

   The FDCPA also prohibits a wide range of harassing and deceptive collection agency behavior, including:

- Communicating with third parties—such as your relatives, employers, friends, or neighbors—about a debt unless you or a court has given the collector permission to do so. Several narrow exceptions to this prohibition apply. Collectors may contact creditors, attorneys, credit reporting agencies, cosigners, your spouse, and your parents if you are a minor. Third-party contacts are also permitted if the contacts are solely for the purpose of locating you and do not reveal in any way the contact's underlying purpose.
- Communicating with you at unusual or inconvenient times or places. The times 8:00 A.M. to 9:00 P.M. (in the time zone where you live) are generally considered convenient, but daytime contacts with a consumer known to work a night shift may be inconvenient.
- Contacting you at work if the collector should know that the employer prohibits personal calls or contacting you at other inconvenient places, such as a friend's house or the hospital.
- Contacting you if you are represented by a lawyer, unless the lawyer gives permission for the communication or fails to respond to the collector's communications.

- Contacting you when you write a letter asking the collector to cease communications. The collector is allowed to acknowledge the letter and to notify you about actions the collector may take.
- Using obscene, derogatory or insulting remarks.
- Publishing your name.
- Telephoning repeatedly and frequently.
- Telephoning without disclosing the collector's identity.
- Making communications that intimidate, harass, or abuse you, such as a threat to conduct a neighborhood investigation of you or telling you that you should not have children if you cannot afford them.
- Making false, misleading, or deceptive representations in collecting debts, such as pretending that letters carry legal authority.
- Falsely representing the character, amount, or legal status of a debt or of services rendered or compensation owed.
- Falsely stating or implying a lawyer's involvement, such as a form letter written on an attorney's letterhead and bearing an attorney's signature that in fact came from a collection agency and was not reviewed by a lawyer.
- Threatening arrest or loss of child custody or public assistance benefits.
- Stating that nonpayment will result in arrest, garnishment, or seizure of property or wages, unless such actions are lawful, and unless the collector fully intends to take such action.
- Threatening to take actions that are illegal or that are not intended. To verify a collector's intention to file suit, you could ask the local court clerk to help you check the plaintiff's index to see whether the company making the threat has a history of filing similar suits. A lawsuit is less likely the smaller the debt (for example, less than $500), the more distant the collector, and the stronger the consumer's dispute of the debt. Other common threats that the creditor may have no intention of fulfilling are that the collector will refer the action to a lawyer, harm your credit rating, or repossess household goods.
- Using any false representation or other deception to collect or to attempt to collect a debt or to obtain information about you.
- Failing to disclose in communications that the collector is attempting to collect a debt.
- Using unfair or unconscionable means to collect debts.

- Collecting fees or charges unless expressly authorized by the agreement creating the debt and permitted by law.
- Depositing post-dated checks before their date. The collector must also give at least three days, but not more than ten days, notice before depositing the postdated check or using the check for the purpose of threatening or filing criminal charges.
- Threatening self-help repossession without the legal right or present intent to do so.
- Creating the false impression that the collector is an affiliate or agent of the government.
- Using any communication, language, or symbols on envelopes or postcards that indicate that the sender is in the debt collection business.

It is illegal for a collector to contact your employer or neighbors about your debt, call you late at night, call you at work, call you repeatedly, make false threats, or engage in any other form of deceptive conduct or unfair harassment.

SUING DEBT COLLECTORS FOR THEIR ILLEGAL CONDUCT

Why Sue the Debt Collector? Debt collection harassment is illegal and you can be compensated for any injury suffered. At the same time, any money awarded may also deter future misconduct by debt collectors.

Suits for All Your Actual Damages *Plus* Up to $1,000 and Your Attorney's Fees for Collector Misconduct. Even when you are subjected to only minor forms of illegal collection action, you can sue the collector and recover up to $1,000 and all of your attorney's fees for any violation of the FDCPA. You can recover up to $1,000 whether or not the conduct caused you any injury.

On top of the $1,000, you can recover for any injuries that were caused by the illegal conduct. Courts may award damages for such emotional in-

139

juries as loss of happiness, loss of energy, loss of sleep, tension headaches, crying spells, and marital problems.

Where the collector's conduct is seriously improper, you may also be able to recover additional punitive damages on top of your actual damages. Examples of such conduct are threats to throw you in jail, to deport you, or have your children taken away. The punitive damages are intended to punish the collector and prevent future misconduct.

If you win an FDCPA case, the collector must pay your attorney's fees. This may encourage a private attorney to take the case without charging you, particularly where the claim appears strong. In fact, the collector may end up paying more in attorney's fees than in damages.

Even though many debt collectors are small operations, you can usually recover your judgments against the collectors. Many collectors carry professional liability insurance to protect themselves against consumer claims. The existence of such insurance is often important in settling claims.

Finding an Attorney to Sue a Debt Collector. It is not always easy to find an attorney to handle an FDCPA claim. Families with low incomes and limited assets may be eligible to obtain free legal services from a neighborhood legal services office, and those offices may pursue such claims. Other consumers can contact local bar associations for pro bono attorneys who might handle the case. Some cities have lawyers who regularly handle debt collection harassment cases. In other areas, you can find a personal injury lawyer willing to pursue the case on a contingent fee basis. The key to convincing a private attorney to take the case will be the availability of an attorney fee award paid by the collector if you win the lawsuit.

The National Association of Consumer Advocates (NACA) is a good resource to help you find an attorney to take your case. Their members specialize in a number of different consumer areas, including debt collection harassment. More information about NACA (including a list of NACA members and their areas of practice) is available at www.naca.net or by writing to NACA, 1730 Rhode Island, NW, Suite 710, Washington, D.C. 20036.

Private attorneys unfamiliar with the FDCPA can find everything they need to pursue an FDCPA claim with a minimum of expenditure in the National Consumer Law Center's book *Fair Debt Collection* (5th ed. 2004 and Supp.). This book is a thorough resource for bringing cases under the FDCPA as well as under other debt collection laws. The manual analyzes and reprints the law and agency interpretations, discusses cases, and includes sample court documents, interview checklists, and other important practice aids.

Sample court documents are also on the companion CD-Rom. Information on how to obtain NCLC's books is contained in the bibliography.

What You Should Tell Your Attorney. Once you find an attorney, your job is to document the extent of collector misconduct and the impact on your family. Although you may not want to discuss your feelings about the harassment, it is key to determining what kind of legal case you have. All symptoms of emotional distress should be discussed, including: anxiety, embarrassment, headaches, nausea, indignation, irritability, loss of sleep, and interference with family or work relationships. Did you consult a doctor? Were there illnesses brought on by the harassment?

Out-of-pocket losses should also be listed, ranging from loss of employment to loss of wages because of time taken off from work to try to resolve the dispute. In addition, telephone charges, transportation, medical bills, and counseling services could all be part of your actual damages.

Keep a record of all expenses related to the collection effort. Prepare a statement describing your physical and emotional response to the collection efforts, and list all costs incurred as a consequence of that response. If you consulted a doctor or counselor, include that expense. Consider whether you can obtain supporting statements from family members, relatives, friends, or coworkers.

A telephone log of collection contacts is also helpful. Pen and paper should be kept near the telephone to record all telephone contacts. Write down as many details as possible. Abusive messages left on an answering machine should be kept if possible.

What If the FDCPA Does Not Apply? The FDCPA applies to collection agencies and lawyers. It does not generally cover creditors or their employees collecting their own debts. That is, the FDCPA only applies to an independent debt collection agency hired by a creditor to collect its debts and when a creditor hires an attorney to collect its debts.

If the FDCPA does not apply to collection efforts, you still have legal remedies for debt collection harassment. These remedies will mostly involve state law, not federal law. While there will be variations from state to state, in every state there will always be at least some remedy for debt collection harassment. For more detail on these other state remedies, see the National Consumer Law Center's *Fair Debt Collection* (5th ed. 2004 and Supp.).

9

Collection Lawsuits

Threats by a creditor or collection agency to sue on a debt can be very frightening. However, most threats of lawsuits are just that—threats. Threats should not lead you to make special efforts to pay a debt unless there is some way in which a lawsuit can hurt you. This chapter provides advice on how to respond if you are sued, including ways you can fight back. You will also learn about what can and cannot happen to you if you lose the lawsuit.

Earlier chapters helped you decide which debts to pay first. If you have decided that there are some debts that you cannot pay, this chapter will help you understand the possible consequences of this decision. You should also review Chapter Nineteen to find out more about whether bankruptcy is a good option.

Here are the basic rules for dealing with lawsuits and threats of lawsuits:

1. *Not all threats of lawsuits will be carried out.*

2. *If you are sued, it is critical that you respond to court deadlines. You may want professional help to evaluate whether you are at risk of losing property in the legal process.* Generally, it is safe to ignore a lawsuit only if you have no defenses and if there is no possibility of being forced to pay a court judgment. You may want professional help to figure this out.

3. *The best way to deal with a lawsuit is to win it. You may have a defense to a lawsuit which can be raised in court.* You may have a good argument that you don't owe money that a creditor is trying to collect. This can offset, in whole or in part, the amount which the creditor is claiming due. Sometimes just raising a defense will lead the creditor to drop the case. It is also cheaper and easier to respond to a lawsuit than to start your own at a later date.

4. *If you lose a lawsuit, there are a variety of ways the creditor can try to use the court judgment to force you to pay. You must remain alert to these tactics and deal with them as they come up.*

Courts also may have special procedures to require you to make payments when there is a judgment against you. You need to comply with orders to appear in court or to make payments. However, you can raise defenses to payment in court if you cannot afford to pay. You can also consider using the bankruptcy process, because you may have more rights to deal with judgments in bankruptcy than in state court. These rights may include eliminating the judgment entirely in many situations. Bankruptcy is discussed in more detail in Chapter Nineteen.

WILL THE CREDITOR ACTUALLY SUE YOU?

Creditors frequently threaten to sue to collect on overdue debts. These threats are likely to cause you a great deal of stress. Usually it is clear that these creditors *can* sue you, but the more important question is whether they *will* sue you. More often than not, the answer is "no," even in cases where the creditor repeatedly threatens to sue.

Creditors do not always make rational decisions. However, the following are good indications that a creditor will *not* sue:

- Creditors typically will not file a lawsuit if they have a better remedy available. The lawsuit process is slow, somewhat expensive, and often unprofitable as a way to recover money from people who have few assets. If the creditor can do something else more effective, it will. For example, a creditor will generally not choose to go to court if, instead, it can repossess your car, foreclose on your house, or terminate your utility service.
- Creditors are unlikely to file a collection suit when the amount of the debt is small. Most creditors rarely sue on debts under $1,000 and some don't sue unless a debt is much higher than that.

- Creditors are unlikely to sue if you dispute the debt and threaten to raise a reasonable defense. When you raise these defenses, collectors will generally view the case very differently. Not only does the collector have to factor in the value of your claim, but also the time and expense it will take to finally resolve the case.
- Creditors are unlikely to sue when you are making small payments even if they are less than the creditor demands.
- Creditors are not likely to sue when that creditor has no history of filing suit. You can check with the local court clerk to see if certain creditors in the area—for example large retailers or finance companies—file a lot of lawsuits to collect money.
- When a creditor is out of state, it is even more unlikely that it will sue over a small amount. It is simply too expensive for most out-of-state creditors to sue you in your home state to try to collect relatively small amounts.

Collectors often threaten other actions instead of or in addition to lawsuits against you. They are unlikely to carry out these threats. For example, a collection agency may threaten to garnish your wages. The truth is that except for a few special circumstances, collection agencies cannot garnish wages unless they first obtain a court judgment. Frequent threats are often a signal that the creditor or collection agency has no real remedy and is trying to intimidate you into paying an otherwise uncollectible debt.

In addition, debt collection agency threats are often illegal under the federal Fair Debt Collection Practices Act (FDCPA). You can sue the collection agency under that statute and receive as much as $1,000 even if you are not injured by the threat. Suits against debt collectors are described in Chapter Eight. If a creditor itself is doing the threatening (not an independent agency hired by the creditor), then the FDCPA does not apply, but you may have other ways to challenge the creditor's conduct, as discussed in Chapter Eight.

HOW TO RESPOND TO
A COLLECTOR'S LAWSUIT

Always Pick Up Your Certified Mail and Accept Notices About Court Actions. You will not escape the consequences of a lawsuit by hiding from notice about that action.

Get Professional Advice If You Think You Do Not Owe the Money or If You May Have a Defense. Fighting back and raising legitimate claims against a seller, collector or creditor can erase some or all of your debt. In many cases, a lawyer can take steps that will significantly improve the outcome for you. The introduction to this book includes tips on finding an affordable lawyer. Keep in mind that neither the cheapest lawyer nor the most expensive lawyer may be the best lawyer. Shop around and find someone you are comfortable with and who is knowledgeable about your legal problem.

If you cannot get the advice you need from a lawyer or counselor, see if a self-help manual has been written for your state on how to defend a lawsuit. Make sure you get a manual for *your* state. Check with the clerk of your local court, local library, or bookstore.

Be careful whom you consult about a lawsuit. There are some unlicensed counselors (some pretend to be lawyers) who claim that they can help defend your lawsuit. Many will take your money and do nothing. Others will file bogus responses to your lawsuit which, in some cases, may cause you to lose valuable rights and defenses. You should contact your local bar association if you are unsure whether someone who claims to be a lawyer is really a lawyer. Even if the person who is trying to help you is a lawyer, you may want to find out from the bar association whether there are complaints on file against him or her.

In addition to professional advisors and self-help manuals, you may also be able to get help by contacting the clerk of the court. Court offices are not just for lawyers—you have as much right to ask questions as someone with a law degree. Don't be intimidated. If you have been sued, you need to know the necessary response requirements and deadlines. It is the job of the court clerk to provide help on these issues.

In some busy courts, clerks may not be very helpful. In others, the advice they give may not be accurate. You may find that the officers in the individual courtrooms are more accurate than the employees in the clerk's office. It certainly cannot hurt to ask several clerks the same question and compare their answers. Whenever relying on information from a court clerk, write down the clerk's name and the answer you received.

Why Am I Getting Notices About The National Arbitration Forum in Minneapolis? At least one credit card issuer (MBNA, now using the name FIA) and several large collectors are bringing actions to collect credit card debt, not in court, but using the National Arbitration Forum

(NAF) in Minneapolis, Minnesota. This is a very troubling practice and at least one state, Pennsylvania, has already put limits on these actions.

A notice about NAF arbitration should be taken as seriously as a court summons. The creditor is claiming you have agreed (in the fine print of your credit card agreement or a change of terms notice) to arbitrate your disputes instead of going to court. The creditor claims its attempt to collect on a debt is a "dispute," allowing it to collect its debt through arbitration instead of going to court. If the arbitrator rules in the creditor's favor, the arbitrator will add, on top of what you already owe, the creditor's attorney fees and arbitration costs. Then the creditor will get a court to help it collect this larger amount from you.

NAF arbitration is just as serious as a court case, and may be even harder to defend. You have the right to an attorney and it is a good idea to get one, if that is possible, but you can also proceed without one. Do not be confused by NAF's address in Minnesota. You can just mail to Minnesota a written statement as a defense, but you can also pay NAF extra for a telephone or in-person hearing. The in-person hearing will be somewhere near your home (not in Minnesota). If you are confused about the process, a local court clerk will *not* help you. Writing or calling NAF may *not* prove that helpful either. Your best option is to find an attorney who can explain things to you, but NAF arbitration may be new to your attorney as well!

If you have a good defense to the debt, you can present it to the arbitrator, but do not be surprised if you do not get a fair hearing. After all, it was the creditor who picked NAF, not you. At one point, MBNA notified its customers that they could choose *not* to use arbitration, by sending a notice to MBNA. If you did this, you should tell that to NAF, MBNA, and the arbitrator. Whether you did this or not, always state in writing at the beginning of any arbitration proceeding in which you participate that you object to arbitration. (In Pennsylvania, it is probably best not to participate, because new court rules there protect you if you do not participate voluntarily.)

Whether you participate or not, the arbitrator will issue a ruling, usually stating that you owe a certain dollar amount to the credit card issuer. After you get notice of that arbitration ruling (called an "arbitration award"), you have the right to go to court to ask a judge to undo that award. *You must act quickly.* In most states, you only have ninety days, but in certain states, such as Connecticut, Massachusetts, and Michigan, you have only twenty-one or thirty days to act.

Usually some months later, if the arbitrator has ruled against you, the creditor will ask a real court to ratify or "confirm" the arbitrator's award.

Only then will the arbitrator's award against you have the same force as a court judgment. It is generally a good idea to oppose the creditor's attempt to confirm the award. You should have a good chance because more and more courts don't like the idea of an arbitrator picked by the creditor deciding a case without a hearing and then asking the court to rubber stamp it. Your chances of winning though are much less than if you had gone to court right after the award was issued. You should consult a lawyer about opposing confirmation of an award. Court clerks may also be able to help with questions about procedures.

DICTIONARY OF COMMON LAWSUIT TERMS

Answer (also called appearance): This is the response to the lawsuit that the defendant must file, usually in writing.

Complaint (also called petition): The document which a plaintiff uses to begin a case.

Default: If the defendant misses the deadline to file an answer, the plaintiff can win by default. Defendants who lose by default have no opportunity to raise any defenses and the plaintiff will be given what he or she requested.

Defendant: The person or business defending against the lawsuit.

Judgment: This is what the court orders after hearing the case.

Plaintiff: The person or business filing the lawsuit.

Small Claims Court: A court designed to decide claims for relatively small amounts of money.

Summons (also called original notice): A document that informs a defendant that a lawsuit has been filed against him or her. The summons contains information about the type of lawsuit, what the plaintiff wants, and the actions the defendant must take to respond to the lawsuit. The summons also states the amount of time allowed to file the answer.

Carefully Read All Court Documents You Receive. The creditor must file a document with the court in order to start a lawsuit. Usually, this is called the petition or the complaint. In this chapter, we will use the word "complaint" to refer to the document which a creditor uses to begin a case. The complaint asks the court to enter an order or judgment that you owe the creditor a certain amount of money.

Along with the complaint filed with the court, the creditor usually must prepare another document to be delivered to you. This document informs you that a lawsuit has been filed against you. It is often called a "summons" or "original notice." We will use the word "summons" here. The summons usually tells you what type of lawsuit it is, what the creditor wants, and the actions you must take to respond to the lawsuit, including the deadline for responding.

Each state has rules on how the summons must be delivered to you. Sometimes a sheriff or constable must personally deliver the summons to you or an adult member of your household. Sometimes mailing it to you is sufficient. Dropping the summons on your doorstep is not sufficient.

Never hide from a court summons; always read it carefully, follow the instructions, meet all deadlines, and attend all hearings.

Each court has its own procedures for responding to a summons. The summons should tell you the proper steps to take to respond to a lawsuit *for that particular court.* Do not assume that a response appropriate for one type of court will be correct for another court or another type of case. Instead, read the instructions on the summons or seek help from the clerk's office. Be especially careful to meet the deadline. Responses received after the deadline might not be accepted by the court.

The summons is often written in legal jargon that is difficult to understand. If something is unclear, ask a lawyer or someone familiar with legal documents to explain what the document means. As described above, a court clerk may or may not be helpful in explaining the documents. In using a publication to understand the notice, make sure the publication is current, applies to your state and to the particular court at issue.

Check Which Court Is Hearing the Case. It is important to direct all questions and your responsive documents to the court that issued the summons. The rules are very different in different courts. Knowing about the court that will hear your case is also helpful in determining if you can handle your own case and how much legal help you need.

The most common court used by creditors to sue is "small claims court," a court designed to decide claims for relatively small amounts of money. For example, in some states, the small claims court can only handle cases involving $5,000 or less. Other states have different limits. If the creditor is seeking more money than the small claims court limit, the suit must be filed in the state's general, all-purpose court. These general courts have different names in different states.

Because small claims courts are set up to handle claims for small amounts of money, the procedure is usually simple and less formal. In many small claims courts, a lawyer is not required. In a few states, lawyers are not even permitted. If a creditor can sue in small claims court, it will often do so without hiring a lawyer. You should also feel confident appearing in that court without a lawyer.

Other state courts usually follow more formal procedures. Creditors are represented by lawyers and formal legal rules apply. Although you may represent yourself in this type of court (this is sometimes called appearing "*pro se*" or "*pro per*"), your wisest course may be to hire a lawyer to represent you.

How to Answer the Summons. To avoid the creditor winning the lawsuit without your having a chance to defend it (this is called winning by "default"), you *must* follow the instructions on the summons. If those instructions are unclear, you should consult a lawyer (not the creditor's lawyer) or other reliable professional. Another alternative is to contact the clerk of the court where the suit was filed.

The summons will tell you to appear at a hearing, file a written response, or file an appearance at the clerk's office. If a written response is required, there will also be a deadline for that response in the summons. If the summons has both a deadline for a written response and a date to appear in court, you must file your written response by the deadline or you may risk losing by default and having your court date canceled.

If the summons requests you to appear at the hearing, it will usually specify a time, a date, and a place at which the hearing will be held. In more formal courts, it is unusual for a hearing to be scheduled immediately, without allowing time for you to file an answer. In some states, hearings are scheduled right away for small claims courts cases. Whichever the court, eviction cases and demands for the immediate possession of property are also usually handled very quickly.

A summons often will tell you to file a written "answer" to the summons (sometimes called an "appearance") within a certain number of days, usually less than thirty. Although the summons may say "appear and defend," this may not mean that you must physically appear on the date mentioned, but only that a written document must be filed with the court by that date.

Many small claims courts that require written answers provide prepared answer forms, which only need to be signed and returned to the court clerk. The answer form states that the defendant (you) deny the plaintiff's (the creditor's) claim. You should return these by the appropriate deadline if you wish to dispute the case. Other small claims courts require no written answer.

In more formal courts, there are usually no prepared answer forms. For these courts, the answer should usually be written by a lawyer and should include reasons why you deny that you are required to pay the creditor's entire claim. If you do not wish to hire a lawyer, you may draft an answer on your own, but you should do your best to follow the court's procedural requirements. Although answers not written by lawyers are accepted by courts, they may be found insufficient on technical grounds.

If you need more time to find a lawyer or to prepare an answer, a time extension is usually allowed, either by written agreement with the creditor's attorney or by a court order. If you reach an agreement for an extension of time (or any other type of agreement) with the creditor or the creditor's attorney, you should confirm the agreement in writing.

Most courts require that you send a copy of the answer and any other document you file with the court to the creditor or the creditor's lawyer, if the creditor is represented by a lawyer. You should indicate on the original court document filed with the court clerk that a copy was mailed to the creditor or its lawyer. You should also keep a copy of the documents you file, stamped and dated by the clerk.

Respond to the Court Summons in a Timely Manner. It is important that you carefully meet all time deadlines set out in the summons, whether the deadline is to appear at a hearing, file an answer or file an appearance.

If you miss the deadline, the creditor can win by default. This means that the court will order you to pay the money plus court costs and, in some cases, any attorney's fees even though there was no hearing on the lawsuit. You will have no opportunity to raise any defenses or explain why you should not have to pay. Instead, the creditor will be granted whatever it requested.

If you reach an informal agreement with the creditor, it is still important to file an appearance and answer. Creditors have been known to proceed with a case and take a default judgment despite having previously reached an agreement with you. Any agreed-upon payment plan or other settlement should be in writing and there should be a clear written statement that the creditor will drop its lawsuit. In fact, the safest course is to file a copy of the written agreement with the court clerk to be entered into the court record.

---

*An oral agreement with the creditor is **not** a substitute for filing an answer to the summons and cannot alone prevent a default judgment.*

Submit Defenses and Counterclaims to the Court. You can tell the court why the creditor should not collect on a debt by presenting a defense, a counterclaim, or both. A defense is a reason why you are not required to pay the creditor, in whole or in part. A counterclaim is a claim that the creditor owes money to you, regardless of whether you owe the creditor on the debt.

Sometimes the difference between a defense and a counterclaim is purely technical. For example, when a dealer finances the sale of a car that turns out to be a lemon, you might use the car's defects both as a defense and as a counterclaim against the dealer.

As discussed earlier in this chapter, it can be extremely effective to raise defenses and counterclaims in debt collection lawsuits, particularly if the amount at stake is small. Frequently, creditors do not want to be bothered with a case and will let it drop simply because you raise a defense.

The creditor is counting on you to give up; creditors often drop lawsuits if you put up a fight.

Each state and each type of court will have its own procedures as to how you present a defense or counterclaim. Some courts require a written statement filed at the beginning of the case specifying your defenses and counterclaims. Some small claims courts require only that you raise the defenses and counterclaims in your statements at the trial.

You should explore *all* of the following six stages related to a transaction to help determine if you have a legitimate defense or counterclaim. *These claims can usually be raised even if someone other than the seller, such as a collection agency, is suing you.*

1. The original advertising and sale of goods or services. Most debts arise from the purchase of goods or services. In the case of loans, the money often is earmarked for the purchase of particular goods or services. Additionally the loan itself should be thought of as a service which the creditor provides.

A first question is always: What statements and written advertisements were made to encourage you to buy the goods or to clinch the deal? Were the seller's statements false? Did the written documents differ from the seller's oral statements? Were high-pressure tactics used? Did the seller hide key information?

DAVID VS. GOLIATH
You may feel that you will lose in a contest with the seller and that a court will always believe an established business person over an individual who is fighting a debt. Actually, the opposite is usually true. Judges and juries may be more willing to believe what you say than what a used car dealer, aluminum-siding, or other disreputable salesperson says. If you have a legitimate claim, the best strategy is often to raise that claim and fight back. However, be prepared for many businesses to accept your challenge and try to get you to give up. If the case goes on for a while, you may need to find an attorney to help you.

Pay special attention to door-to-door sales. High-pressure tactics and oral misrepresentations are common in those transactions. In addition, door-to-door salespeople have to give you written notice that you have the right to cancel the sale for any reason within the first three days. Were you given such a notice?

The National Consumer Law Center's *Unfair and Deceptive Acts and Practices* (6th ed. 2004 and Supp.) provides the best description of the many types of claims and legal theories available to consumers relating to sales abuses. The book lists thousands of practices, categorized by type of sale, that have been found to be deceptive or unfair.

2. Warranties. Goods or services often do not turn out as expected. The goods are later discovered to be defective, work is not completed, or the work is found to be substandard. These problems provide a strong basis for claims.

A warranty is a guarantee about the quality of the goods or services you buy. There are two different types of warranties, express and implied. You get the protection of an express warranty only if the seller or manufacturer makes a specific statement about the quality of the goods or services. Express warranties can be written or oral. An example of an express warranty is: "This product is warranted against defects in materials or workmanship for three years."

Almost every product or service comes with an "implied warranty of merchantability." This is a promise that the product will work if you use it for a reasonably expected purpose. For example, if you buy a car, you should feel secure that you will be able to drive it on the road.

A common mistake consumers make is to assume that, when a product is sold "as is" or "without warranties," they cannot complain about problems with the product. In fact, "as is" disclaimers often do not prevent you from winning court awards from sellers.

You should always raise claims when goods or services are not delivered, the wrong services are performed, or the work is not completed. Similarly, when goods or services come with a warranty, you should have a claim if the seller fails to comply with the warranty. For more detail on consumer claims based on the performance of the goods or services, see two National Consumer Law Center publications, *Consumer Warranty Law* (3d ed. 2006 and Supp.) and *Unfair and Deceptive Acts and Practices* (6th ed. 2004 and Supp.).

3. Loan terms. Most debts begin with a loan contract—often called a "note." Anything that you find to be outrageous, unfair, unjust, or deceptive about the terms of the loan agreement may form the basis of a valid claim. High-pressure tactics should also be challenged.

You may also have a claim if a creditor made a loan to you that you could not afford from the outset or if, by refinancing your loan, you ended up in worse shape than if you had stuck with the original debt. Abusive practices such as bogus charges, double-charging, and the sale of useless insurance may also form the basis of legal claims. Common problems with home equity and refinancing loans are discussed in Chapter Six.

In addition several laws, including the federal Truth in Lending Act, state installment sales laws, and other state credit legislation, create various requirements as to what the creditor must tell you about a loan. These laws are technical and you may need the assistance of a lawyer. The National Consumer Law Center's *Truth in Lending* (6th ed. 2007) is the best volume available about your rights under the federal Truth in Lending statute.

Many states have usury laws that set maximum interest rates and limits on certain types of credit charges. Creditors who violate these "usury" laws will have to pay significant damages, but again, a lawyer is usually necessary to press such claims. National Consumer Law Center's *The Cost of Credit* (3d ed. 2005 and Supp.) fully discusses a variety of types of credit overcharges.

4. Creditor's subsequent conduct.

You can also raise claims and defenses based on a creditor's conduct after a loan is made. You should check whether payments have been properly applied, whether escrow amounts are handled correctly, and whether late charges are appropriate.

Car loan creditors and home mortgage lenders often purchase property insurance for you if your coverage runs out. Make sure this substitute coverage was not purchased for periods when you had your own insurance in place, did not contain unnecessary coverages, and was not sold at an inflated price.

5. Debt collection tactics.

Chapter Eight discusses what types of debt collection practices are illegal.

6. Attempts to enforce a court order or security interest.

You may have problems with the way a creditor attempts to collect on a judgment, repossess a car, seize household property, foreclose on a home, evict you, or terminate utility service. Creditors often are sloppy in the way they sue, garnish wages, repossess or seize property. Their failure to follow proper procedures may lead to legal claims. In most states, these claims give rise to

---

FIGHTING BACK: AN EXAMPLE

Ms. P was sued for the balance owed on a car loan after her car had been repossessed and sold. When she took out the loan, she was told the interest rate would be 8%, but the actual rate from a finance company was 15%. Also, the car never worked properly even though the salesperson told her it drove "like a dream."

Ms. P received no notice prior to repossession and she was sued, not where she lives, but in the next county.

In defending the lawsuit, Ms. P should raise all of her available claims. These might include the seller's misrepresentations about the car and the credit terms, problems with the car's performance, and the seller's failure to repair the defects. The creditor may also be responsible for illegal repossession and for failure to give required notices. Finally, the lawsuit itself may violate federal law by not being brought where Ms. P resides.

All of these claims may be used to offset the amount Ms. P owes the creditor on the debt. In fact, it is not uncommon for an aggressive attorney to be able to settle a case like this one so that Ms. P owes the creditor nothing. The creditor might even be made to pay her several thousand dollars together with her attorney fees and court costs. If these defenses and counterclaims are not raised, the creditor might get a judgment against Ms. P which it could enforce by garnishing her wages or selling other property.

---

damage awards. You will probably need the help of a lawyer or counselor to discover whether the creditor has followed the proper procedures.

Other common defenses to consider include:

- Money was paid by you but not credited to the account;
- The debt is not owed or that you are current on your payments;
- The creditor miscalculated the amount due. For example, the creditor may be seeking attorney fees or collection costs that are too high or possibly not allowed by law;
- The creditor is collecting more than you agreed to pay;
- You never agreed to pay the debt (if, for example someone fraudulently used your name);
- The debt has been discharged in bankruptcy; or
- The debt was incurred so long ago that under state law the creditor has waited too long to bring the lawsuit.

SPECIAL RIGHTS IF YOU ARE ON ACTIVE DUTY WITH THE MILITARY

If you are notified of a lawsuit against you while you are on active duty with the military, or within the first ninety days after you get off active duty, you can ask the court for a "stay." If you succeed in getting a stay, the lawsuit will not be dropped, but the case will not move ahead while the stay is in effect. Once the stay ends, you have to defend the case as if you were not serving in the military.

To request a stay, send a letter to the court explaining how your current military duties prevent you from appearing in court. The letter must state when you will be able to appear. It must also include a statement from your commanding officer that your current military duties prevent you from appearing in court and that military leave is not authorized for you. Once the court gets this letter, it must order a stay for at least ninety days. If you need more time, you can ask for it in the original letter, or send a second letter. The second letter must include the same information as the initial request. If the court refuses to give you a longer stay, it has to appoint a lawyer to represent you. A JAG Corps attorney may be able to help you ask for a stay.

If the creditor has sued other people in the same lawsuit, the court can, but does not have to, order a stay for them too. However, the creditor must have court permission to proceed against the non-servicemembers.

MEDICAL DEBT DEFENSES

Medical debt is an enormous problem. There are about 45 million uninsured Americans, and close to half of them may have outstanding medical bills. There are a number of special strategies that can be used to deal with cases involving medical debt:

- **Discriminatory Pricing.** Uninsured consumers are sometimes charged two or three times more than someone covered by an HMO or Medicaid/Medicare for the same medical procedure. Finding out and presenting evidence of discriminatory pricing may help your case with a court. It might also help in negotiating a lower bill or better payment plan.

- **Charity Care Funds.** Nonprofit hospitals have a duty because of their tax-exempt status to provide a certain amount of charity or "free care" to low-income patients. Apply for charity or free care funds to be applied toward your hospital bill.

- **Hospital Errors.** Hospital bills are notorious for containing overcharges, errors, and double billing. Another source of errors are hospital mistakes that increase costs, such as delays which lead to unnecessarily long stays. These errors may be the hospital's responsibility.

The courts also have the authority to stay enforcement of judgments, including orders for attachment and garnishment, against servicemembers. A court may stay collection of a judgment if it finds that military service impairs the servicemember's ability to comply with an order to pay the debt.

The federal law protecting servicemembers may stay other proceedings in addition to collection lawsuits. The law also protects servicemembers facing repossessions as well as lawsuits for eviction and mortgage foreclosure. You will find more information about these protections in the chapters of this book dealing with these specific areas.

GOING TO COURT

Attend All Court Proceedings and Respond to All Papers You Receive. You should attend all hearings that are scheduled in your case. If you don't show up, a default judgment will be entered against you even if you filed an answer or appearance earlier. If you cannot attend, you should send someone else to ask for a delay (usually called a "continuance") and to explain the reasons why you could not attend the hearing that day. This will usually be allowed if you had a good reason for not attending (such as illness, family emergency, preexisting and unavoidable work conflict, or unusual transportation problems). In small claims court, you usually only have to go to court once to resolve the case.

Whenever possible, you should let the creditor or the creditor's attorney know in advance if you have a good reason for not attending the hearing. Often, they will agree to a delay in the case. If a delay is agreed to, you should put it in writing in the form of a letter confirming the agreement.

Understanding "Discovery." Cases are often complicated in courts other than in small claims court. In these cases, the creditor could, but rarely does, take your deposition or send you other paperwork (called "discovery"). A deposition requires you to appear, usually in the creditor's attorney's office, to answer questions under oath without a judge present. Your answers are written down by a court reporter and can be used against you later if the case goes to trial and you give different answers. If you get requests for documents or questions about the case (usually called "interrogatories"), you will need to respond to these in writing as best you can. Keep copies of any responses you provide. As a participant in the case, you also have a right to hold a deposition or to send discovery to the other side. Because the requirements for doing so are technical, you will usually need a lawyer to set this up for you.

What Is Summary Judgment? In more formal courts, either side can ask for a judgment before the trial if there are no important facts in dispute. This is usually called a "motion for summary judgment." If you receive a copy of a motion for summary judgment, you will need to respond to it. Otherwise, it may be granted automatically by the court. When you file a response, always send a copy to the creditor or to the creditor's lawyer if they have one.

How to Prepare for a Court Hearing. The hearing is the opportunity for both parties to tell their story to a judge or magistrate. In many small claims courts, the hearing is informal. Usually, the creditor first explains why it is suing. In most cases, the creditor gives the judge a copy of the purchase contract and the accounting records that show any missed payments.

You will then present your response. Because attending a court hearing can be intimidating to many consumers, it is best to be as prepared as possible. You may want to consult a lawyer for advice on how to prepare. Here are some tips to help you prepare for a court hearing:

- *Bring all relevant documents.* It is unlikely that you will have another chance to present documents other than at the hearing. Remember that courts generally pay a lot of attention to written documents. Examples of written documents include complaint letters you have written to the creditor or cancelled checks showing you paid money on the account that wasn't credited. It will be helpful to have extra copies available, because the court and the creditor will keep copies of the documents you present.

- *Bring witnesses if there are any.* Witness testimony may be important, especially if the witnesses are not friends or relatives. For example, if the dispute is about an item which does not work properly, a mechanic or another witness can testify from their own experience in using that item.

- *Do not rely on the written statements of your witnesses,* because the court usually will not allow them into evidence. Have the witnesses attend the trial.

- *Consider going to court beforehand* to get a feel for where the court-room is, how the court works, how people dress, when to stand, how to tell when your case is called, where you sit during the hearing, whether a microphone is used and how to use it, the judge's personality, whether an interpreter is available, etc.

- *Take a companion to the actual hearing* if possible to offer emotional support, to give you feedback and other help, keep track of your documents, and offer a second opinion if you must respond on the spot to a settlement offer.

- *Prepare a written chronological report of events in advance,* together with a checklist of points to make, and a checklist of documents to be given to the court, and take these checklists with you. Many judges will be impatient if you are disorganized.

- *Assume that the judge has not read any of the documents* already presented to the court and does not know the facts of the case. Start at the beginning and tell your story in a clear and organized fashion in the order it happened.

- *Do not be afraid to be forceful, but do not make personal attacks on individuals,* including lawyers, witnesses, or the judge. A display of anger will usually hurt you more than it helps.

NEGOTIATING OR SETTLING DISPUTED CLAIMS

Your claims against a creditor give you the chance to settle your debt. Most commonly, a formal settlement involves a written agreement between you and the creditor where the creditor cancels some or all of the debt in exchange for your agreement to drop your claims. However, you may also want to think about other settlement terms which could benefit you. For example, you might want to ask a creditor to "cancel the delinquency." Even if the total amount you owe does not change, you benefit if the creditor agrees to ignore a delinquency and treat your debt as if it is current. This would protect you, at least temporarily, from debt collection actions such as foreclosure, repossession, or lawsuits.

Any type of agreement you reach with a creditor should be documented in writing. If you reach an informal agreement with the creditor, it is still important for you to go to court to file an appearance and answer. In fact, the safest course is to file a copy of the written agreement with the court clerk to be entered into the court record.

If you are not represented by an attorney, you may need help to determine if a settlement of a disputed debt is fair and reasonable. Depending on the amounts involved, it may make sense to hire an attorney to help you evaluate the settlement. If the amounts are small, advice from an objective but trusted friend or relative may be helpful.

Never agree to anything you do not understand or which you think is unfair. Whenever possible, wait until you see the terms of the settlement in writing before you agree. If a creditor has cheated you once, it may be possible that you are being cheated again.

Accord and Satisfaction. One final tactic to consider if you want to arrange a settlement on favorable terms is based on a legal doctrine known as "accord and satisfaction." The most common use of accord and satisfaction for consumers is when you write "payment in full of a disputed debt" on the back of a check and a creditor endorses and cashes that check. As long as there was a valid basis for the dispute, the law treats your check as final payment.

In order to protect yourself if you wish to try to settle a dispute by "accord and satisfaction," you should follow all of these steps:

- Make clear to the creditor that you have a dispute by sending a letter to the creditor and keeping a copy;

- The letter you send should clearly set out the basis of your dispute (for example, "you were hired to paint three rooms and you only painted two");
- The letter should make clear that the amount you are enclosing is the total amount you believe you actually owe, and state the basis on which you calculate that amount;
- Carefully mark your check on the reverse in big block print: "payment in full of a disputed debt";
- Keep a copy of the front and back of the check you send in case the creditor alters it in any way before cashing it; and
- Keep a copy of the canceled check when it is returned by the bank, together with the letter you sent accompanying the check.

As long as they give you proper notice, companies can require that you send the check to a particular "disputed claims" branch of their office.

Your letter and copy of the canceled check is your record that the creditor accepted the check as payment in full. Not all states allow you to use this tactic.

WARNING ABOUT COUPON SETTLEMENTS
If you are owed money by a creditor, one type of settlement you may want to resist is a store coupon or an additional extension of credit from that creditor. Coupons or new credit from a lender will only get you back into a relationship with a company that has given you problems. It is usually better to take a smaller amount of cash than to accept a store coupon.

Dealing with a Default Judgment. As explained earlier, by not filing a written answer or appearance within the specified time, or by failing to attend the hearing, or by missing other deadlines, you may lose the opportunity to raise your defenses. This is usually called a "default." It is important that you avoid losing by default unless a lawyer has evaluated your case for you.

Even if a default has been entered against you, you may still be able to get another chance to be heard. When this happens, it is called setting aside a default. Usually, a default can be set aside only for specific reasons and within a short time after the judgment has been entered into the court records.

Reasons for setting aside a default commonly include not having proper notice of the case or other unavoidable circumstances that made you unable to answer within the required time. In some courts, you will also have to tell the court briefly about your defenses or counterclaims so that the court will know that you have a chance to get a different result if the default is lifted.

Usually, a request to "remove," "lift," or "set aside" a default has to be made to the court in writing. A copy of your request should always be mailed to the creditor or to its lawyer.

It may be very difficult to set aside a default. You should not assume you will be able to do it. You can avoid this problem by responding on time to all deadlines.

The Judgment and Your Appeal Rights. A party that loses a lawsuit at the first court level can appeal to a higher level. For cases heard in small claims court, this usually means appealing to the state's trial court. This may be the only appeal that is allowed from a small claims court decision. Further appeals can be granted only if a higher court specifically says that it wishes to hear the case.

If a case starts in a more formal trial court, the losing party can appeal to another court which has power to hear appeals. In some states, more than one appeal is possible because there are several levels of courts. Deadlines for filing an appeal are generally short and strictly enforced. You may need professional assistance in bringing an appeal.

The costs of an appeal vary widely but can be significant. Typical costs include a filing fee, fees for a transcript of the trial, and posting a bond to cover the judgment being appealed. In some circumstances, a party unable to afford these fees can request that some of them be waived.

Appeals rarely involve a completely new presentation of the case. Usually, an appeals court will review the case only on the facts presented in the court below it.

WILL YOU LOSE YOUR PROPERTY IF A COURT JUDGMENT IS ENTERED AGAINST YOU?

Significance of a Court Judgment Against You. The judgment is what the court orders after hearing the case. If the creditor wins, the judgment gives the creditor the right to force you to pay using a variety of methods. If a creditor has not taken your property as collateral for the loan, you cannot be forced to pay a debt until a judgment is entered.

Even if you lose a lawsuit, this does *not* mean you must repay the debt. If your family is in financial distress and cannot afford to repay its debts, a court order to pay may not really change anything. If you do not have the money to pay, the court's judgment that you owe the debt will not make payment any more possible.

The court order does let creditors use several special collection tools to try to squeeze money from you. How effective these tools are will depend not only on how much income and property you have, but also on the *types* of income and property you have. In some cases these collection tools are effective in recovering money and may even result in loss of your home. In other cases, these special tools will have *no* impact on you. In still others, the creditor will not spend the money to take further action against you even if they have a judgment.

Even a court order cannot make you pay a debt if all
your income and property are exempt from seizure.

What It Means to Be Collection Proof. When losing a lawsuit cannot hurt you, you are called "judgment proof" or "collection proof." This means that your assets and income are small enough and are protected by federal and state law from seizure by creditors. In that case, you do not really have to worry about the judgment unless your financial situation substantially improves. Being "collection proof" is not a permanent condition. If your financial situation improves, the creditor may still be able to collect money from you in the future.

If you are faced with a collection lawsuit, you should know in advance whether you are collection proof. If you can be hurt by a judgment, there is even more incentive to defend against the lawsuit. Whether or not you are collection proof will depend on whether all your income and property are protected by federal and state "exemption" law. This section discusses whether your property is protected from seizure. The next section discusses whether your wages, benefits, or other income are protected from seizure.

Exemptions May Protect Your Car, Household Goods, and Other Property from Seizure. State exemption laws protect certain types of property from seizure after a court judgment and permit you to keep the basic necessities of life. However, exemption statutes provide little or no protection from a creditor seizing *collateral*. For example, if you agreed to put up a home or car as collateral on a loan, exemption laws do not prevent the creditor from seizing the home or car if you get behind in your loan payments.

Exemption statutes give you important rights if:

- You have not put up any collateral when taking out the loan;
- The creditor has a court judgment against you saying that you owe the debt; and
- The creditor seeks an additional court order against you which would allow the creditor to seize your property.

Some exemption statutes specify dollar amounts of property that are exempt from seizure. For example, the statute may specify that $8,000 worth of your personal property is exempt from seizure. This would allow you to choose which items of your personal property you want to keep, as long as what you keep is worth $8,000 or less. Such a statute will apply to your personal property, and not to your home, which is considered real estate. What types of property are considered your personal property will be specified by your state law.

Some states list certain types of property that are totally exempt from seizure, no matter how much money they are worth. A list of totally exempt property typically includes items such as tools and supplies required for your occupation, clothing, a car (usually with a value under a specified amount), a bible, and household goods.

If you file for bankruptcy in some states, the amount of property exempted from seizure may increase because you can choose federal bankruptcy exemptions rather than state exemptions. The federal bankruptcy exemptions may or may not be better than your state's exemptions. But some states have "opted out" of the federal exemptions, meaning that even in a bankruptcy, the federal exemptions are not available and you must rely on your state exemptions. The 2005 amendments to the bankruptcy laws created new rules that apply to exemptions claimed by individuals who have moved to a new state within certain time periods before they file bankruptcy. For example, the exemptions of your old state may apply if you moved to your new state within two years of your bankruptcy filing. These rules are discussed in Chapter Nineteen.

Some creditors try to force you to turn over property that is exempt under law from seizure. The creditor will point to small print in the contract that says you agreed to waive rights under state exemption laws. Do not give in to these aggressive creditors. These types of waivers are illegal under federal law.

Even if exemption laws fully protected your property at one point in time, you may be at risk if your equity in your property increases. Court judgments remain on the books for many years. If your equity in property increases beyond the exemption limit or if you acquire nonexempt income or property, creditors may be able to reach it at some point in the future. At that point, if the judgment is still unpaid, you will have to work out a payment plan with the creditor or reconsider a bankruptcy filing.

State exemption laws can be very complicated. You may want to get professional help to understand the exemption laws available in your state. At a minimum, you should try to find a publication that explains your state's laws. This type of publication may be available from the local bar association, a legal services office, or a nonprofit consumer credit counselor. Make sure any source you rely on is up-to-date. See Chapter Three for warning signs of unscrupulous credit counselors.

How the Law Protects Your Home from Seizure After a Court Judgment. Homestead exemptions protect your residence, and can be as high as $100,000 or more in some states, but can also be significantly less in others. Under some state's laws if husband and wife own property jointly, that property may be entitled to special protection from the debts of one spouse or the other, but not from joint debts. Joint owners, whether married or not, usually may each obtain a separate exemption which covers their share of the property and doubles the amount of protection.

To benefit from the homestead exemption in some states, a declaration of the homestead must be filed with the property registry in your community. In a few states, this paper must be filed before the credit is granted. You should always file your declaration as early as possible if you live in a state where a declaration is required. In other states, protection is automatic.

Exemption amounts stretch a long way because they apply only to your equity in property, not to the property's value.

Homestead Exemptions. A homestead exemption allows you to exempt only a certain portion of the equity in your property. However, a relatively small exemption amount may be enough to protect property worth a lot more. If you have equity above the exemption limit, the creditor can force a sale and you are only allowed to keep the amount of the exemption from the sale proceeds. For example:

1. Mr. J lives in a state with a homestead exemption of $30,000. His home is worth $150,000.

     Mr. J has a first mortgage of $100,000 and a $20,000 home equity loan. The total liens on his property = $120,000.

     Equity equals the value of the home minus the liens. In this case, $150,000 - $120,000 = $30,000 in equity.

     Since the homestead exemption is $30,000, his home is fully protected from execution by a judgment creditor. He doesn't have to worry that a creditor can force a sale of his home.

2. If Mr. J's home increases in value to $200,000, his equity also increases. The new amount of equity would be $200,000 - $120,000 = $80,000. The homestead exemption of $30,000 no longer protects all of Mr. J's equity.

The creditor in this case could force a sale. The first $100,000 from the sale would go to the mortgage holder. The next $20,000 would pay off the home equity loan. Mr. J. would get to keep $30,000, the amount of the homestead exemption. This leaves $50,000 of sale proceeds available to pay off the creditor that initiated the sale. If the creditor is owed less than $50,000, Mr. J will get any balance left.

A creditor can force a sale in example #2 but won't necessarily do so. Forcing a sale is expensive. The creditor may instead wait to collect on the lien until Mr. J sells the property.

How to Fight the Creditor's Attempt to Use a Court Judgment to Seize Your Property. A creditor with a court judgment can arrange for the sheriff to seize certain items of your property. Because the creditor is armed with a court judgment and is asking the sheriff to do the seizure, the creditor can seize your property even though the creditor had not taken that property as collateral for its loan. This is called "attachment and execution."

This creditor right is sharply limited by federal and state exemption law. You can prevent the seizure of exempt property by filing a notice of exempt property or by taking similar steps specified by your state law. In some states, you will need to file papers with the sheriff or a public official by a certain deadline in order to get the benefit of an exemption. In other states, the sheriff gives you permission to set aside exempt items at the time of seizure or sale.

Additionally, the sheriff cannot seize property in your possession which does not belong to you. To stop its seizure, the property's rightful owner may have to file a declaration of ownership with the appropriate office.

If the sheriff is able to seize your property, it will then be sold at public auction, and the proceeds will go to the creditor to help pay off the judgment. These auctions are usually poorly attended and bring low bids. For this reason, creditors rarely seize used household goods, which will have minimal resale value. Limits on taking your household goods are discussed in Chapter Seventeen. If property is sold at auction, you or your friends can attend the auction and re-purchase the possessions at a bargain price.

After a sale, the creditor may seek the remainder due on a debt if the sale price is less than the amount you owed. This is called an action to collect the "deficiency." You may raise the types of claims and defenses discussed earlier in this chapter in response to a deficiency claim. In fact, you should fight a deficiency claim in the same way you would fight any other debt collection case.

Judgment Liens Can Stay on Your Property for Years. Any unpaid judgment generally becomes a lien on any real estate you own in the county where the judgment is entered (or statewide in some states). Creditors also may have the right to transfer judgments so that they cover your real estate in other locations.

Unless the real estate is legally exempt from execution, as discussed above under the homestead discussion, creditors can force its sale in much the same way as they can force the sale of other property. Even if the real estate is exempt from execution, the creditor's lien on your property usually remains in effect until you sell it.

In most states, when you sell the property, mortgages are paid off first. Then you get to keep what is left, up to your state's maximum exemption amount. Anything over that amount goes to satisfy all or some of the creditor's judgment against you. Even if your property is exempt from seizure today, if the property's value increases enough in the future, it may no longer be exempt from seizure.

One possible way of getting rid of judgment liens is to file for bankruptcy. To the extent the property is exempt when you file for bankruptcy, the lien can be permanently removed. Bankruptcy is discussed in Chapter Nineteen.

WILL YOU LOSE YOUR INCOME AND CASH IF A COURT JUDGMENT IS ENTERED AGAINST YOU?

Exemptions May Protect Your Income and Cash from Garnishment. A creditor with a court judgment against you has the right to "garnish" money belonging or owed to you that is in the hands of a third party. In this context, to "garnish" means to take. Most often, garnishment takes money from your wages or bank account.

Garnishment can only take place *after* the creditor obtains a judgment against you. (One exception is for collection of student loans and other debts owed to the government, where garnishment is allowed without a judgment, but only after a notice and hearing process. For more information, see Chapter Eighteen.)

After obtaining a judgment, the creditor can file a request for garnishment with the court clerk, sheriff, or another local official depending on state practice. A notice is then issued to the "garnishee" (a bank, an employer, or another third party holding your property), directing that party to turn over the property at a specified time.

You must be given notice of the garnishment. You can then request a hearing to prove that state or federal law protects your money from garnishment. The law protects you from garnishment in two ways:

1. A portion of your wages is protected from seizure. Current
federal law provides that the first $175.50 from weekly take-home pay, after taxes and Social Security are deducted, cannot be garnished at all. This $175.50 is based on a formula that is linked to the minimum wage. The minimum wage in 2007 is $5.85/hour. It will go up to $6.55 on July 24, 2008 and to $7.25 on July 24, 2009. The amount of wages protected from garnishment will go up when these minimum wage increases occur.

If the weekly take-home pay is more than the amount protected from garnishment, an employer, in response to a garnishment order, must pay the *smaller* of the following amounts to a sheriff:

- The weekly take-home pay (after deductions) minus $175.50; or
- 25% of that take-home pay.

For example, if your weekly income after deductions are taken out is $200, your employer would be required to calculate the amount due under the two formulas: (1) ($200 − 175.50 = $24.50) or (2) (25% of $200 = $50) and pay the creditor the smaller amount. In this case, your employer would pay the creditor $24.50 from your take-home pay. A higher amount can be garnished if the debt is for child support or alimony.

The standard described above is based on federal law and sets out minimum wage protections for debtors in all fifty states. In some states, you have even greater protections against wage garnishment. Some states prohibit all wage garnishment or allow a smaller amount of wages to be garnished than the federal standard. Federal law and some state laws forbid employers from firing employees solely because their wages are being garnished.

2. Certain types of income, primarily government payments, are completely exempt from garnishment.
Even if your income is large enough so that a portion may be garnished, certain sources of income are *completely* protected under federal or state law. For example, federal law almost always exempts Social Security payments, Supplemental Security Income, and veteran's benefits. States with TANF (Temporary Assistance for Needy Families) and unemployment insurance programs usually exempt those benefits from garnishment as well.

Social Security Offsets. Because Social Security is considered so essential for survival, it has traditionally been protected from attachment by creditors. A 1996 law takes away some of this protection, but only when federal agencies are collecting debts owed to them. Examples include money owed to the Department of Education for student loans and money owed to the Department of Agriculture for food stamp overpayments.

This is an important change to the law, but it is not a reason to panic. It will not apply to everyone and not all benefits can be taken.

Certain amounts of other federal benefits may also be taken under this law, including:

- Social Security Retirement and Disability Benefits;
- Certain Railroad Retirement Benefits;
- Black Lung Part B Benefits.

Supplemental Security Income (SSI) cannot be taken under this law. Other benefits that the law says cannot be taken include Veterans Benefits and benefits under Part C of the Black Lung law.
Even if your Social Security payments may be taken through this program, you do not have to worry that the government will take your entire check. The government cannot touch the first $750/month ($9,000 over the

course of a year) of your benefits. In addition, no matter how much money you get, the government cannot take more than 15% of the total benefit.

For example, Mr. A receives a monthly Social Security benefit of $850. The first $750 is completely protected from offset. The government can only take the lesser of (1) 15% of the total benefit = $127.50 or (2) the amount left above $750. In this case, this amount is $100. Since this is less than $127.50, the amount of the offset would be $100.

You are supposed to get a number of notices warning you that your benefits are going to be taken. The notices give you information about your right to request a hearing with the agency that is collecting the money. You should especially consider this strategy if you think you have defenses to repayment or if you are facing financial hardships that may make you eligible for a reduction in the amount of offset.

The I.R.S. can also take Social Security benefits to collect tax debts. The rules are different for this program. Not all of the same protections apply. You should contact a tax professional for more information. More information about tax debts can be found in Chapter Eighteen.

Funds such as Social Security are exempt from seizure if you keep them in a bank account. However, problems sometimes arise when your bank account contains both exempt and nonexempt money because it is hard to trace which portion of the funds is exempt. In many cases, creditors will improperly seize money, such as Social Security payments, which should be exempt. You will then need to fight back and show that the seizure was illegal and that those funds were protected. If you are threatened with a court judgment, you must weigh the benefits of opening or keeping a bank account against the risk of having the money seized.

More information on garnishments and available defenses is contained in National Consumer Law Center's *Fair Debt Collection* Ch. 9 (5th ed. 2004 and Supp.). This book also provides information about situations where the bank is trying to collect fees from your account. This is called a bank right of "set-off" and there are special rules that apply.

HOW TO RESPOND TO A DEBTOR'S EXAMINATION

Debtor's Examination. After obtaining a judgment, a creditor can ask a judge to order you to appear in court to answer questions about your income and assets. The purpose is to find income or property that is not protected by law and which the creditor may seize.

In some states this procedure is called a debtor's examination, but the procedure goes by other names in other states. Some creditors routinely request a debtor's examination. Others never do. There are three important things to remember about a debtor's examination:

- It is a court-ordered appearance. Failure to show up can result in arrest, citation for contempt, and a jail sentence. A notice to appear for a court examination should *never* be ignored. You should always appear or make a written request to the court for a postponement. The court will usually grant a postponement if the creditor agrees to the request or if you have a good reason.
- Your answers are made under oath and often are recorded by a court reporter. Lying under oath is perjury, a crime punishable by jail.
- If the creditor which holds a judgment finds assets or income not protected by law, the creditor can obtain a court order requiring you to turn over those assets. Failure to comply with the order could be considered contempt and could result in jail.

DEBTORS PRISONS??

There are no debtor's prisons in the United States. This is the good news. The bad news is that there is a rarely used collection tactic usually called a body attachment (also known as a civil arrest warrant, bench warrant, or writ of *capias*) that can lead to the same result.

A body attachment means arresting a debtor who doesn't show up in court, usually for a debtor's examination. In most cases, the body attachment is not an active arrest warrant. This means that a debtor can be arrested only if she comes into contact with the police for some other reason. It is considered so extreme that it is not used in many parts of the country. But be advised—body attachments are making a comeback, particularly in medical debt collection cases. This is yet another reason to respond to court papers and to show up for court dates.

The first step in responding to notice of a debtor's examination is to review your assets *well before the examination.* Determine if all your property is protected by law and if all your income is exempt from garnishment. If so, immediately tell the creditor. This may be sufficient to get the creditor to drop the request for an examination since it will just be a waste of everyone's time. If the examination is canceled, be sure to get this in writing. Do not rely on the creditor's oral promise that it will drop the examination.

EXEMPTION PLANNING

If you have property that legally can be seized, you may want to think about "exemption planning." This is a way of maximizing the protection of existing laws by converting property that can be seized (for example, cash) into property that cannot be seized (for example, household goods or equity in the home).

For example:

Mrs. Q owns a home. She has $10,000 equity in the home. (Equity equals the amount of cash she would keep if she sold her home and paid off all the liens on it.)

Mrs. Q also has $10,000 in cash.

The homestead exemption in her state is $20,000. Other exemptions in the state allow her to protect $3,000 of the cash.

The $10,000 equity in Mrs. Q's home is less than the $20,000 homestead exemption and is therefore completely protected from seizure. However, only $3,000 of the $10,000 of her cash is exempted.

Instead of losing $7,000 to the creditor, Mrs. Q can use the cash to prepay the mortgage in part. If she prepays the mortgage, she will owe less on the home. This increases the equity in the home. The higher amount of equity in the home will be protected up to the $20,000 homestead exemption limit.

The idea of exemption planning is that you keep the total value of all of your property but trade one type of property that is not exempt from seizure for another type that is. This is different than an improper transfer of property where you try to give away property to a friend or relative or sell it for a less than it is worth to someone who will later return it. Among other problems with these improper transfers, creditors can have them cancelled under your state law covering "fraudulent transfers" or "fraudulent conveyances."

If there is property important to you that a creditor can seize, you can approach the creditor about a "workout" agreement. You can offer to pay all or a portion of the amount due over a period of months or even years. The amount you offer to pay should be directly related to what the creditor could seize after the debtor's examination. Do not offer to pay $3,000 over twelve months when the only items the creditor could seize have a market value of $500.

You should always get a workout agreement in writing. The written agreement should excuse you from attending the debtor's examination if it has not already been held, and contain the creditor's promise not to use wage garnishment or execution on your property as long as you continue to make payments. You can also ask for an agreement to waive the remainder of the debt if part is paid. Some creditors will accept partial payment if they know they can't get payment in full. From the creditor's perspective, some payment is better than none. See Chapter Eight for more information about negotiating with creditors.

A final option to prevent loss of property after a debtor's examination is to file for bankruptcy. The bankruptcy will immediately stop any seizure and may allow you to keep your property permanently. Since bankruptcy is a right under federal (national) law, your rights in the bankruptcy process will take precedence over the state court collection process. Chapter Nineteen discusses consumer bankruptcy filings.

10

What You Need to Know About Your Mortgage— Even If You Are Not Delinquent

---

TOPICS COVERED IN THIS CHAPTER

- Why Your Servicer May Be More Important Than the Lender Holding Your Mortgage
- What to Do About "Exploding" Mortgages
- Getting Credit for Your Payments When Servicing Is Transferred
- Surprising Facts About What Happens to Your Partial Mortgage Payments
- How to Find Out the Amount You Owe and Dispute Errors
- Straightening Out Your Escrow Account
- Cancel Unnecessary and Expensive Insurance
- Dealing with the Servicer from @#!&

Recent years have seen an epidemic of sloppy, greedy, and downright fraudulent practices by lenders and those they hire to process your mortgage and escrow payments. Even worse, loan brokers and others who initiate mortgage loans have been hiding some truly dangerous terms in the fine print of your mortgage. It is not surprising that the newspapers are filled with stories about the mortgage crisis, and it is important for you to aggressively investigate your own mortgage situation.

Does the fine print in your mortgage mean your monthly mortgage payments will skyrocket in a year or so? Is the lender properly applying your mortgage payments to reduce your obligation? Is the lender asking for too much to be put in escrow and does it promptly pay your insurance and tax bills out of that escrow? Are you being charged for insurance you do not need?

Answering these questions is vital. This may not only save you a lot of money, but also help you save your home. Failing to keep on top of these issues may eventually lead to foreclosure on your home. Keep in mind that quite often the person who helped you get your mortgage, the company that takes your mortgage payments, and just about everyone else involved in your mortgage are more concerned with making money off you and your mortgage than they are with keeping you in your home.

This chapter helps you resolve various types of mortgage problems that could eventually lead to foreclosure, even where foreclosure is not imminent. This chapter provides important advice you need even *before* you get into major trouble, even *before* you get seriously delinquent in your mortgage payments. (Of course, this chapter also provides important advice if you are in trouble with your mortgage already.) By contrast, Chapter Eleven explains how you may be able to obtain a workout agreement from your lender if you are significantly behind in your mortgage payments, and Chapters Twelve and Thirteen examine your rights to slow or prevent the actual foreclosure.

In some ways, this is the most important chapter of the four because there is more you can do to prevent foreclosure before you get behind on your payments than when you later become seriously in default. Of course, much of the discussion in this chapter will also help you if you are facing foreclosure. But it is best to start working on these problems as early as possible. For example, the lender has up to sixty days to respond to certain of your inquiries, so resolving problems could take a while.

WHY YOUR MORTGAGE SERVICER MAY BE MORE IMPORTANT THAN THE LENDER HOLDING YOUR MORTGAGE

Whatever your mortgage problem—the lender's failure to credit your mortgage payments, confusion about what must be paid in escrow, or that your monthly payments are about to skyrocket—it is important that you identify your mortgage "servicer" and understand what a servicer does. The servicer is generally responsible for preparing and sending mortgage and escrow statements, collecting payments and making sure they are applied correctly, handling escrow accounts and dealing with other day-to-day activities on your mortgage account. Thus it is usually easy to identify your mortgage servicer—it is the company where you send your mortgage payments.

The servicer often is not the original lender and is typically not the company to whom you really owe your mortgage payments. Instead, it is a company hired by the owner of your mortgage to service your loan. Over the course of your mortgage payments, you may have to deal with more than one servicer, as the owner of your mortgage may change servicers, or the owner may sell your loan to someone else, and the new owner may hire a new servicer.

The original lender on your mortgage, the lender today holding your mortgage, and the company servicing your mortgage may be two or even three different companies. For example, you may have taken out a mortgage from the Third National Bank, which then sold your loan to Fannie Mae. The Third National Bank may continue to service the loan for Fannie Mae, or the loan servicing may be transferred to ABC Servicing Company. In many cases, the servicer will be an out-of-state company that deals with thousands or hundreds of thousands of mortgages. Although your parents may have had one bank that originated, continued to own and serviced their mortgage, this is rarely the case today.

WHAT TO DO ABOUT "EXPLODING" MORTGAGES

In recent years, many mortgage loans have been written with hidden traps that spring on the consumer several years later. Your monthly payment will literally explode two or three years into the mortgage, whether or not general interest rates go up. The lender offered you a "teaser" rate that is guaranteed to go up after two or three years, causing your mortgage payments to "explode" at that point.

Even if you are keeping up with your mortgage payments, sometime soon you may suddenly find you cannot afford the new higher payments, and will face potential foreclosure. It is essential that you determine as soon as possible whether your mortgage loan contains this feature. You will have more options and more time to investigate those options if you act promptly.

If you have been making mortgage payments for five or ten years with the same lender, it is highly unlikely you have an exploding mortgage loan, *unless you refinanced that loan within the last few years.* Many of these exploding mortgages were refinancings of existing mortgages or second mortgages for home improvements or similar expenses.

If you took out a mortgage loan within the last few years, you should check what happens to your monthly payments in the future. Ask the servicer or lender. Another way is to show all your loan documents to a counselor or other person familiar with mortgage loans. A disclosure form accompanying the loan will usually show a complex payment flow, indicating the exploding payments.

You may be among the millions whose monthly mortgage payments are about to skyrocket. You have options if you act now.

If you do have an "exploding" adjustable rate mortgage loan, immediately explore the following options:

- *Ask your lender to freeze your existing interest rate* so that monthly mortgage payments stay at the same amount. It is possible that your lender has a program to eliminate or postpone the interest rate jump, at least for certain qualifying borrowers. If the servicer resists this, it may pay to contact the entity that owns your actual mortgage loan. More on how to persuade the lender to modify your mortgage loan is found in Chapter Eleven. If the lender does agree to modify the mortgage, look to see whether the lender requires you to waive any rights. If you think you were defrauded when you took out the loan and have a good case against the lender, you may want to consult an attorney before waiving your rights.

- *Try to refinance the loan with another lender.* If you find another lender to refinance your present mortgage, you may have to pay more now than under your present "teaser rate," but you will save lots of money later on. It is more important to establish a mortgage payment plan you can afford in the long run than save a few dollars now, only to lose your home in a few years. There are some loan programs, including reverse mortgages for older homeowners, which can also reduce or eliminate your monthly payments. Refinancing options should be evaluated carefully, possibly with professional assistance. Avoid high-rate refinancing loans and do not consolidate other substantial debts with your existing mortgage. These choices will only make your problems worse in the long term. See Chapter Six for information about refinancing your mortgage. But explore refinancing now—do not wait. Your chances of getting another lender to let you refinance is far greater while you are still current on your mortgage payments. If you wait until the payments explode, you may become delinquent, and this will seriously impede any attempt to refinance. Nevertheless, mortgage underwriting requirements may now be tougher than when you took out the mortgage, and you may have difficulty qualifying for a new mortgage, particularly if your home has gone down in value.

■ *Putting money aside to help pay future mortgage payments.* If you are stuck with much higher mortgage payments in the future, putting away money now can help you weather the storm for a while. Hopefully, this will get you through until your income increases, you build up more equity in your home so that you are able to refinance with lower payments, or you decide to sell your home. Obviously, pressures of other bills make it difficult to put away savings now. But you should seriously consider postponing payment on other bills to build up enough savings to pay future increased mortgage payments. Mortgage payments are high-priority debts because the mortgage company has the right to foreclose and take your home, while other creditors generally do not. See Chapter One about prioritizing debts.

■ *Cutting expenses and increasing income now* may help you afford higher payments in the future and for the long run. Tips on cutting back on unnecessary insurance related to the mortgage is described later in this chapter. Also consider other approaches to cutting expenses, set out in Chapter Two. Look at whether there are ways to increase your income, including loans from pension plans, food stamps, fuel assistance, property tax abatements, and unemployment or disability income. See Chapter Two for a discussion of income-related issues.

■ *Ask a lawyer to look over your mortgage* and the facts that led to your getting into the exploding adjustable rate mortgage. If a loan broker defrauded you or if there are law violations in the loan, these may provide you with viable legal claims to help you recover damages, cancel the loan, or work out a beneficial settlement that lowers your mortgage payments in the future.

GETTING CREDIT FOR YOUR PAYMENTS WHEN SERVICING IS TRANSFERRED

During the time you have your mortgage, there is a good chance that the company that collects the payments and services your mortgage will change several times. Reports of consumer complaints about mortgage servicing show that many problems occur when servicing is transferred. It is important that you know your rights when this happens. These rights are provided by a federal law, the Real Estate Settlement Procedures Act, commonly known as RESPA.

Before a new mortgage servicer takes over servicing your loan, your current servicer is required under RESPA to send you a notice at least fifteen days before the transfer takes effect. In addition, the new servicer must send you a similar notice not more than fifteen days after the transfer. These notices from the old and new servicers can be combined into one notice as long as it is sent at least fifteen days before the transfer.

The transfer notice must include the following information:

- The effective date of transfer;
- The name, address, and toll-free telephone number of the new servicer;
- A toll-free telephone number the consumer can call for answers to questions;
- The date when the old servicer will stop accepting payments and the date when the new servicer will begin accepting payments;
- Additional information about insurance coverage.

The law also creates a sixty-day "safe harbor" period after the transfer date. If you send a payment before the normal due date to the old servicer during this sixty-day period, it must be treated as a proper payment made on time. This means the new servicer cannot charge a late fee, cannot claim your account is in default, and cannot report the payment as late on your credit report. This protection applies even if the old servicer does not send the payment in a timely way to the new servicer.

SURPRISING FACTS ABOUT WHAT HAPPENS TO YOUR PARTIAL MORTGAGE PAYMENTS

When you make a mortgage payment for less than the total amount due (a partial payment), one of two surprising things often happens—neither of them being that the payment is applied toward your mortgage. Even more amazing, in many cases this may be permitted by the loan documents.

The one thing servicers commonly do with your partial payment is send your check back to you un-cashed. You might wonder why they are refusing to accept money. One theory is that they want to put pressure on you to make the full payment. In any event, if the partial payment is returned to you, you should set the money aside and *not* use it to pay other bills. The money that is set aside will help you get caught up on your mortgage payments later, or, if you cannot do that, at least help you negotiate a workout agreement with the mortgage company later (see Chapter Eleven). In the worst case scenario, if foreclosure becomes inevitable, you will have some money saved for moving expenses.

Other servicers do not return a partial payment, but also do not apply that payment to the amount due. Instead, they keep the amount in a "suspense account" to be held until you pay the remaining amount due for that one monthly payment. So, the next month, if you send in a full payment, part of that payment is used to complete the payment for the prior month and the balance (being only a partial payment) goes into the suspense account. So at this point, the prior month's payment will be credited, but *not* the current month's payment—even though it was paid in full. This can get quite complicated, particularly where the lender is assessing late fees and the like. As a result, it is easy to get confused as to how much you owe and you might be surprised how much the lender thinks you have to pay to keep the mortgage payments current. The next section explains how to find out how much you owe and how to dispute errors.

The safest course is to make full payments and quickly catch up on any partial payments. Your home mortgage payment is more important than virtually any other bill, so it makes sense to keep that current and delay payment of other bills, if necessary.

HOW TO FIND OUT THE AMOUNT YOU OWE AND DISPUTE ERRORS

It is quite common for a lender or servicer to claim more than you believe is owed. Federal law provides you the right to accurately determine the balance due. As a side benefit, if you discover that the lender or servicer is asking for more money than it should, and you are facing foreclosure, you may be able to delay the foreclosure. A housing counselor or an attorney will be able to help with this.

Some common disputes about the amount claimed as due include:

1. Failure to credit all the payments you made;

2. Crediting payments you made in a way which is inconsistent with the accounting principles required by the contract or your state law;

3. Compounding interest when compound interest is not permitted;

4. Failing to properly reduce interest rates as required in a variable rate mortgage;

5. Crediting amounts paid by you in ways which are not permitted by the contract (for example, applying payments to credit insurance which you did not authorize);

6. Failure to properly manage escrow balances (for example, failing to make timely tax payments and thereby incurring late charges);

7. Charging the mortgage account for things not permitted by the loan contract or for amounts which are not reasonable under the circumstances (for example, excessive property inspection fees or a fee for calculating the amount needed to pay off the loan in full, called a "discharge" or "pay-off" fee);

8. Charging excessive attorney fees or costs for foreclosure (only real costs can be charged to your account—the lender should not be able to profit by padding foreclosure fees);

9. Double counting foreclosure fees and costs by including them in the escrow balance and then also separately breaking them out as individual charges;

10. Charging late fees in amounts which are not permitted by the contract (for example, applying a late charge to a missed payment more than once);

11. Charging for force placed insurance when the lender has proof you already have insurance;

12. Refusing to accept payments without a valid reason (for example, when a payment is short by a few dollars or does not include an amount to cover a late fee).

Occasionally a lender will have caused you to default by making one or more errors in accounting or by otherwise mishandling your money. As mentioned earlier, problems commonly arise when servicing is transferred from one lender or servicer to another. Payments get lost and accounting can be confused. In some cases you may be able to prove that you aren't delinquent at all.

The first thing to do is to contact the servicer. Provide the documentation they request and keep copies for yourself. If the servicer does not provide you with the information you requested or if you dispute how the servicer is handling your account, you may send the servicer a more formal request, called a "qualified written request," to ensure that they respond in a timely manner and correct any errors.

Sending a Qualified Written Request to Obtain Information and Dispute Errors on Your Account. If you are having trouble obtaining information from your servicer or if you have a dispute concerning your account, you may be able to force the servicer to respond to your request or complaint. Under RESPA, your servicer must respond to any written request for information or investigate any claims of error concerning your account, including your escrow account, so long as you provide certain information regarding your account.

This is called a "qualified written request." You must include enough information in your request to allow the servicer to identify your account. Usually an account number, along with your name and the address of the property is sufficient. You must also include a statement of the reasons why you believe the account is in error or provide clear information about your question. Be as specific as possible.

Your request should not be written on a payment coupon or included with your payment, but rather should be a separate letter sent to the customer service address for your servicer. Send the letter return receipt requested, so that you will have a record of when the servicer receives it. If the servicer has given you a notice that lists the address where qualified written requests are to be sent, then you must send it there. This address may be listed on the original loan documents, a transfer of servicing statement, an annual escrow statement, or a monthly billing statement. If you did not get such a notice or don't remember if you did, you should call the servicer's customer service center (a toll-free number may be listed on your account statements or you can check the servicer's website) and ask for the address to send the request.

If you cannot confirm the proper address and you have several addresses for the servicer, then send it to all of these addresses. However, you should not send the request to the "lock box" address on your payment coupon as this may be the post office box for a third-party company hired by the servicer to process payments.

The servicer must acknowledge that it received your request within twenty days of receipt (not including Saturdays, Sundays, and legal holidays).

The servicer has up to sixty days after receiving your request (not including Saturdays, Sundays, and legal holidays) to conduct an investigation, if you claim that there was an error in your account, or provide the information you requested, if available. During this time the servicer must correct your account, if necessary, and inform you of its actions. In addition, during this sixty-day period, the servicer cannot give any information to credit reporting agencies that a payment related to your inquiry is overdue.

If the servicer receives your letter but does not respond to your request, you may consider filing a lawsuit. If you are successful and have suffered harm because of the servicer's conduct, you may be able to recover damages, costs, and the fees you paid to your attorney. An example of a "qualified written request" follows on the next page.

Request Validation of the Debt. When an attorney for the lender or servicer sends you a letter threatening foreclosure, announcing that you are in default, or for any other reason, the letter should describe your right to dispute the mortgage debt. An explanation of this right will usually be included in the first notice or letter you get from the attorney, or within five days after the attorney first communicates with you about the debt. If you then dispute the debt in writing within the next thirty days, the attorney must stop collection efforts while your dispute is investigated. See Chapters Eight and Nine for more information about your rights under the Fair Debt Collection Practices Act.

Setting Up a "Tender" Defense. If you have a real dispute with your lender or servicer about the amount you are delinquent, you may want to set up the defense of "tender." To "tender" means to offer the undisputed amount that is delinquent, while not paying the amount you dispute. That way, if you are right about what is owed, you are not delinquent and the lender should not be able to foreclose. On the other hand, if you withhold both what is disputed and what you agree is owed, the lender can argue that, even if you are right, you still are behind in payments, and the lender can proceed to foreclose. It is *not* required that you tender the balance in order to dispute the amount claimed due, but your effort to tender will help prevent foreclosure and will make your case more sympathetic to a judge, if matters reach that stage.

If you can afford to do so, tender is usually achieved by mailing the undisputed amount of the debt (by check or money order) to the lender or

SAMPLE "QUALIFIED WRITTEN REQUEST"

Ken and Susan Consumer
12 Budding Bloom Lane
Elizabeth, New Jersey

June 1, 2008

Last Dollar Mortgage Co.
398 Rockefeller Drive
St. Albans, WV 25177

Attention: Customer Service Department

RE: Account #123234

Dear Last Dollar Mortgage Co.:

We are requesting information about the foreclosure fees and costs and escrow accounting on our loan. Please treat this letter as a "qualified written request" under the Real Estate Settlement and Procedures Act (section 2605(e)). Specifically, we are requesting the following information:

- The payment dates, purpose of payment, and recipient of all foreclosure fees and costs which have been charged to our account;
- The payment dates, purpose of payment, and recipient of all escrow items charged to our account in the last 24 months;
- A breakdown of our current escrow payment showing how it was calculated and the reasons for any increase or decrease in the last 24 months (include a copy of any annual escrow statements prepared within the last 24 months); and
- A payment history that can be easily read and understood listing the dates and amounts of all payments for the last 24 months, and showing how they have been applied or credited.

Also, on March 1, 2008, we sent our March payment to First Dollar Mortgage Co., which had been servicing our mortgage before it was transferred to you. Our March payment was never credited to our account. Please correct this error.

Thank you for taking the time to acknowledge and answer this request as required by the Real Estate Settlement Procedures Act (section 2605(e)).

Very truly yours,

Ken and Susan Consumer

[certified mail]

servicer with a letter explaining that you dispute the balance. The letter should also state that the amount you tender is offered in "full satisfaction of the dispute."

Most often, your tender will be returned. If it is returned, you have the defense that the money was offered and refused. Keep your letter and the lender's response as proof. You should set the money aside, if possible in a bank account, while the dispute is being resolved. You can add the claim of tender to your defenses in the legal process, if the matter reaches foreclosure.

In some states, if your tender is accepted, you can then claim that acceptance by the lender settles the dispute in your favor. This defense is usually called "accord and satisfaction."

One disadvantage of tendering is that, if the money is kept and later you cannot afford to keep the property or the dispute is resolved against you, you will not be able to get the money back. Sometimes, in foreclosure this can mean that you are further investing in a home that you cannot afford in the future.

Even if you cannot afford to tender, or choose not to do so for other reasons, it is a good idea to put money aside during a dispute. The money can be used to cover as much as possible of the mortgage payments if you lose the dispute or to cover any undisputed portion if you win. In the worst case scenario, if foreclosure goes forward, you can use this money to move.

Raising the Dispute in the Foreclosure Process. Whether you have tendered the undisputed amount or not, it is very useful to raise any dispute about the amount owed in the foreclosure process, if things have progressed that far. This will often slow up the foreclosure, and can reduce what you have to pay in order to get caught up. Even if you don't have the financial resources necessary to get caught up, you will want to minimize the amount you owe the lender. This will increase your potential to recover some of your equity if you cannot get back on track with your payments.

Often your ability to effectively dispute the amount owing on a mortgage will require you to have legal representation, which may not always be practical. But if you are in foreclosure, it is particularly important to have an attorney, and you can ask that attorney to investigate the disputed amount. Your attorney will have the ability to review the lender's records in a process known as "discovery" in the court foreclosure case or in a case brought by you against the lender. If your attorney needs a resource to help investigate the matter, the National Consumer Law Center's *The Cost of Credit* (3d ed. 2005 and Supp.) addresses many of these issues.

STRAIGHTENING OUT
YOUR ESCROW ACCOUNT

If your monthly mortgage payment includes an amount to cover property insurance and taxes on your home, you have a mortgage with an "escrow" or "impound" account. Your lender or servicer puts these extra payments into an escrow account and then is supposed to pay the insurance and tax bills for you when they are due. You want to be careful to understand what is in your escrow account, you want to correct any errors before they lead to trouble down the line, and you want to make sure that the payments are getting to the insurance company and tax authority in a timely manner.

Escrow Account Statements. The amount your servicer can require you to pay into an escrow account each month is set by a federal law called the Real Estate Settlement Procedures Act (RESPA). Your servicer also has a duty under RESPA to give you information about your escrow account. It must give you an initial statement when the account is first set up and periodic statements at least once per year. These statements must include information such as the amount of your current escrow payment, the amount your escrow payment will be for the next year, the total amount you paid into the escrow account during the past year, and the total amount paid out of the escrow account during the past year for taxes, insurance premiums, and other escrow bills.

Unfortunately, your servicer is not required by RESPA to send you an annual escrow statement if at the time the yearly escrow analysis is done you are more than thirty days behind on your mortgage payments or your mortgage is in foreclosure. You may still be able to obtain information about your escrow account by making a written request (discussed earlier in this chapter). In addition, if your mortgage account is later reinstated or becomes current, your servicer must then send you the annual escrow statement within ninety days.

Escrow Payment Limits. Your servicer cannot require you to pay a monthly escrow amount greater than one-twelfth of the total estimated escrow bills (taxes, insurance, etc.) that will need to be paid during the upcoming year. The servicer may also require a "cushion" be added to each monthly payment in case your actual escrow bills are slightly higher than estimated, but the amount per month of this cushion usually cannot increase your monthly escrow payment by more than one-sixth (16.67%). For example, if you have a tax bill of $1,200 and an insurance premium of $360 that will have to be paid during the next year, the total of these annual escrow bills is $1,560. This means that you will need to make escrow payments of $130 per month ($1,560 divided by 12 = $130). If your servicer also requires the maximum cushion, then it can demand that you pay an additional $21.67 per month (16.67% of $130), making the total escrow payment $151.67 per month.

A common lender error is to miscalculate how much escrow you owe. Watch out also for lender failure to pay your tax or insurance bills promptly.

The exact amount of your escrow payment depends upon the time when each of the escrow bills will need to be paid. For more information on how to calculate the maximum amount your servicer can charge on your escrow account, check the website for the United States Department of Housing and Urban Development (HUD) at www.hud.gov.

Escrow Surplus. If your annual escrow account statement shows that there is a balance in your escrow account ("surplus") from the previous year, you may be entitled to a refund. If the surplus is $50 or more, your servicer must return it to you within thirty days after it prepares the annual escrow statement. If you often get a large refund, this suggests there is a problem with how your servicer is calculating your escrow payment. To avoid being charged too much during the year, you should ask your servicer to correct this problem.

Escrow Shortage or Deficiency. Errors sometimes occur when servicers fail to take into account changes in escrow bills from year-to-year, most often when there have been property tax bill adjustments based on reassessments or tax rate increases. When these changes are significant, your escrow payment may be set too low. However, as long as you are current with your payments, RESPA requires your servicer to pay the escrow bills even if there is not enough money in your escrow account.

The problem is that you are still responsible for paying these bills. Your servicer will include these amounts in your next annual escrow statement as an escrow "shortage" (when your account has a balance smaller than expected) or "deficiency" (when your account has a negative balance because the servicer had to use it own funds to pay an escrow bill). The servicer is required to send you a notice listing any shortage or deficiency amounts, which may be provided as part of the annual escrow statement or sent as a separate letter. The notice must also tell you how your servicer expects you to repay these amounts.

If your account has a shortage that is greater than one month's escrow payment, your servicer must give you twelve months to pay it back in future escrow payments. For example, if your account has a $240 shortage, your new escrow payment will increase by $20 per month for the next year ($240 divided by 12 = $20).

If your account has a deficiency (negative balance), RESPA unfortunately is not that helpful. Your servicer can require you to pay this back in as little as two months, but you can ask for more time. You may have good reason to ask for at least twelve months to repay the deficiency, especially if your servicer caused the deficiency by not updating its escrow records with the correct amounts for your taxes and insurance. Some servicers have a "secret" policy to allow even longer repayment periods, but you will probably need to ask a supervisor in the servicer's escrow or collection department.

Servicer Must Pay Your Taxes and Insurance Promptly. RESPA requires your servicer to pay your taxes, property insurance, and other escrow bills on time, before the deadline for avoiding penalties such as interest or late fees. Some servicers are not careful about making escrow payouts on time. To make matters worse, they may simply pay any extra penalties using your escrow money rather than their own money. You should compare your tax and insurance bills with the actual escrow payouts shown on the annual escrow account statement. If these show that you paid additional interest or late charges because the servicer took too long to pay the bill, you should send the servicer a dispute letter and demand a refund (discussed earlier in this chapter).

If you get a bill for interest or some other penalty from the tax collector's office because your servicer did not pay the taxes on time, you should send this bill to your servicer (keeping a copy) and insist that they pay it with their funds. If something more drastic happens because your servicer did not make timely escrow payouts, such as a tax sale of your home or a loss after your insurance was canceled, you should consult with an attorney about filing a lawsuit against the servicer or servicer. You may be able to recover damages, costs, and the fees you paid to your attorney.

CANCEL UNNECESSARY AND EXPENSIVE INSURANCE

There are several types of insurance related to your mortgage that you may be able to cancel to help reduce your monthly payments. Some of this insurance only protects the lender, not you, and you are always better off cancelling it if you can. Other insurance, such as credit insurance, provides some protection for you, but it is very expensive and there are cheaper alternatives that may offer you even better protection.

Force Placed Insurance. If your mortgage does not have an escrow account, then you are responsible for paying the taxes and insurance on your own. You will need to set aside money each month to help pay these bills. It is very important that you not allow your property insurance to be canceled. Not only does this insurance help protect you from fire and other hazards to your home and possessions, it is required by your mortgage.

If you allow your insurance to be cancelled or do not make sure your lender has proof of your coverage, your servicer will get a new insurance policy that usually protects only the lender's interest. This insurance is called "force placed insurance." It is very expensive (three to four times or more what you would pay on your own) and your servicer will require you to pay for it either in a lump-sum or by adding an amount each month to your mortgage payment.

If you get a notice from your insurance company or servicer stating that you do not have property insurance, you must take this seriously and act immediately. If the servicer made a mistake and you do have insurance, you should still provide the servicer with proof, by giving the servicer the policy number and name of your insurance company or agent. You should also send written proof, such as a summary of the insurance policy (certificate of insurance). You should refuse to pay (or ask for a refund if already paid) any premiums for force placed insurance that the servicer got because of its mistake. For more information on disputing charges, see the earlier section in this chapter.

If your servicer is correct that you do not have insurance, you should get coverage on your own as soon as possible. Once you have your own coverage, you should provide proof to your servicer and request that they cancel any force placed insurance. You should not have to pay for any force placed insurance premiums once you have given the servicer proof of your own insurance coverage, and you may be entitled to a refund for any overlapping coverage when both your policy and the force placed policy were in effect.

Private Mortgage Insurance. If the down payment you made when buying your home was less than twenty percent of the purchase price, you are probably paying for private mortgage insurance (PMI). This insurance protects the lender if there is a default on the mortgage by allowing it to get paid some of the monies not recovered from the foreclosure process. The cost of this insurance is added to your mortgage payment and is handled like payments for taxes and property insurance in an escrow account.

Federal law gives you certain rights to cancel this insurance, and your servicer may agree to cancel it in certain situations even when not required by law. This insurance is expensive and it only protects your lender, so cancelling the insurance will bring down your mortgage payments and not have any downside for you. Doing so can save you hundreds or even thousands of dollars.

Canceling your private mortgage insurance
can save you thousands of dollars and
you will not even lose any protection.

In general, as you bring the balance owed on your mortgage down over time, the lender is more secure in its loan, and will not need the PMI as much to protect its interests. To compute when you cancel this insurance, you need to know two numbers. The first is the value of your home when you first obtained the mortgage. You must use the *lesser* of the original purchase price of your home or its appraised value at the time you got the mortgage.

The second number is the amount of principal still owed on your mortgage. You can get this number by checking your mortgage statements or calling your servicer.

Next figure out what percentage the second number (the amount still owing) is of the first number (the original value of the home). Compute the percentage by doing division and multiplying by 100. For example, if the amount still owed is $80,000 and the original value was $100,000, the percentage is 80%.

If the percentage is 80% or less, and you are current on your payments, you can cancel the PMI by right of federal law. You must make the request in writing to the mortgage lender or servicer. This law does not apply to mortgages made before July 1, 1999 and it does not apply to all mortgages (for example, FHA mortgages are not covered, though FHA has its own rules for cancellation of PMI).

When the percentage gets to 78%, or if you are past the midpoint of your original payment schedule (for example, after seven and a half years on a fifteen-year mortgage), it is the servicer's obligation under federal law (with the same exceptions in the prior paragraph) to cancel it for you. If they did not do it for you at that point, you may be entitled to a refund.

Even if you have an older mortgage or this law does not apply for some other reason, your servicer may be willing to cancel the PMI or your state may have a law that requires it to do so. When you get your percentage down to 80%, always ask your servicer if you can cancel PMI.

You can also try to cancel your PMI even earlier if your home has gone up in value since when you purchased it, and the percentage of what you still owe compared to the *current market value* of your home is 75% or less. You do not have a right to do so under federal law, but some servicers may agree to do so. They will first require an appraisal of your home.

Credit Life and Disability Insurance. If you did not look closely at your loan documents when you bought or refinanced your home, you should check them now to see if you signed up for credit insurance. You can also check your monthly mortgage statements, if your lender sends them, and look for a breakdown of your monthly payment. If some of your payment is going for credit life insurance, you should consider less expensive alternatives. This insurance will pay some or all of the balance owed on your mortgage if you die. It can cost three to four times as much as a term life insurance policy. And the amount credit life insurance pays out as a benefit goes down over time as you pay down the mortgage. You should try to replace credit life with a term life or similar insurance policy.

You may also be paying for credit disability, unemployment, or other types of credit insurance. You should check these policies carefully to figure out exactly what they cover. Once again, you may find less costly options or decide that you do not need the insurance.

DEALING WITH THE SERVICER FROM @#$%

In too many cases, servicers totally fail in their responsibilities, and mess things up so badly that you may find your home being foreclosed even though you are current on your payments. These servicers are eager to be paid for their work, but less eager to actually provide any service. Warning signs of mortgage servicing abuse include:

- Multiple demands for cure amounts that the servicer claims are insufficient after they have been paid by the borrower.
- Inconsistent demand letters.
- Unjustified and unreasonable late fees, interest charges, property inspection fees, property preservation fees, attorney fees, foreclosure expenses, etc.
- Unexplained "corporate advances" and "other fees."
- Unnecessary force placed insurance when the homeowner has coverage.
- Excessive charges for force placed insurance.
- Returned payments.
- Improper posting of payments to a suspense account.
- Late posting and misapplication of payments.
- Failure to make timely payments out of escrow.
- Threatened foreclosure based on non-existent default.
- Failure to provide complete and accurate accounting of charges.
- Failure to provide timely and complete responses to qualified written requests from the homeowner.
- Failure to give the borrower timely notice of a transfer of servicing rights and to properly apply payments during the transfer period.
- Failure to reasonably exhaust loss mitigation options.
- Double-counting of fees in forbearance agreements.
- Failure to honor forbearance agreements.
- Inclusion of waiver of rights clauses in forbearance agreements.
- Unnecessary demands for electronic debit or wire transfers for payments.

If confronted with such a servicer, you must act decisively and aggressively to protect your rights, because servicer ineptitude and greed could even result in your losing your home. The best approach here is to find attorney representation, if possible. Next best would be to find a housing counselor or someone else who can help you straighten out the mess caused by the servicer.

11

Mortgage Workouts

TOPICS COVERED IN THIS CHAPTER

- When You Should and Should Not Negotiate a Workout Agreement
- How to Prepare for the Negotiation, How to Start the Process, What to Ask For, and What It Will Cost You
- What to Do If the Workout Negotiation Is Not Going Well
- Tax and Credit Consequences of Workout Plans
- Special Standards for Workouts for FHA/HUD, VA, and RHS Mortgages

---

One of the most effective ways to prevent foreclosure when you are having trouble making mortgage payments is to see if your lender will agree to a "workout." A workout is a temporary or permanent change to your mortgage terms. There are many types of workouts discussed in this chapter—repayment agreements that let you get caught up over time, loan modifications that reduce your monthly payments, and even arrangements that allow you to sell the house in a more advantageous way than through foreclosure. The lender will not agree to all workout proposals. The key is finding a workout plan that meets your needs and whose obligations you can meet, and which is acceptable to the lender.

Many lenders now realize it is better for them
to accept what you can afford to pay
than to foreclose on your home.

It is not in the lender's self-interest to have large numbers of foreclosures on small properties. After a glut of foreclosures in the late 1980s and early 1990s, lenders were left with the problem of managing large numbers of deteriorating properties. Although some foreclosures were very profitable because lenders purchased property cheaply at foreclosure and then sold it at full fair-market value, large portfolios of foreclosed property generally lost money. Now that this foreclosure crisis is being repeated—only more so—most lenders are now willing to discuss loan workouts to avoid foreclosure. Lenders with government-backed mortgages are required to do so, and this is the policy for most conventional loans as well. The extent to which subprime lenders are willing to offer workouts is a developing story.

THE IMPORTANCE OF GETTING HELP

It is not impossible to try to arrange a workout on your own. If you have a good idea of what you want, an ability to work with numbers, and an aggressive approach, good results are possible. However, arranging workouts is a tricky business. Too often, the lender will have far more information than you about available options. The lender may push you to choose an option that is not what you want or that is really too expensive for your family to afford.

It is a good idea to try to find a nonprofit counselor or a lawyer who has experience with mortgage workouts to help you through the process. Having an advocate will help you get a fair deal by balancing the bargaining power between you and the lender. If you cannot afford or find a lawyer, nonprofit counseling may be a good alternative. You may be able to find a nearby HUD-approved counseling agency with experience doing mortgage loan workouts by calling HUD at 800-569-4287 (TDD 800-877-8339) or by checking its website at www.hud.gov.

Some lenders have also established programs to provide special counseling assistance to homeowners facing foreclosure—usually through local nonprofit organizations. These programs are generally free. Other lenders may offer assistance through a nationwide toll-free telephone hotline. Remember, if you feel more comfortable speaking to a counselor in person, you can ask to be referred to a local housing counseling agency. That agency will also be the most knowledgeable about local programs or sources of funds which may be available to homeowners facing foreclosure.

Counselors in these programs will guide you through the process of presenting an application to the lender for a loan workout or temporary delay of foreclosure. In many cases, counselors will have access to programs and lender personnel that you cannot reach yourself directly. It can't hurt to ask the lender if it has a program for homeowner assistance in your community.

Free foreclosure counseling assistance is especially common for homeowners who bought their homes with the help of first-time homeowner education programs. If you received prepurchase education about homeownership, contact the organization that provided your classes to find out if they also provide foreclosure prevention assistance or can refer you to an organization that does.

You can also call a local nonprofit housing organization and ask if they do foreclosure counseling. Many cities and states are developing programs to assist homeowners in default. Contact your local government housing office or a community group that addresses housing and homeownership to see if they can refer you to a counselor.

If someone unsolicited offers to help, make sure you are dealing with a legitimate nonprofit agency with experience in default and delinquency counseling. Too often, someone who advertises or approaches you about mortgage counseling is really just a con artist who will get you into more trouble.

Whether you go it on your own or with a counselor or lawyer, we recommend reading this chapter carefully, so you understand the process. In addition, a new National Consumer Law Center book, *Foreclosure Prevention Counseling* (2007) is highly recommended. This book is geared to help housing counselors advise consumers on how to obtain a workout. The book goes into much more depth than is possible in this chapter, including how to go about getting a workout and also detailed standards that government-backed lenders, conventional lenders, and subprime lenders use in deciding for what type of workout you qualify.

SHOULD YOU CONSIDER A WORKOUT AND, IF SO, WHEN SHOULD YOU SEEK IT?

For many homeowners facing foreclosure, negotiating a workout is the best strategy for saving their home. But it is not always the best approach for all homeowners and, even when it is, care must be taken to start negotiations with the lender at the best time. This section provides guidelines to help you decide whether and when to start discussions with the lender about a workout agreement.

You Should Determine If You Have Defenses to Repayment. As discussed in Chapters Ten, Twelve and Thirteen, there are some situations in which you have defenses to repayment of a mortgage. You should never agree to repay money that you do not owe unless you can work out a compromise of the amount in dispute or you can obtain an agreement to eliminate the improper charges. You should remember, however, that a lender who took advantage of you in making the original loan also may look for ways to take advantage of you in arranging a workout. You should try to get legal help in this process.

Do Not Initiate a Workout When There Are Other Financial Problems That Are Equally Pressing. A workout does not make sense if you will lose the home anyway because of another mortgage problem which cannot be worked out. You do not want to throw away money on a mortgage workout if you are going to lose your home anyway.

Sometimes, if you have a large number of pressing financial problems, bankruptcy will be a better option than a workout because the bankruptcy process will allow you to deal with all your financial problems at the same time. The bankruptcy option is discussed both in Chapters Twelve and Nineteen.

Do Not Initiate a Workout When It Is Too Late to Finish the Process Before the Sale. If your foreclosure sale is coming up very soon, a workout process can be risky. Workout negotiations almost always take at least thirty days to complete. If you are within thirty days of a scheduled sale date, always obtain a *written* agreement to postpone the sale as one of the first steps in the workout process. Without such an agreement, you will be better off filing bankruptcy since bankruptcy gives you the benefit of an automatic stay of the foreclosure sale.

Start Workout Discussions As Early As Possible. In situations other than those described above, a workout is usually a good approach after you default on a home mortgage. Always begin a workout discussion as early as possible after the default. There are five reasons to start early:

1. It is easier to negotiate a workout before you get too far behind in payments.
2. Starting early avoids the difficulty of negotiating at the last minute with a potential foreclosure sale date pending.
3. You will appear more responsible if you try to prevent the problem from getting out of hand.

4. Beginning early avoids potential foreclosure fees and costs, which can be substantial.

5. It is better to begin negotiations before the lender has turned the matter over to a foreclosure lawyer.

You may also consider starting workout discussions *before* you default on your mortgage. If the default is reasonably foreseeable—for example, if you lost your job and you will not have enough income going forward to make your monthly payment—then the lender may consider restructuring your mortgage to make the payments more affordable. A default may also be foreseeable if you have an adjustable rate mortgage that will reset to an unaffordably higher monthly payment due to an increase in the interest rate. The lender may offer to maintain your interest rate and the current level on a temporary or permanent basis. Some lenders may have to be pushed to consider your workout proposal if you are not currently in default. However, they do have the authority to do a workout if your default is imminent, and in fact, some programs currently being developed by the mortgage industry to assist homeowners will target homeowners who are not yet behind on their mortgage.

As discussed above, when a foreclosure is pending, careful attention must be given to preventing the sale. A foreclosure sale will cut off your ownership, your ability in most cases to cure the default in bankruptcy, and your right to raise most defenses to the validity of the mortgage.

If you are thinking about bankruptcy, workouts should generally be considered prior to filing. Once bankruptcy is filed, lenders may not be willing to negotiate an agreement, or will not offer an agreement better than what you could get in bankruptcy.

TIPS FOR PREPARING FOR A WORKOUT

Gather Information Before You Contact the Lender. An important key to success is preparation. This begins with understanding your own financial situation, how much you can afford to pay on the mortgage, and what you will need to make things work in the long and short term. Throughout the process, remember that no proposed solution makes sense if you cannot really afford it.

Prepare a Reasonable Budget for the Future. You will need to provide detailed information about your debts, assets, income, and expenses.

Realistic income and expense projections are particularly important. You will also need to provide documents such as tax returns which illustrate your financial circumstances.

After gathering this information, you and your family should agree on a strategy before you contact the lender. You should base your strategy on a budget for the future which is as realistic as possible. This budget should detail both your income and expenses. More information about budgeting can be found in Chapter Two.

Re-Examine the Budget to Determine If You Have Any Way to Increase Your Income or Reduce Your Expenses. Ways to reevaluate your budget in times of financial stress are discussed in more detail in Chapter Two. Careful budgeting is important to the workout process for two reasons. First, you may find that you have more (or less) money that you thought to devote to the mortgage. Second, if you are living a luxurious lifestyle, the lender is likely to reject your proposal. Since workout agreements are voluntary alternatives to foreclosure, lenders want to see that homeowners are doing as much as they can to cut back on expenses to concentrate on making the maximum possible mortgage payments.

In setting up your budget, remember your priorities. You should not spend any money, for example, to pay unsecured debts such as credit card and medical bills at the expense of making your mortgage payments. Although you will need to tell the lender about your credit card bills and other debts, you should inform the lender that these creditors will not be paid in any month before the mortgage payment is made. Only food, utilities, necessary current medical expenses (not past-due debts), property insurance, and essential transportation costs should come ahead of the mortgage. Nonessential costs such as private school expenses, charitable contributions, costs of eating out, and entertainment are likely to cause a problem when you are seeking a negotiated agreement from a lender. See Chapters One and Two.

At the same time, you should look at all your expenses, even those for necessities, to see if there are ways to reduce them. There may even be ways to reduce your monthly mortgage payment without a workout. You should also evaluate your income to see if there are options for increasing it.

Seek Out Any Available State or Private Sources of Funds for Foreclosure or Disaster Assistance. In times of foreclosure crises, states sometimes set out special foreclosure assistance funds, that provide low-cost loans to homeowners who are threatened with foreclosure, to help them get caught up on overdue payments and make some future payments. Pennsylvania, Maryland, Connecticut, and New Jersey are states that at least at one time had such programs. Massachusetts and Ohio have recently established programs, and several cities and at least one federal agency are considering implementing similar programs. Check if your state or city presently has such a program.

If you receive a notice about the availability of special assistance with foreclosure, you should apply if you think you have any chance at all of meeting the program's requirements. These programs have early deadlines which you must meet. Failing to meet the deadlines will disqualify you.

There are also a variety of private programs for financial assistance with mortgage payments in different parts of the country. To find out about these programs, you should contact a local nonprofit housing counselor or other specialist. One problem, however, is that some scam artists have learned to design their rip-offs to look like assistance offered by a nonprofit. Before getting into a deal too deeply, investigate to make sure the program is legitimate. Never sign away rights to your home in order to get help.

If the default on your mortgage was caused by a natural disaster (either because it affected your income or required unusual expenses for home repairs), you may be able to obtain state or federal disaster relief. Check with your local government or a local Federal Emergency Management Assistance (FEMA) office. FEMA will publicize a toll-free telephone number in the disaster area. Call that number or visit their local office for information about FEMA's "mortgage assistance program."

Develop a Plan to Deal with Other High-Priority Debt Problems. Workouts on one mortgage will have little benefit when there is no plan in place to deal with other mortgages on the same property or to keep utility services for the residence. Similarly, if you need a car to get to work, you will need a plan to pay those bills to prevent repossession. On the other hand, if a creditor can do little to hurt you (such as credit card debts when you have not been sued), you can plan to pay nothing on those debts until your situation improves. Possible consequences of not paying your unsecured debts are discussed in Chapter Nine.

Prepare a "Hardship" Letter Which Explains Why You Defaulted. One of the things the lender will want is a short letter which explains the reasons why you fell behind in your payments. Sympathetic aspects of your situation should be emphasized and thoroughly explained. The lender may also want documentation on issues which can be verified. For example, the lender may want proof that you have been laid off and have applied for unemployment compensation. Lender representatives are human beings and they will often go farther to assist you if they feel some sympathy for you based on the reasons you fell behind.

Gather Certain Information About the Property and Its Value.
It is also important to obtain information about your property, particularly its condition and its value. You might consider having a broker evaluate it for the purposes of sale. Other potential sources of information about value include what you know about prices of nearby homes that are similar to yours. The lender's willingness to discuss a deal may depend in large part on the real value of the property in the event of foreclosure. Physical problems with the property, including deterioration or liability associated with ownership (such as lead paint liability), make foreclosure a less desirable option for the lender. As discussed below, such information may be an important bargaining chip.

Decide Before You Contact the Lender What You Want and Why You Should Get It.
You should know before you contact the lender what type of workout you need to resolve your situation. A variety of options are discussed below. Think about what you realistically need to make things work.

For example, if you are experiencing a temporary lay-off, you may need only a period of temporary help on mortgage payments. However, if you have a permanent income reduction (because of retirement, for example), you may require a complete loan restructuring. You also may see from the beginning that you have little choice other than to sell your home but need time to arrange a full value sale that will allow you to get your accumulated equity.

In general, the rule is to ask for what you need to make things work out, but not for more than what you need. Lenders will be turned off if you seem too greedy. Where your needs are so unrealistic as to be out of the question for any reasonable lender (if for example, you cannot afford to pay any interest at all), consider the possibility that you need to sell your home before foreclosure rather than lose it involuntarily.

Understand the Details of Your Loan and the Amount of the Default.
An understanding of your existing loan terms and the amount of your default is essential to a workout negotiation. A high interest rate, for example, might be negotiated down to market rates.

Obtaining a breakdown of the default amount from the lender between principal, interest, late charges, insurance escrow, tax escrow, and foreclosure fees will also help. It is easier to negotiate reduction of late charges than reduction of actual costs like property taxes paid by the lender.

Additionally, in some cases, a breakdown of the default amount will reveal that some charges claimed are not proper. For example, the lender may not have credited a payment you know you have made. You may also find that the lender is charging you unreasonable fees and costs associated with default or foreclosure. See Chapter Ten.

HOW TO START THE WORKOUT PROCESS

You should always start the workout process as soon as possible. You need to know about the various parties involved with your mortgage to understand whom you should contact and what that individual's role is in the foreclosure process. There may be a mortgage holder, a mortgage servicer, a foreclosure attorney, and a mortgage insurer all involved with your mortgage. In some cases the mortgage holder has a separate servicer for foreclosures.

Usually, You Do Not Contact the Mortgage Holder. The mortgage holder is the lender who actually owns your mortgage. The mortgage holder is the person or company that has the right to foreclose. Since many mortgages are transferred after you borrow the money, the mortgage holder is not likely to be the bank or mortgage company which made the loan to you originally.

A high percentage of mortgages are now held by investors, including Fannie Mae (the Federal National Mortgage Association) or Freddie Mac (the Federal Home Loan Mortgage Corporation). Other mortgages are gathered together ("pooled") and sold under trust agreements so that the mortgage holder acts as a trustee for a larger group of investors. This process is referred to as "securitization." As described below, you generally do *not* initially contact the mortgage holder directly unless you cannot otherwise get help.

Usually, Contact the Mortgage Servicer First. Although the mortgage holder has the final authority to decide whether to accept a workout, very often some or all of this authority is given to one or more companies that are responsible for dealing directly with customers. The role of servicers is discussed at Chapter Ten.

Sometimes a loan is transferred to a special servicer for the purpose of foreclosure. There is often a lot of confusion when servicing is transferred, although the law requires that you get notice of who is servicing the mortgage and where to send your payments. See Chapter Twelve.

In many cases, the servicer will be an out-of-state company that deals with thousands or hundreds of thousands of mortgages. Fannie Mae, Freddie Mac, and a variety of mortgage holders give their servicers differing amounts of authority to act on their behalf. This authority is spelled out in writing in servicing guides and contracts.

Frequently, the servicer will be the only party with whom you have any contact. Only on investigation will it become apparent that the servicer is acting on another company's behalf. If you request it, the servicer must tell you the name, address, and telephone of the mortgage holder. In addition, servicers are required by Freddie Mac to tell you on their own initiative if Freddie Mac is your mortgage holder.

It is almost always appropriate to begin the workout process with the servicer. The servicer should have workout specialists who will tell you what you need to provide, take your application, and provide information on the normal requirements for a workout. Contact the servicer, explain that you are interested in a loan workout and ask to get any available information packages as well as any forms the lender will want you to submit.

You may want to keep a record of contacts with the servicer, including the names and phone numbers of the people you speak with, as well as a record of what you are told. You should confirm in writing any important communications or decisions, such as an agreement to postpone a foreclosure.

You will rarely have any contact with the mortgage holder. The mortgage holder will rely on the servicer to deal with you directly. So in this chapter, even where we refer to the lender, it will be the servicer who will be communicating any decisions regards workouts, and often the servicer will be the one making decisions.

If You Are Referred to the Foreclosure Attorney. The foreclosure attorney is usually hired by the servicer, although the attorney also works for the mortgage holder. Some servicers will ask you to speak only to their attorney once the legal process of foreclosure has begun. When the servicer tells you to do so, you have little practical alternative.

Although some attorneys will readily participate in workout discussions or give you permission to speak with their client directly, others will need to be pushed. Unresponsive attorneys should be reported to the servicer or to the mortgage holder if necessary.

You Should Also Contact Any Mortgage Insurer. Mortgage insurance is increasingly common in residential mortgage transactions. It is referred to as "private mortgage insurance" (PMI) and is different than property insurance because it protects the mortgage holder from losses if you default on the mortgage. If your down payment was less than 20% of the purchase price, private mortgage insurance was probably required. In other cases, mortgages are insured by the federal government (FHA, RHS (formerly FmHA), or the Department of Veterans Affairs) or by a state housing finance agency.

If you default and your property is sold, the mortgage insurer generally will pay the mortgage holder part of your debt not recovered in the foreclosure process. The good news is that mortgage insurers realize they have an interest in preventing foreclosure in many cases. They will sometimes step in to insist that the mortgage holder accept proposed workout terms. Alternatively, they may agree to pay a small arrearage (or part of it) or provide other limited relief in order to help you keep your home. They do so in order to prevent a potential larger loss in the event of foreclosure.

If you are paying for private mortgage insurance, it is a good idea to find out the name of the insurer and to send them copies of anything you send to the lender to keep them informed of the progress of workout negotiations. The name of the mortgage insurer should not be kept secret from you; you are the one paying for the mortgage insurance. Check your original mortgage documents or ask the lender. Even if the mortgage insurer is not willing to participate in the workout discussions, keeping them informed will keep the mortgage holder and servicer on their best behavior.

HUD, VA, and RHS (formerly FmHA) Guaranteed Mortgages. If your mortgage is insured (guaranteed) by a federal or state funded entity, the lender may be subject to special servicing requirements designed to help you avoid foreclosure. Check your loan papers. HUD (FHA insured mortgages), the Department of Veterans Affairs (VA), and the Rural Housing Service (RHS) (formerly the Farmers Home Administration (FmHA)) have substantial programs to avoid foreclosures. These are described briefly at the end of this chapter, but are presented in more detail in a new National Consumer Law Center book, *Foreclosure Prevention Counseling*. These programs are often similar to, but in some respects better than workouts offered for conventional loans.

Make Partial Payments on Your Mortgage If the Lender Will Accept Them. If you can afford to make partial payments on your mortgage and want to try to arrange a workout, you should start submitting partial payments to the lender. You can then try to formalize partial payments under a workout plan. Keep a careful record of any partial payments you send so that you can check later that they have been credited properly.

If the Lender Refuses Partial Payment. The lender may have no obligation to accept partial payments and your payments may be returned to you. If payments are returned to you, it is crucial to save this money (as well as to continue to put aside as much as possible) while you are attempting to arrange a workout agreement.

If possible, any funds saved should be placed in a special account. At a minimum, they should be placed in a savings account which earns interest. You should resist the temptation to dip into these funds as other financial problems come up.

Many lenders will provide much more favorable workout terms if you have a lump sum saved to help you get caught up on the default. Over a period of time, the lender's incentive to agree to a workout may increase based on a lump sum, even if you are actually further behind.

If a workout is arranged, you will pay this savings to the lender to reduce your future obligations on the mortgage. If a workout is not possible, you can use the money to move.

The Workout Application Process. Different lenders have different workout application processes and forms. Every lender will require you to provide financial information about your debts, assets, income, and expenses with appropriate verification. You will also need to submit a hardship letter explaining your reasons for default. Many lenders require a property appraisal and/or a credit report. It is usually a good idea to get any necessary forms from the lender and an understanding of what kind of supporting information will be required prior to submitting a workout application. Otherwise you may have to submit an application twice. In general, you should always confirm with the lender that your application package is complete and that they have all the information necessary to make a decision regarding your workout.

Your income is usually verified by documents such as pay stubs, unemployment compensation award letters, and back-tax forms. You may have to submit verification of your expenses as well, such as utility bills, tax payments, and other fixed costs of homeownership. Since a workout involves giving you a second chance on a defaulted loan, it is not unreasonable for the lender to expect information similar to that required for qualifying for a mortgage. Additionally, it is not unfair for a lender whose collateral is at risk to want an appraisal or, at minimum, a property inspection.

The application form may not have a space to describe what workout terms you are seeking. If it does not, you should include your request in the hardship letter or in a cover letter to the application. You should also explain the reasons you have for making your proposal.

Once the application is made, you may have to follow up with the lender. It is not uncommon for applications to be swallowed up. It is a good idea to find out who has the application at any given time (as well as the name of that person's supervisor) and to make polite but regular follow-up phone calls. Some give-and-take may be required. Remember that proposals are subject to a negotiation process.

WHAT TO ASK FOR IN A WORKOUT

General Considerations. The most important part of a workout negotiation may be deciding what terms to request from the servicer or lender. There are a variety of workout terms available and servicers use all kinds of different names for their workout programs. Try using the names for workouts used here. You may need to offer a further explanation if the lender does not understand what you are talking about.

You should always propose workout terms that are sufficient to address the problem which caused your default. There is little value to you or the lender in negotiating terms which, if accepted, will not resolve your problems for both the long and short term. For negotiating purposes, you might consider asking for a little more than you need at the outset in order to get to an agreement you can live with.

This section includes a variety of different potential workout options. Some servicers or lenders may not offer each of these options, while others may offer options which are not listed here. The rule of thumb is to ask for what you want. Do not assume a particular option is not available.

It may also be necessary to use a combination of options. For example, if you are currently unemployed but you have found a lower paying job which will not start for three months, you may need a temporary moratorium on payments and a permanent interest rate reduction. All of these options are discussed in more detail below.

Request a Delay of Any Impending Foreclosure Sale. At the outset, the most important request may be for a delay of the foreclosure sale process long enough to make a workout application. A completed foreclosure sale will generally cut off all workout possibilities (although there are some exceptions).

You should always request a delay when a scheduled sale is less than thirty days away. If the sale is not yet scheduled or if it is more than thirty days away, you usually have time to complete a workout negotiation before the sale is held. Nevertheless, it is important to keep track. When you get inside the thirty-day window, ask for a postponement of the sale.

A request for delay is more likely to be granted when you provide preliminary information about your circumstances and your ability to make a reasonable workout proposal. For example, if you have recently returned to work, documentation of employment would usually justify postponing a sale. Similarly, an offer of partial payment may help delay the sale for several months.

Servicers have different approaches to handling requests for delay. Some may not agree to a delay until the sale date is fairly close. One pitfall to avoid is leaving the decision to grant a delay in the lender's hands to the very last minute. The risk is that you will assume that the application is being acted upon even if it is not, and you will lose the opportunity to pursue other strategies prior to sale.

When you request a delay well before the foreclosure, try to obtain a response to your request at least seven days before the foreclosure sale date. If not, this is a good indication that the lender is not really serious about negotiating a workout. When you receive an agreement to delay a sale, you must get it in writing. In most cases, it is sufficient if the lender puts the agreement in a letter to you. But, if the foreclosure sale is a court-supervised process, you should make sure that you meet the appropriate procedural requirements to delay the sale—including notice to the court. These will vary from state to state. Whatever the process, it is a good idea to verify that the sale is actually canceled.

Be careful that your home is not foreclosed while you are waiting to finalize your workout agreement.

If there is no sale date or if that date is a long way off when you begin workout negotiations, it is still important to keep an eye on the sale process. It is not unheard of for a property to be sold while a workout application is pending.

Traditional Payment Agreements. A payment agreement (or "forbearance agreement," "reinstatement agreement," or "deferral agreement") involves curing a default by making regular monthly mortgage payments as they are due together with partial monthly payment on the arrears (past-due amount). A typical agreement might call for making one-and-a-quarter monthly payments until the default is resolved. For example, if your regular payment is $600 per month and you are 3 months behind, the agreement might have you pay off the arrears of $1,800 by making payments of $750 ($600 regular payment + $150 for arrears) for 12 months. Most lenders used to limit payment agreements to no more than one year for reinstatement. Agreements longer than one year and up to thirty-six months are now more common.

This type of agreement is most similar to a cure of arrears that you would get in a chapter 13 bankruptcy. It may be easier to negotiate than other workouts because most servicers have authority to approve payment agreements without first checking with the mortgage holder.

You are most likely to benefit from this traditional payment agreement if you have experienced temporary financial difficulties which are now resolved. You need to have some excess income in your budget to commit to the mortgage beyond the regular monthly payment.

EXAMPLE OF A PAYMENT AGREEMENT

Mr. and Ms. Smith are three months behind on their monthly mortgage payment because Ms. Smith lost her job. Ms. Smith has now returned to work so the family budget is more flexible, but not flexible enough to get caught up by paying a lump sum.

Step 1: How much are the Smiths in the hole?
Their monthly mortgage payment is $1,000
They have missed 3 payments for a total of $3,000
The lender has pre-foreclosure court costs (the Smiths
may need to check with the lender about costs) $600
Total Amount the Smiths are Behind **$3,600**

Step 2: How much will it cost each month for the Smiths to get caught up?
Over One Year:
       Total delinquency ($3,600) divided by 12 months $300

Over Two Years:
Total delinquency ($3,600) divided by 24 months $150
Over Three Years:
Total delinquency ($3,600) divided by 36 months $100

Step 3: What will the Smiths total payment be while they get caught up?
They will need to make their regular payment each month $1,000
Together with a payment to cure the delinquency:
One-year cure (total payment) $1,300
Two-year cure (total payment) $1,150
Three-Year cure (total payment) $1,100

Step 4: The Smiths must return to their budget to determine which plan they can afford. If the plan they need is longer than one year, they will need to provide information to the lender that establishes that they cannot get caught up over a shorter period.

One problem with this type of arrangement is that you may fail to account for the extra initial expenses associated with recovery from temporary financial difficulties. Homeowners often have substantial budgetary pressures for several months after dealing with a temporary financial problem. Other bills including utilities may have fallen into arrears and expenses such as urgent clothing needs for children may have been deferred. The agreement must realistically take these expenses into account—perhaps by proposing graduated payments on the delinquency at the beginning of the workout plan.

Temporary Interest Rate Reduction. You may want to seek a temporary interest rate reduction if your financial problems are likely to last for a limited period of time but you cannot presently meet your mortgage payments. You generally must have a reasonable plan for increasing your income so that you can make full payments by a certain date.

The theory behind a temporary interest rate reduction is that, if you get help by lowering payments in the short term, you will be able to keep from falling further behind while waiting, for example, for a recall from a lay-off. Some lenders want assurance that, if you can't return to paying the full rate within a reasonable time, they will then be allowed to go forward with the foreclosure.

Typically, rates can be reduced fairly easily to the market rate of interest or, with a good reason, below market. You should make certain that any temporary interest rate reduction agreement does not just lower your payments but actually lowers the interest rate used to compute the outstanding principal. Otherwise, the lender may add the interest you have been forgiven back into the loan amount you have to eventually repay.

Recasting of Missed Payments. Another form of temporary mortgage relief is known as "recasting" or "deferral." Recasting involves excusing your present obligation to catch up on missed payments, and instead delaying your obligation to make those payments until the end of the loan term. This allows you to start making your regular monthly payments again, without having to immediately address the problem of your back-due payments. It is ideal for those whose financial situation has improved enough to start making regular mortgage payments but not enough to allow them to get caught up on their mortgage default.

This option is becoming increasingly rare because lenders are often unwilling to make the necessary accounting changes on a temporary basis. When recasting is available, lenders are much more willing to recast payments you have already missed than to recast payments not yet due. In addition, most lenders are unwilling to recast more than six past-due monthly payments.

Permanent Modification of Loan Terms. In some cases, lenders will agree to permanent changes in loan terms, such as permanent interest rate reduction, extension of the loan's payment period, reamortization, capitalization of arrears, cancellation of principal, or some combination of these. An agreement of this type occurs most frequently when you can no longer afford the original loan terms due to a permanent change in your circumstances (for example, your retirement or death of a spouse), and it is not in the lender's financial interest to foreclose. These types of agreements are usually called "loan modifications." Some lenders may use the terms "loan refinance" or "note change."

The lender generally does not have a financial interest to foreclose when a forced sale of your home will bring in significantly less than what you owe. This might occur where your property's value has gone down since taking out the mortgage, where lead paint or other hazards may create liabilities for someone foreclosing on the property, where you have a large, senior mortgage with another lender, or where the property is unmarketable for some reason.

A loan modification may also be available if you have legal claims or other leverage to exchange for the change in loan terms. As discussed briefly below, you also may achieve the same change in loan terms by a complete refinancing with a new lender. There are at least five ways to permanently change the loan terms:

EXAMPLE OF A WORKOUT PLAN THAT EXTENDS THE LOAN TERM, REAMORTIZES, AND CAPITALIZES ARREARS

Ms. Jones is five months behind on her mortgage payments after an expensive divorce. She has found a higher paying job, but her income will still be less than the total household pre-divorce income.

Step One: What is the current situation?

Total principal now owed to pay off the debt
    (based on original balance of $120,000) $96,000
Back-due interest $3,400
Pre-foreclosure costs $600
Total Amount Owed $100,000
Interest Rate 8%
Current Monthly Payment (without escrow) $880.50
Total Delinquency (5 monthly payments = 5 x $880.50)
    (without escrow) $4,402.50
Months remaining in loan term (out of original 360) 240

Step Two: What would this loan cost if the lender agrees to extend the loan for another thirty years (360 months), and also reamortizes the loan and capitalizes the arrears?

New (modified) loan amount (same as Total Amount Owed Above) $100,000
Months in Modified Loan Term 360
Interest Rate (same as above in this example) 8%
New Monthly Payment (without escrow) $733.75

The advantage of this plan is that Ms. Jones would save approximately $150 each month. She also would not have to arrange to pay the delinquent payments separately, since these amounts are part of the new total loan amount on which interest is calculated.

Step 3: Ms. Jones must return to her budget. She must determine whether she can afford the payments necessary to get caught up in this way. To determine whether the plan is affordable, Ms. Jones will have to budget for the new monthly payment and for any fixed monthly payment (of escrow) to the lender for taxes and insurance. These charges cannot be modified. If taxes and insurance are not paid to the lender under an escrow account, these charges must be listed separately in a monthly budget.

---

1. Interest Rate Reductions. The most common scenario for a permanent interest rate reduction is when the existing rate is above market and is permanently unaffordable due to financial hardship. The lender recomputes the loan payments based on the lower interest rate, resulting in a lower monthly payment. In some cases, this may involve converting your variable-rate to a fixed-rate loan or vice versa. For example, if your adjustable rate mortgage is about to reset and you are unable to make the higher monthly payment, the lender may agree to permanently convert your loan to a fixed-rate mortgage using the initial introductory interest rate or the market rate. The lender may recognize that, if it forecloses on the property and then makes a loan on the property to sell it to someone else, it can obtain no more than the market rate of interest. Some lenders will allow a combination of temporary and permanent rate reductions. A lender may temporarily reduce your interest rate to a below-market rate and then, at some point in the future, raise it back to a market rate. This is sometimes called a "step-up" plan.

2. Extension of the Loan Payment Period. An extension of the loan payment period is a change in the loan term which helps some homeowners by allowing them to repay the principal over a longer term, thereby reducing the monthly payment. For example, an older homeowner who borrowed $100,000 in 1985 on a thirty-year mortgage might owe only $20,000 today. Payments might be $750 monthly based on the original note. By extending the term back to thirty years on the $20,000 balance, and reamortizing the loan over the longer payment period, the monthly payments can be reduced to $175 dollars (even if there is a slight change in interest rate). The lender does not lose out as long as the rate is at least as high as the market rate because the entire current principal will be repaid with the applicable interest.

3. Capitalization of Arrears. When arrears are "capitalized," the past-due amount is added to the principal balance before the interest rate is applied and the payment is recalculated, to come up with a new fixed monthly payment over the remainder of the loan. The theory behind this is that the arrears are owed anyway. It is easier to repay them over the remaining length of the loan rather than in a lump sum or even in monthly payments over a few years. In most cases in which there has been a default, "capitalization of arrears" will also be necessary in connection with any other reamortization that the lender has agreed to do.

Capitalizing the arrears, even without extending the period or changing the interest rate, may help you because it lets you spread out whatever payments you have missed over the remaining term of the loan while canceling your arrears. If the lender does not agree to adjust the loan interest rate, term or principal, your monthly payments will go up slightly. If reamortization is combined with an interest rate reduction, an extension of the term of the loan, or a cancellation of a part of the principal, your monthly payments may go down significantly, even though your total outstanding balance is higher. See example on previous page.

4. Reduction of Principal Balance. A reduction of principal balance may be available in some cases where the loan amount is more than the value of your home because reasons beyond your control have lowered its value. You may also be able to reduce your principal balance if you have legal claims against your lender. The lender recognizes that it is better to receive mortgage payments on a lower principal than to foreclose on property worth far less than the amount of the mortgage. Most lenders will require an appraisal of your home before considering an agreement to modify the principal. Once your principal is reduced, if the loan is reamortized, your payments will be lower.

5. *Deferred Junior Mortgages.* Some lenders will only reduce their principal if they are allowed to keep a "deferred junior mortgage" (also called a "silent second mortgage") in the amount that the principal is reduced. For example, if your principal balance is lowered by $20,000, the lender would ask for a second mortgage for $20,000, which you do not have to pay immediately. This junior mortgage protects the lender in the event that the property value later goes up. Deferred junior mortgages typically require you to pay the principal on that mortgage only if you transfer your home to someone else. Granting the lender such a junior mortgage may be a bargaining chip to obtain a modification involving reduction of principal.

Other Creative Workout Terms. Some servicers or lenders will consider other offers of workouts involving temporary or permanent relief, even if they are highly creative. Some examples include making a home equity loan for emergency home repairs (particularly if your failure to make the repairs will reduce the value of your home and thus the lender's mortgage), cancellation of arrears, or substitution or surrender of other property in exchange for a modification. However, some lenders may be uninterested if the proposal is too complicated.

Pre-Sales for More Than You Owe the Lender. A pre-sale is a sale or transfer of your home in lieu of a foreclosure. Some lenders also refer to deeds in lieu of foreclosure and refinancings by third-party lenders (discussed below) as pre-sales.

In many cases, it is in your interest to sell the property rather than to have it foreclosed, since the property is likely to sell for a higher price through a realtor than in the foreclosure process. This is especially true if you have substantial equity and little likelihood of being able to afford reinstatement through a payment plan or modification of your loan.

The biggest potential problem in arranging a pre-sale is time. If you decide it is in your interests to sell the property, you should list it for sale with a realtor immediately. You must complete your pre-sale before the lender holds a foreclosure sale.

In some cases you will want to ask the lender for a short delay in the foreclosure sale process to give you an opportunity to complete a pending sale. This will usually be approved only when you can show the lender that you have made substantial progress toward a sale which will pay off the loan balance in full. Many lenders will not consider a pre-sale arrangement as grounds to postpone a foreclosure sale until you find a buyer and sign a "purchase and sale" agreement.

When you have equity in your home because the pre-sale price exceeds the amount owed the lender plus the costs of sale, you get to keep your equity from the sale proceeds after paying off the lender and your costs. But remember, you will have to pay off not only the first mortgage but also other liens and mortgages, if any, or your sale will not go through.

Short Sales. Some lenders, particularly in a depressed real estate market, will agree to let you sell your home through a realtor rather than a foreclosure sale, and will agree to cancel all or almost all of what you owe after the lender receives the sale proceeds, even if the sale proceeds will not cover the amount due on the mortgage. This is called a "short" sale. A short sale may help the lender avoid additional foreclosure costs which cannot be recouped in the foreclosure sale process. It allows you to pay as much of the loan as possible by selling your home. It also avoids a foreclosure notation on your credit report.

You will always need to get agreement from the lender if you want to sell your property in a short-sale situation. The lender will want to make sure that you are obtaining the best price possible because, the higher the price, the more of the amount you owe is paid. At the time of an agreement for a short sale, make sure you also get an agreement in writing that the lender will not seek payment on the balance of the debt (cancel any deficiency). Realtors, particularly those who have experience dealing with a particular lender, may be able to help you convince the lender to agree to a short sale. The realtor's incentive is the commission on the sale.

In some cases, the lender will insist that you make a cash contribution to any deficiency because it thinks you can afford to do so. This is negotiable. Explain the financial difficulties you are in and the purposes for which you have set aside any available savings.

A short sale is not a miracle cure. You are losing your home just as you would if a foreclosure was completed. What you get is freedom from worry about being sued to cover the deficiency and perhaps a slightly improved credit record for the future. (Although there will be no foreclosure notation, the sale will be reported to the credit bureaus as a "short sale" and the fact that you missed monthly payments will also appear on your credit record.) In rare cases, if the lender thinks the price is high enough or if you can show hardship, it may agree to let you have between $500 and $2,000 from the sale proceeds to help you move. It can't hurt to ask.

Mortgage Assumptions and Other Transfers. Some mortgages can be assumed (taken over) by a third party. When a mortgage is assumable, the property can be transferred, and the person to whom it is transferred can pick up the payments on the mortgage. If payments were behind when the mortgage was assumed, absent a workout agreement, the person assuming the mortgage will be in default and subject to foreclosure. The advantage may be that the assuming party is in a better position to deal with the default than you.

A mortgage is always assumable if the contract documents say it is or, in most states, if the documents are silent on this issue. Other mortgages contain a "due on sale" provision, which is a clause specifying that transfer of the property creates a default. There are a number of situations in which assumption can take place despite attempts by the lender to enforce a due on sale provision. For example, lenders cannot block a transfer from parent to child or from one spouse to another.

Your lender may let another person assume your mortgage even if your loan documents say otherwise.

Even if a mortgage is not assumable, lenders will sometimes agree to what are usually called "delinquent assumptions" so that they can start getting payments from someone. If you want to transfer the property to someone who can better afford the mortgage payments, it does not hurt to ask the mortgage company for permission.

MODIFICATION FEES, FORECLOSURE FEES, AND LATE CHARGES

Many lenders charge a modification fee for handling workout applications. Some want this fee at the beginning of the workout process regardless of the application's outcome. Fees can run as high as $750 or more plus costs. There are a number of approaches you can take in dealing with this request. One approach is simply agreeing to pay the fee, which may be a small price to pay for an agreement to lower the interest rate or to make serious modifications to your mortgage.

Where possible, however, you should try to minimize your modification fees. Request a waiver or a fee reduction to make the modification affordable. Remember that a modification can sometimes save the lender thousands of dollars in foreclosure fees, loss of principal, and resale costs after foreclosure. In some cases a mortgage insurer will agree to step in and pay the fee or pressure the lender to waive it.

The lender's out-of-pocket costs to modify your mortgage, such as appraisal fees and credit report charges, probably will not be waived. However, these fees should be examined to make sure that they are reasonable. If the fees exceed $200–300, they should be reduced. You can also request an agreement to pay some or all of the modification fees in installments or to have the fee lumped together with the loan balance if your workout is a modification involving capitalization.

Related problems arise when the lender has already begun to incur foreclosure fees and costs when you request a workout. The lender will expect reimbursement from you for these fees and costs. These should be reviewed to make sure that they are legitimate and reasonable. They should be minimized whenever possible. A typical problem arises when you are required to pay for an attorney's retainer for foreclosure and the foreclosure does not take place due to your workout agreement. These fees should then be credited back to your account. Refunds or credits for fees paid to auctioneers, sheriffs or court officials, or for legal advertisements, should also be made depending upon when the foreclosure sale is canceled. To the extent foreclosure fees and costs are valid, they need to be paid or otherwise accounted for in the modification process.

Late charges will often be waived if you ask, especially if it is necessary to the success of a workout agreement. You should push for waiver of late charges whenever possible.

DOCUMENTING A WORKOUT AGREEMENT

The lender generally has forms that it requires for finalizing a workout agreement. These should be reviewed carefully to make sure they are consistent with the agreement.

Even if there is a delay in signing the forms for the workout, you should make sure that the basic terms of the agreement are spelled out in writing. If a sale needs to be postponed while you are finalizing the agreement, make sure postponement takes place and make sure that you have a record in writing. A trained professional can be very helpful in this part of the process.

Many workout forms include an agreement under which you give up all legal claims that you may have against the lender. You should never sign that type of agreement (which may be labeled "release") until the actual workout agreement is finalized because, if you do not complete a workout agreement, you may want to pursue other legal remedies. Once a workout agreement is reached, it may make sense to give up your legal claims as part of the final agreement, but you should first try to convince the lender to take the release provision out of the workout agreement. If the workout was intended to deal only with your default and did not include negotiation of any legal claims you have against the lender, you should tell the lender that the release is unreasonable. If the lender will not take out the release and you believe you may have legal claims against the lender, you should not sign the release without first consulting with an attorney.

To complete a workout agreement, you should make sure all the forms are properly signed by the lender and recorded, if necessary, with the mortgage in the property registry.

IF YOUR WORKOUT NEGOTIATION IS NOT GOING WELL

Appeals to Higher Ups. If you feel you aren't receiving sufficient cooperation in negotiating a workout agreement, ask to speak to a supervisor. It is also appropriate to go over the head of the loan servicer and complain directly to the mortgage holder or mortgage insurer. Fannie Mae, Freddie Mac, and some institutional investors have "loss-mitigation" departments which will intervene, if pushed, to address a proposed workout. The applicable Fannie Mae offices are regional. Freddie Mac's loss mitigation is done on a national basis. If you are having a problem with the servicer, it is a good idea to learn the location of the mortgage holder's office and to find a person in that office to call or write with specific complaints about the servicer's conduct. It is best to ask to speak with someone in "loss mitigation" or "workouts."

Who to Contact at Fannie Mae and Freddie Mac. Fannie Mae's customer service number is 800-7-FANNIE and its home office can be reached at 202-752-7000. Usually, though, you should try to contact the regional office where the mortgage servicer is located (not the regional office near where you live):

- The Midwestern Regional Office, 312-368-6200, serves Illinois, Indiana, Iowa, Michigan, Minnesota, Nebraska, North Dakota, Ohio, South Dakota, and Wisconsin;
- The Northeastern Regional Office, 215-575-1400, serves Connecticut, Delaware, Maine, Massachusetts, New Hampshire, New Jersey, New York, Pennsylvania, Puerto Rico, Rhode Island, Vermont, and the Virgin Islands;
- The Southeastern Regional Office, 404-398-6000, serves Alabama, District of Columbia, Florida, Georgia, Kentucky, Maryland, Mississippi, North Carolina, South Carolina, Tennessee, Virginia, and West Virginia;
- The Southwestern Regional Office, 972-773-HOME (4663), serves Arizona, Arkansas, Colorado, Kansas, Louisiana, Missouri, New Mexico, Oklahoma, Texas, and Utah; and
- The Western Regional Office, 626-396-5100, serves Alaska, California, Guam, Hawaii, Idaho, Montana, Nevada, Oregon, Washington, and Wyoming.

To lodge a complaint about a Freddie Mac servicer, it is necessary to call 800-FREDDIE and access the customer service representative from the initial menu. Ask the customer service representative for the name and number of someone in the loss mitigation department who can review your workout proposal.

Refinancing with Another Lender. If your existing home mortgage lender will not agree to a reasonable workout, consider refinancing your existing mortgage with a new lender. If your existing mortgage is at a high interest rate, refinancing at a lower interest rate and/or with a longer payment period can greatly reduce your monthly payments and bring the payments within reach. Similarly, if the new loan is significantly longer than the remaining term of your existing mortgage, this will bring payments down, because the loan will be amortized over more years.

Refinancing a low-interest first mortgage and high-interest second mortgage into a single low-interest first mortgage can also reduce payments. For example, a family with a twenty-five-year, $10,000 first mortgage at 8% interest and a fifteen-year, $30,000 second mortgage at 18% interest has combined monthly payments of $560.31. Refinancing what is left owing on those two mortgages with a twenty-five-year, $30,000 first mortgage at 10% will result in new monthly payments of $272.61. This is $287.70 per month less.

On the other hand, many refinancing schemes are frauds. Even legitimate refinancing options that look helpful may, on closer inspection, be far more costly than the existing mortgage. Whatever choice you make about refinancing, it is never a good idea to pay off other presently unsecured debts with a debt secured by a mortgage. It is essential that you carefully review Chapter Six to decide whether refinancing makes sense.

If you decide in favor of refinancing, you should make every effort to obtain a loan at a reasonable rate, usually from a savings bank, a commercial bank, a credit union, or a legitimate mortgage company. Most finance companies and certain mortgage companies do not make residential loans at reasonable rates and terms.

You should *not* assume that legitimate lenders with low interest rates will turn you down because you are in financial distress. Only by applying can you determine the availability of a loan from a particular lender. Chapter Three sets out guidelines that mortgage lenders may utilize in reviewing your credit rating in conjunction with a mortgage application.

When applying for a residential loan you should present your financial problems in the best possible light. The presentation should show how the problems are being solved and how refinancing will provide substantially lower payments. You should stress your past financial, residential, and employment stability, and indicate your plans for the future.

If your application is rejected, you should obtain the reasons for the rejection and determine whether the reasons are legitimate. You should try to cure any problems so that the next application will be successful. Your rights under federal law to be notified as to the reasons for your rejection are detailed in National Consumer Law Center's *Credit Discrimination* (4th ed. 2005 and Supp.).

Some lenders actively solicit financially distressed families for refinancing loans by phone or mail. Usually the terms of their loans are not just unfavorable but disastrous. In general, avoid such offers unless reviewed by a counselor, lawyer, or accountant you trust.

Refinancing with a Reverse Mortgage. If you are an older homeowner (usually over sixty-two years old) and workout negotiations do not seem to be working, another possibility is to refinance with a reverse mortgage. You will only qualify if you have lots of equity in your home (that is, the home is worth a lot more than the mortgage payout). A reverse mortgage pays off your existing mortgage, may even provide you will additional monthly payments, and lets you keep the home without any mortgage payments until you sell the home, move out, or are deceased. At that point, the home will be sold and much if not all of those proceeds will go to pay off the reverse mortgage loan.

The most popular reverse mortgages are insured by the Federal Housing Administration under its Home Equity Conversion Mortgage (HECM) program. To obtain a HECM mortgage, you will need counseling from an agency certified by the U.S. Department of Housing and Urban Development (HUD). Call HUD at 1-800-569-4287 or go to www.hud.gov/offices/hsg/sfh/hecm/hecmlist.cfm. Plus it is a good idea to get counseling before you take out any type of reverse mortgage—there are lots of pitfalls to reverse mortgages in general and those offered by certain unscrupulous lenders in particular. The HUD counseling is free, even if you are not seeking a HECM reverse mortgage. Never agree to pay someone to give you advice on a reverse mortgage, since you can get probably better advice from a HUD counselor for free.

Deeds in Lieu of Foreclosure. If a lender will not agree to a workout, it may consider taking your deed "in lieu of foreclosure." That is, you voluntarily turn over your home to the lender as an alternative to foreclosure. Lenders will not be interested in deeds in lieu if there are junior mortgages or other junior liens on your home because, in that case, foreclosure is necessary for the lender to obtain clear title to your home.

Deeds in lieu are usually, but not always, a bad idea. A deed in lieu of foreclosure will voluntarily terminate your ownership. You should not agree to a deed in lieu unless the lender agrees to something in exchange for the deed in lieu agreement, such as eliminating a negative credit reference or giving you an extra period of time to remain in the property before eviction. Some lenders will even agree to pay a small amount of cash (under $2,000) for a deed in lieu to help you move. The lender may agree to these terms in order to save the time and expense of foreclosure. If you do decide to give a lender a deed in lieu of foreclosure, be sure to get the agreement in writing, including anything the lender agrees to give you in exchange for the deed.

Deeds in lieu are almost always a poor choice if you have significant equity in the property. The only way to get that equity is through a sale, perhaps even a foreclosure sale. If you give a deed in lieu, you cannot get cash back from the lender's sale of the property.

TAX CONSEQUENCES OF SHORT SALES AND WORKOUT PLANS

Some workout plans and almost all short sales involve an agreement by the lender to cancel some part of your debt. Cancellation of a debt can have tax consequences, although in many cases you will not owe taxes, you will just be required to properly complete certain tax forms. In general, the IRS treats a loan as income to you which is offset by the obligation to repay, so that no tax is owed. If you are forgiven from repaying some or all of the debt, the IRS may treat the amount forgiven as taxable income in the year in which the forgiveness takes place. This is true for other types of debts that might also be forgiven, such as credit card debt.

Some lenders file a 1099C form with the IRS any time they agree to cancel or forgive a debt. You should get a copy of this form from the lender when it is filed. You should not ignore this 1099C. The IRS also gets a copy of the 1099C and will charge you a penalty for not paying the taxes on the amount the lender forgave if you do not file. Even if you do not get a 1099C, you are still supposed to report the discharged debt to the IRS. You will have to file a long form 1040 tax return. You report the discharged debt to the IRS on Form 982.

You can attach to Form 982 an explanation of why the discharged debt should not count as income. There are two common situations when the IRS will not count the discharged debt as income, as long as you let the IRS know which of these situations apply to you. The first of these only recently became available to you because of a new law passed in December 2007.

This first situation where you can exclude forgiven debt from your taxable income is an important one. It excludes from your income debt incurred to purchase your home, even if you later refinanced. This excluded forgiven debt is called "qualified principle residence indebtedness." This exclusion does not apply to loans you took out to refinance any debt other than your mortgage, but it may apply in some cases if you took out a loan to do home improvements.

The other situation where you can exclude from your taxable income forgiven debt is equally important. You can exclude forgiven debt to the extent to which you were insolvent at the time the debt was forgiven.

To establish insolvency, you need to send the IRS a statement concerning the discharged debt listed on the 1099C form together with a list which shows that, at the time of forgiveness, you had more debts (including the forgiven debt) than assets. All debts and assets must be listed. Even if you were only partially insolvent, the discharged debt will be excluded from income to the extent you were insolvent.

To figure out how much of the discharged debt can be excluded from income due to insolvency, subtract your debts from your assets. If you subtract your debts from your assets and you get a negative number, you were insolvent. If so, subtract the amount by which you were insolvent (converted to a positive number) from the amount of your forgiven debt. If you still get a negative number or zero, then none of the forgiven debt counts as taxable income. If the amount is more than zero, that amount may be taxable income.

There are other situations where forgiven debt should not be counted as income. For example, in most consumer transactions, only principal amounts canceled should be counted as income. Canceled interest and fees are generally not counted as income. There are other exceptions as well. Because these tax issues are complicated, you may want help from a qualified tax professional.

CALCULATING TAX ON FORGIVEN DEBT

Example 1: Purchase Money Mortgage: Mr. and Mrs. Green buy a house with a mortgage for $120,000. The house is only worth $100,000. After a new appraisal, the bank agrees to reduce their mortgage principal balance from $120,000 to $100,000. The Greens have no other debts.

Since the entire debt was used to acquire the house, any amount forgiven is qualified principal residence indebtedness and excluded from income. The qualified principal residence indebtedness is the full amount of the debt discharged, $20,000. The Greens do not owe tax on any of the amount discharged. The Greens must still file a tax return and explain the situation to the IRS.

Example 2: House Sale and the Insolvency Exception: Mr. and Ms. Brown owed $120,000. They bought the house many years ago and have refinanced several times. They sold the property for $100,000 and the bank canceled the balance.

The Browns have forgiven debt of $20,000
The Brown's total assets upon sale of the home are worth $35,000
They have debts totaling (including the forgiven debt) $50,000

Step One: Subtract debts from assets:
Assets $35,000
Minus Liabilities $50,000
Total . . . . (15,000)

The Browns are insolvent by $15,000. (If they sold every asset and used the money to pay debts, they would still owe $15,000.)

Step Two: Subtract the amount of the insolvency from the amount of the forgiven debt.

Forgiven Debt $20,000

Minus Amount Insolvent $15,000

Total Amount on which Tax May Be Owed $5,000

The Browns owe tax on $5,000 in forgiven debt. If the total had been less than zero, they would owe no tax on the forgiven debt.

Information to establish the insolvency must be provided to the IRS.

Example 3: Refinance of Purchase Money Mortgage: Mr. and Mrs. Smith buy a house with a mortgage for $120,000. When their mortgage balance is $100,000, they refinance with a new mortgage of $120,000. The house is only worth $100,000. After a new appraisal, the bank agrees to reduce their mortgage principal balance from $120,000 to $100,000. The Smiths have no other debts and only $5,000 in assets other than the house.

The qualified principal residence indebtedness exception does not help the Smiths. They now owe the same amount of the original loan that they refinanced, so the IRS won't treat this as a forgiveness of an acquisition loan. However, the insolvency exception will help them,

Step One: Subtract debts from assets:

Assets (including the value of the house) $105,000

Minus Liabilities (the principal balance before debt forgiveness) $120,000

Total .... (15,000)

The Smiths are insolvent by $15,000. (If they sold every asset and used the money to pay debts, they would still owe $15,000. Note that this insolvency is due largely to the over-appraisal of the home.)

Step Two: Subtract the amount of the insolvency from the amount of the forgiven debt.

Forgiven Debt $20,000

Minus Amount Insolvent $15,000

Total Amount on Which Tax May Be Owed $5,000

The Smiths owe tax on $5,000 in forgiven debt. If the total had been less than zero, they would owe no tax on the forgiven debt. The Smiths must be sure to indicate on Form 982 that they are electing the "insolvency exception" and attach a balance sheet.

CREDIT CONSEQUENCES OF FORECLOSURE AND WORKOUT PLANS

There is no easy way to know how a foreclosure will affect your credit. Your mortgage delinquency is likely to be reported by credit bureaus for seven years. If you cannot avoid a foreclosure sale, the fact of the sale will also be reported for seven years.

There is a great deal of information in Chapter Three about credit reporting and how to improve a bad credit report. As discussed in that chapter, there are no hard and fast rules about how any individual lender will evaluate a notation on your credit report. Each creditor evaluates credit reports differently. A notation which is fatal to an application for credit with one lender may not keep you from getting credit on reasonable terms from a different lender.

Some general information about foreclosure and future credit may be useful if you are worried about your long-term prospects:

1. Concerns about future credit should rarely influence how you address your current problem. You cannot control how your credit report is evaluated by those who check credit reports. Any significant delinquency will usually mean "bad credit risk" to most creditors even if it is paid in full relatively quickly. There are generally more important concerns in the foreclosure avoidance process than the small improvements which will result from one type of workout plan over another.

2. A completed workout plan of any type is likely to look better on your credit report than a completed foreclosure sale. Any effort which prevents a foreclosure from being completed will show a creditor that you have made an effort. Repayment plans and loan modifications, if you cure the arrears, will show that you have gotten back on your feet.

3. A completed foreclosure sale or bankruptcy is usually fatal to applications for new mortgages from reputable lenders for at least two years. The completed foreclosure will be an important consideration for most lenders until the notation is deleted from the credit record after seven years. However, after two years, you should qualify if you can show a lender that your financial problems are behind you.

4. A deed in lieu of foreclosure is not a big improvement over foreclosure. One myth about credit reporting is that a deed in lieu of foreclosure is going to keep you in good standing on your credit record. A deed in lieu of foreclosure is a strong negative mark on a credit record; it is only slightly less damaging than a foreclosure. A deed in lieu should be considered where appropriate, but it should not be seen as a "miracle cure" for future credit.

5. It is a good idea to explain the reason for any mortgage delinquency and/or a foreclosure when applying for credit, if you know it appears on your credit report. Explain why the delinquency or foreclosure occurred if there was a good reason, the efforts you made to deal with it, and the ways in which you are in a better position now to pay your debts. This can be done either with a letter to the credit reporting agency for inclusion with your credit report as discussed in Chapter Three or with a written explanation directly to lenders who are evaluating your report.

6. Unsecured credit, such as credit cards, is often available even if you have a recent foreclosure on your credit record. There is a great deal of competition in the credit card business. Companies even compete for borrowers with bad credit records. It is a good idea to shop around for reasonable terms rather than simply accepting the first offer. Lower interest rates and fees may be available. (See Chapter Five for more information.)

7. If you are in a high-risk credit group, it is especially important to shop around when you apply for credit. Many finance companies and other abusive lenders prey on people's beliefs that they have no other potential source of credit. If you are offered credit only at high rates, shop around. You are likely to obtain better terms if lenders know you are shopping. Read the terms of credit carefully when it is offered to you. Use the APR (annual percentage rate) to compare it to other offers you have received. Lower APR's are better, unless there are other terms of credit (such as the type of collateral you must give) which are worse. You can walk away from a deal even at the last minute.

WORKOUTS FOR FHA/HUD-INSURED MORTGAGES

At present, families with mortgages insured by the Federal Housing Administration (FHA) and the United States Department of Housing and Urban Development (HUD) have some workout rights not available to families with conventional loans. (We will refer to all of the FHA and HUD loan programs as "FHA/HUD mortgages.")

How to Tell If You Have an FHA/HUD Mortgage. If you have an FHA/HUD mortgage, you are likely to be paying government insurance premiums with your mortgage payment. If you don't know whether this is the case, look at your original mortgage or loan documents. Since some lenders use the HUD forms for all mortgages, you cannot assume that you have a HUD mortgage just because your forms say FHA or HUD at the top or bottom. Look to see whether your payment includes a government mortgage insurance premium. You can also check whether there is a box marked "FHA insured" that is checked off on your settlement statement. If you have any doubt, call and ask your lender. Their records should be clear on this issue because the existence of the insurance is a benefit to them.

Help Getting a Workout with Your FHA/HUD Mortgage. When you get behind on a FHA/HUD loan, you may be sent a pamphlet published by HUD entitled *How to Avoid Foreclosure*. This pamphlet contains useful information, and is also available on HUD's website at www.hud.gov/foreclosure/index.cfm. In addition, another National Consumer Law Center book, *Foreclosure Prevention Counseling* (2007), has a separate chapter on obtaining a workout on a FHA/HUD mortgage.

In-person help with your rights under a HUD mortgage can be found by asking your HUD regional office for information about how to obtain HUD-funded foreclosure prevention counseling. You can also get help through HUD's automated phone line. It will identify HUD-approved housing counselors that are close to your community. Call 800-569-4287 (TDD 800-877-8339). A list of HUD-approved housing counseling agencies is also available on HUD's website at www.hud.gov. Not all HUD-approved agencies provide foreclosure prevention counseling. Be sure to check the agency's description on the website.

You can also try calling a local housing or credit counseling organization that you identify on your own. Be sure to contact a reputable organization. You may be approached by organizations or individuals offering counseling or other services for a fee. These services may include things you could do on your own for free, or may be provided for a small fee or no charge at a HUD-approved agency. Chapter Four has more information on counseling services.

Getting Started to Obtain a FHA/HUD Workout. Lenders must give you notice of your default of a FHA/HUD mortgage loan no later than the end of the second month of your delinquency. This notice must explain what you must do to get reinstated. Lenders must also make reasonable efforts to arrange face-to-face interviews with you before three full monthly installments are overdue. Telephone interviews are also possible. These interviews give you an opportunity to talk to the lender about a loan workout or other alternative to foreclosure. The lender may not initiate foreclosure until it has considered whether you qualify for one of the workout plans discussed below. Chapter Thirteen discusses other limits as to when a FHA/HUD mortgage can be foreclosed, and this chapter briefly outlines your rights to a workout to get out of default.

Special Forbearance Workout Plans. If you have defaulted on a HUD loan, you are eligible for a special forbearance plan if you have recently experienced a reduction in income or an increase in living expenses for reasons beyond your control. You must show the lender that you have a reasonable ability to pay in the future under the terms of such a forbearance agreement.

If you qualify for a special forbearance plan, your payment may be reduced or suspended for the period of time agreed upon by you and the lender. The amount of your payment in that period can be based on your budget. However, the total amount of the forbearance cannot exceed the equivalent of twelve monthly payments. This means that you can get reduction of your payments for at least twelve months, depending on the amount of any partial payments you can make.

At the end of the forbearance period, you must begin paying at least the full amount of the monthly mortgage payment due under the mortgage. You must also agree to a repayment plan to catch up on any amounts that you have fallen behind. These payments on the arrears can be made in small installments over any part of the remaining period of your loan. If you are unable to repay the arrears, you may combine a forbearance plan with a modification or partial claim discussed below.

If you are currently unemployed, HUD has made this option easier to use if you have a reasonable prospect of re-employment. A lender may enter into a special forbearance agreement with you if you have a good payment record and a stable employment history, but have not received a commitment for employment at the time the lender reviews your financial information. The lender may require that you make partial monthly payments if you have the ability to do so. The lender is also required to renegotiate the terms of the agreement when you are reemployed.

You can negotiate a special forbearance agreement even if foreclosure proceedings have started. In that case, the lender may stop the foreclosure proceedings before entering into the forbearance agreement. Be sure you get the lender to confirm in writing that the foreclosure proceedings have been stopped. It is not unusual for a foreclosure to proceed while a homeowner is waiting for a decision from the lender on a request for forbearance.

Negotiating a special forbearance agreement can be a difficult process. Many lenders resist following the rules that HUD sets for special forbearance. A HUD-approved housing counseling agency can help you with the negotiation. Help is also available from HUD's Servicing and Loss Mitigation Division in Oklahoma City at 888-297-8685.

Mortgage Modification. HUD will allow some homeowners to modify their mortgages, usually to change the loan term and lower the monthly payment. You may qualify if you have recovered from a financial problem but your income is less than it was before default. This option is essentially the same as the mortgage modification options discussed earlier in this chapter.

Partial Claims. In some cases, your lender will loan you money to get your monthly payments caught up to date. Lenders then seek reimbursement from (or file a "partial" claim with) HUD for the amount of the loan. The total amount of the loan cannot exceed 12 monthly payments.

To be eligible for a partial claim, you must be at least four months behind and no more than twelve months behind. You must also have sufficient income to resume making full monthly mortgage payments. Before offering a partial claim, your lender must determine that you are not able to pay the past-due amount using the special forbearance agreement or modification options (described above). The lender may also require that you make at least three full monthly payments before entering into the partial claim.

You must agree to give HUD an interest-free mortgage in the amount of HUD's payment on your behalf. You will not need to pay this mortgage, unless you choose to do so, until you sell or transfer ownership of the property or pay off the original mortgage.

Short Sales and Deeds in Lieu of Foreclosure. A lender may also agree to allow you to sell or give up your property voluntarily. Unlike other workout options, you must submit an application to participate in HUD's pre-foreclosure sale program. In HUD's pre-foreclosure sale program, you may sell your home and use the proceeds to pay off your mortgage even if the proceeds are less than the amount you owe the lender. This is also called a short sale and these options are discussed earlier in this chapter. HUD may also give you a small amount of money to help you move. To be eligible for a pre-foreclosure sale, you must be at least two months behind and you must be able to sell your home within three to five months.

The "deed in lieu of foreclosure" option allows you to transfer your home to HUD in exchange for a release from all obligations under the mortgage. HUD will generally not accept a deed in lieu if you have a tenant or other liens (such as a second mortgage) on your home. Prior to accepting a deed in lieu, the lender will require that you attempt to sell your home through the pre-foreclosure sale process described above. HUD pays you a small fee for completing this option. However, if there are any other liens on the property, the fee may be used to help pay off those liens.

WORKOUTS ON VA MORTGAGES

The Department of Veterans Affairs (VA) guarantees loans made by private lenders to veterans for the purchase, construction, or refinancing of homes owned and occupied by veterans. The VA has established guidelines and procedures for workouts of delinquent loans insured by the agency. The VA expects the lender to exhaust all possible alternatives before pursuing foreclosure. Here are the current options for VA-guaranteed loans:

Important Note: In 2005, the VA issued proposed extensive changes to its workout rules, but has not yet adopted them in final. Ask whether new rules have been implemented. If they have, the above guidelines may not all still be the ones in effect.

Forbearance. The lender may grant forbearance by allowing payments to remain delinquent for up to twelve months. Forbearance is followed by a lump-sum repayment or a payment plan. A written forbearance is required if the forbearance will extend beyond the first sixty days of a missed installment. Under written repayment or forbearance plans, lenders must accept partial payments of installments. However, they may return the partial payments if the foreclosure process has started. The guidelines do not limit the repayment period, which can make repayment very flexible.

Modification. A delinquent loan or one where default is imminent may be modified. The lender may extend the term or reamortize the loan provided that at least 80% of the loan balance extended will amortize over the remaining term of the loan, or, for loans with terms of less than thirty years, the lesser of the economic life of the security or thirty years from the date of origination. Unpaid interest, taxes, and insurance may be added to the newly modified balance. Lenders are not allowed to increase the interest rate on a modified mortgage. Modifications will be offered to homeowners whose incomes have been reduced making them financially unable to pay their loan or make up the arrears.

Assumption. If a workout is unsuccessful, a lender may grant a homeowner forbearance for a reasonable period of time to permit the sale or transfer of the property. For loans made on or after March 1, 1988, the approval of the VA is needed for an assumption. In addition, most buyers must pay a funding fee equal to one-half of 1% of the loan balance as of the date of transfer. There is also a processing charge, whose maximum is the lesser of: (1) $300 and the cost of a credit report; or (2) the maximum fee prescribed by state law.

Compromise Claim. If the proceeds of a private sale are insufficient to pay the loan, or to pay the delinquency in the case of the assumption, the VA may pay the buyer a "compromise claim" to facilitate the sale. This option is akin to a "short sale" and the lender claims payment from the VA for any deficiency between the sale price and the amount due on the mortgage. If the loan is assumed, and the fair market value of the property is less than the unpaid principal balance, the payment may be applied to the principal to reduce the loan balance and the amount the third party has to assume. The VA, not the lender, processes a compromise claim payment. Any purchaser assuming a VA loan involving a compromise claim must be qualified by the VA, assume responsibility for repayment of the loan, and indemnify the VA against loss in the event of future default.

Refinance. A homeowner may refinance a high interest rate loan at a current, lower rate under the VA's interest rate reduction refinancing program. If the loan is current, no underwriting is necessary. If the loan is delinquent, the VA must approve this option.

Refunding. The VA has the authority to buy a loan in default from the lender and take over its servicing. However, this option, called "refunding," is to be exercised at the VA's discretion. Though the VA makes very limited use of this option, the VA says it reviews every loan in default to determine whether to refund the loan. There is no formal application process. The objective of refunding is to avoid foreclosure when the VA determines that the default can be cured through various relief measures and the lender is unable or unwilling to grant further relief. Other loss mitigation options may then be available to the homeowner.

Deed in Lieu. The VA must approve any deed in lieu, although it strongly encourages lenders to accept the voluntary transfer of the property if there is no alternative to terminating the loan. But the deed in lieu will usually not be accepted if there are any junior liens on the property.

WORKOUTS ON RURAL
HOUSING SERVICE MORTGAGES

The Rural Housing Service (RHS) (formerly known as the Farmers Home Administration or FmHA) also runs programs designed to help you avoid foreclosure. To tell whether your mortgage is RHS insured or guaranteed, look at the mortgage papers or loan documents or call the lender. Older loans may refer to FmHA insurance or guarantees. You also may find a reference to the "Section 502 Single-Family Housing Program."

If your loan is insured or guaranteed by RHS, you can use many of the options described above for HUD mortgages. You may qualify for a special forbearance, modification, short sale, or deed in lieu of foreclosure. The RHS does not offer a partial claim option. In addition, if you qualify, RHS will assist you in paying the interest on your loan (described below). However, eligibility for this option must be established at the time your loan guarantee was authorized.

The RHS also provides direct loans to borrowers under its Section 502 Single-Family Housing Program. The RHS's Centralized Servicing Center in St. Louis, Missouri, handles all servicing. That office can be reached at 800-793-8861. It is easier to get assistance if you have your account number handy.

RHS Assistance Programs. If you have a loan made directly by RHS and a financial setback interferes with your ability to make payments, RHS has special servicing programs designed to assist you. These include "payment moratoriums," "delinquency workout agreements," and "protective advances." In addition, if you have an Interest Credit and Payment Assistance subsidy, RHS can increase your subsidy within certain limits to make your payments more affordable.

232

Payment Moratorium. A payment moratorium is available when you can show that, due to circumstances beyond your control, you are unable to continue making full payments without substantially impairing your standard of living. Under the moratorium program, your scheduled monthly payments may be reduced, based on need, for up to two years. At the end of two years (or earlier if RHS determines that you no longer need moratorium assistance), your monthly payments will be recalculated based on the existing balance at that time. If you are unable to afford the payments after they are recalculated, some or all of the interest that came due during moratorium may be canceled. Eligibility for the moratorium program is reviewed at least once every six months and you should be provided with sixty days' notice before the moratorium is terminated.

Other RHS Options. A Delinquency Workout Agreement (DWA) allows you to make a delinquent account current, either by making a single lump-sum payment or by paying a portion of the delinquent amount, in addition to your scheduled mortgage payment, over a period of no more than two years. This works like a payment agreement as discussed earlier in the chapter.

A "protective advance" occurs when RHS advances money to pay for taxes or insurance and then recalculates the loan balance and payments. When the loan is recalculated, if the payment period is extended, your loan payments may go down. This is illustrated with an example earlier in the chapter.

Many RHS loans come with interest rate subsidies to make the payments affordable. If you are experiencing financial problems, the subsidy may be increased for a period of time while you get back on your feet. The RHS will first consider an increase in your subsidy before considering a payment moratorium discussed above.

You Must Apply Quickly When These Options Are Offered. RHS will not offer these special servicing options until your mortgage payments are at least two months overdue. You should apply for these special servicing options very quickly, because foreclosure can start just a month later.

Appeals. If a request for special servicing is denied, you can appeal to a higher RHS official. If your application and your appeal are improperly denied, it may be possible to challenge the lender's decision to foreclose on your home.

12

Defending Your Home from Foreclosure

FIRST CONSIDERATION IN DEALING WITH A FORECLOSURE

Your home is typically your most valuable possession and loss of your home can have devastating effects on your family. The prior two chapters provided advice on how to keep your home despite problems with your mortgage payments. This chapter and the next provide information you will need if the foreclosure process becomes imminent.

Distinguishing Four Different Types of Foreclosure. This chapter examines four different types of foreclosures, and it is important to understand which type of foreclosure applies to you. Most foreclosures are by the lender holding the mortgage on your home, and much of this chapter explains how that type of foreclosure works and provides advice on delaying or stopping that foreclosure. The end of this chapter also discusses your rights

235

relating to the other three types of foreclosure. One is where your city or town tries to seize the home for unpaid property taxes. A second is where someone *without* a mortgage on your home obtains a court judgment against you and then uses that judgment to try to seize your home. The third is where you do not pay your condominium fees and the condominium association puts a lien on your condominium and then attempts to foreclose for those unpaid fees. Your rights are different for these three types of foreclosures, so it is important to determine who is seeking to take your home and for what reason.

Your Goals in Responding to a Foreclosure on Your Mortgage.

You are not powerless if your home is being foreclosed based upon your non-payment of your mortgage loan, but you need to be realistic in defining your objectives. You often have a good chance of achieving the following three objectives:

1. You can delay the sale to give you enough time to find a solution to the foreclosure problem.
2. You can use your legal rights at various stages in the process to cure your default or to redeem your home. You can usually also exercise those rights by filing a chapter 13 bankruptcy.
3. You can find out the valid amount you owe on the debt, and dispute improper charges, so that you are not repaying more than you should.

This chapter focuses on various steps you can take to meet the first two objectives: to delay the foreclosure or to cure a default or redeem your home. Chapter Ten provides advice on disputing improper charges your lender claims you owe—either before or after foreclosure proceedings have begun.

You also have additional important rights in certain situations, discussed in the next chapter (Chapter Thirteen):

- If your mortgage is backed by the government—FHA/HUD or VA;
- If you are now active duty military;
- If the mortgage resulted from a home improvement scam;
- If the mortgage terms themselves were unfair or oppressive;
- If the mortgage resulted from a refinancing or was not to purchase the home;
- If the mortgage is on a manufactured home.

In those specific situations you may be able to keep your home even though you defer payments for a while, or you may even be able to wipe out your mortgage in whole or in part.

The previous chapter (Chapter Eleven) discussed saving your home with a workout agreement. Usually, your first step should be to try to negotiate a workout agreement if you do not have defenses to the foreclosure. A workout may accomplish your goals without resorting to a legal process. However, a foreclosure sale may be so close at hand that a workout agreement is not possible, or the lender may not agree to an acceptable arrangement. In these situations, you should consider the options laid out in this chapter and the next.

While Chapters Ten through Thirteen provide a good overview of your rights to protect your home, we also recommend another National Consumer Law Center book: *Foreclosure Prevention Counseling*. That book is written primarily for housing counselors, but will be useful for most readers. And, while it focuses on how to obtain a workout, the book also describes the foreclosure process and discusses legal protections against foreclosure.

YOUR RIGHTS IN THE MORTGAGE FORECLOSURE PROCESS

Preliminary Notices. In every state, you will be entitled to some notice of a pending foreclosure on your home. However, the type, amount, and timing of these notices varies considerably. You cannot necessarily rely on the lender to send notices and, because of problems with mail delivery, you may not receive them. For this reason, if you know you are behind on your mortgage payments, you will need to stay on top of things by reading any notices you do receive carefully, by keeping track of deadlines, and by contacting the, servicer, lender or the foreclosure attorney at regular intervals, if necessary, to get information about what is going on.

In addition, since many foreclosure notices are sent by certified or registered mail, you should make sure to pick up these notices from the post office. Refusing to pick up notices and not knowing what is in them does *not* protect you.

Some of the typical types of notices that may be received if foreclosure is pending are discussed here. However, remember that each state has different procedures.

Notice of Default. You will almost always get a notice from the lender or lender's servicer that says that you have fallen behind on your payments. This is usually called "notice of default" or "notice of delinquency." It may look like any other collection letter.

This notice will usually tell you how many payments you are behind and the exact amount of money you need to catch up and "cure" the default. This amount is often called "the arrears." It will also state when you must make this payment of the arrears to avoid foreclosure, usually a date which is at least thirty days after the notice. In many states and under most mortgage contracts, if you offer to pay the total amount of the arrears at this stage, the lender must accept the payment. Even if the law or your mortgage does not require it, almost all lenders will be very happy to take your full payment at this point if you have it. Partial payments are often rejected unless they are made as part of a workout agreement.

You should treat the notice of default as an important warning that there is a problem. It will be easier to address the problem if you begin looking for a solution at this early stage. If you can resolve the problem before it goes any further, you may be able to save considerable money by avoiding the legal fees and costs that the mortgage company will charge you for a foreclosure. Chapter Eleven examines how to obtain a mortgage workout agreement that may resolve the problem.

Notice of Acceleration. When you are behind on your mortgage, lenders in most states must take a legal step known as "acceleration" before they can foreclose on your home. Acceleration means that you are far enough behind on your mortgage that the law allows the lender to treat the whole loan balance as due right away. In many states and under most mortgage contracts, the lender must give you notice when this occurs. In some states, this notice may be combined with the notice of default. The notice will typically say that the whole balance (sometimes with the actual amount written into the notice) is due and payable immediately or after the period for "curing" the default has passed.

Receipt of a notice of acceleration is a good indication that the foreclosure process is moving quickly. This letter, if you receive it, should therefore serve as an important warning that you must put a strategy in place to prevent foreclosure or give up your home.

The Right to Reinstate and the Right to Redeem. Many states and mortgage contracts allow you a second chance. In these states you can avoid foreclosure by "reinstating" the mortgage after acceleration. Usually, this means getting caught up on the arrears (missed payments together with foreclosure fees and costs). Many mortgage contracts give you this "right to reinstate" up until five days before the foreclosure sale, and some lenders and servicers may accept payment even after that period if it is offered before the sale. Your lender or servicer may require that this "reinstatement" payment be made by certified or bank check and sent to the law firm handling the foreclosure. Occasionally, lenders may claim that you did not meet your obligations in some other way, such as failing to keep the property insured. These defaults can also be "cured" by taking care of the problem.

Even in states which do not allow you to reinstate after acceleration, many lenders will agree to reinstate voluntarily, although others will not. Some lenders prefer foreclosure, either because they think foreclosure will be profitable or because they no longer want to deal with a borrower who has had financial problems. But even in this situation, you can usually force the lender to allow a reinstatement by taking the matter to court.

You can usually stop a foreclosure
if you are able to pay all past-due
mortgage payments plus certain costs.

If you have money to get caught up or to pay off the full balance owed on the mortgage, you can usually use the legal process to force the lender to accept it—even if, at first glance, it looks like your state's law permits the lender to refuse the money. In most states, because judges have the ability to direct fair resolutions of disputes, they will sometimes order things like a reinstatement.

Most judges will not want to allow a family to be put on the street when the family has money to pay the arrears or the full balance owed. Even in states where judges do not have this power, offering a cure to the lender in court in front of a judge will sometimes embarrass the lender into accepting.

In every state you are also allowed to "redeem" the home up to the time of a foreclosure sale (and in a handful of states for a limited number of days after the foreclosure sale). To redeem, you must pay off the full amount of the loan in one payment plus the lender's foreclosure fees and costs. That is, instead of just catching up on the delinquent payments, you have to pay the whole remainder of the mortgage. Since most people don't have enough cash to redeem the home outright, the most common method of redemption is taking out a new loan to pay off the existing lender (refinancing).

Some states also allow you to redeem your home *after* the foreclosure sale, by paying the sale price and other costs to the person who purchased your home at the foreclosure sale. As discussed below, concerning your rights after foreclosure, this redemption right as to the foreclosure purchaser is different than redeeming with your mortgage lender before or just after the foreclosure sale.

Additionally, you have bankruptcy rights under federal (national) law rather than state law. You always have a right to redeem and a right to cure in bankruptcy before a foreclosure sale is completed. This is true even if your state law places limits on your right to cure and reinstate after acceleration. In fact, as discussed below and in Chapter Nineteen, the bankruptcy right to cure in a chapter 13 case includes a right to pay back any amount in default in installments over a period of time. This can be as long as three to five years. This means that, if you are behind, you can use chapter 13 bankruptcy to get caught up over a manageable period of time, even if your state's law does not allow it.

How Long Does Foreclosure Take? The length of time you have before your property is sold varies a great deal from state to state. The amount of time also varies because some lenders move more quickly than others. Depending on these factors, together with any response you put in place, foreclosure can take as little as three months from the time you default to as long as a full year or more. You should check local practice and stay on top of any information you receive in foreclosure-related notices, as discussed above.

Whatever the length of time it takes for
foreclosure in your situation, your rule for
action should always be: **it is always better**
to act sooner rather than later.

Delays can lead to a serious loss of legal rights, reducing your options for preventing foreclosure. Although delaying a sale will always help you, delay in taking action to prevent the sale will not. You will need both a short-term strategy to evaluate your options and a long-term strategy to prevent the foreclosure.

How a Lender Gets Permission to Foreclose. Foreclosure procedures vary from state to state. The procedures are established by state laws and by local practice. In some states, foreclosures involve court proceedings. In these states, the lender first files suit in a court—usually in the county where the property is located. Unless you successfully fight the foreclosure in court, a judgment is entered for the lender. This gives the lender permission to hold a foreclosure sale unless you can work out an agreement or take some other action (such as bankruptcy) to prevent it.

If the lender has to go to court to foreclose upon your home, you will receive a summons or a similar notice usually brought to the house by a sheriff, constable, marshal, or process server. This notice gives you a certain period of time to respond to the foreclosure lawsuit and to raise your defenses if you have any. You should take this deadline seriously. If you do not respond, the court will enter a foreclosure judgment against you. Although this is not the end of the process, you lose important legal protections once a court judgment is entered. Most importantly, you lose the right to raise defenses in most cases. For this reason, receipt of a summons or other court papers is always a good time to review your legal options and to see a lawyer if possible.

Other states have "non-judicial foreclosures." In those states, lenders foreclose without a court action and without official permission to go forward. They advertise the home for sale, using a legal notice in a newspaper. If you want to challenge this type of foreclosure, you must file a lawsuit and ask the court to stop the sale. You may have to file a bond to protect the lender. You may also stop the sale by filing bankruptcy. Some states allow both judicial and non-judicial foreclosure.

The Foreclosure Sale. In all states, lenders are required to send you a notice of the date and time intended for sale of your property. In some states, this notice may be combined with the notice of acceleration, discussed earlier in this chapter. The sale date is the most important deadline in the foreclosure process because the sale will cut off all of your rights as owner. Sale of the property will also generally cut off your opportunity to obtain a workout or to use the bankruptcy process to help prevent foreclosure.

Generally, a foreclosure sale is a poorly advertised and poorly attended auction. In many cases, no one attends except the foreclosing lender, who bids no more than the balance of the debt and maybe significantly less. Depending on state law, the auctioneer might be a sheriff or other court official. In other states, usually where there is "nonjudicial foreclosure," the auction is conducted by a lawyer or an auctioneer hired by the lender. Depending on state law, the sale may be held on the property itself or at a local courthouse or government building. Although you can attend the auction and bid on the property, every state has rules about making a down payment at the auction and paying any balance in a limited period of time.

---

*Notice of sale is generally sent **very late** in the foreclosure process. It usually represents your last chance to do something about foreclosure.*

Once the sale is held, you should ask for information about who bought the property and the sale price. This will help you determine if you are owed money from the sale or if you are likely to face a deficiency claim. Unless you ask, you may not receive this information.

After the Foreclosure Sale and the Mortgage Deficiency or Surplus. Once a foreclosure sale is completed, you may receive a variety of different types of notices. These may include notice of the outcome of sale (who bought the property and for how much), eviction notices, and court papers related to eviction. It is important to remember that, after a foreclosure sale, you are rarely able to do much to recover your home. However, in a few states, you retain the right to redeem the property from foreclosure. In addition, you can occasionally challenge the procedures under which the sale was held and, in extreme circumstances, have the sale declared invalid. Your options after a foreclosure sale are discussed later in this chapter, and this section just explains about mortgage deficiencies and surpluses.

If the sale does not bring in enough to pay off the lender, in many states you remain responsible for the balance, and the lender can seek a "deficiency." A deficiency is the remainder due on the loan plus costs, minus the amount the lender was paid from the sale proceeds. Some state laws prevent lenders from seeking this deficiency or place certain conditions on lenders before they can seek the deficiency. You may also receive a variety of notices about the deficiency, including collection letters and court papers. Some states limit the amount of a deficiency or do not allow it at all, but you may need to respond to notices and court papers to get these protections.

If lenders can collect a deficiency under your state's law, the deficiency will be an unsecured debt (unless the lender has collateral other than the foreclosed home). You may be sued in court for the mortgage deficiency, and you will have the right to defend against the lawsuit. For a discussion of dealing with collection lawsuits, see Chapter Nine.

On the other hand, if the sale brings in enough to pay off the lender and pay for all foreclosure costs, you are entitled to any amount by which the sale price exceeds that. This is called a surplus. Although most foreclosure sales bring in far less than home's value, if you think you are entitled to a surplus, you should contact the lender or servicer (or its foreclosure attorney). If the lender or servicer tells you that you are entitled to a surplus, be sure to give them your new address when you move, since they will need to find you to pay you your share of the foreclosure sale receipts.

If the lender or servicer does not cooperate and does not tell you whether you are entitled to a surplus, then send a Qualified Written Request to the servicer, as described in Chapter Ten, above. You may find that the sale brought in much more than owed on the mortgage, but that the lender claims various fees and costs that eat up the difference. If these are excessive, you can hire a lawyer to challenge this.

GETTING LEGAL ADVICE TO STOP A FORECLOSURE; ADVICE TO AVOID

Foreclosure is a harsh legal process and, when you are threatened with fore-closure, you should immediately try to obtain legal help. Possible sources of low-cost legal help are the neighborhood legal services office and a bar association panel of pro bono attorneys. A small number of other community lawyers may handle foreclosure defense cases for a fee and many lawyers will handle bankruptcies. You should exercise care in hiring a lawyer to help you with foreclosure defense, just as you would in hiring any professional. Find someone you trust to do what you need them to do; if possible, get a referral from a friend or relative. More information about finding a lawyer can be found in the Introduction to this book.

The size of the lawyer's fee does not represent the quality of the lawyer's work. A free legal services lawyer may be the best in town. A costly lawyer may rip you off. The important thing is to find someone you feel comfort-able with, at a price you can afford (when free help is unavailable).

One thing to avoid is "quick fix" attorneys who may advertise or solicit through the mail from published foreclosure lists. Many times, these lawyers will push you to file a bankruptcy before other options are considered. A bankruptcy may be necessary at some point. But, as with many things, proper timing is critical.

There are also businesses that offer help to people facing foreclosure in order to rip them off. By law, foreclosure of your home will be advertised to the public. These scam artists find you name from this advertising and contact you, offering to save your home. Their offers of help are often fraudulent. You may be told you are getting a loan or that they have arranged a payment plan for you with your lender. Instead the papers you are asked to sign will have you selling your home to them with an option to buy it back. These are not solutions to your foreclosure problem and will only make things worse. You should reject any offer to sell your home with an option to buy it back.

Requests for high fees or for money to pay the mortgage (payable to someone other than the mortgage company) are also signs of scams. In addition, offers of new mortgages as a way out of foreclosure can lead to disastrous deals which will make your situation impossible to resolve. Even if they do give you a loan, it will likely be a high-rate, high-cost loan with other bad terms. If you do sign a new mortgage under pressure of foreclosure, remember that you have three business days to cancel.

A more legitimate source of help in some cases is nonprofit foreclosure prevention counseling (sometimes called "default counseling"). Contact a local nonprofit housing organization to find out where this service is offered in your community. Try calling 800-569-4287 (TDD 800-877-8339) or visiting the HUD website at www.hud.gov to find a HUD-approved housing counseling agency near you.

Too often, homeowners postpone getting help until it is too late to assert their legal rights. Others prematurely walk away from their homes in frustration, leaving themselves without any equity and vulnerable to deficiency claims. For each foreclosure situation, a counselor or lawyer must carefully evaluate your goals and interests. It is better to get this help too soon rather than too late.

DELAYING THE FORECLOSURE PROCESS

Foreclosure can move very quickly. One advantage of exercising your legal rights is that you can slow down the process. In the short term, delay can be helpful because it will give you more time to put into place a long-term solution to the problem.

If you succeed in delaying the foreclosure, you should do everything possible during that time to put money aside toward your mortgage to avoid falling further behind. You should also act diligently to try to deal with your underlying financial problems.

You cannot properly delay foreclosure just because you need more time. The actions you take must be based on some underlying legal claim or defense which is raised in good faith.

Procedural Defenses May Delay the Process.   In most areas of the country, foreclosures are rarely contested, and lenders' attorneys tend to assume that there is no defense to foreclosure. Consequently, lenders may be sloppy in their procedures and sometimes do not comply with pre-foreclosure requirements. Lender errors can be to your benefit when you are contesting foreclosure, forcing the lender to start over, or, at the very least, forcing the lender to comply with required procedural requirements. This will provide you with additional time to refinance, sell privately, or arrange a workout agreement. (See Chapter Eleven.)

Foreclosure procedures and defenses to foreclosure vary significantly from state to state. Therefore, a lawyer or some other professional will have to determine whether the lender has complied with all the required procedures and whether defenses to foreclosure are available.

Examples of possible defenses include failure to give you the proper notice, failure to give you a fair chance to correct the default, failure to properly advertise the sale, failure of a lender to introduce the original documents in the foreclosure proceeding, failure to sue all the proper parties, failure to bring the foreclosure proceeding in the name of the real mortgage holder, or discouraging bids at the foreclosure sale.

In states where foreclosure cases are resolved by court action, you can raise defenses in that action. If the creditor can foreclose without a court case because your state allows nonjudicial foreclosure, then you will have to bring a legal case of your own and ask the court to stop the foreclosure. Many of the legal remedies discussed here are covered in more detail in National Consumer Law Center's *Foreclosures* (2d ed. 2007). In addition, special rights to defend against a foreclosure for certain types of loans or borrowers are detailed in the next chapter (Chapter Thirteen).

The Lender's Acceptance of Partial Payments May Be Grounds to Delay a Foreclosure.   Late or partial payment on a mortgage generally triggers the lender's right to "accelerate" the loan—to call the full amount of the mortgage due immediately. Failure to pay the full amount then leads to foreclosure.

Nevertheless, many courts refuse to allow foreclosure if the lender surprises you by suddenly calling the whole loan due when the lender has been lenient in accepting late or partial payments in the past. If a lender usually accepts late or partial payments, it must warn you that it will no longer continue to accept those payments before it calls the whole loan due and attempts a foreclosure. Failure to do so may provide you with grounds to stop a foreclosure and give you another opportunity to catch up. The delay can be substantial.

Similarly, if the lender accepts a payment after foreclosure has started, you can argue that there is no longer a default. In some states, this will require the lender to restart the foreclosure process from the beginning.

Asking the Court for More Time. In some states, courts have the power to delay foreclosures for other reasons. Two situations where delays may be granted are if there is serious hardship and if there is a substantial amount of equity in the home which protects the lender against losses on its claims.

Serious hardship claims must be documented and they must involve more than the unfortunate circumstance of homelessness. If a family member has a serious illness, for example, a temporary delay may sometimes be granted. Usually the hardship must be temporary as well. If the hardship will last forever, the judge may feel that now is as good a time as any to allow the foreclosure.

Filing for bankruptcy will delay a foreclosure, but only some bankruptcies will permanently prevent foreclosure.

If you have a great deal of equity in your home, a court may allow you a short period of time to sell the home without foreclosure. This will allow you to get the best possible price and recover your home equity. Even if you are unable to make payments during this time, the lender is not hurt because there is enough value in the property to eventually pay the lender's full claim.

A Chapter 7 Bankruptcy May Create a Temporary Delay. As discussed in more detail in Chapter Nineteen, a chapter 7 bankruptcy case cannot address a foreclosure problem in the long term. This is because mortgages and other liens (with a few exceptions) survive chapter 7 bankruptcy. However, if you file a chapter 7 bankruptcy case, you will delay a foreclosure because the automatic stay in the bankruptcy case will temporarily prevent the foreclosure process from continuing. The lender cannot continue foreclosure without permission of the court (this usually takes at least sixty days) or until the case is over. However, the stay may not automatically prevent a foreclosure in some cases, such as when the consumer has had other previous bankruptcy cases dismissed or there is an order by the bankruptcy court in an earlier case that prevents the stay from going into effect.

Two things are important to keep in mind. First, you cannot file a chapter 7 bankruptcy solely to delay foreclosure. You must have some other legitimate purpose for filing bankruptcy. For most homeowners in financial distress, this is hardly a problem because there are lots of other debts outstanding. Second, if you want a more permanent solution to your mortgage problem, you will need to file under chapter 13. This is discussed in more detail below.

FILING A CHAPTER 13 BANKRUPTCY MAY STOP A FORECLOSURE PERMANENTLY IF YOU MAKE REQUIRED PAYMENTS

You should carefully consider filing a bankruptcy case if you are in financial distress and about to lose your home. This can stop the foreclosure process and allow you time to regroup and try to work out a plan to keep your home. Chapter 13 of the bankruptcy law always requires lenders to accept cures even when state law says otherwise. In fact, in chapter 13 bankruptcy, you can cure a default or pay off a mortgage in installment payments over time rather than by having to come up with a lump sum.

Bankruptcy is covered in detail in this book's Chapter Nineteen and in even more depth in National Consumer Law Center's *Consumer Bankruptcy Law and Practice* (8th ed. 2006 and Supp.). Only some of the most important aspects of bankruptcy and foreclosure will be discussed here.

Bankruptcy may not be effective unless it is carefully planned and timed. For example, a premature bankruptcy filing may eliminate your right to receive special state assistance or may prevent the lender from discussing more favorable workout options. If you file too late, your ability to keep your home and cure or pay off the mortgage may be lost. You will almost always have to file before the foreclosure sale. In addition, you will need to have a credit counseling briefing with an approved credit counseling agency before filing bankruptcy, so it is *important to plan for this so that you will have sufficient time* to file bankruptcy before the foreclosure sale. Some HUD-approved housing counseling agencies are also approved to give the bankruptcy briefing. See Chapter Nineteen for more information about this requirement and how to locate an approved bankruptcy counseling agency. See Chapter Four for other potential problems with credit counselors.

The Automatic Stay. The "automatic stay" is the primary reason bankruptcy is such a powerful method of dealing with a foreclosure. The filing of your petition in bankruptcy automatically stops most creditor actions against you and your property, including foreclosure, foreclosure sales, and the filing of liens against your property. If you have filed other bankruptcy cases that were dismissed within the previous year, however, you may not get an automatic stay or it may only last for the first thirty days of your bankruptcy case. This is discussed in more detail in Chapter Nineteen.

The lender cannot do anything without first asking the bankruptcy judge's permission to do so. The bankruptcy judge will often *not* give the lender permission to proceed—especially if you have proposed a plan in chapter 13 to cure or redeem the debt on the mortgage.

Curing Delinquent Payments and Reinstating the Mortgage. The automatic stay gives you time to take advantage of other aspects of the bankruptcy law. In a chapter 13 bankruptcy filing, called a "debt adjustment" case, you can "cure" (pay back) the delinquent payments gradually over a period of years so long as you also keep up on future mortgage payments as they come due each month. In a chapter 13 case, you may have up to three years to pay back-due mortgage payments, but that can be extended to five years if there is a good reason.

The following example of a cure in a five-year chapter 13 case shows how helpful a bankruptcy filing can be. Assume you are six months behind on $500 monthly mortgage payments, so that your total arrears is $3,000. In a five-year chapter 13 case, you can cure by making future $500 payments as they come due and catching up on the past due $3,000 in sixty monthly payments of $50 each.

You may also have to pay interest on the $3,000 while you cure the default and a commission to the bankruptcy trustee for handling your payments. This will add about $16.00 a month to your obligation. Although a few courts require you to get caught up in less than five years, many will allow a five-year payment plan if it will take you that long to get caught up.

You can cure delinquent payments in a chapter 13 bankruptcy case even if a lender has already accelerated payments so that the full loan amount is due or even if the lender has obtained a foreclosure judgment. You can also pay off a mortgage in bankruptcy even if the last payment has already become due or if it will be due during the bankruptcy case itself.

Another important issue when using the bankruptcy law to cure a mortgage delinquency is the extent to which lenders can collect attorney's fees and costs as part of the amount needed to cure. The lender is only entitled to attorney's fees and costs if the mortgage loan agreement clearly provides for collection of such charges. Even then, many state laws either place significant limits on fee arrangements or prohibit them entirely.

When fees are appropriate, they should be assessed only if they are reasonable, necessary, and actually paid. A lender whose litigation is unsuccessful or unnecessary should not be allowed to collect fees.

If the amount you owe is small, keeping your home by paying off the full debt is another option in a chapter 13 bankruptcy. You can do this over the full three- or five-year term of the chapter 13 plan and, depending upon the type of mortgage you have, you can reduce the interest rate on your loan principal from the rate originally specified in the loan to interest rates prevailing in your community today for similar loans. This can be a big savings.

Raising Disputes in Bankruptcy. The bankruptcy process gives you another opportunity to raise defenses to the lenders' claim (if they have not already been raised and rejected by another court). You do not lose your right to raise disputes about how much you owe or about fraud or unfairness when you walk into bankruptcy court. These defenses and others can be raised as "objections to claims" as part of determining how much you have to pay under your chapter 13 bankruptcy plan.

Sale of a Home in a Chapter 13 Bankruptcy. If you can no longer afford your mortgage payments, you will not benefit from bankruptcy's ability to cure past delinquencies. However, you can use the bankruptcy process to sell the home on your own in an orderly fashion, thereby keeping your equity and avoiding the problems of a foreclosure sale. This strategy is probably only available to you if you will earn enough from the sale of the property to pay both the creditors secured by your home and some portion of your unsecured creditors from the sale proceeds.

If you want to sell your home after filing bankruptcy, you usually have to request that the court approve your realtor. When a sale is arranged, you will also have to file a "Complaint to Sell Property Free of Liens" with the bankruptcy court and obtain an order from the bankruptcy court approving the sale and allowing the property to be sold free of liens. Many title insurance companies require this order for the sale to go through.

This section has provided only a brief overview of your options in bankruptcy. If you want to use bankruptcy to help prevent a foreclosure, you should also read Chapter Nineteen.

STATE TEMPORARY BANS ON FORECLOSURE

While no state, as of the date this book went to press, has instituted a temporary ban on foreclosures, this has happened in the past and it may happen again. States today are looking at various possible fixes for the foreclosure crisis facing their citizens. Some states, by the time you read this book, may in fact institute a temporary ban on foreclosures. It is certainly worth checking it out. When there is a state ban on foreclosures, you only will be temporarily protected, but this will give you an opportunity to get back on your feet.

During the economic depression of the 1930s, many states enacted moratorium laws postponing foreclosure sales of homes and farms. Where still in effect, these laws sometimes prevent foreclosures by requiring lenders to accept smaller payments during moratorium periods. For example, the Iowa foreclosure law provides general relief in cases of natural disasters and when the governor declares an economic emergency.

Occasionally, a state will declare a temporary local emergency and allow foreclosure relief in areas of widespread distress. During a plant closing crisis in the early 1980s in Pennsylvania, local judges and sheriffs postponed home foreclosures against dislocated workers without resorting to a moratorium law. Massachusetts had a temporary moratorium in 1991 on foreclosures, responding to widespread instances of home improvement fraud and other second mortgage scams. Most recently, Mississippi imposed a moratorium on foreclosure after Hurricane Katrina left many homes destroyed.

IF YOU DECIDE TO GO TO COURT

If you decide to go to court for one of the reasons discussed in this chapter, keep in mind that there are strict time deadlines to do so. At the very latest, any defenses you have must be raised before the foreclosure sale process is completed. And in many states, defenses are cut off even earlier.

When evaluating how to raise claims in court in your state, keep in mind that there are significant differences between states that have a court process for foreclosure (often called "judicial" foreclosure) and states that do not (often called "nonjudicial" foreclosure).

In a judicial foreclosure state, you should receive notice that the lender started a court case. You will then have a short period of time to file an "answer" to the foreclosure case or to file motions to raise procedural issues. Sometimes, this deadline can be extended if you make a request. If you miss this deadline, it may be more difficult to raise defenses. At the least, you will have to explain in your court papers why you missed the deadline. If a court order has been entered in the case (usually called a "judgment"), you will have an even greater obligation to show why you did not file your response on time.

In nonjudicial foreclosure states, time restrictions until the date of sale may be less severe. However, raising your defenses is substantially more complicated because there is no court process in which to do so. This means that you have to begin your own case in court to prevent the foreclosure. You may have to pay court fees and other court costs to do so.

Access to the bankruptcy court is discussed in more detail in Chapter Nineteen. More discussion about court procedures is contained in Chapter Nine.

YOUR OPTIONS AFTER THE FORECLOSURE SALE

All is not necessarily lost after the foreclosure sale. You may be able to buy the home back from the purchaser, particularly if the buyer was your mortgage lender. You will need to obtain funding from a third party. However, if the house does not sell at the auction, government lenders occasionally will be willing to refinance your loan and let you stay in the home.

Redemption and Setting Aside the Sale. Some states, for a very limited number of days after the foreclosure, allow you to redeem the home back from the lender. Another option in some states is to redeem your home from the person purchasing it at the foreclosure sale. State law may provide you only a very limited number of days to redeem in this manner, but other states give you up to a year to redeem from the purchaser. (State laws in this area are summarized in NCLC's *Foreclosure Prevention Counseling* Appendix E, or you can ask a lawyer or housing counselor what the law is in your state.)

If you redeem from the purchaser at the foreclosure sale, you will have to pay the purchaser the total purchase price plus interest and allowable costs. You will, of course, have to obtain funding to do this. If you cannot find funding for yourself, one option is to find another purchaser for your home willing to pay more than the redemption amount. You still lose your home, but you get to keep the difference between what you sell the home for and the redemption amount. You come out financially better off than if you did not exercise the redemption right, and this difference may be very helpful in your finding new housing. But redemption has strict time deadlines and strict procedures, so it is best to try to have an attorney to assist you in redeeming the home.

If you have a right to redeem after the foreclosure, you may also have important rights to save the home if you file bankruptcy. You must act quickly and you almost certainly will need a bankruptcy attorney to help you use the bankruptcy process to save your home.

You can also ask a court to set aside the foreclosure sale because proper procedures were not followed or because the price was unconscionably low. This is a long shot and you will have to act very quickly and almost always with the help of an attorney.

Your Rights As a Tenant in Your Own House. If all else fails, you will be a tenant at will in your own home, now owned by someone else. Before the new owner can evict you, the new owner in most states must follow the state's landlord-tenant eviction law. In some states, this can be very quick, while in others it may take a while.

You can also offer the new owner two options in lieu of eviction. One is that the new owner gives you "cash for keys." To save the new owner of the difficulty and time of the eviction process, you offer to vacate voluntarily if the new owner gives you cash to help in the move and to find new housing. The other option to offer the new owner is that you will pay rent if you are allowed to stay in the home. Even a short extension can be helpful in finding a new place to live.

FORECLOSURES FOR UNPAID TAXES, COURT JUDGMENTS AND CONDOMINIUM FEES

Most of this chapter talks about foreclosure by your mortgage lender. You also have to worry about foreclosures by your town or other local government seeking to take your home for nonpayment of real estate taxes. This section will provide some tips on reducing what you owe in property taxes and avoiding seizure.

Most foreclosures are by creditors holding a mortgage on your home. But you also have to be concerned with home seizures that may be instituted by other creditors, creditors who do not have a mortgage or lien on your home. Nevertheless, you have important protections against this type of seizure. As discussed below, such a creditor first has to obtain a court judgment against you for money, and even then you have protections against your home being seized to pay that judgment.

Another type of foreclosure to be concerned about happens in some states where you do not pay your condominium fees. If the condominium association has a lien on your condominium because of unpaid condominium fees, it may be able to foreclose upon that lien. Whether or not the condominium association has this power, there are steps you should take to deal with your condominium fees, as discussed below.

Foreclosure Based on a Tax Lien. Once you default on property taxes on your house and a lien has been imposed, the government will move quickly to sell your house. In most states, you will not be summoned to court prior to the sale. You should seek legal help as soon as you fall behind on your taxes to have the best chance of preventing or delaying the sale. A lawyer may also help overturn the sale, if there are proper legal grounds, or redeem your property if it has been sold.

Before you fall behind on your taxes, there are many things you can do to reduce the amount of property tax you owe. Every state has a special property tax abatement or exemption program which allows you to reduce the amount of taxes that you owe. These special programs apply based on your age, disability, income level, or personal status (for example, veteran, surviving spouse of fire fighter or police officer killed in the line of duty).

You may also reduce your taxes by challenging the assessed value of your home if you believe the assessment does not reflect the true value of your home. You may contest the assessment if, for example, you believe that your property is assessed at a higher value than similar properties in your area. Each state has a procedure for challenging tax assessments. Usually you must file your appeal shortly after you receive the bill with the new assessment. It is important that you follow the time guidelines or you may lose your ability to challenge the assessment.

In most states, if your home has already been sold at a tax sale, you may redeem your home by paying the buyer whatever he or she paid for the property or for the taxes owed, plus interest. The law in each state varies as to how long you have to redeem your property, but usually it is at least one year after the sale. Often the amount you will need to redeem will be less if you do it sooner rather than later. This is because interest and additional fees may accrue during the redemption period.

Foreclosure Based on a Judgment Lien. If a creditor does not hold a lien or mortgage on your home, it cannot seize your home until it first obtains a court judgment against you for money owed. It first has to go to court to sue on a debt you owe that creditor, and you are entitled to a hearing on whether you owe the money. (See Chapter Nine for tips on defending such lawsuits to collect a debt.)

If the judge rules for the creditor, a lien, called a "judgment lien," may be placed on your home. The creditor can later "execute" that judgment by asking a court to sell your home and use the proceeds to satisfy the amount of the judgment lien.

Even then, state homestead laws usually prevent such a sale. Although the amount varies by state, these laws do not allow seizure of your home unless the equity you have in that home is over a certain amount. Additionally, bankruptcy is likely to give you the opportunity to remove the lien entirely if you do not have substantial equity in your home.

Further discussion of these and other protections against judgment liens is contained in Chapters Nine and Nineteen. Because you have strong protections against losing your home because of a judgment lien, it is particularly important for you to get expert advice and pursue your rights aggressively. This can be the difference between keeping and losing your home.

FORECLOSURE AND OTHER ACTIONS BASED UPON UNPAID CONDOMINIUM FEES

If you are having trouble paying the mortgage on your condominium, you are probably also behind on your condominium fees. It is important for you to understand the consequences of your overdue condo fees.

Condominium owners own their unit, but the building, the land on which it sits, and the other "common areas" are owned by the association of unit owners. Each unit owner has a percentage interest in the common areas, and the condominium association collects a fee (usually monthly) from each unit owner to pay for upkeep of the common areas and for certain other services such as landscaping and snow and trash removal.

The condominium association will have collection remedies for failure to pay your condominium fees and may pursue them aggressively. State laws vary in terms of how associations may go about collecting the debt.

The law in many states gives condominium associations a priority lien for the payment of fees. A priority lien means that the condominium association may foreclose and collect a certain amount of its fees through the sale of your unit. This means that you can lose your condominium unless you pay your fees or reach some type of agreement to get caught up over time.

When condominium association liens are put on your property records, they may complicate the process of arranging a workout with your other mortgage lenders. This is because the mortgage may be at risk if there is a foreclosure on the condominium liens. For this reason, when pursuing a workout agreement in a state that allows associations to take a lien, you will need to pay off your fees or negotiate with the condominium association at the same time as you deal with your other lenders.

Another common way for an association to get its fees is through legal action. The association's trustees may file suit and then seek to enforce the court's judgment if they win. If your unit is rented, they may also be able to collect rent from your tenants until the overdue amount is paid. If your condo association pursues this remedy, the lawsuit will be just like any other lawsuit to collect a debt. Your options for dealing with debt collection lawsuits in general are discussed in Chapter Nine.

It is important to communicate with the association's trustees or property manager if you are unable to pay your condominium fees. Let them know the reason you fell behind and try to arrange an agreement which will address the problem based on your financial circumstances. Remind them that you have to make your mortgage, food, and utility payments first and then you can apply funds toward the condominium fees. Since the other owners are your neighbors, they may be willing to work out an agreement with you that will help you through difficult times.

13

Important Additional Protections Against Foreclosure

ADDITIONAL PROTECTIONS COVERED IN THIS CHAPTER

- If Your Mortgage Is Backed by the Government (FHA, VA, RHS)
- For Active Duty Military
- Where a Mortgage Resulted from a Home Improvement Scam
- For Refinancings or Where Mortgage Not Used to Purchase Your Home
- Where a Lender's Actions Are Fraudulent or Oppressive
- Manufactured Home Mortgages

Chapter Twelve examines your basic rights to delay or prevent a foreclosure. This chapter examines additional rights that apply only to certain situations: for certain types of mortgages, for certain types of borrowers, or where the loan transaction or a related consumer transaction involved fraud or unfairness. These are often your best protections against foreclosure, so it is important to review this chapter to see if any of these special rights apply to you.

PROTECTIONS IF YOU HAVE A GOVERNMENT-BACKED MORTGAGE

Many mortgages are backed by the U.S. Government—FHA/HUD insured mortgages, VA guaranteed loans, and Rural Housing Service (RHS) loans. The government provides you special rights to obtain a loan modification or workout and also provides special protections against foreclosure. For more about workout options specific for each of these types of loans, see both Chapter Eleven and also National Consumer Law Center, *Foreclosure Prevention Counseling* (2007). This section discusses some special rights you have to stop a foreclosure for FHA/HUD and VA loans. RHS loans are examined in *Foreclosure Prevention Counseling*.

You may be able to tell whether you have one of these mortgage loans by your loan paperwork that will include on certain pages a symbol for one of these government agencies. For example, to tell whether you have a VA mortgage, look for the VA logo on the top corner of the mortgage or other loan documents.

Nevertheless, if a form says FHA or HUD, this does not guarantee it is a FHA/HUD mortgage because some lenders use the HUD forms for all mortgages, whether they are government insured or not. A better way to tell is: if you have an FHA/HUD mortgage, you are likely to be paying government insurance premiums with your mortgage payment. If you don't know whether this is the case, look at your original mortgage or loan documents to see. You can also check whether there is a box marked "FHA insured" that is checked off on your settlement statement.

If you have any doubt whether you have a VA, RHS, or FHA/HUD mortgage, call and ask the company servicing your mortgage loan. Their records should be clear on this issue because the existence of the insurance is a benefit to them. FHA/HUD loans are insured by the Federal Housing Administration, which is part of the U.S. Department of Housing and Urban Development. VA loans are guaranteed by the Department of Veterans Affairs, and RHS loans are with a part of the U.S. Department of Agriculture, the Rural Housing Service.

Special Protections Against Foreclosure for FHA/HUD Loans.

Lenders cannot begin legal foreclosure proceedings on a FHA/HUD insured loan until at least three monthly payments are overdue. Such lenders also cannot foreclose if your only default is an inability to pay an escrow shortage in a lump sum.

If your home has been destroyed or damaged by a hurricane, earthquake or other natural disaster, your lender on a FHA/HUD-insured mortgage may be required to temporarily stop foreclosure proceedings. HUD imposes a ninety-day moratorium on foreclosures of homes directly affected by disasters declared by the President. This means that the lender may not start or continue a foreclosure on your home for ninety days after the date the President declares a disaster.

Foreclosure Defense Based on Improper Servicing of FHA/HUD Loans. A servicer's failure to meet HUD's servicing requirements can be a defense to foreclosure. (See Chapter Ten for a discussion of servicers.) Some of the servicing requirements include:

- Servicers must give you notice of your default no later than the end of the second month of your delinquency. This notice must explain what you must do to get reinstated.
- Lenders must make reasonable efforts to arrange face-to-face interviews with you before three full monthly installments are overdue. Telephone interviews are also possible.
- Most importantly, the lender may not initiate foreclosure until it has considered whether you qualify for one of the FHA/HUD workout plans, discussed in Chapter Eleven.

More often than not failure to comply with these servicing requirements will delay rather than permanently prevent foreclosure.

Get Help from a HUD-Approved Counselor. If you have a FHA/HUD mortgage and are threatened with foreclosure, and you do not have an attorney, you should at least contact a HUD-approved counselor. Sometimes a counselor can convince a lender to give you a second chance. HUD also has an office in Oklahoma City whose responsibilities include helping you if you are facing foreclosure on a HUD mortgage. The telephone number for that office is 888-297-8685. Stay on the line until a HUD field officer picks up.

Restrictions on Lender's Right to Foreclose on a VA Mortgage. Families with VA mortgages have certain protections against foreclosure. The lender cannot foreclose unless you fail to make three full monthly payments. The lender must give the VA thirty days' warning of its intent to foreclose and must make all reasonable efforts at forbearance before actually foreclosing on the property. Forbearance will usually not last beyond 12 months. In addition, the VA may assist you if you are an active servicemember and if a job transfer requires relocation, and you lack time to adequately market your home. Active members of the military also have special rights under the Servicemember's Civil Relief Act (discussed later in this chapter).

The lender must consider temporary suspension of payments, extension of the loan, and acceptance of partial payments. If the lender still intends to foreclose, you can stop the foreclosure by paying all overdue payments, all late charges, and any of the lender's foreclosure expenses to date.

The lender's failure to meet its obligations in this area can be a defense to foreclosure. If you hope to use this defense, it is a good idea to send a letter to the lender which asks the lender to consider one or more of these foreclosure avoidance strategies. The lender's failure to respond appropriately would then be evidence of its failure to meet its responsibilities.

In recent years, the Department of Veterans Affairs (VA) has devoted more resources to helping homeowners with workout plans. Contact a local VA office and ask to speak to an employee who deals with the VA's mortgage guarantee program. It is helpful to be ready to explain the reasons for your default and what you see as the best plan for getting your mortgage payments back on track.

SPECIAL PROTECTIONS FOR ACTIVE DUTY MILITARY

If you are on active duty in the military, you have special protections from foreclosure under the Servicemembers Civil Relief Act. This Act applies to all loans—conventional, insured by the FHA, or guaranteed by the VA or RHS. The key limitation to know about is that these protections *only apply* if you entered into the loan before your current period of active duty.

In order to qualify for the protections of this law you must be a member of the Army, Navy, Marine Corps, Air Force, Coast Guard, or a Public Health Officer in the Army or Navy. Members of the Reserves or National Guard who are called to active service also qualify. Spouses or other dependents of anyone listed above qualify for many of the protections, but usually they have to apply to the court to enforce the protections.

This section outlines briefly the significant protections from foreclosure for which you may qualify. Because these rights will often help you save your home, you should seek legal help to enforce the protections of this law. You can get more information about the law on the website for the U.S. Army's Judge Advocate General's Corps at www.jagcnet.army.mil.

Restrictions on Lenders' Right to Foreclose. If you are on active duty, a lender must obtain a court order or your written permission to foreclose on your home. (Remember, this protection only applies if you took out the mortgage loan *before* your current period of active duty.) The lender must comply with this requirement even if state law normally allows nonjudicial foreclosure. This protection also applies for a period of ninety days after the end of active duty.

If the lender files a foreclosure case, the court is required to stay (suspend) the case for ninety days if you make a written request to the court. The request should explain why your military duties affect your ability to appear in court, should state the debt when you will be able to appear, and should include a statement by your commanding officer that your military duties prevent you from appearing in court and that leave is not authorized. You can request a longer stay if your military duties will have a continuing effect on your ability to appear. In addition, the court has the authority to stay the case for a period of time, or make adjustments in your obligations under the mortgage, if your ability to pay the mortgage was materially affected by your military service. If you request a stay, you should ask for confirmation in writing that the foreclosure proceedings have been suspended.

If the lender has already obtained a default judgment against you, you may be able to challenge that judgment, but you or your representative will need to do that while you are on active duty or within sixty days after the end of your active duty. Any rights you have under state law to redeem a property after a tax sale will also be extended by an amount of time equal to your active military service, or 180 days after you leave active duty, whichever is longer. The law also provides protections for other attempts to seize or sell your home, such as when a local government tries to enforce a property tax lien by holding a tax sale or a creditor tries to enforce a judgment lien.

Change in Interest Rate. In addition to relief from foreclosure, a lender may not charge more than 6% interest on the loan of a servicemember during a period of active duty. This includes any fees or other charges payable on the loan (late charges, for example). Any interest above 6% that would normally be charged must be forgiven, not simply deferred. The lender must also reduce your regular payment amount to give you credit for the interest forgiven. The 6% cap on interest rates applies to other types of debts entered into before beginning active duty, such as credit card debts, car loans, and some student loans. See Chapter Five for more information about this protection.

To take advantage of this law, you should call your lender and tell them that you have been called to active duty. When you or your representative contacts the lender, you may want to have on hand a copy of the order from the military informing you of your activation, any other orders extending your military service and proof that your loan was entered into before the date of activation. You or your representative must also send a written notice to the lender stating that you are on active duty and include a copy of your military orders.

PROTECTIONS WHERE MORTGAGE RESULTED FROM A HOME IMPROVEMENT SCAM

A widespread and vicious scam is to pressure you into a home improvement contract—vinyl siding, basement waterproofing, replacement windows, roofing, etc.—and then have you signpay for this improvement by signing up for very unfavorable financing and a mortgage on your home. If the home improvement contractor never completes the work or the work is shoddy or wildly overpriced, you will then have legal claims against the home improvement contractor. A different company, often a finance company or a mortgage company, will nevertheless try to collect on the loan and foreclose when you refuse to pay or get behind.

If a contractor ripped you off, you may not have to repay a loan that the contractor arranged for you to pay for the work.

In almost all such situations, you can fight the foreclosure based on the misconduct of the home improvement contractor. That is, even though the contractor and lender are not the same company, there is enough of a connection between the two of them so that you can raise the contractor's misconduct as a reason why you do not have to repay the loan, so that the foreclosure should not be allowed.

While raising the conduct of a contractor or salesperson is a very effective defense to a foreclosure, it is best to obtain legal representation to make sure that the defense is raised correctly. More detailed information (than what is presented below) about raising the contractor's misconduct as a defense to a foreclosure is found in another National Consumer Law Center publication, *Unfair and Deceptive Acts and Practices* (6th ed. 2004 and Supp.).

When Is Your Lender Responsible for Your Contractor's Misconduct? You can almost always defend a foreclosure based on the home improvement contractor's misconduct. In most cases the loan documents will say that any holder of the loan is subject to all claims and defenses that you have against the seller (that is, the contractor). In other words, the very loan the lender is trying to enforce will say that you can raise the contractor's misconduct as a defense to the foreclosure.

Where this provision is not in the loan documents, you still should be able to raise the contractor's misconduct as a defense. First check whether the contractor signed the loan as the original lender, and then sold the contract to another company. You can tell that the contractor is the original lender because the contractor's name will be on the loan as the lender, and the contractor will then have sold the loan to another lender. In that situation, the law *always* allows you to raise in a foreclosure by the second lender all the defenses that you could have raised against the home improvement contractor.

The situation is not so clear-cut when another lender (not the contractor) was the original lender. In that case, some other company's name will be on the loan agreement as the lender. You will need a lawyer to press your defenses, but there are a number of grounds why the lender still should be subject to your defenses against the contractor.

Defending a Foreclosure Based on Contractor Misconduct. If the contractor never did any work, failed to complete required work, or did the work in a very sloppy or inadequate way, that should be sufficient to stop a foreclosure. These situations create warranty or deceptive practices claims. It is also possible to have a partial defense based on a warranty or deceptive practice which would reduce the amount you owe and prevent foreclosure. On the other hand, small errors or minor problems with the work probably will not be enough as a foreclosure defense. In some cases, these problems can be fixed by calling the contractor.

Similarly, door-to-door sellers (including contractors who go door to door) have to give you a three-day cancellation right, either under the Truth in Lending law or under door-to-door sales laws or both. If this right to cancel was never given or if work began before the three-day period ended, you may be able to cancel the home improvement contract. A canceled sales contract would be a complete defense on the loan.

You may have claims against the contractor that are smaller in amount than the total amount you owe on the loan. The loan will still be a binding obligation even though you have a defense to repayment of part of it. In that case, if you are in default, the lender may be able to foreclose because of your obligation to pay part of the loan. Nevertheless, some courts will delay the foreclosure until the amount owed is established. You can often negotiate so that you need only keep current on smaller payments based on the new loan amount. Alternatively, you can consider refinancing with a reputable company for the amount which is still owed.

PROTECTIONS AGAINST FORECLOSURE FOR REFINANCINGS OR WHERE MORTGAGE NOT USED TO PURCHASE YOUR HOME

Truth in Lending Rescission Provides Powerful Relief in Certain Circumstances. Federal law provides you with an extraordinarily effective means of stopping a foreclosure in certain special situations. Instead of giving you more time to make reduced payments, this federal remedy allows you to permanently *cancel* your mortgage and significantly reduce the amount of the debt you owe the lender. Once the mortgage is canceled, there can be no foreclosure.

If you can legally rescind your loan under
Truth in Lending, you, not the lender,
will be in the driver's seat.

This remedy, called Truth in Lending rescission, is not available to cancel a mortgage used to purchase or build your home. But it may be available to cancel other types of mortgages, such as second mortgages, first mortgages not used to purchase your home, refinanced mortgages, debt consolidation loans involving mortgages, and home equity lines of credit.

Truth in Lending rescission is a powerful tool particularly when dealing with credit contracts imposed by home improvement contractors, finance companies, and mortgage companies that prey on families in financial distress. In fact, in 1994, Congress amended the law by adding the Home Ownership and Equity Protection Act (HOEPA) for just this purpose. This law provides special rescission rights for high interest loans and loans with high up-front costs.

While Truth in Lending rescission sounds almost too good to be true, there are four catches.

1. Truth in Lending rescission does not apply to certain types of loans.

2. The lender must have made one of a list of basic mistakes when providing information to you about your mortgage or when setting the terms of your mortgage.

3. You will not be able to rescind in most cases if your loan is more than three years old.

4. You must usually go to court to convince the lender to honor your Truth in Lending rescission rights.

A lawyer is almost always necessary in order to successfully utilize Truth in Lending rescission. Contact your local bar association referral service, your local legal services office, or seek a recommendation from a local nonprofit. You may want to ask for a specialist in consumer law. If your case is successful, the home will be free from the mortgage, your indebtedness may be reduced by thousands of dollars, and the lender may have to pay for your attorney.

This section is not a detailed analysis of Truth in Lending rescission, which can be quite technical. This section does help you identify when Truth in Lending rescission is definitely not available and when it may be. This section also helps you decide whether it is worth contacting an attorney to discuss your rescission rights. More detailed information is available in National Consumer Law Center's *Truth in Lending* (6th ed. 2007). Besides a detailed analysis of all aspects of the law, the volume reprints the key sources of Truth in Lending law—the Truth in Lending Act (TILA), the federal TILA regulations, and the official federal TILA interpretations, as well as sample letters and pleadings. NCLC also publishes *Stop Predatory Lending* (2d ed. 2007), covering TILA and other strategies for dealing with high-rate loans.

When Does Truth in Lending Rescission Apply? Truth in Lending rescission applies to most home mortgages except the ones taken when you buy or build a home. When more than one person has the right to rescind a transaction (such as husband and wife), any one of the individuals can exercise the right and cancel the transaction on behalf of all.

TILA rescission does *NOT* apply if:

■ The mortgage loan was used to purchase or build the home;

- The mortgage loan was not for consumer purposes, but was for business or agricultural purposes;
- The lender was only involved in a very few loans within the last year;
- The mortgage is on investment property, a vacation house, or other property *not* your principal residence at the time the loan was extended (a manufactured home, condominium, cooperative, two- or three-family home, trailer, and even a houseboat *can* be a principal residence);
- You no longer own the home that the mortgage relates to;
- The mortgage is a refinancing of an existing loan where no new money is borrowed and the same property stays mortgaged; or
- The mortgage is more than three years old (although there may be extensions of this time period in some states).

When Can You Rescind a Mortgage? There are three different situations where you can use TILA rescission to cancel your mortgage. You can rescind for any reason within three days after taking out a loan that uses your home as collateral. This will be too late to stop an impending foreclosure, but it is very useful if you ever are pressured into refinancing your mortgage or contracting to improve you home, and it is a bad deal. You have three days to back out of the deal.

You can also cancel a mortgage loan if you did not receive proper notice that you could rescind the loan. Lenders must deliver two copies of the notice of the right to rescind. The notice must be on a separate document that identifies the transaction, discloses that the lender has a mortgage on specified property of yours, and that you and joint owners have a right to rescind. The notice must also give directions on how to rescind, provide a form for that purpose with the appropriate addresses, and explain the effects of rescission and how long you have to rescind. Failure to include all this information or failure to give you this notice is grounds for you to cancel the loan even several years later.

The third basis for canceling the loan is if the lender makes a mistake in its disclosure of certain important terms of the loan. If the disclosure is improper, you can rescind the loan even several years later, unless you are given a corrected disclosure. Other protections may apply if you have a high-cost loan and the lender did not give you additional disclosures or your loan includes certain unfair terms. In practice, since lenders rarely correct mistakes, you can cancel just before the foreclosure unless the loan is more than three years old. You only have three years to rescind the loan if you did not receive notice of the right to rescind the loan or if the lender made a mistake in its disclosure of certain important terms. A few courts allow rescission even for loans older than three years if you are trying to prevent a foreclosure.

Uncovering Truth in Lending Errors. For many loans, the key issue will be whether the lender made a mistake on the disclosure form sufficient to allow you to cancel. Errors are often made in important calculations, especially when there are a variety of costs and charges in connection with the loan.

Nevertheless, this issue can be quite complicated. Any decision to pursue Truth in Lending rescission should be made with the assistance of an attorney experienced with financial calculations and Truth in Lending issues. In fact, the analysis necessary to uncover lender mistakes may be intimidating for many. Nevertheless, there are several steps that you or your attorney can take to explore whether your home can be saved through Truth in Lending rescission. What you do is review the numbers and other terms on the Truth in Lending disclosure form and related paperwork:

- *Check the numbers.* Based on the payment schedule, is the total of payments accurate? Is the annual percentage rate calculation correct? Does the amount financed and finance charge add up to the total of payments? The National Consumer Law Center's *Truth in Lending* manual explains what mathematical errors to look for and how to show that the lender made a mistake.
- *Review the calculation of the amount financed.* See what happened to the "amount financed" that is, the money you borrowed, by reviewing the contract and any itemization you received. Be suspicious if large portions of the amount financed did not go to you or for your benefit. When a loan is loaded with broker fees, points, insurance, and assorted fees, it may pay to ask a lawyer familiar with Truth in Lending law to review the contract. The National Consumer Law Center's *Truth in Lending* gives a step-by-step analysis as to whether the existence of these charges in the amount financed will allow a homeowner to rescind.
- *Prohibited terms in some loans.* If you have a high interest rate loan or a loan with high fees and costs, the lender is subject to extensive additional regulation under the HOEPA amendments to the Truth in Lending Act. Additional disclosures are required. Many unfair terms

267

are prohibited in those loans including most balloon payments, negative amortization, and most prepayment penalties. Failing to make necessary special disclosures or including a prohibited term in these loans is a ground for you to rescind.

■ *Did you receive information about your right to cancel?* If not, you can rescind the loan. For home improvement contracts, did the contractor begin working before the three-day period elapsed?

How to Cancel. Cancellation is straightforward if you cancel within three business days of signing the papers. Unfortunately, anyone threatened with foreclosure is well past that point. If you think you may have a right to cancel, but more than three days have passed, you should check with an experienced consumer lawyer. You will need to send a notice of rescission to the lender, but the requirements for doing so after the three-day period has expired are somewhat technical. Several sample forms related to cancellation are included in National Consumer Law Center's *Truth in Lending* (6th ed. 2007).

The Effect of Cancellation. Sending the rescission notice automatically voids the mortgage. As long as the rescission was proper, the lender no longer has the right to foreclose on your home. This applies to the current lender or mortgage holder even if it was not the original lender on the mortgage. Within twenty calendar days after the lender receives the notice of rescission, the lender must cancel the mortgage and file that release on the public record. Although you may later have to return to the lender the amount borrowed (not including interest and other charges) if you cancel after the three-day period has expired, you do not need to do so right away.

A lender who receives a cancellation notice but no loan payments will usually ignore the notice and begin the mortgage foreclosure. What this means is that you will have to retain an attorney to fight for enforcement of the right to rescind. Your lawyer can raise the Truth in Lending rescission as a defense to the foreclosure.

There is much misunderstanding as to a consumer's financial responsibility after rescinding a loan. It is true that rescinding a loan does not mean that you necessarily get to keep all the loan proceeds. On the other hand, many people mistakenly believe that the consumer, when rescinding, must immediately pay the full amount of the loan.

The exact answer as to when and how much you must pay after rescission will depend on many factors. You should not have to pay anything back before the mortgage is voided, meaning that the home will be safe from foreclosure at least temporarily.

The amount you do pay back will often be significantly less than the amount borrowed. If your rescission is proper, you will not have to repay interest, most fees, closing costs, points, insurance payments, and other charges. Any payments you have made (even those originally applied to interest or fees) will be credited to the principal. Furthermore, the lender's violation of Truth in Lending law will usually mean that you can knock off at least another $2,000 from the amount owed and perhaps significantly more. Moreover, for a home improvement contract, you may just have to return the value of the work done, which is often much less than what you paid for it.

You will probably need to go to court for a decision about whether your cancellation was proper. In such a case, you should also raise whatever other legal claims are available, such as breach of warranty and deception, as additional reasons why the amount owed should be further reduced.

If you still have to return a sizeable amount to the lender, you can seek to refinance the amount owed (which should be much less than the original loan amount) with a different lender and at lower interest rates. This may well result in affordable payments. See Chapter Six for what to look out for if you decide to refinance.

While the details of any payment you will have to make are being worked out, you should keep making your monthly payment—or as much of it as you can afford. Your lawyer may advise you to deposit the payments into an escrow account or savings account rather than paying them directly to the lender. That way, you will build up a sum of money toward whatever amount you are required to repay.

WHERE LENDER'S ACTIONS ARE FRAUDULENT OR OPPRESSIVE

In today's mortgage industry, a number of different companies may have defrauded you or taken unfair advantage—mortgage brokers or others who help you originate a loan, the original lender, the company servicing your mortgage, and the company that presently holds your mortgage loan. An important question is whether you can raise as a defense to foreclosure the conduct of all of these different companies. For example, if you were misled when you took out your mortgage loan, can you raise this as a defense to foreclosure where an entirely different lender is seeking to foreclose upon your loan?

If you were deceived or treated unfairly, you will often have a claim against the company that deceived you or treated you unfairly. The key question though is whether you can raise this as a defense in a foreclosure action or whether you have to bring a separate lawsuit to recover your damage. You may feel less happy years later upon receiving a check from someone who ripped you off if in the meantime you have lost your home.

Conduct That May Void Your Loan No Matter Who Holds Your Mortgage. Look for the following, which may eliminate your obligation to repay the loan and thus stop the foreclosure, even if a different company is holding your mortgage loan and is seeking to foreclose:

- The lender misrepresented the nature of the document you signed, for example, saying, "this is just an application";
- The interest rate exceeds the legal maximum;
- The lender is not licensed to do business in your state;
- The lender coerced you into signing the loan;
- The person who signed the mortgage was not the real owner of the mortgaged property (usually this involves forgery);
- The person who signed for the loan was not legally competent to do so (for example, children below a certain age or people who are mentally infirm).

Some defenses based on state law, however, may not apply to certain lenders because the defenses are "preempted" by federal law. Where these defenses are available, you can have the loan declared void. Often, you will need the help of a lawyer to do so.

Figuring Out If the Same Lender Originated and Now Holds Your Loan. For other types of lender misconduct, not listed above, you will have to deal with the problem whether the lender who engaged in the misconduct is the same lender that seeks to foreclose. This is because, in today's mortgage marketplace, mortgage loans are typically sold from one lender to another. Of course, the lender may remain the same, and then you can raise all defenses to that lender's foreclosure. But it is not so easy to tell whether the lender stays the same (typically it is not the case).

Remember that there are two different functions: being the lender holding your mortgage and being the company servicing your mortgage loan. The servicer is sending you correspondence and foreclosure notices and has accepted payments, but the servicer usually does not own your mortgage loan. The mortgage servicer will not be seeking to foreclose in its own name, but in the name of the lender holding your mortgage.

In the easy case, Bank A gave you a loan, still owns the loan, and performs its own servicing. Then any defense you have against Bank A for deception, fraud, non-disclosure, and the like may be raised as a defense in Bank A's foreclosure.

Another possibility is that Bank A gave you a loan and still owns that loan, even though Bank A has hired Servicer B to accept your payments and send you notices. While Servicer B is sending you letters about your foreclosure, Bank A still owns the loan, and Bank A will be the one really foreclosing. In that case, any claim you have against Bank A or its agent, Servicer B, for deception as to the loan terms, mistake in applying payments, misrepresentations about whether they will seek a foreclosure, oppression in originating the loan, and the like are all available defenses to foreclosure.

Unfortunately, another situation is more common. In that case, Bank A originated your loan, but sold the mortgage to Lender C, who then hired Bank A to service the loan for Lender C. Even though you are getting correspondence still from Bank A, any foreclosure will really be in the name of Lender C. It may be more difficult now to raise in Lender C's foreclosure Bank A's misconduct in first giving you the loan. On the other hand, you can raise as a defense the conduct by Bank A in *servicing* the loan, because for that function, Bank A was the agent for Lender C.

Potential Defenses Based on Fraud and Misconduct Can Be Grouped into Three Categories.

From the examples above, you can see that your defenses to foreclosure really can be grouped into three categories. The first type are described above in "Conduct That May Void Your Loan No Matter Who Holds Your Mortgage." These defenses apply no matter who holds your mortgage.

Second are your claims involving your servicer, which are discussed in Chapter Ten. These might include promises from your servicer to give you more time to catch up payments or their misapplication of your payments. Since the servicer is the mortgage holder's agent, you can raise all these defenses in the foreclosure.

The third type are claims you have that you were deceived about the terms of the loan when you first took it out, or that the lender hid important information from you. Another defense might be that the lender knew you could not afford the loan but recommended it anyways, or gave you a variable rate loan whose payments would explode in size after a few years, even knowing that you were on a fixed income. Yet another might be that the lender gave you a consolidation loan that actually made you worse off than if you had not consolidated various obligations, or continually refinanced a mortgage making you somewhat worse off after each refinancing. In fact, there are numerous other possible defenses you may have concerning the original loan and its compliance with federal and state laws. You will need an attorney versed in this area to identify these defenses.

This third category of defenses can be raised to stop a foreclosure if the original lender still holds the loan. On the other hand, you will need an attorney to figure out whether the defenses can stop a foreclosure if the original lender has since sold the loan to another lender. If you cannot raise these claims in the foreclosure, you can always raise them in an action for money damages against the original lender. But this may not be enough if you lose your home in the meantime.

MANUFACTURED (MOBILE) HOMES

Is a Manufactured Home Considered Real Estate or Personal Property? Manufactured homeowners face some unique issues when dealing with a threatened foreclosure. The first question is whether the manufactured home is considered like other homes as real estate or as personal property (similar to a vehicle) once the home is purchased and put on a lot. If the home is treated as real estate, the lender who wants to foreclose will have to use real estate foreclosure procedures. If the home is treated as personal property, the lender may be able to repossess it through a judicial procedure, commonly known as replevin, or through self-help repossession (discussed in Chapter Sixteen).

Whether a manufactured home will be treated as real property or personal property depends on your state's laws. All states, for example, treat a manufactured home as personal property before it is purchased and put on a lot. You will need to get information about your state's approach to this question. In most states, there is no clear answer because the treatment of a manufactured home depends on a variety of factors, including where the home was when the loan documents were signed. Was it on the dealer's lot or attached semi-permanently to land? If it was attached to land, was it your own land or was it in a manufactured home park? Is there a title to the home, or are ownership documents recorded in the local land records?

It is important to know that the law in some states may treat your manufactured home as personal property in some circumstances and as real property in others. You may need legal help to answer this important question. Some states also allow you to take steps to convert your manufactured home from personal property to real property.

You should consider discussing the possibility of a workout agreement with the lender if you are behind on payments, whether your manufactured home is real estate or personal property. A variety of options for workouts are discussed in Chapter Eleven.

If a workout is not possible and your manufactured home is treated as real estate under your state's law, then your legal rights will be consistent with the legal rights of other homeowners, as discussed in this and the previous chapter. If your manufactured home is treated as personal property, then your legal rights will compare more closely to the rights of automobile owners facing repossession, as discussed in Chapter Sixteen. A lender may send a representative to repossess your manufactured home; more likely, however, your lender will take you to court and try to have the court order a sheriff to seize your manufactured home. This proceeding is called replevin, but in some states has other names, such as detinue. Like other court actions, you should get legal help as soon as possible to defend against the lender's claims. No matter how your state law treats manufactured homes, filing bankruptcy can stop a foreclosure, repossession, or replevin, and provide options for curing the default. See Chapters Twelve and Nineteen.

Special Rights for Manufactured Homeowners. Manufactured homeowners may have certain rights not available to other homeowners. Federal protections apply to certain manufactured home loans. You may have thirty days to get caught up on a default after notice of the default is provided.

A lender does not have to provide this federal protection, but the federal government offers certain incentives for lenders to do so, and many choose to do so. If so, the lender must send you a notice of default by certified mail, return receipt requested. The notice must state the nature of the default, what you must do to cure the default, the lender's intended actions if you fail to cure, and your right to redeem the property under state law. The lender may not repossess your manufactured home or call the rest of the note due until thirty days after the notice is mailed. To cure, you must pay the past-due amounts due plus any late or deferral charges.

Since issues related to manufactured home foreclosures and repossession vary significantly from state to state, it is recommended that you also consult with someone who is knowledgeable about the laws in your state. Pamphlets may also be available from your state's attorney general or at a local counseling agency or legal services office.

Owners of manufactured homes have certain extra protections, but they also have added problems if they do not pay their park rent and fees.

Manufactured Home Lot Rent. If you rent the land on which your manufactured home sits, failure to make your lot payments can result in eviction. Typically, the manufactured home park or other landowner that owns the lot will have to bring a legal action to evict you. In some states, this legal action will be similar to other landlord and tenant actions, as discussed in Chapter Fourteen. About half the states have special legislation dealing with manufactured home park evictions, and that procedure will apply instead.

If the owner of the lot evicts you after a court action for failing to pay rent, at a minimum you will have to move the manufactured home. Sometimes this presents practical problems because the home is not really movable, is expensive to move, or you have nowhere else to put it.

Equally important, in many states, the lot owner has special remedies allowing it to take action to repossess the manufactured home in the event you fail to pay your lot rent. In many states, this process is the same as for any other creditor with a claim against you. The lot owner can seek a money judgment and then use that judgment as a lien on your manufactured home. These issues are discussed in Chapter Nine. In other states, however, special laws give the lot owner the right to an automatic lien and special repossession rights ahead of other creditors.

You will need to check with a specialist who is knowledgeable about these issues in your state. You can also ask a manufactured home park tenant's association or manufactured home owner's association for advice. But it is important to deal with your lot rent as a priority debt just as high as your manufactured home loan payment.

Consumer Issues Associated with Manufactured Homes. Manufactured homes are the source of a variety of abuses. It is not uncommon for mobile homes to be defective, for loans used to purchase manufactured homes to be made on unfair terms, or for manufactured home park owners to exercise abusive collection tactics. These practices may give rise to defenses against foreclosure, replevin, or eviction. They may also create legal claims for which you have the right to recover money.

If you think you have a defense to foreclosure, replevin, or eviction or a claim for damages, it is a good idea to check with a lawyer or manufactured home park association sooner rather than later. Delay can cost you your legal rights. In some locations, local legal service organizations will advise you about your rights or represent you for free.

Manufactured home-related debts raise unique issues which can be very complicated. Further information can be found in National Consumer Law Center's *Repossessions* (6th ed. 2005 and Supp.) and *Foreclosures* (2d ed. 2006 and Supp.). Other useful publications include National Consumer Law Center's *Unfair and Deceptive Acts and Practices* (6th ed. 2004 and Supp.); *NCLC Guide to Mobile Homes;* and *Manufactured Housing Park Tenants: Shifting the Balance of Power* (AARP 2004).

14

Evictions and Other Disputes with Landlords

TOPICS COVERED IN THIS CHAPTER

- Strategies to Get Out of a Lease
- Breaking a Lease If Necessary
- Responding to Eviction Attempts
- Possible Defenses to Evictions
- Special Rights for Military Servicemembers
- Using Bankruptcy to Stop Eviction

If you cannot afford your rent payments, you are likely to be facing one of these significant problems: (1) you want to move out, but the landlord wants you to pay for breaking the lease; or (2) you want to stay in the residence, but your landlord is seeking to evict you. This chapter provides advice on the best way to deal with each of these problems.

GETTING OUT OF A LEASE

Getting Out of Your Lease As an Alternative to Eviction. Affordable rents can quickly become unaffordable when you lose your job or when, for some other reason, your financial situation worsens. Moving to a less costly apartment or house may be your best option, at least until your situation improves. This is usually better than being evicted and then being forced to find another residence under severe time pressure.

If you break a lease, you may owe your landlord rent not just for those months you are in the apartment but for some number of months after you leave. Nevertheless, switching apartments on your own time schedule, even with this penalty, may still be a better choice than waiting to be evicted.

Eviction can be a devastating and disruptive experience. Eviction makes the financial hardships you already have even worse because it puts extra costs and pressures on you. The speed of the eviction process may force you to make unwanted choices, to pay extra expenses and to accept a less than satisfactory alternative living arrangement. Frequently, the only other housing available is more expensive or less desirable than that from which your family was evicted. Also, being evicted may make it harder for you to rent elsewhere in the future, and may impair your credit rating.

You can avoid most of these problems by moving out on your own. This is almost always better than an eviction. While you may owe your landlord some compensation for breaking the lease, there are steps you can take to lessen this amount, as set out below.

Read the Lease. The first step in terminating a lease is to read the rental agreement carefully. If the agreement provides that either party can terminate the lease by giving advance notice, you need only give the notice specified in the lease. Then you may move without responsibility for additional payments.

Check to see if the lease is for a specified amount of time, usually one year, or if it is a month-to-month lease. If you have lived in the apartment for a long time, the lease might have started out as a one-year lease but may have turned into a month-to-month lease after that year ended. Be sure to read the terms of your lease carefully to see whether the lease has become month to month or has renewed for a year. State landlord-tenant law sets the rules for terminating month-to-month agreements. In most states, you must give thirty days' written notice before moving, unless something is seriously wrong with the property, making it unsafe to remain there.

Negotiate with Your Landlord to Reduce What You Owe. If the lease requires you to pay for all rent due until the end of your lease, try to get a better deal from the landlord. If you want to try to stay in the apartment, start by asking for a rent reduction, explaining why the rent is no longer affordable. Lowering the rent may be less costly for the landlord than going to the expense of evicting you and finding a new tenant. This is less likely if you live in an area where it is very easy to find new tenants. Still, even if the landlord will not reduce the rent permanently, he might do so for a few months until you get back on your feet.

Landlords will often forgive back-rent payments
or reduce the penalty for terminating the lease
early in exchange for an agreement to move.

Landlords may also allow you to break the lease without penalty so that they can rent to others who are better able to pay. You can even try to get the landlord to agree not to charge you for back-rent if you move out by a certain date. Landlords will often do this to get you out of the apartment more quickly and avoid expensive court costs. Be sure to get in writing any deal you make with the landlord! This will protect you if the landlord breaks his or her word.

Find Someone Else to Take Over the Apartment. There are two different ways that someone else can take over your apartment and the rent payments for you. One way is a sublease, where someone else takes over your apartment and agrees to pay the rent. In a sublease, you are still obligated to pay the landlord any rent your subtenant fails to pay. The other way is for someone else to take over not only the apartment but the whole lease. This is called assuming the lease. If you can find someone to assume the lease, you will be able to wash your hands of the lease forever even if the new tenant does not pay the rent.

Look at the language in your lease to see if subleasing or lease assumption are allowed and whether the landlord must approve the new tenant. Whatever the wording of the lease, the landlord may let you move out early with no penalty if you have arranged for responsible tenants to sublet or assume the lease. Even when a lease permits subletting or assumption, landlords should be consulted before you begin looking for new occupants. Landlords are more likely to cooperate with a sublease or an assumption if you let them know what you are trying to do.

BREAKING THE LEASE

If it is impossible to negotiate a friendly early termination, assumption, or sublease, you should evaluate the financial cost of breaking the lease. Although there may be financial consequences of breaking a lease, the alternative of eviction or of continuing to pay rent for an apartment you can't afford is usually worse.

When a lease is broken, the amount you will owe the landlord is limited in most states. The landlord must try to find a new tenant for the unit right away. If the landlord does not try, or has refused to allow you to permit someone to sublease or assume the lease, this may provide you a defense if the landlord tries to collect additional rent from you.

If you have a month-to-month lease and you give proper advance notice that you are leaving, you have no financial liability to the landlord. If you have a one-year lease, you can only be obligated to pay rent until the end of the one-year lease period. Be sure to check your lease to see if you must give notice that you are not renewing it.

If there are still a number of months left on your lease and there are no state laws that limit how much you owe, breaking your lease may mean that you will owe the monthly rent for the remainder of the lease or until the landlord finds a new tenant, plus any costs associated with the landlord finding a new tenant (whichever is less). If a new tenant is found who will pay rent, but only in an amount lower than you would have paid, you may be responsible for the difference.

If the landlord does not sue, your loss will be limited to the security deposit and the last month's rent or other money held by the landlord (together with anything you agree to pay voluntarily). You can only be forced to pay more than this if the landlord goes to court. On the other hand, landlords who take their cases to court may recover not only all their losses, but sometimes also court costs and attorney fees if such fees are allowed by the lease agreement and state law.

Even if the landlord sues and obtains a judgment against you, he must find non-exempt property or income to satisfy the judgment if you refuse to pay it. If you are "collection proof," there will be nothing for him to take from you to collect the judgment. A bankruptcy may also eliminate the landlord's right to collect on the judgment. (See Chapter Nine for more information about protecting your property from judgments.)

However, even if you are collection proof and your old landlord can't collect anything from you, having a judgment on your record may still cause you problems in looking for a new apartment. Some landlords subscribe to "tenant screening services" which gather information from court records and sell this information to landlords who want to find out more about prospective tenants. If you live in an area where landlords frequently use these services, it is even more important to try to reach an agreement with your landlord before you move out. It is also important to try to get a copy of your credit report to make corrections if necessary. See Chapter Three for more information about credit reports and how long negative information will appear on your report.

Other Things to Do If You Decide to Break the Lease. If you decide to break the lease, here are some steps to take to minimize your liability for damages:

- You should give the landlord plenty of notice, preferably thirty to sixty days, so the landlord will have time to advertise for new tenants.
- You should consider advertising the apartment yourself. Even if a sublease or lease assumption is not permitted, offering a suitable substitute tenant will make it hard for the landlord to argue that no other tenants were available.
- The premises should be cleaned thoroughly and left in good condition when you move so that there are no claims of damages against your security deposit. It is also to your advantage to minimize any delays before the next tenant moves in. You should request that the landlord go over the property after you clean it to prevent any dispute over damages. You may also want to have a neutral party review the condition of the property before you move, in case you need a witness later. You can also take pictures or video of the clean apartment to use in the event of a dispute.
- Check newspaper, Internet, and other ads to verify that the landlord is making an effort to find new renters.
- After you move, you may also want to go by the rental unit from time to time to look for signs of new occupants.

The bottom line is that, if you break a lease, you will probably lose your security deposit. However, if you plan carefully, making sure that the landlord suffers no loss of rent and has no unplanned expenses, you may recover some or all of the deposit.

State landlord-tenant laws provide specific procedures for recovering your security deposit if the landlord does not voluntarily return it. These state laws usually specify the number of days or weeks after you move out during which the landlord must return the deposit. The landlord must send you an itemization of costs that were deducted from the original deposit if the entire deposit is not returned. Check this itemization over carefully as landlords will very commonly try to charge you for damage to the apartment that was not your fault. If you are dissatisfied with the amount returned, you can sue the landlord in small claims court yourself or seek help from a lawyer. In most states, you can recover damages and possibly attorney fees in a court case if the deposit is wrongfully withheld.

Special Considerations If Your Apartment Is Unlivable. In some cases, you may be able to break the lease due to substandard conditions in your apartment. If there are serious problems with the apartment, you may want to call the housing inspector to come out and look at the conditions. In general, rental property must meet local housing, health, fire, and building ordinances. Heat and hot water must be available. Appliances must be safe and in working order. Usually the property must be free of insect and rodent infestation.

If you have serious problems with your apartment, you may also be able to withhold rent until repairs are made. Be careful—only some state laws allow you to withhold rent to pay for necessary repairs. These laws almost always require you to follow specific steps in withholding your rent. The most common rule requires you to give notice to the landlord, usually in writing, about the problems with the apartment so that the landlord will have an opportunity to make repairs.

Sometimes, if conditions become so bad that you are forced to break the lease and move, a landlord may be required to reimburse you for the cost of temporary substitute housing. You will usually have to go to court to get an order against your landlord to make repairs, refund your rent, or pay for damages due to substandard conditions. It is best to consult a lawyer before choosing to break the lease, withhold rent, or sue a landlord for substandard conditions.

Special Considerations for Military Families. If you are in the military on active duty, you have the right to get out of a lease in some circumstances. This right applies if:

- The lease is for a place where you or a dependent live or planned to live, or that you or a dependent used or planned to use for a profession, a business, farming, or something similar; and
- You signed the lease, or someone signed it on your behalf.

If those two requirements apply, you can get out of the lease if, *after you signed the lease:*

- You entered active duty;
- You were given orders for a permanent change of station; or
- You were given orders to deploy with a military unit, or to support a military operation, for ninety days or more.

To get out of the lease, you have to notify the landlord and enclose a copy of your military orders. You can use U.S. mail (you must request a return receipt), or a commercial mail service, or you can deliver your notice by hand.

If your rent is payable monthly, you still have to pay the monthly rent on the next due date after you notify your landlord that you are terminating the lease. After that, you should no longer owe the rent, and any rent you have prepaid has to be refunded to you. If you do not pay your rent on a monthly basis (for example, if it's payable weekly or quarterly), then the termination of the lease is effective on the last day of the month in which you notify your landlord. If your dependents signed the lease along with you, they are automatically relieved of their obligations under the lease if you exercise your right to get out of it.

RESPONDING TO A LANDLORD'S EVICTION ATTEMPTS

Unfortunately, if you are unable to pay your full rent on a regular, ongoing basis, you almost inevitably will have to move. Although some defenses to eviction are available, landlords can nearly always remove you eventually for nonpayment of rent. The best potential outcome to an eviction proceeding is generally to make sure you have enough time to find alternate housing that is both affordable and adequate, with minimal disruption to your life.

Be wary of attorneys or other professionals who claim that they can keep you in an apartment indefinitely. These services are often rip-offs. Some will take your money and never file any papers on your behalf. Others will file inadequate defenses or improper bankruptcy petitions. Even though you may feel desperate to stay in your apartment, your best strategy is to determine on your own, or with the assistance of a reliable attorney or counselor, whether you have real challenges to your landlord's eviction action. Possible defenses are discussed below.

If you don't have any defenses and your problem is that you simply can't afford where you are living, you should avoid getting yourself into more trouble by paying money to a bogus eviction defense service that is just trying to profit from your desperation.

If You Are Sued for Eviction, You Have the Right to a Fair Trial. The legal steps for an eviction vary from state to state, so you must become familiar with local rules. Most eviction proceedings take place very quickly. The entire process may be completed in as little as two weeks. In some states, the process can take considerably longer, particularly if you have reasons to argue that you should not be evicted. Appeals are also possible if you lose.

If you lose an eviction case, the court will usually order that you move out immediately. If you do not move out, court officials or the sheriff will come to put you and all your belongings out. How long that takes depends on your state. It may be days, weeks, or even months. The local legal services office or the court clerk should be able to tell you how long you usually have. Remember that court officials and sheriffs rarely take breaks for holidays or weekends. You should assume that you will have the least amount of time.

Here are some general rules about the eviction process:

The Notice to Quit Is a Warning. In most states, the first step in an eviction is a notice from the landlord telling you that you must move within a short time. This is usually called a "notice to quit" or a "notice to vacate." If you have not paid your rent, the notice usually instructs you either to pay rent or to get out.

This notice does not, by itself, require that you move. It is illegal for a landlord just to put your things out or to call the police to force you to move out. Instead, landlords who want to put legal teeth behind the notice must first go to court after the time allowed in the notice has expired. (In a few states, this notice is not required and the landlord may go directly to court.) A notice to quit should be seen as a warning, not a final notice.

Generally, the notice will give you a specified number of days in which to vacate the premises. In many states, the notice must also give you the right to stay in the apartment by "curing" your failure to pay rent. "Curing" means that you pay the back-rent within a specified number of days. State law usually requires landlords to accept rent during this "cure" period if you offer them the full amount.

Sometimes the landlord will also claim other violations of the lease, such as excessive noise, damage to the premises, or keeping a pet forbidden by the lease. These violations may sometimes be cured by taking care of the underlying problem within the allotted time.

Negotiating with the Landlord. Even after receiving a notice to move out, you should consider talking to the landlord about a mutual agreement which would resolve the problem. For example, if you are having trouble paying your monthly rent in a lump sum, some landlords agree to accept weekly or biweekly installments. Landlords sometimes also agree to lower the rent, at least temporarily. Whether a landlord will agree to work something out depends upon the landlord and your relationship with the landlord in the past. Remember that landlords are not required to work things out with you if you are behind on your rent.

At the very least, you can suggest that the landlord exchange lower rent for your agreeing to move out in a certain number of months. This would let you leave on your own terms without the threat of an immediate eviction. Landlords who know that their tenants will definitely move usually allow them some extra time. This saves the landlord the expense of a court case.

Temporary and Permanent Rent Assistance. You may also want to look into various sources of temporary rent assistance that can buy you some time. Emergency rental assistance is available in some states, usually through the local public assistance office. In other places, you may want to call local community action agencies.

Public assistance programs also can help tenants. Most programs provide housing payments to needy individuals in certain circumstances, at least for short periods. In addition, church groups and private charitable organizations are potential sources of financial assistance. Some programs will help you pay back-rent. Others will help by giving or loaning you moving expenses and money for a new security deposit.

Tenants who do not already receive a government housing subsidy can also apply for various kinds of government housing assistance, including special rental assistance, state or nonprofit housing programs, Section 8 subsidized housing, and traditional public housing. Waiting lists are quite long. Urgent circumstances, such as homelessness, illness, or small children, sometimes move applicants higher on waiting lists.

Priorities for assistance and the length of waiting time vary from program to program and from community to community. Needy individuals should promptly apply for any assistance for which they may be eligible. The first place to contact for more information is your local or regional housing authority.

RESPONDING TO THE EVICTION CASE

If you have not paid the full back-rent and have not moved out by the time specified in the notice to vacate, the landlord can file an eviction action in court. This is sometimes called a forcible entry, detainer, or ejectment action. (In this book, we refer to these actions as "eviction actions.")

Eviction actions are usually scheduled for a hearing right away. State laws require that you be given the landlord's complaint and a summons to appear in court—generally by a process server or a local official. State law also specifies a minimum number of days, often as few as five, between when you are served and when the hearing takes place. Therefore, you should promptly take steps to respond, or consult a lawyer.

If you disagree with a landlord's complaint, or if you have any defenses, you should immediately contact the court and file an answer or counterclaim. Some common defenses and counterclaims are discussed briefly below.

Many landlord-tenant cases are held in less formal housing courts or state district courts. This should make it easier for you to file your own answers or counterclaims without using a lawyer or sophisticated legal terminology. Most courts charge a fee for filing papers, but may waive the fee if you can show that your income is low (taking into account your family size) and that you therefore cannot pay it.

Attending the Eviction Hearing. If you have been served with notice of an eviction proceeding, you should always attend—whether or not you have already moved out. Even if you believe you have no defenses, you should attend the eviction hearing to make sure you know what is going on. You want to be certain, for example, that the landlord does not misstate the amount of rent you owe or ask that you be put out by a quicker than normal process.

Even if you have no defenses, you can request that the judge give you additional time before moving if there are special circumstances. Some examples might be illness of a family member or unavailability of emergency shelter. The judge will be more likely to grant additional time if you are able to offer at least partial rent or if other housing has been arranged. Judges are also more inclined to grant delays for compelling circumstances, such as for families with small children or for the elderly.

At the hearing, you will need to be prepared to present your defenses, if any, to the eviction. Be sure to include relevant documents and witnesses, if any. Preparing a case for court is discussed in Chapter Nine. Some defenses which may be available in an eviction case are discussed below.

Raising Defenses. Tenants with defenses to an eviction must raise those defenses at the eviction hearing (or earlier in some states by filing required papers—usually called an "answer" or an "appearance"). Defenses will always be lost if you do not appear at the hearing.

Most courts require that an evicting landlord strictly comply with all the technical requirements of the eviction law, including the content, timing, and service of all required notices and court documents. Any mistake in complying with these requirements, including misstatement of the amount of rent owed, may cause a landlord's petition to be dismissed if it is pointed out to the court. The landlord will then be required to begin the procedure over again. Remember that, if you don't have any other defenses to the eviction, the landlord will usually be able to correct the technical problem and still end up evicting you in a relatively short period of time.

State law sometimes allows other defenses or claims that might defeat or delay an eviction. For example, some states recognize a defense called "peaceable possession." This defense states that if a landlord fails to file an eviction action promptly after the expiration of the notice to vacate time period, the landlord has consented to continued occupancy. Peaceable possession may result in dismissal of the eviction, although the landlord can send a new notice to vacate.

Another possible defense is that the landlord routinely accepted late or partial payments of rent, and then, without warning, started eviction proceedings based on another instance of late payment or nonpayment. The eviction is then improper because there was a custom of late or partial payment of rent, and the landlord consented to this practice.

Other issues may be present when a landlord is subject to federal housing laws. These laws establish specific requirements for a landlord's eviction case in addition to those mandated by state law.

Legal advice may be necessary to understand specific procedural requirements for the landlord's action and for your potential responses. In many communities, eviction clinics or legal pamphlets on tenants' rights are offered by the local legal services office, the bar association, or the court clerk.

Substandard Housing Condition As a Defense. In most states, courts will recognize defenses or counterclaims based upon the property not being "habitable" (in livable condition) or properly maintained. These claims are based on the landlord breaching the rental agreement by not keeping the property in good repair.

The availability of defenses and counterclaims based on the condition of the apartment varies widely from state to state. Almost everywhere, you will have a defense if the apartment has been cited for housing code violations.

If a citation for housing code violations is issued, you should make sure to get a copy to take with you to court. A "certified" copy may be required in some courts. Ask the housing inspector how to get a certified copy of the report.

Even if there are no housing code violations, problems with the apartment can still partially or fully offset your obligation to pay rent. In some cases, you may be able to afford the lower amount. In others, you may still end up getting evicted, but the court may lower the amount of back-rent you owe because the apartment was never in proper condition. Take pictures or videos of any problems, if possible. In the alternative, for problems like lack of adequate heat, a disinterested witness may testify.

Many states require that you give prior notice to the landlord of the bad conditions before the conditions can be used as a defense to eviction. The notice requirement is designed to give the landlord an opportunity to correct the problem. It is always a good idea to provide notice in writing with a copy for your records. This notice should be sent by certified mail. You should bring several copies with you to court in order to prove that you have complied with the law.

You may have withheld rent at some point due to problems with the apartment. Your landlord may still be able to sue you in these circumstances if you did not follow the proper rules for your state. However, if you did follow the rules, in most states you have the right to terminate your rental agreement and move elsewhere.

Retaliatory Evictions. If you can show that an eviction action is in retaliation for your exercise of your legal rights, this will generally be a defense to the eviction. The classic example of a "retaliatory eviction" is an eviction case which is brought because one tenant has organized other tenants in the building and submitted joint complaints to the landlord. Similarly, some landlords routinely evict tenants who contact housing inspectors to report problems with the property.

Retaliatory eviction cases are hard to prove—especially when there is also a back-rent issue. This is because you will have to show that the landlord is really evicting you because you stood up for your rights and not because you didn't pay rent. If a retaliatory eviction has occurred, it is a good idea to consult a lawyer.

Appeals. If you lose an eviction case and the court orders an eviction, one possibility is to appeal the case to a higher court. This may buy you more time to move in a more orderly fashion. The threat of an appeal may also allow you to negotiate more time with the landlord.

An appeal may require that you pay certain filing fees or other court charges. Sometimes these fees can be waived if you can show you cannot afford to pay them. However, regardless of your income, you will probably have to post a bond to cover the rent while your case is on appeal. In any event, you should only consider an appeal if you honestly believe you have a case. Frivolous appeals can result in fines or other sanctions against you.

Other Responses to a Court's Eviction Order. You should respond to a court order of eviction by making arrangements to move before you are forced out into the street. It is always a mistake to ignore the eviction order.

In some states, but not all, you will get notice of an actual eviction date. You may want to consult the sheriff, a court clerk, or your local legal services office about how long you are likely to have. Often, you will have only a very short period of time to move before you are put out.

In some cases, arrangements to move by a certain date can be made directly with the landlord or by the court with a judge's approval. Sometimes, you can get assistance with moving costs from the public assistance department in your community or from a local charity.

If you have not vacated by the time specified in a court eviction order, a sheriff or a similar official may move your belongings onto the sidewalk or, if you are fortunate, place them in storage. You will then have to pay moving and storage costs.

In some states, landlords can place a lien on your furniture and other possessions to cover moving and storage charges. Until you pay those charges, you cannot get your property back. It is better to avoid this problem entirely by moving voluntarily.

Seizures of Personal Property and Unauthorized Lockouts. As described above, seizures of your personal property as part of a court-ordered eviction process may be legal. On the other hand, in most states, it is illegal for a landlord to seize your personal property without court permission.

A tenant whose property has been seized should seek legal advice. Even in those states that allow such seizures, certain property will be listed as exempt from seizure. There may even be grounds for a constitutional challenge to the procedure itself.

Without permission from a court, landlords cannot padlock your apartment, shut off your utilities, or otherwise force you to leave.

Lockouts, utility shut-offs, and eviction-related harassment are illegal in all states. When landlords take these actions, they are generally known as "self-help evictions." If you are locked out or if your landlord is harassing you to move out (including the common practice of shutting down utility service to your property), you are likely to be entitled to get back into the property and to have the harassment ended by a court. You also may be entitled to damages. Legal assistance for a case of this type is a good idea.

When you are locked out or if your utilities are shut off, your landlord may claim that you have abandoned the apartment. You may want to let the landlord know in writing that this is not the case. If the landlord does not let you back in or turn on the utilities, a copy of the letter will serve as proof that the landlord knew that you had not moved out. Remember that, even if you are not able to pay your rent, landlords are not allowed to try to put you out without court approval. Landlords must go through the legal process and allow you to have your day in court if that's what you want.

The Landlord's Suit for Back-Rent. Landlords sometimes sue for back-rent or property damage after a tenant moves or is evicted. As part of that suit, a landlord may also ask that the tenant be required to pay the landlord's attorney fees.

A case for back-rent may or may not be included with the eviction. If you are sued for back-rent, it should be treated just like a suit for money by any other creditor. A general discussion of ways to address lawsuits is included in Chapter Nine. In addition, some special considerations apply.

Some of the claims that you may raise in evictions are also potential defenses or counterclaims in suits for back-rent. Common defenses include:

substandard housing conditions; miscalculation of the amount owed; illegal attempts by landlords to seize your property; a landlord's attempt to lock you out; or a shut-off of utility service. Landlords, collection agencies, management companies and their lawyers are also potentially responsible for debt collection harassment. For any of these claims, you should consider consulting a lawyer.

Special Eviction Defenses for Military Families. If you are on active duty with the military, your landlord cannot evict you, your spouse, or your dependents from a residence you are renting unless he or she gets a court order. This protection does not apply, however, if your monthly rent is more than $2,721 in 2007 dollars.

If your landlord goes to court to evict you, consider asking the court to postpone the case or adjust the terms of the lease. The court must postpone the case upon your request if your ability to pay the agreed rent is materially affected by your being on active duty. As an alternative, the court can adjust your obligation under the lease in a way that preserves your interests and also takes into account the landlord's interests. For example, the court might revise the lease to allow you to take in a paying subtenant, revise the due dates for the rent, or make other orders that will preserve your tenancy.

USING THE BANKRUPTCY PROCESS
TO STOP EVICTIONS

In most cases bankruptcy will, at best, only delay an eviction. In some cases it will not even do that. There are some limited situations in which filing a bankruptcy case can be a very effective way to preserve a tenancy. This section will help you to recognize those situations.

The general aspects of bankruptcy, including the differences between chapter 13 and chapter 7, are described in Chapter Nineteen of this book. You may find it helpful to review that chapter in considering this discussion.

Your rights as a tenant will be very limited if you start a bankruptcy case after a state court has entered an eviction judgment against you. You will lose substantial rights as a tenant in bankruptcy if you start your bankruptcy case after a state court has entered an order for your eviction, usually called a "judgment of possession." Chapter Nineteen gives more information about how this works. Most important, if a state court judge has already ordered your eviction, the eviction can proceed despite the bankruptcy unless you are careful to satisfy certain legal requirements. These requirements include paying one month's rent to the bankruptcy court immediately and paying all rent due within thirty days of filing bankruptcy. You also must have the right, typically through a state law, to reinstate your tenancy after a state court eviction judgment. If you do not meet all these requirements, the bankruptcy filing will not stop or delay the eviction.

If you file for bankruptcy before a state court has ordered your eviction, you may be able to cure a rent default through a long-term payment plan. Your rights as a tenant remain more flexible if you file for bankruptcy relief before a state court has entered a judgment for your eviction. If you start a chapter 13 bankruptcy case before the state court's eviction judgment, you may be able to "cure," or pay back, the rent arrearage under a payment plan that could extend for several months or even years. In order to take advantage of this procedure, you have to be in a financial position to afford both the payments for current rent and monthly payments to go toward the rental arrearage.

In addition to these financial considerations, you must meet two other important requirements.

1. First, you must have a long-term lease. Leases for federally assisted housing programs, manufactured home parks lots, and leases for some rent controlled apartments usually create these types of long-term tenancies. Some state laws also prohibit landlords from refusing to renew residential leases unless there is a serious ground for termination. It is important to keep in mind that filing a bankruptcy petition does not give you a longer lease term than you would have if you had not filed bankruptcy.

2. Second, you must have a right under your state law at the time you file your bankruptcy petition to reinstate your tenancy by paying any money you owe. Many states have special laws that allow a tenant to "pay and stay" up to a certain stage in the eviction process. A chapter 13 bankruptcy filing is a way of stretching out this right over a much longer period of time. A chapter 13 case is a substantial commitment, but if it preserves the benefits of a long-term affordable lease, such as a lease with income-based government subsidies, the commitment may be worthwhile.

Unless you rent from a government agency, a chapter 7 bankruptcy may delay an eviction, but it will not preserve a tenancy that has been terminated for nonpayment of rent. Once a lease has been terminated for nonpayment of rent, a chapter 7 bankruptcy will usually not preserve the tenancy for the long term. If you file a chapter 7 bankruptcy case before a state court has entered a judgment for eviction, the automatic bankruptcy stay may delay the state court eviction proceedings for three to five months while the bankruptcy case is pending. However, even during this time the landlord can ask the bankruptcy judge for permission to complete an eviction in the state court. The bankruptcy judge will usually grant the landlord's request. In the alternative, the landlord can wait the several months for the chapter 7 bankruptcy case to end. When the case is over the landlord cannot try to collect the back rent, but may proceed with an eviction from the property.

The only exception to this rule for chapter 7 cases is for evictions from public housing or similar rental properties where a government agency acts as the landlord. A special section of the bankruptcy law applies to these government agencies. Tenants of government agencies, such as housing authorities, may be protected from eviction for nonpayment of rent if they file a bankruptcy petition that discharges the rent-debt owed to the government agency. Courts around the country have come to different conclusions on this issue. A local legal services office or tenant organization would be a good source of information about the availability of this option in your area.

15

Utility Terminations

Everyone needs utility service to survive. We need electricity to light our homes and run the furnace; we need water to drink and bathe and clean with; we need gas or other fuels to heat our homes; and we need telephone service to make and receive essential calls.

Utility providers have a powerful method of forcing their customers to pay their bills. They can impose the drastic remedy of terminating service to force payment of back-bills. When faced with a large utility bill, you may feel that you have nowhere to turn—pay an unaffordable bill or lose essential service. This chapter explains the tools you have to help you manage these debts and avoid termination of service.

CHOICES IN UTILITY SERVICE PROVIDERS

In the past, customers had no choice about which company to use for local or long-distance telephone service and electric and gas service. Today, depending on where you live, you may be able to shop around for some or all of these utility services.

All households in America can choose their provider of long-distance telephone services. Some consumers can also choose their provider of local telephone service. For some, it may even make sense to drop traditional long-distance service and switch to pre-paid calling cards or dial-around services (10-10 numbers). In many states, consumers also have choices about their providers of electric or gas service. Making decisions about which providers are best for you can be tricky.

The choice of your utility provider will not only determine the price you will be charged but may also affect the protections you have. The availability of bill payment assistance and conservation programs, as well as the amount of basic information that you will receive about your rights and obligations, may also differ. When choosing between utility service providers, ask questions about the company's special programs for elderly, disabled or low-income homeowners, and policies regarding late payments and protections from shut-off. Also, for all these utility services, make sure to ask for both the current price and how long that price is good for. Many of the newer companies change their prices frequently and with little advance notice. This chapter explains many rights and benefits that are available to utility customers. If you have a choice in the provider of your utility service, find out from the different providers which rights and benefits each has to offer you.

WAYS TO REDUCE
YOUR UTILITY BILLS

Even if your most pressing concern is getting *past-due* utility bills paid to maintain service, you should still be interested in reducing your *future* bills. This section will provide specific ideas on how to reduce the bills, by

- Reducing the amount you are charged for the utility service you use;
- Changing the type of service you receive;
- Changing the way you are billed to make the bills easier to pay;
- Reducing *energy and water usage* through weatherization and water conservation measures; and
- Obtaining cash assistance in paying your bills.

You May Be Eligible for a Discount Plan. Often, utilities have special programs which will allow certain customers to reduce the *charges* for the utility service. It only takes some investigation to see what the different utilities have to offer and whether you are eligible for any of the programs.

Discounted Rates for Financially Distressed Households. Many utilities have special programs for low-income households, households with seniors, or households with members with disabilities to help them pay their utility bills. Many of these programs are available to households which are receiving some sort of public assistance or energy assistance payments. Some of these programs reduce the bills by a set amount each month; others provide discounts based on the amount of the bill. Check with your utility to see what is available and how to enroll.

PIPPs or Energy Assurance Programs. Utilities in Ohio and a few other states have plans by which families pay a certain percentage of their income for utility service if that amount is less than what they would otherwise pay. This results in lower bills. Typically, consistent payment of the lower amount is rewarded by gradual forgiveness of old, unpaid bills.

These plans are sometimes called Percentage of Income Payment Plans (PIPPs) or Energy Assurance Plans (EAPs), but each utility has its own unique name for the program. The best way to determine if a utility has such a program is to contact the utility or the public utility commission's consumer division in your state.

Telephone Discounts. There are federal and state programs for discounts on local telephone rates for low-income households. In all states, eligible households in financial distress can obtain a significant monthly discount, ranging from around $10.00 to $20.00 (depending on the state), on local telephone bills under the "Lifeline" program run by your local phone company. There is a related "Linkup" program that discounts the cost of installing new telephone service. Much larger discounts are available for low-income consumers living on Native American reservations. Some phone companies also offer discounted rates to disabled consumers. Contact your state's public utility commission's consumer division or the local telephone company for details.

Eligibility. Eligibility for these programs varies considerably. Most states require you to show that you receive or are eligible for governmental benefits such as Social Security, SSI, public assistance, Food Stamps, or the Low Income Home Energy Assistance Program (LIHEAP). New York and some other states automatically place households on Lifeline once they are enrolled in any of the programs listed above. Recently, eligibility for the federal Lifeline assistance program was expanded to include households with incomes at or below 135% of poverty (for example, a household with an annual income of $27,878 for a family of 4 in 2007). Families receiving TANF or who are enrolled in the national free school lunch program are also eligible. Check with your local phone company to see if you are eligible for the discounted local phone rate.

If you don't have phone service, you may be eligible for temporary access to a voicemail account though a Community Voice Mail™ (CVM) program. Local agencies in 40 cities in 19 states run CVM programs to help those without phone service in their efforts to get jobs, contact support services, and stay in contact with families and friends. Participants are given a voice-mail number where callers can leave messages. These messages can be retrieved from any phone by using a personal phone number and private security code. To see if there is a CVM program in your area, look for the latest updates on the Community Voice Mail's website at www.cvm.org (you can get on the Internet for free at your local library) or call 206-441-7872 (a local call if you are in Seattle).

Changing the Type of Service Can Reduce Your Bill. You may be receiving some utility services which you could do without. While the charges for each of these individual services may not seem like a lot, together they can add up to quite a few dollars each month. A careful review of your bills and a discussion with each utility company may yield some real savings.

Electric Service. Many states (including Maine, Massachusetts, New York, Pennsylvania, Ohio, Texas, and others) have "restructured" their electricity markets. This means that your utility company may have sold its generating plants to other companies and that now you may be able to buy your electricity from more than one company. While consumers in these states have more choices, they will also need to shop more carefully. Your own utility may now offer different residential rates, sometimes called "standard offer" (or "price-to-beat") and "default" (or "provider-of-last-resort"). Make sure you're on the lowest rate you are eligible for by calling the company or your state utility commission. In some states, low-income customers are eligible for a discount or may be protected from being on the more expensive rate plans.

If you have the ability to choose which company provides your electricity, make sure to shop around. In some states, the state utility commission prepares a list of companies that allows you to compare prices and other terms for service (for example, any penalties for switching to another supplier). If you have Internet access, these lists are usually posted on the commission's web page. If not, call the commission and ask for a copy.

Cable/Satellite TV Service. Are there cable or satellite TV services that you can drop? During your period of financial difficulty, can you return to using an antenna for your television and eliminate the entire bill? Even if you need cable or satellite to get reception, you should ask your company about less expensive "basic" plans.

Local Telephone Service. Examine your telephone bill. Are you paying for call waiting, call forwarding, Caller ID, and other extra services? You could do without these services and save $5 to $20 or more a month. Another way to shave some dollars off your local phone bill is to cut back on using directory assistance. Phone companies generally charge for these calls after the first or second use. Instead, whenever possible use a phone book. Also check your phone bills to make sure you are not leasing your phone, as it is cheaper to buy your own. You could also save money by buying an inexpensive answering machine rather than paying a monthly fee for voicemail.

Another consideration is whether you are paying a lot for local measured service, which is when you are billed separately for each local call. Contact the telephone company and ask for the least expensive plan that meets your calling needs.

Long-Distance Telephone Calls. How much does your long-distance service cost? Many people don't know that the "basic rate" for long-distance service is often the most expensive rate. It is a good idea to shop around with the different long-distance carriers and look at the different calling plans. Long-distance companies are required to post their calling plans on their website. You should also shop around for the best rate on local toll calls (calls made outside your calling area that are still within the state, also called intra-LATA calls). Their various deals are often complicated but can result in significant savings depending upon your calling patterns. Some programs have less expensive calls during the day, others at night. Look for the long-distance service which best fits your actual calling patterns.

Be cautious of those programs that require you to pay a flat monthly charge regardless of how many calls you actually make, and then charge what seems to be a low per-minute amount. Generally, these plans only benefit heavy long-distance users. Also factor in the numerous fees and taxes in your cost comparisons, as these are often not included in the advertised per minute rate.

Sometimes, your long-distance bill includes calls you did not make. If you are billed for calls that you did not make (also called cramming) or if you do not feel you owe the full long-distance bill, ask the long-distance company to delete these charges from your bill. You should also make a note that you are only paying the undisputed charges when you send your payment.

If you rarely make long-distance calls, it may make more sense to drop your long-distance plan and avoid the extra charges and fees common in these plans. You can still make long-distance calls using pre-paid calling cards and dial-around (10-10) services. If you'd like to cancel your long-distance plan, contact your local phone company and your long-distance company. You may be charged a fee to drop your long-distance service.

If you use a cell phone, be sure and shop around for the most affordable plan to suit your needs. And keep track of any limits on minutes or calls. Cell phone fees can pile up quickly and cost you a bundle.

Pre-Paid Phone Cards. Pre-paid phone cards are a convenient way to control long-distance costs, especially for those calls made away from home, since you can use a pre-paid calling card with most other phones. Pre-paid phone cards may be much less expensive to use than the calling cards given to you by your local and long-distance companies.

Pre-paid phone cards are often shaped like a credit card and made out of plastic or paper. On the card is a telephone number to access the long distance service provider and a personal identification number (PIN) that acts like your account number.

Pre-paid cards differ in the amount of minutes or units that are covered by the card and the amount the cards cost. You can get a rough idea of how much a minute of a long-distance call will cost by dividing the cost of the card by the number of units or minutes (for example, a $20 card for 200 units is roughly 10 cents a minute). This is not an exact calculation because some calls, such as a long-distance call from a payphone, are billed extra units and some pre-paid cards deduct extra units per call made. Note that some cards charge much higher rates than are advertised, so it's also a good idea when trying out a new company's card to track your minutes to see if you are getting your money's worth.

Not all pre-paid phone cards are alike in quality of service, rates, or value. Because you might not get your money back if there is a problem, it is important to be careful when buying a pre-paid phone card. Look for information on who issued the card. Ask yourself: Is this a reputable company? Is there a toll-free number to call if there is a problem? How much will a minute of long distance cost? Are there additional charges, fees, or taxes added to each call made? Has the PIN information been hidden so that it can't be stolen before you purchase the card?

If you don't have a chance to do any research before buying a pre-paid card, you may want to buy just a small amount of time to try out a company. Also keep in mind that pre-paid phone cards often have an expiration date, so you should not buy more time than you will be able to use within that timeframe.

Dial-Around (10-10 services) Long-Distance Services. Another way to make long-distance calls without a long-distance calling plan is to use a dial-around service (10-10 numbers). This is a way to pay for long distance service on a call-by-call basis. Long-distance calls using a dial-around service appear on your local phone bill. There are also dial-around services for international calls.

There are many different dial-around long-distance services and not all of them offer good rates or service for your particular calling patterns. It is important to go slow and choose wisely until you find a dial-around service that is right for you. When selecting a dial-around service, check for any additional charges, fees, or taxes included in a call. You should also find out the rate for the call. Some dial-arounds have a minimum charge per call, which can increase the price of a short call. Also find out if the dial-around service charges a monthly fee. This is not a bargain if you rarely make long-distance calls.

Other Telephone Charges. Watch out for calls to 1-900 and 1-976 services (also called pay-per-call services). These calls can be very expensive. Examples of 1-900 services include calls to psychic hotlines or adult entertainment lines. **Local phone companies are prohibited from terminating your *local service* for nonpayment of these pay-per-call services.** If you are disputing 1-900 charges, make a note to the phone company that your payment is only for the local and, if applicable, long-distance charges and that none of the payment is to be applied or credited to the disputed 1-900 charges. You can also put a block on 1-900 calls so that these calls cannot be made from your phone. Call your local phone company for more information on 1-900 blocks. The block should be free for new accounts or a reasonable one-time fee for established accounts.

REDUCING YOUR BILL BY CHANGING YOUR BILLING PATTERNS

Level Payment Plans. If you are able to pay your *average* utility bill but have difficulty meeting your heating bills in the coldest months of winter or your electric bills in the hottest months of summer (because of air conditioning), a level payment plan might make sense for you. A level payment plan allows you to avoid running up debts during high-usage months by averaging your expected bills so that you can pay the same amount each month. Many states require their regulated utilities (gas and electric) to provide these plans.

In a level payment plan, your projected yearly bill is divided into equal monthly installments. Monthly bills reflect this amount rather than each month's actual use. For example, a customer whose total gas bill for a year is $1,200, would pay $100 each month instead of $200 to $300 a month in the winter, and $30 to $40 a month in the summer.

Dealing with Quarterly or Bi-Monthly Bills. In some areas, utility services are billed quarterly or every other month. If financial problems cause you to live month to month, you may find it difficult to deal with large quarterly or bi-monthly bills. Contact your local utility company to explain the difficulty and ask them to bill you on a monthly basis. In the alternative, ask them to accept monthly payments from you, even if they won't send you a separate bill each month.

If you make this choice, ask about "service charges" or "finance charges." If the cost is too high, this type of payment plan may not be the best solution for you.

Avoiding Late Payment Charges by Changing the Date Your Bill Is Due. If your main source of income arrives in the mail on the fifth of the month, but your utility bill is due to be paid on the fourth, it is obviously going to be very difficult for you to pay your utility bill on time. The result may be that you not only have the high utility bill to deal with but you will also have to pay additional interest or late charges. Generally, utility companies will help you deal with this problem if you explain the situation. Although they may insist that you pay the late charges that have already been billed to your account, the utility company should agree to change the date your bill is due each month so that late charges don't keep accruing.

REDUCING YOUR BILL BY REDUCING YOUR UTILITY USAGE

Utility Company Sponsored Weatherization or Conservation Programs. Many utilities have programs that provide free or low-cost weatherization or conservation services. Sometimes these programs are available to all households, sometimes they are limited to the elderly or homes with disabled persons and/or children. In other areas, eligibility for the program may be based on your household's income or eligibility for a government program such as Energy Assistance (also called Low Income Home Energy

Assistance Program or LIHEAP) or the Weatherization Assistance Program (also called WAP).

Different utility companies offer very different types of programs. In the best programs, the utility sends someone who conducts a full energy audit of your home and provides extensive weatherization services. Other programs simply provide hints on how you can reduce usage, or they supply conservation products such as special energy efficient light bulbs, insulation for hot water tanks, "low flow" efficient faucets, or other conservation products. Even the less ambitious programs which provide only some conservation advice should be helpful to you. Investigate by calling your local energy and water providers and finding out what programs they have available.

You should be very cautious before investing more than a few dollars of your own money in any weatherization or conservation efforts with a contractor, however. While it might make sense in the long run for households with extra cash, it is often not the wisest use of funds for households which are strapped to pay for rent and food. To know whether an energy conservation investment is a good use of money, you must analyze the cost of the investment against how long you expect to live in your current residence and your anticipated energy savings. This type of analysis should be done by an expert.

Government Sponsored Weatherization Programs. Several programs are designed to provide weatherization assistance for owner-occupied housing as well as rental units. The primary program is the Weatherization Assistance Program. Households that qualify generally receive up to $2,500 in actual weatherization benefits, which are provided at no cost.

Additionally, many states have their own weatherization programs. Cities also have Community Development Block Grant money which is often used to help low-income households weatherize their homes. Although there may be a long waiting list for all of these programs, the benefits are often so great that it is worthwhile to add your name.

Self-Help Weatherization and Water Conservation. If you are unable to find or qualify for any programs through your utility or the government, there are still a number of practices which may help reduce your usage. In some situations, these relatively inexpensive procedures reduce energy and water bills by a surprising amount.

On a windy day check for air leaks around your windows and doors. You can use a lit stick of incense to detect leaks around windows and doors by moving the stick around the frame and watching to see if there is any wind blowing the smoke.

If you are a tenant, try to get the landlord to fix these leaks properly. If the landlord does not fix the problems, or you own your own home, try a number of homespun fix-ups.

- Use caulk, or weather stripping for air leaks around windows. In the winter you can seal windows with heavy-duty clear plastic sheets or clear plastic film. In a pinch you could use clear plastic tape to seal the cracks.
- For leaks around doors, leave a rolled up towel next to the bottom of the door. If necessary, use weather stripping or tack up a blanket or large towel to stop leaks around the top and sides of doors.
- If there are holes in the walls, try to plug them up by stapling plastic sheeting over the holes and caulking the edges of the plastic. You will be surprised how much warmer a house or apartment can be without the heat loss from cracks between openings and walls.
- If you have a fireplace, make sure the flue is tightly closed. As the home warms up, you can consider turning down the heat.

Turn off lights and heat or cooling when not at home. Also close the door for any rooms you are not using, and don't try to heat or cool them.

Toilets are often the largest source of water use inside a home. Leaks from the toilet and the faucet waste water and money. Remember that your sewer bill is generally determined by how much water you consume. By saving water, you are saving twice—on your water bill and your sewer bill. Your water utility may provide free toilet leak detection kits. You can also purchase several inexpensive leak detection dye tablets at the hardware store. The hardware usually necessary to fix a toilet leak can cost from just a few dollars to around $20.00. If you have water leaks that you cannot afford to fix, call your water company. Many water companies have programs that assist homeowners with low-cost plumbing problems.

Putting an inexpensive displacement bag (a special strong plastic bag for your toilet tank that you can buy at a hardware store) or a heavy plastic bottle in an old toilet tank will cut down on the amount of water consumed each time you flush.

Turn off the water while you are brushing your teeth.

Reducing Your Bill Through Government and Other Assistance.

If you have a low income and high utility bills, you are probably eligible for one or more of several sources of assistance with your utility bills. These programs vary a great deal. Some types of aid are only available at certain times of the year, others are available only if you have a certain type of fuel. Some programs only help you if you are facing a termination of utility service; other programs only help you if you are not facing a termination. All programs have eligibility requirements, but they differ considerably in their specific terms.

The Federal Low Income Home Energy Assistance Program (LIHEAP), which is run by each state, helps low-income families pay their utility bills. All states provide this assistance for winter heating bills; some states also use LIHEAP funds to assist families with summer cooling expenses. LIHEAP benefits are also provided to renters and some public and subsidized housing tenants whose heat is included in their rent.

Guidelines for LIHEAP eligibility vary by state, but most states require that family income over the past three or twelve months be below 150% of the federal poverty guidelines. (In some states, income must be even less and in some states the income can be more.) The size of a family's LIHEAP benefits generally depends on the family's income and the number of household members, and may also depend on housing type, fuel type, fuel prices, weather conditions, or actual energy consumption.

To apply for LIHEAP benefits, you should contact the local agency in the community administering the program. This is usually a nonprofit agency, such as the local community action program (CAP) or a county department of social services office. Benefits are sometimes paid directly to the utility company or fuel vendor, and your utility or fuel bill is reduced accordingly. Other times, joint checks are made out to you and the utility. In a few states, fuel assistance checks are provided solely to the customer.

In many states, the Salvation Army or some other charitable organization may operate a "fuel fund"—a fund which helps people pay their bills if they make a little too much money to qualify for LIHEAP or if LIHEAP funds have run out. To find out if there is a fuel fund in your area, contact your state utility commission or the agency that distributes LIHEAP funds in your area.

YOUR RIGHTS WHEN THE UTILITY THREATENS TO TERMINATE YOUR SERVICE

Utilities Must Follow Rules Before Terminating Your Service. In most states there are laws which provide a variety of significant protections when utility companies threaten termination of your utility service. Many of the larger utilities are regulated by commissions called public utility commissions or public service commissions. Utility companies can only shut off your service if they have met the requirements set out by these commissions.

Utility termination rules generally have the following basic requirements, but not all states have all of these provisions:

- Notice of the proposed termination;
- A right to a hearing;
- A limit on circumstances permitting termination;
- A limit on the times or days when shut-offs can occur;
- The right to a deferred payment plan;
- Protection from terminations during the winter months or extreme weather;
- No terminations if there is serious illness in the household;
- The right to information about places to go for assistance with paying the utility bill;
- Protections for tenants from termination of service by landlords.

The utility's failure to follow required termination rules typically allows you to demand that the termination process start all over. Utility service must be maintained throughout the process. If your utilities were wrongfully terminated, you might also have a claim for damages. An attorney can often get a special court order (an injunction) to stop termination or to have service restored when the utility has failed to follow the rules on termination procedures.

Often utility representatives refuse to negotiate a payment plan or fail to give notice of all your important rights, such as the opportunity for appeal or the right to participate in a payment plan. Generally, because your only information provider is a company representative, you should not hesitate to contact a local legal services attorney or the consumer services division of the state public utilities commission to find out whether the utility has complied with the termination rules. Public utility commissions generally have the power to resolve complaints and a call to the appropriate person can often stall or prevent a termination altogether.

The state public utility commissions offer consumers other protections. Commissions typically have a legal division (or general counsel's office), a consumer complaint division, and separate divisions to handle problems with particular types of service, such as electric, gas, and telephones. Individual customers can often obtain help with utility disputes directly from the staff of the state commission.

In addition, you have certain rights to stop a termination when you file for bankruptcy. Finally, you may be eligible for certain emergency funds you can use to stop the shut-off.

The following is a more detailed explanation of your rights concerning a threatened utility termination:

Notice. Prior to termination of your utility service, you must be given notice that the service is subject to termination and of the various rights that you have to prevent termination. Usually written notices are required, but face-to-face notice may also be required in certain parts of the country.

Limit on Circumstances Warranting Termination. Regulations typically permit disconnection for nonpayment but often prohibit disconnections for very small amounts or for amounts which have been owed for less than a certain number of months. Furthermore, if you dispute that you owe the bill which the utility says must be paid, the utility is generally prohibited from terminating service until the dispute is resolved. If you dispute part of the bill, you must pay the undisputed amount to preserve your rights. It is a good idea to make a note that the payment only covers the undisputed charges when you pay your bill.

Limit on the Times or Days When Shut-Offs Can Occur. Many states allow shut-offs only at times when the consumer can reach the utility commission (for example, Monday-Friday from 8 A.M. to 5 P.M.). Some states prohibit shut-offs on holidays or the day before a holiday or weekend. Call your state utility commission to find out when shut-offs can occur.

Right to a Hearing. Before or after termination, you have a right to appeal to both the utility and to an independent third party such as the public utility commission. In many states, informal appeals can be made by telephone prior to termination and, often, utility service will be maintained or reconnected during the appeals process.

A utility commission's consumer division responds to phone calls, letters, and visits by residential customers. Many of these complaints are resolved informally by consultation between the consumer division and the utility. Consumer divisions also hold hearings on complaints that cannot be resolved informally.

Consumers generally have a legal right to a hearing whenever they have grounds to contest a utility termination. Simply request the utility commission to provide a hearing before service is terminated. (If you dispute only part of a back-bill, you will usually have to pay the undisputed part to keep your service on while the dispute is being decided.) While city-owned utilities are generally not regulated by the utility commission, customers of municipal utilities also have a constitutional right to a hearing before termination.

You do not need the services of a lawyer at the hearing. However, it may be helpful to have a paralegal or experienced utility counselor assist with the hearing. To support the claim, it is important for you to bring all relevant documents, such as a physician's affidavit or past bills. It may also be helpful to have witnesses such as friends and neighbors.

Right to a Deferred Payment Plan. Before utility service is shut off, most states require that you be informed about the option to pay all overdue bills over a period of months through a reasonable installment plan. Often this payment plan has a six-month or a one-year limit for bringing the account up-to-date.

The plan may be designed so that you pay current usage and slowly catch up on the amount you are behind. However, if your financial circumstances require it, you can sometimes negotiate a lower cost plan whereby the monthly payments do not completely cover current bills and do nothing to catch up on past-due bills, but you are still making regular payments to the utility.

To make a successful payment plan, develop a budget that you can reasonably meet and be assertive with the utility company employee who negotiates the agreement. Payment plans need not require the same payment each month. For example, seasonal workers may want to pay less toward arrears in the winter and more in the summer, or vice versa.

The utility company may want a payment plan that requires larger payments than you can afford. Large payments are in the company's short-term interest because it recovers past debts more quickly. Too many customers, believing they have no choice, agree to these payments.

It is usually a bad idea to agree to a payment plan which you know you cannot afford. This will only make things worse in the long run. It is better to explain your financial circumstances and push for an affordable agreement from the beginning.

Unrealistic plans harm both you and the utility company in the long term. You may not be able to make the payments and may lose the service, and the company will not collect its debt. In some states, utilities are not required to enter into a second payment plan with consumers who have defaulted on a first payment plan. If a company refuses to agree to a reasonable payment plan, help can be obtained from the consumer division of the utility commission.

Winter Moratorium on Terminations and Other Termination Bans. In many northern states, heat-related utilities are prohibited from terminating any residential customer between November 1 and March 31st (or some similar period). In other states, there is usually a limited moratorium to prevent utility terminations for households with elderly or disabled residents, and occasionally for households with infants. Generally, financial hardship must be shown. Some of these rules require that all efforts to obtain state energy assistance must have been pursued before a household can be considered for the moratorium. In some states terminations are forbidden during periods of extreme weather, but once the temperatures return to a certain degree, the terminations can move forward.

Note that a moratorium only prevents disconnection of service. Your bill will still be charged and you will be responsible to pay for service used during the moratorium period. For this reason you should pay, if you can, even if your service is not subject to being disconnected.

No Termination If There Is Serious Illness. State law or public utility commission regulations often restrict termination of service for households whose members face a serious illness, are threatened with serious illness, or depend upon life support systems. Often, the illness must be certified by a doctor. A family with very young children or a pregnant woman may also be able to use the health risk to the children as grounds to stop utility termination.

Information About Sources of Assistance. Before a disconnection, utility companies often must provide consumers with information about the existence of energy assistance programs, such as LIHEAP or local crisis intervention programs. (See the discussion above concerning these sources of emergency assistance.)

Tenants Protected from Termination of Service for Landlord's Failure to Pay. When a landlord is responsible for providing utility service it is all too common, particularly in difficult economic times, for a landlord to fail to pay for that service. This puts tenants at risk of losing their utility service. Tenants in this situation sometimes have special protections. In some states, tenants must receive a special shut-off notice if the landlord is delinquent. Then, tenants make utility payments directly to the utility and deduct those payments from their rent.

Tenants Protected from Shut-Off by Landlord. It is illegal in almost every state for a landlord to cut off your utility service as a way of making you move or pay your rent. Landlords must go through the courts to evict tenants. They cannot make the residence uninhabitable by terminating the heat or water service to force the tenant to move. Generally, a tenant can stop a "self-help" eviction by going to court. The tenant is often entitled to recover damages for the landlord's wrongful actions. See Chapter Fourteen for more information.

No Termination of Local Telephone Service for Bills for Other Services. Many, but not all, states prohibit the local telephone company from terminating service for nonpayment of long-distance service. However, every local telephone company is prohibited from terminating local telephone service for nonpayment of 900 calls or pay-per-call services.

Bankruptcy Protections. Although it is rarely a good idea to file bankruptcy solely because of your utility bills, you may have other financial problems which lead you to consider bankruptcy. When you file a bankruptcy petition, there is an automatic requirement that the utility company must restore service or stop a threatened termination. The bankruptcy filing starts a twenty-day period during which you are entitled to service from all applicable utilities. The utility can only terminate service after that twenty-day period if you fail to pay bills arising *after* the bankruptcy is filed. Then, if you successfully complete your bankruptcy case, you never have to pay the past-due arrears. The utility, though, can also require that you provide adequate assurance that *future* bills will be paid, such as providing a new security deposit. Bankruptcy is explained in more detail in Chapter Nineteen. The process is complicated, so professional advice is a good idea.

Sources of Emergency Assistance. There are several sources of emergency assistance that may provide you with funds to prevent a utility termination. The following sources should be pursued:

- *LIHEAP crisis assistance.* Contact your local CAP (community action program) agency or the county department of social services to find out who provides these funds in your area.

- *Emergency assistance for families with children.* If you have children and you are about to lose essential utility services (water, heat in the winter months, etc.), contact your county department of social services to see if special emergency funds are available to help you.

- *State emergency assistance.* Some states have special funds to help prevent utility terminations. Also, many counties have "homeless prevention" funds which can be used to prevent utility terminations. Contact your local CAP agency or the county department of social services.

- *Utility fuel funds.* Many utilities collect money from their customers and their shareholders for a special fund to help people pay their utility bills. Contact both the utility which is threatening to shut off your service and any other utility from which you receive service to see if they have a fund that might be of some assistance to you.

- *Salvation Army, local churches and other places of worship.* The Salvation Army and other local religious and charitable organizations often have money that is available to help needy people in the community with emergency bills such as utilities. Check with the utility company, the public utility commission, or the department of social services. Many churches, synagogues and mosques that have these funds do not limit them to their own members.

WAYS TO GET YOUR UTILITY SERVICE TURNED BACK ON

Everyone has the right to receive utility service from the regulated provider in their area. Establishing new service after a move or after previous service has been terminated can be difficult and expensive. However, regulated utility companies are prohibited from discriminating in service and are required to establish *reasonable* rules for customers to follow.

If you have had your prior utility service terminated for nonpayment, it may be difficult to establish renewed service. You will generally have to pay the old bill plus late charges, a reconnection fee, and often a deposit. However, there are a number of things you can try to reduce the amount of money you have to pay to obtain new utility service.

Dealing with an Old Bill. If the bill is *very* old, such as more than three or four years, it is possible that the utility cannot legally require you to pay it before providing you with new service. Check with the utility commission or a local attorney if you have a very old bill.

The best method to deal with back-bills which must be paid may be to request the utility to allow you to pay off the old bill in installments over a period of six to twelve months or longer. So long as you maintain your payments on the new service you will be receiving, there is no reason for the utility to refuse to provide you service under this arrangement. After all, a utility provider is generally permitted to terminate utility service only as a way of avoiding future losses. If you are ready and willing to pay for future service as it is provided, and to pay for the old service over time, the utility does not have reasonable grounds to deny you this new service. Many states have specific rules addressing how much you'll have to pay to get new service.

Late Charges. Generally, a utility will charge late fees for paying a utility bill after it is due. There are usually specific rules on how much these late charges can be, and state law and regulations generally limit the late charges to reasonable amounts. The purposes of the late charges are to compensate the utility for its extra costs in collecting the overdue bill and to discourage you from missing payments.

If the late charges are so high as to be unreasonable, try contacting the consumer services division of your state public utility commission to challenge the amount. Otherwise, try to negotiate with the local utility about the amount. If you lost your job, went through a separation or divorce, or suffered an illness in the family which caused you to be late on your payments before, you can show that this was a temporary difficulty which has now passed. Bargain with the utility; in many cases, they will reduce all or part of the late charges, especially if you had a good reason for missing payments.

Reconnection Fee. This is a fee which may be imposed on a household after its service has been terminated for nonpayment. The purpose of this fee is similar to late charges. Try the same type of arguments and negotiation. Some states prohibit or limit these charges.

Deposits. Before establishing new or renewed service, many utility companies ask households with poor payment histories to pay a deposit, usually equal to the average bill for one or two months. Utilities are prohibited from discriminating against certain types of customers in setting the deposit requirements. Customers who believe that a deposit is being requested unreasonably, or that a requested deposit is too large, should not hesitate to complain to the public utility commission's consumer division.

If the issue is not reasonableness but affordability, some of the sources of assistance listed earlier in this chapter may be available to help pay deposits. Later, when you have established a good payment record, or when you decide to terminate service, request that the utility return the deposit with interest. This should always happen if you did not fall behind again after the deposit was made.

Instead of a deposit, some utilities accept the signature of a cosigner or guarantor, who agrees to be responsible for payments you fail to make. In some states, the cosigner is responsible for all payments you fail to make. In other states, the cosigner's responsibility is limited to several months' worth of unpaid bills.

Failure to Pay Bills from Prior Address As Grounds for Denying Service. Utility companies often require customers to pay outstanding bills from a previous address before connecting service at a new address. An unpaid bill is the most common reason for refusing new service. But, in many states, it is not always legal for a utility to do this. Check with a local legal services attorney or the public service commission. If you are given no choice and you must pay the bill from the previous address in order to obtain new service, you should be able to pay for the old service under an installment agreement.

If you are obligated to pay an old bill before service will be connected and you have filed for bankruptcy, the old obligation will likely be discharged in the bankruptcy. The utility will have to provide new service as long as you provide a reasonable assurance, such as a deposit, of the ability to make *future* payment. The filing of the bankruptcy will immediately entitle you to service at the new address.

You Cannot Be Forced to Pay Someone Else's Bills. Even in those states where the utility is permitted to require customers to pay for their outstanding bills from other addresses, a utility generally cannot insist that one customer pay another customer's bill. For example, you are not obligated to pay the delinquent bills of the prior tenant of your new residence or bills that your old landlord was obligated to pay. Similarly, you may not have to pay an old bill if the service was in someone else's name (for example, an old roommate, a former spouse, or even a current roommate) but the service is now in your name.

Failure to Provide Information As Grounds for Denying Service.
Sometimes companies refuse to hook up service because you have not provided requested forms of identification or proof of residence. The company will use this information for various reasons, including to make sure that you do not owe money for service received at a previous address. This is generally not an unreasonable request unless the company carries it to extremes, such as demanding a birth certificate or information about all previous residences.

When a utility refuses to provide service in your name, look for a rental that comes with utility service or have another household member sign the lease and apply for utility service.

Avoiding Utility Company Restrictions on New Service.
When you are unable to pay a prior bill with the utility or cannot afford the security deposit, there are still ways to obtain utility service. Look for a house or apartment that includes utilities in the rent. Another option is to establish utility service in the name of someone else with a good payment history. However, since that individual becomes responsible for any unpaid bills, this approach must be considered carefully and with full disclosure of the risks to the individual assuming responsibility for the bills.

Special Telephone Lifeline and Link-Up Programs.
In most states, households in financial distress can obtain steep discounts on new service installation charges under the "Link-up" program run by the local phone company. You may also be eligible for a significant discount on telephone monthly charges under the "Lifeline" program. Contact the public utility commission or telephone company for details.

16

Automobile Repossessions

WHEN TO WORRY ABOUT REPOSSESSION

When you buy a car on credit, you are almost always required to put up the car as collateral. Consumers can also put up their cars as collateral for loans unrelated to the purchase of the car, but this is less common.

If your car is collateral, then, if you get behind on your payments at any point, you risk the immediate loss of your car. A repossessor may legally break into your car one night and simply drive or tow it away.

The car may be repossessed only by a leasing company or by a lender that has specifically taken the car as collateral. For example, if you do not pay a credit card bill, the credit card company cannot repossess the car. All the credit card company can do is sue you, obtain a court judgment and, if the car is not protected by a state law exemption, ask the sheriff to seize the car. This rarely happens in practice and if it does, it might occur a year or more after default. For car loans and leases, the situation is very different. Miss one or two payments and the car may be gone.

Losing your car may be particularly disastrous if you are recently laid off and looking for work. The loss of your car makes it much harder to look for and get a new job. But that is only the beginning of your problems after a car repossession. After the creditor repossesses your car, it will then sell it for much less than it is worth and your equity in the car will be wiped out. On top of all that, you may find yourself being sued for thousands of dollars that the creditor claims is the difference between the amount owed on your loan and the price for which the car was sold. This is sometimes called a deficiency action.

This chapter provides advice on how to avoid repossession and what to do if a car is repossessed. While repossession law varies somewhat from state to state, this advice is generally applicable nationwide. Most of the advice here also covers motorcycles and trucks, including trucks that you use for business purposes. Manufactured home repossessions are discussed in Chapter Thirteen.

HOW TO TELL IF A CAR CAN BE REPOSSESSED

A car can be repossessed only if you have put up the car as collateral or if you have leased the car. Usually this is easy to check. Look at the documents for the purchase of the car. Examine the front page of the loan or look for a separate one-page disclosure statement and see if the car is listed under "security." Sometimes the documents will clearly state that the transaction is a lease, in which case the car is also subject to repossession.

Next, examine the car's certificate of title. The title will usually list the names of creditors who have rights to the car. If the title is not in your name, but in the name of a company, you are probably leasing the car.

HOW SELF-HELP REPOSSESSION WORKS

Self-help repossession is a very real and dangerous threat whenever you fall behind on even one car payment. Creditors in most states have the right to seize the car even when you are only a few weeks late in making payments and, in some cases, even if the creditor just thinks you will not make payments when due.

The process is called "self-help" because the creditor is not required to get court permission to repossess the car. The creditor can have one of its own employees or a hired "repo man" seize the car. In most states, the creditor does not even have to notify you that a repossession is about to take place. As long as the seizure does not "breach the peace" (discussed below), it is usually legal.

There are important exceptions to a creditor's right to use "self-help" repossession:

- The creditor must have taken the car as collateral.
- In some states, the creditor must first give you notice of the right to catch up on delinquent payments. (See *Curing a Default* below.)
- Self-help repossession is generally illegal on certain Indian reservations. In Louisiana, self-help repossession is illegal except for repossession of a motor vehicle by a financial institution that is licensed, chartered, or regulated by the state or federal government. In Wisconsin, before repossessing a motor vehicle (or retaking a lease vehicle), the creditor must send the consumer a notice giving the consumer fifteen days to object. If the consumer objects, the creditor must obtain a court order before repossessing the vehicle. Self-help repossession is legal in Maryland only if the credit agreement allows it.
- A creditor cannot use self-help to repossess a car owned by active duty military personnel if the debt was incurred *before* the individual entered active duty. Children, spouses, and other dependents of active duty military personnel can apply to a court for an order prohibiting repossession. A court may prohibit repossession when military service impairs the servicemember's or a dependent's ability to make the loan payments. The servicemember or a dependent may also ask the court to modify the payment obligation, such as by restructuring the payment schedule. In some circumstances, active duty military personnel also have the right to cancel a vehicle lease or to ask a court to order vehicle lease payments postponed. The servicemember cannot be made to pay an early termination charge after canceling the lease.

These exceptions prevent a creditor from seizing a car you own but may not prevent a lessor from repossessing a leased car.

STRATEGIES TO PREVENT YOUR CAR FROM BEING REPOSSESSED

Keeping Current on Car Payments. You should stay current on all your bills if possible. Falling behind on any bill hurts your credit report or score. However, if you cannot pay all of your bills, do not pay credit card debts, doctor bills, or other low-priority debts ahead of car payments. If you skip payments on low-priority debts for several months ahead of car payments. If you skip payments on low-priority debts, you will not lose any property for at least several months. Skip one or two car payments and you risk losing the car. See Chapter Nine for more information about the consequences of not paying credit card and other debts.

Keep Your Car's Damage Insurance Current. If your damage insurance is cancelled, the creditor can repossess your car. Or it can decide to buy insurance for you that is *much* more expensive and protects you *much* less.

Curing a Default. Many states give consumers a second chance to make up late payments on cars before repossession. This is called a right to cure. California, Colorado, Connecticut, the District of Columbia, Iowa, Kansas, Maine, Massachusetts, Missouri, Nebraska, New Hampshire, Puerto Rico, South Carolina, South Dakota, Virginia, West Virginia and Wisconsin all require creditors to offer consumers the right to cure in auto transactions. The information about how much you need to pay to cure the default will be in a notice the creditor is required to send you. You can prevent repossession by paying just for the months you are past due and some late charges. Rights to cure auto *leases* are also available in some states.

In other states making all back-payments may *not* prevent a repossession. Creditors generally insert into their agreements the right to call the whole loan due if you miss a payment. This is called "accelerating" a loan and means that the entire amount borrowed must be repaid immediately.

In these states, paying just the delinquent payments may not stop a repossession unless the creditor agrees in writing to accept the back-due payments and reinstate the loan. That agreement should specify that the lender will not repossess the car unless you fail to make future payments. Otherwise, the creditor may keep the back-due payments and still repossess the car.

Negotiate a Work-Out. Many creditors are willing to negotiate a work-out arrangement, where your monthly payments are lowered and the creditor agrees not to seize the car. Particularly where the debt is more than the car is worth, a work-out may ultimately be less expensive for the creditor. The work-out can be a good deal for you as well if you want to keep the car.

Carefully evaluate any work-out proposal before taking it to a creditor. You should balance the importance of keeping your car against the cost of doing so. Consider how much you have already paid, the risk of a deficiency if the car is repossessed, and the importance of keeping the car. For example, a well-running car worth $5,000, with only $2,300 still owed on it, is worth trying to save. The same may not be true of a $17,000 car with $18,000 still owed where the car payments and insurance payments are beyond what you can afford. Do not let the creditor pressure you into agreeing to payments that you cannot afford.

Work-out arrangements should also take into consideration whether you have any claims or defenses relating to the car loan or to the car purchase. Was the car a lemon? Were promised repairs made? Were illegal debt collection contacts made? See Chapter Nine for more information on raising these types of complaints as a defense to loan repayment. An attorney representing you may be able to raise these claims and defenses more effectively than if you do so yourself.

Whether or not you have an attorney, it is important to document your work-out arrangement in writing. Getting the creditor to sign an agreement or send you a letter spelling out the agreement is best. At the very least, you should send your own letter to the creditor to confirm the agreement. Whatever form it takes, your letter should be specific about what you have agreed to do *and* what the creditor has agreed to do or not to do.

Sell the Car. It may be that you simply cannot afford car and insurance payments and maintenance costs or you cannot afford a car as expensive as the car you own. One option is to sell the car yourself. When you sell the car yourself, you will get a *much* higher price than a buyer would pay at a repossession sale. Just as important, you avoid repossession, storage, selling and other expenses which the creditor would otherwise eventually charge back to you. You also get a rebate on car insurance when the coverage is canceled early.

Before trying to sell your car, be sure to find out whether you own it or are merely leasing it. Since you do not own a leased car, you cannot sell it. If you do own the car, you must still obtain the creditor's permission to sell it. If you do not, you might get into trouble for an illegal sale.

It is critical that you coordinate the car's sale with the creditor. The creditor is unlikely to allow a new purchaser to assume the car loan and may require you to pay off the car loan in full to give the new purchaser clear title.

If you cannot sell the car for as much as is owed on the loan, the lender is unlikely to cancel the lien. It will hold out for payment in full. Point out to the creditor that this is not in its own self-interest because it will actually get less money if it repossesses the car.

319

If a creditor still refuses to go along with the sale, make sure you have a written record of the offer for the car. If the creditor eventually seizes the car, the creditor may have difficulty justifying a sale price significantly lower than the bid you received.

Avoid anyone who offers to "broker" a sale or lease (that is, act as a go-between between you and someone who will buy the car). In many states car brokerage is illegal. A widespread scam is for con artists to take money from both you and the new "purchaser" but not complete the paperwork for a real transfer in ownership. Instead, you will still owe the creditor or lessor the full amount. These brokers do not get the lessor's permission or release a creditor's lien on the car. The broker may not even forward monthly payments to the lessor or creditor.

Turn the Car in to the Creditor, But Make Sure You Get a Fair Deal. This strategy is similar to selling the car, only you let the lender sell the car. Although generally not a good idea (because the lender will do such a bad job selling the car), it is a good strategy if you get a *written agreement* from the lender that you do not owe anything else on the loan.

Make sure the agreement is in writing. You should also consider asking the creditor to state in the agreement that it will not report the default to a credit reporting agency.

Your agreement to turn in the car voluntarily is attractive to the lender because then the lender does not need to go to the expense of seizing the car, possibly followed by a legal battle to justify the repossession. The lender may not mind giving up the right to collect additional money if your assets are protected from seizure, meaning that you are "collection proof." (See Chapter Nine.)

Too often consumers voluntarily surrender collateral without trying to negotiate fair terms. Voluntary surrender of collateral requires less effort, sometimes creates good will with the creditor, and generates fewer expenses (for towing, attorney's fees, and other fees) than self-help repossession.

However, voluntary surrender has serious disadvantages. Voluntarily surrendering the car will not prevent the creditor from seeking a deficiency claim (the amount of the debt minus the re-sale price of the car), unless you get a specific agreement (preferably in writing) to this effect. The creditor will normally sell the car for a low price and then come after you for the difference. In addition, a surrender can mean that you unintentionally waive some of your claims or defenses.

The situation is similar when you turn in a leased car. It is a common mistake to believe that you will have no further obligation after you return the car. You will have no further obligation only if you turn the car in at the *scheduled* termination of the lease. Your liability at *early* termination may be thousands of dollars. Before turning in a leased car, negotiate with the lessor to reduce or eliminate your early termination liability. Make sure to get this agreement in writing.

Resisting the Repossession. This strategy is possible but risky and may be only a temporary solution. Repossessors are required by law to obey you if you resist their efforts to take your car. They are only allowed to seize your car if they can do so without "breaching the peace."

Breach of the peace is a technical term and the law sets out some strict rules about how a repossession may be conducted. A repossessor breaches the peace in the following circumstances:

- The repossessor cannot use bodily force or threats. Physical contact is prohibited.
- The repossessor can seize the car from the street or even a driveway but cannot break open a locked garage door to get at a car.
- Most courts agree that the repossessor cannot take property over your oral objections.
- The repossessor cannot be assisted by a government official, such as the police, unless the official has a court order.
- Courts are divided over whether a repossessor can use tricks to seize the car, such as agreeing to make free repairs just so that it can seize the car.

In most states you can stop a repossession by politely objecting—as long as you are there when the car is seized—or by storing the car in a locked garage.

In practice, this means that the repossessor cannot take a car if you or a family member (or in some cases, someone else who is acting for you) is present at the repossession and objects to the seizure just *before* the seizure takes place. Your objection should *not* involve force. You do not even have to scream. Just politely and firmly tell the repossessor not to take the car. You should definitely refuse to turn over the keys when requested to do so. Do not be swayed by any legal advice offered by the repossessor. You have an absolute right to object to the repossession. In most cases, a third party can object for you.

Never resort to force. Never meet force with force. Never use force to object. Never use force to impede a government official. If the repossessor uses force or threats, or otherwise breaches the peace, call the police. Do not take matters into your own hands. After the fact, consult an attorney. There are significant legal remedies available to challenge an illegal repossession.

To avoid consumers objecting to the seizure, repossessors tend to take cars away in the middle of the night. This is perfectly legal, even if the car is parked in your driveway or in a company parking lot. On the other hand, repossessors cannot break open a garage door lock and force themselves into your garage.

Even though you should never resist government officials in the performance of their duties, it is appropriate to verify the identity of any alleged government official appearing at a repossession and the reason why the official is there. Government officials should only operate pursuant to written court orders and should not assist self-help repossessions. (For advice about situations when a government official does have a court order to take your property, see Chapter Seventeen.)

Sometimes, repossessors will try to trick you into believing they have a court order by waving around papers that look like official documents. You should always ask to inspect the documents. Remember that people in uniforms are not necessarily government officials. If the "official" does not provide proper identification, politely object to the seizure—but do so orally, not physically.

Repossessors cannot seize a car they cannot find. There are ways you can try to hide the car, but you should know that in most states there are laws that make it a criminal offense to conceal collateral (such as your car) or to move it out of state.

If you do not want your car repossessed, you should never turn it over for repairs to the dealer or anyone else the creditor would know. Do not drive the car to the creditor's place of business to discuss a work-out agreement. You may have to walk home if you fail to reach a satisfactory arrangement.

File for Bankruptcy Protection. It may not make sense to file for bankruptcy solely to stop a car repossession, but you may have other reasons to file for bankruptcy. In that case, you should know how bankruptcy can deal with the threatened repossession.

As discussed in detail in Chapter Nineteen, filing proof that you received a credit counseling briefing and several other simple forms with a bankruptcy court (with the rest of the forms to be filed later) starts the bankruptcy case and automatically triggers what is known as "the automatic stay." (If you have filed other bankruptcy cases that were dismissed within the previous twelve months, however, you may not get an automatic stay or it may only last for the first thirty days of your bankruptcy case.) Under the automatic stay, no one, including car repossessors, can take any action against your property. Although a lender can later ask the bankruptcy court for permission to take the car, any attempt to repossess while the stay remains in effect is illegal.

In practice, most creditors are careful not to seize cars once they learn that a consumer has filed bankruptcy. If your car has already been repossessed but not yet resold, bankruptcy can help you get it back. This is discussed in more detail below.

After the automatic stay freezes everything, you will need to take several steps to keep your car for the long term (discussed below). See also Chapter Nineteen for a more detailed discussion of your bankruptcy rights.

MINIMIZE THE LOSS OF PERSONAL PROPERTY INSIDE THE CAR

Property left in a car has a way of disappearing after the car is seized. If you have received a repossession notice or anticipate a repossession for other reasons, remove personal property such as tools, tapes, CDs and radio, clothes, and sporting equipment from your car. Remove any important records from the glove compartment. There are some items, however, such as childrens' car seats and spare tires, that need to be in the car when you drive it. Make a list of these items so that you will be in a better position to claim them if the car is repossessed. It is also helpful to take photos or videos of these items in the car or have a friend verify these items and their condition. For some items, like childrens' car seats, you may be able to remove them every night and put them back when you need them. This will make it less likely that the creditor will get the car with those items in it.

If you are present when the car is repossessed, you should remove your personal property from it, whether or not you protest the repossession. If other people are present and you are not able to retrieve all of your personal property, ask them to make note of the property that is left in the car.

WHAT TO DO *AFTER* YOUR CAR IS REPOSSESSED

Get Back Personal Property Left in the Car. Creditors cannot keep property left in your car when it is repossessed. The lender can only keep the car itself. As soon as possible, demand any property left in the car.

A lender's failure to return the property promptly is illegal. (A gray area is whether certain improvements to a car have become so much a part of the car that you do not have a right to their return, such as a tape deck, CD player or radio semi-permanently installed.)

Make the request by phone and put it in writing. Specify everything left in the car. Make the request *quickly*. Some credit contracts require (probably illegally) that you request return of your property within a certain number of days.

You Can Reinstate the Contract in Some States. California, Connecticut, the District of Columbia, Illinois, Mississippi, Ohio, and Wisconsin allow a consumer to reinstate the contract after repossession in at least some circumstances. Reinstating the contract allows you to recover the repossessed car and pay only the back-due payments, not the full amount of the debt. You may also have to pay the costs of the repossession and any storage charges, plus possibly one or two payments in advance. You must act quickly. In most states, you have only a few weeks to reinstate after repossession.

You Can Redeem the Car. In every state, after a repossession, you can redeem the car as long as you were buying the car rather than leasing it. The creditor must send you written notice of the date of the car's sale or a date after which the car will be sold. The notice has to give you a telephone number you can call to find out how much you have to pay to redeem the car. You can redeem the car up until the very moment before the car is sold.

To redeem the car, you must pay off the whole debt for the car in one lump sum, plus reasonable repossession and storage charges. Be sure to get a breakdown from the lender of how much you owe. The breakdown should include a refund for unearned interest and insurance charges that are not owed because the debt has been paid off early.

Redeeming the car is rarely a practical solution. Most owners of repossessed cars could not afford the monthly payments, never mind paying off the whole debt in one lump sum. But where the car is important to you and worth more than the debt, consider whether you can borrow from another source, including friends or relatives. It is rarely a good idea to mortgage the house to get the car back because defaulting on that loan may result in your losing your home.

Try to Negotiate with the Creditor. If your car has just been repossessed, you might be able to negotiate to get the car back. The creditor might agree to reinstate the original payment schedule or even agree to a new schedule. The same considerations apply as when negotiating a work-out arrangement prior to repossession.

You are in a particularly strong position if you have significant claims or defenses relating to the car, its credit terms, or its repossession. If a car has minimal resale value, the creditor should also prefer a work-out agreement to a worthless asset.

If you do not want the car back, it is still worthwhile to try to get the creditor to permit you to sell it privately. If you can't sell it yourself, check the notice of sale to see whether the creditor plans to sell the car at wholesale or retail. Encourage a retail sale, which will produce a price significantly higher than a wholesale auction.

Get the Car Back by Filing Bankruptcy. Even after a car is "lost" through repossession, you can get it back in most states by filing bankruptcy. If the loss of the car is your only problem, a bankruptcy filing may not be justified. But if you have other financial problems, a bankruptcy may be justified and you should know how bankruptcy can help to get your car back.

You will have to file for bankruptcy before the lender resells the car or takes any other steps to cut off your property rights in the car. The lender should return the car voluntarily once you file for bankruptcy. If not, then you may be able to obtain a court order directing the creditor to "turn over" or return it. (In a few states, courts have ruled that the creditor does not have to return a car that was repossessed before the bankruptcy case was filed. While the authors believe that these decisions are wrong, other courts might follow them and it is safest to file bankruptcy before a vehicle is repossessed.)

Once you get the car back, you will need to pay for it if you want to keep it for the long term. If you file a straight bankruptcy (known as a chapter 7 bankruptcy), you can keep the car by "redeeming" it. Redeeming a car in bankruptcy is different than redeeming a car outside of bankruptcy. Outside of bankruptcy, you would have to pay the full balance of the debt plus all the creditor's costs. In bankruptcy, if the car is worth less than you owe on it, you merely pay what it is worth.

Even with this reduced obligation, most consumers will not be able to come up with the cash. Some creditors will let you redeem in installments. However the court cannot order installment payments if the creditor insists on a lump sum payment. Additionally, since other debts are wiped out by the bankruptcy, you will have fewer other debts to pay after bankruptcy, so you will have more money available to apply to redeem the car. Of course, you may have more pressing needs for your cash, such as rent or utilities.

Another way to keep a car in the long term is to file a chapter 13 bankruptcy, sometimes known as a "reorganization." In a chapter 13 bankruptcy, you have several ways of keeping the car. Probably the best one is to set up a plan to pay off the car loan in monthly installments over a period as long as five years.

The interest rate charged in this plan can in some instances be lower than what you are paying on the car loan. You may even reduce the amount owed on certain loans to the current value of the car if the car's value is less than the amount you owe. You may be able to keep the car and significantly lower the car payments. However, changes made to the bankruptcy laws in 2005 may limit your ability to modify car loans in a chapter 13 case in this way. Most courts interpret the new law to mean that you cannot reduce the debt to the value of the car if you took out the loan to buy the car within 910 days of your bankruptcy filing. See Chapter Nineteen for a more detailed discussion of your bankruptcy rights.

Where the Repossession Was Wrongful. Sometimes cars are seized even though the creditor has no right to seize the car or no right to take the car at that time. Other times, the repossession company does not follow proper procedures in seizing the car.

In each of these situations, you have a right to get the car back and be paid money damages. As a practical matter, enforcement of your rights will usually require a lawyer. The first four items in the next section provide an overview of this law. Items five and six deal with situations where the creditor or lessor has already sold the car.

CREDITORS' COLLECTION EFFORTS *AFTER* THE REPOSSESSION SALE— THE DEFICIENCY ACTION

After repossession, the creditor will sell your car and apply the sale price (after deducting all repossession and sale expenses) against the amount you owe. Creditors then often come after you for any remaining amount due on the debt. This is called a deficiency action. When a lessor repossesses a leased vehicle, the result is the same. The car is sold and the lessor seeks a further amount under the lease, called an early termination charge.

Many consumers feel especially victimized in this situation. They have already lost their car and now the creditor is trying to get more money. You should realize two things about the creditor's claim for a deficiency that might make you feel better. First, the obligation is no longer backed up by any collateral but is just an unsecured debt. The creditor can take no immediate steps if you do not pay. The deficiency debt is just like a hospital bill or a credit card debt. You should not pay this unsecured debt ahead of more pressing obligations, such as rent or utility bills. (For more on collection of "unsecured debts," see Chapter Eight.)

Second, many defenses are available to you when a creditor attempts to collect this deficiency amount. Creditors who repossess cars are required to follow strict technical requirements. In many states, if the creditor trips up on even one technical requirement, the deficiency action may be thrown out or the creditor may even end up owing *you* money.

Because creditors frequently make mistakes, it is always a good idea to get legal advice before agreeing to pay any deficiency. This section provides an overview of six types of defenses you may have when the creditor seeks a deficiency. It also reviews claims relating to other aspects of the sale and repossession that can often be raised as counterclaims when you are being sued for a deficiency.

1. Claims concerning the car or the credit terms. In many cases you can fight a deficiency claim by showing the car was a lemon, the dealer misrepresented the quality of a used car, the credit terms were illegal or not disclosed accurately, or the creditor engaged in debt collection harassment. These types of defenses are summarized in Chapter Nine.

If you have a claim along these lines, the mere threat that you will raise it is helpful in negotiating a resolution of the deficiency claim. Depending upon the value of your defenses, you may be able to negotiate a "wash-out." This means that both parties agree to call the debt even, or a "wash," and release each other from liability for further payments.

2. Is the car collateral on the loan? If the creditor has not taken the car as collateral, it cannot repossess the car, even if you defaulted on a loan used to purchase the car.

Your agreement to put up the car as collateral must be signed by you. The agreement must also correctly identify your car, and the car's title must be in your own name. Otherwise, the creditor has no right to seize the car.

For example, if a husband alone signs a loan and security agreement but has the seller put the car in his wife's name, the creditor may not have a valid security interest in the car. A repossession may also be illegal if the lender explicitly took the car as collateral only for an earlier loan, but not for the loan at issue.

Another common dealer tactic is to try to get you to buy a car "on the spot" before the financing arrangements are completed. This practice is called "spot delivery" or a "yo-yo sale." Dealers will allow you to take the car home while they supposedly try to find a good financing deal for you. Often, the financing never comes through, and the dealer will then try to repossess the car. A claim you might have in this situation is that the dealer never properly took the car as collateral because the financing arrangements were never final, or that you are not in default (see item #3).

For more analysis as to whether a creditor has properly taken a car as collateral, see National Consumer Law Center's *Repossessions* (6th ed. 2005 and Supp.).

3. Were you in "default" when the car was seized? Creditors can repossess your car only if you are in default on the car loan. Being late on payments does not necessarily place you "in default."

For example, if a creditor routinely accepts your late payments, the creditor cannot surprise you and seize the car just because a payment is late. You sometimes can also avoid a default by giving the lender notice that you are withholding payments because the car is a lemon.

In some states, the law gives you the right to cure the default (discussed earlier in this chapter). The creditor cannot repossess the car before the right to cure has expired. More detail on when a consumer is actually in default can be found in NCLC's *Repossessions* (6th ed. 2005 and Supp.).

4. Did the car's repossession breach the peace? Whether a seizure breaches the peace has already been discussed earlier in this chapter under *Strategies to Prevent Your Car from Being Repossessed* and *Resisting the Repossession*. See also *How Self-Help Repossession Works*, above, for situations where self-help repossession is not permitted at all. When a seizure is wrongful, the creditor generally should not keep the car or collect a deficiency. The creditor may owe you money instead.

5. Improper repossession sale or miscalculation of the deficiency. Creditors must either keep the cars they repossess or sell them. If it keeps a car, which is rare and allowed only in certain circumstances, the creditor cannot seek any more money from you.

Creditors usually sell cars after repossessing them. The law is very strict on the exact procedure the creditor must use in selling a repossessed car. You can challenge the creditor's attempt to collect a deficiency simply by showing that the creditor did not take the correct steps in selling the car. Tripping up on one technical requirement is usually enough to stop a deficiency. While these technical requirements are very briefly summarized below, see National Consumer Law Center's *Repossessions* (6th ed. 2005 and Supp.) for more details.

Failure to meet these requirements may prevent collection of a deficiency if they are raised in court:

- After a repossession or if you turned the car in voluntarily, you must be sent advance notice of the creditor's plan for selling the repossessed car. The notice must describe the car, state how the creditor plans to dispose of it, and state the time and place of a public auction or the date after which the car will be sold privately. It must also give certain information about your rights and responsibilities, and tell you how to get more information about the sale and the debt. This notice is very important. Many consumers have prevented a deficiency merely by showing errors in the notice of sale.
- The sale cannot be too rushed and it cannot be overly delayed. On the one hand, there must be time for you to receive the notice of sale and for others to read advertising about the sale. On the other hand, the creditor cannot wait too long to sell the car or the car's value will depreciate.
- *Every* aspect of the sale, including the manner, the time, the place, and the terms must be "commercially reasonable." Particularly if the

sale price was unreasonably low, look at every aspect of the sale, including the decision to sell at retail or wholesale, and the decision to use an auction rather than to sell the car off a lot. Advertising for the sale must be sufficient; an auction must use competitive bidding; and the car should be available for advance inspection. Consider attending the sale, along with a witness if possible, to see how your car is actually sold.

- Look out for low-price sales to insiders. If the sale price seems unreasonably low, check with the motor vehicle department to see who the car was sold to. If the car was sold at an unreasonably low price to the creditor itself, an officer or director of the creditor, a relative of an officer or director, or the dealer, then you have the right to be credited with the fair price of the car. Be especially suspicious if the car was sold at a private sale. The law prohibits the creditor itself from buying the car at a private sale, but some creditors use private sales to sell cars at low prices to employees or relatives.

- Check to see if the creditor correctly calculated the amount of its claimed deficiency. If the creditor asks you to pay a deficiency after the car has been sold, in most states it must send you a summary of its calculations, along with an address or phone number where you can get additional information. Go over this summary and ask the creditor for any details that are missing. Were you given proper credit for all payments? Were the late charges correctly calculated? Did the creditor give you a proper rebate for unearned finance charges and insurance premiums? Were you credited with the car's actual sale price and not the car's "estimated" cash value? Were the creditor's expenses (repossession, reconditioning, sale, attorney's fees) reasonable and accurate?

6. Auto leases. Special laws and rules apply where you leased the repossessed car instead of buying the car on credit. The lease will specify the formula used to calculate how much you owe upon default or early termination. The formula is usually quite complex and difficult to understand, and may be unreasonable or not properly applied by the lessor. Federal and state laws provide you with powerful remedies when lessors apply unreasonable formulas or do not clearly disclose the formulas they use.

Although it is not uncommon for a lessor to demand $5,000 to $10,000 at early termination of a car lease, proper legal advocacy can often get car leasing companies to drop the whole claim. For more detail on challenging auto lease early termination penalties, see National Consumer Law Center's *Truth in Lending* Ch. 10 (6th ed. 2007).

YOUR RIGHTS WHEN THE CREDITOR MAKES A MISTAKE

The penalties are severe when creditors trip up in repossessing cars. In many states, any mistake will lead to the creditor being barred from seeking any deficiency.

Moreover, if the creditor trips up on one of the requirements, it may have to pay you as a penalty 10% of the car's original purchase price plus the whole finance charge on the car loan. This penalty can run into many thousands of dollars.

If repossessor conduct is seriously improper, you may also be able to recover punitive damages running into many thousands of dollars. Sometimes, the creditor will even have to pay your attorney fees. Legal representation is usually essential to recover any of these penalties.

FOR MORE INFORMATION

To learn more about consumer repossession rights, the best legal practice manual is the National Consumer Law Center's *Repossessions* (6th ed. 2005 and Supp.), which is the source of much of the information in this chapter. The manual covers all the federal and state laws governing consumer repossessions. *Repossessions* includes step-by-step checklists for different types of repossession situations and samples of different documents a lawyer will have to prepare in a repossession case. The manual covers both car loans and leases.

17

Seizure of
Household Goods

UNDERSTANDING CREDITOR THREATS
TO SEIZE HOUSEHOLD GOODS

One of the most frightening creditor practices is the threat to seize your household goods, such as your television, wedding rings and bedroom furniture. These threats can be effective because of these items' special personal significance, even if they have minimal resale value.

In most cases, you should not take such threats seriously. The goods' limited economic value means the creditor has no financial incentive to follow through with the threat. Additionally, federal and state laws limit the types of household goods a creditor can take and how it can seize those goods.

This chapter explains the limited situations in which a creditor can legally seize your household goods, how it must conduct the seizure, and what steps you can take to prevent such seizures. There are only four situations in which a creditor can try to seize your household goods:

1. Purchase money security interests. When you get credit specifically to purchase certain household goods and agree to have those goods serve as collateral for the debt, the creditor has a "purchase money security interest" in those household goods. For example, if you buy a dining room set on credit offered by the furniture dealer, the dining room set is likely to be collateral for the debt. Another common example is a car loan, discussed in Chapter Sixteen.

Some stores which have their own credit cards take a purchase money security interest in the things you buy at their store with their card. This would be reflected in your credit card agreement and on your charge slips. Non-store cards such as Visa, MasterCard, Discover, or American Express typically do not take security interests in the items sold.

If you default on a debt with personal property collateral, the creditor can seize those goods. However, you do not have to let repossessors into your home without a court order and creditors usually do not find it worth the expense to get a court order.

2. Non-purchase money security interests. When a loan is *not* used to purchase household goods, but the creditor insists that you put up household goods as collateral for the loan, the creditor has a "non-purchase money security interest." For example, a finance company may insist that you give a lawnmower or living room set as collateral for a loan you take out to pay for car repairs. A non-purchase money security interest will be reflected in your loan papers and in your disclosure statement concerning the cost of the loan. Under federal law, creditors cannot take non-purchase money security interests in basic household goods such as clothing, furniture and appliances. More discussion of this issue is found below.

3. Execution on court judgment. If you have not put household goods up as collateral for a loan, creditors can still ask a sheriff or other official to seize these goods, but only *after* suing you and obtaining a court judgment on the debt. The creditor uses that judgment to try to "execute" on the household goods. Even then, state exemption law (discussed below) generally protects most of your household goods from such executions.

4. Rent-to-own transactions. When you rent goods with the option to purchase them after all payments are made, this is called a "rent-to-own" or RTO transaction. Although the RTO merchant has the right to take the goods back if you get behind on payments, the merchant does *not* have the right to enter your home without your permission to take the goods.

No Other Rights to Seize Household Goods. These are the *only* four situations in which a creditor has *any* legal right to follow through on a threat to seize household goods.

You can usually determine if one of these four situations applies by looking at the loan or credit documents. The documents will indicate if household goods are taken as collateral and if the credit was used to purchase those goods. Sales agreements will also indicate if they are rent-to-own transactions.

Ways to deal with each of these potential threats to your personal property are discussed below.

NINE STRATEGIES TO PROTECT YOUR HOUSEHOLD GOODS

This section lists nine strategies that can help you keep your household goods when a creditor threatens to seize them. For more details, see the National Consumer Law Center's *Repossessions* (6th ed. 2005 and Supp.).

1. Do not panic; determine if the threat is false. The first thing to realize is that a creditor threatening seizure is usually bluffing. The value of most household goods after deducting repossession, storage, and selling expenses is very small. The creditor has no economic interest in the goods and therefore is unlikely to pursue repossession.

The creditor is using the threat of repossession to frighten you into paying off that creditor's debt first, even though it may be in your overall best interest to pay off other debts instead. Sometimes a creditor also makes these threats to build up its reputation as being tough on defaulters.

A threat to seize household goods is false if the debt does not fall within any of the four categories of allowable seizures listed at the beginning of this chapter.

Even if one of these four situations applies, the threat is still usually false. This is particularly the case where the creditor is threatening to execute on household goods under a court judgment, since state laws usually protect most common household goods from seizure.

Beyond that, evaluating a threat will often depend on the value of the collateral, the difficulty of seizing it, and the nature and reputation of the creditor. For example, a consumer electronics store is more likely to seize $2,000 worth of the stereo and video equipment it sold you a few months ago than a loan company is to seize the family photo album or the five-year-old lawnmower.

If the threat is false, you should not worry about it. False threats are illegal and you may be able to recover as much as $1,000 plus your attorney fees even if you are not injured. See Chapter Eight.

Even if the threat is not false, you have a series of strategies to protect the goods or make it very difficult for the creditor to seize them. In protecting your household goods, you have the upper hand in dealing with the creditor. Do not be frightened into doing something you will regret.

2. Determine if the creditor can take the household goods as collateral.

Federal law prohibits creditors from taking "non-purchase money security interests" in most household goods. This rule is particularly important in dealing with finance companies but usually not helpful in dealing with furniture or appliance dealers that are seeking to seize the goods you purchased from them.

A creditor *can* take household goods as collateral if you used its credit *to purchase those particular goods,* although it may choose not to do so. The only way to tell is to check your credit agreement to see if the creditor is claiming a security interest in the goods purchased.

Under federal law, a creditor *cannot* take the following household goods as collateral for a loan which is *not* used to purchase the goods: clothing, furniture, appliances, one radio, one television, linens, china, crockery, kitchenware, and other personal effects such as your wedding rings and photographs. But the law probably allows the following types of goods to be taken as collateral, even if the loan is not used to purchase these items: art, lawn equipment, tools, audio systems, a second television or radio, cameras, boats, sporting goods, typewriters, firearms, bicycles, musical instruments or jewelry (other than wedding rings).

No creditor can claim a security interest in all of your household goods or all items located at your residence, because this will include many types of prohibited collateral. In addition, creditors cannot take as collateral goods which you do not yet own at the time of the loan but will own in the future. As a consequence, for example, a creditor cannot take a security interest in all tools or audio systems you will ever own, only in identified items you own at the time of the loan or acquire within ten days after the loan.

Some merchants sometimes try to take a security interest in all goods you purchase in their store with their credit card. (This applies to the stores' own cards, but not to other cards accepted by the stores, such as Visa or Master-Card.) The store may or may not be successful in taking purchased items as collateral, depending on how it complies with various technical requirements. You will have to ask an attorney whether the security interest is valid.

3. Do not consent to the creditor coming into your home. This strategy applies *only* if the person coming to your home works for the creditor or a collection agency. See the next item if a sheriff or other government official comes to your home.

No creditor, collector, or hired repossession agent may come into your home without your express permission in order to repossess property. You can easily stop them by politely, but firmly, refusing permission to enter.

Repeat your objection to entry each time a repossession threat or effort is made and instruct landlords, spouses, children, and/or roommates *not* to consent to repossessors entering your residence. This protection also applies to a locked garage on your premises. If you have property outdoors, consider bringing it inside or placing it in your locked garage.

You can stop a creditor's self-help repossession by refusing to allow the repossessor to enter your home. The creditor has no right to enter unless invited by you.

Do not physically resist the entry, just politely and firmly object to the entry. Even walking uninvited through an open door makes the repossession illegal.

If repossessors do force themselves in or break a lock to gain entry, your first concern should be for the safety of individuals in the house. After the repossession, contact the police and an attorney because the repossessor's action was an illegal breach of the peace. Witnesses are helpful. Other evidence, such as a broken lock, should be retained.

4. *Do cooperate with the sheriff.* In rare cases, it will not be the creditor who is seizing the goods but a government official such as a sheriff, bailiff, or constable. (This chapter will refer to all these types of officials as "the sheriff.")

This situation is unusual because a creditor has to get a court order before the sheriff will come. Obtaining a court order is likely to cost more than the goods are worth. If it is the sheriff (and not the creditor claiming to be the sheriff), ask for identification and then comply with any order the sheriff makes.

Find out from the sheriff which creditor has asked for the goods to be seized. The steps you can take after the seizure will depend on whether or not you put the goods up as collateral for the loan from that creditor. (See the next two sections.) Ask the sheriff if he or she has copies of any papers for you, or where you can get copies.

5. Challenge the creditor in court if you have defenses.
If you put your household goods up as collateral for a loan, usually it is not worth the creditor's time and money to get a court order for the sheriff to seize the goods. But some furniture and appliance stores, and occasionally other creditors, will get court orders sending the sheriff to seize this collateral.

To get a court order, the creditor goes to court (sometimes without even telling you) and claims that you are behind on your payments and that the sheriff should seize the collateral. (Depending on what state you are in, this proceeding may be called "replevin," "sequestration," "detinue," "claim and delivery," or "bail.")

Sometimes you will be given notice and the opportunity to fight this seizure before it happens and sometimes you can only do so after it happens. (If your hearing is not until after the seizure, the creditor will not obtain permanent custody of the property until *after* your hearing.) In either case, just as in other types of lawsuits, the creditor is not expecting you to contest the matter or to be represented by an attorney. Raising a serious defense, such as that the goods which the creditor seeks to repossess are not the same goods which serve as collateral for the loan, may be enough for the creditor to drop the suit. This will allow you to keep or recover your property.

Exemptions discussed in the next section generally do *not* apply to property that was collateral for a loan.

6. Claim that the household goods are exempt.
If you did not put up the household goods as collateral for the debt to a creditor, the only way that a creditor can have the sheriff seize them is to get a court judgment against you—a ruling from a court that you owe the debt. You have important rights under state law when the sheriff seizes goods to pay a judgment.

Almost all states protect certain household goods from seizure to satisfy a court judgment.

The state laws offering this protection are usually called exemption laws. They may provide protection for all household goods, for household goods under a certain dollar figure or for certain types of household goods. It is important to know the exemption law for your state. Ask a legal services office or other attorney or a reputable credit counseling agency. Often the information is available in pamphlet form. See Chapter Nine for more details about exemption rights.

In addition, property in your residence owned by someone else should not be seized to satisfy a judgment against you. This applies even to property owned by other family members.

If property is exempt or owned by someone else, this should be pointed out to the sheriff or, even better, to the court before the sheriff comes. Usually, there is a form which will be sent or delivered to you before or at the time of the seizure. It should be returned as soon as possible and definitely *before* the scheduled date for the seizure.

If the sheriff still takes the goods, *quickly* go to court to explain that the household goods are exempt under state law or belong to someone else. The court clerk's office or sheriff's office may have a form to fill out to help you with your claim. If the clerk's or sheriff's office cannot help you, see an attorney immediately.

7. Negotiate an agreement. Since the goods the creditor is seeking are likely to have very little value if seized, the creditor may be willing to agree to a very fair voluntary repayment plan. You should approach this negotiation based on what you can reasonably afford and with a complete understanding of what you can do to prevent repossession if the creditor does not accept your offer. You should never agree to make voluntary payments in an amount larger than you can afford or if you have other higher-priority debts which will remain unpaid.

8. Preventing RTO repossessions. Rent-to-own (RTO) contracts give you ownership of rented goods after you make all the payments. If you stop making payments, the RTO company has the right to take the rented property. But most states prohibit the RTO company from repossessing over your objection or entering your home without permission. This is true even if you gave permission in the small print of the sales agreement to the repossession

339

or entry into your home. Be careful of the "switch out" technique where the RTO company claims it is taking an item in for repair, maintenance, or upgrading, when it is actually repossessing it.

RTO companies may also threaten criminal action if you do not return rented goods. But it would be very unusual for a court to hold that failure to let RTO personnel into your home was a crime. In addition, the RTO company usually has no intent to pursue a criminal action.

Nevertheless, unless you have made substantial payments on a rent-to-own contract, it is usually a good idea to return the goods and stop paying. There will be no liability except for back-due payments. And, typically, the rented item is significantly overpriced. You will pay for the goods many times over before you own them.

9. File for bankruptcy. The cost and other complications of filing bankruptcy may not make sense just to protect certain household goods. But a bankruptcy filing also offers you benefits in dealing with other debts, so bankruptcy may make sense for other reasons. For this reason, it is important to know how bankruptcy can protect your household goods.

Filing for bankruptcy provides immediate relief by automatically stopping *any* threatened seizure of the household goods. This applies to seizures of collateral and even to rented items. (If you have filed other bankruptcy cases that were dismissed within the previous twelve months, however, you may not get an automatic stay or it may only last for the first thirty days of your bankruptcy case.)

Bankruptcy can usually protect your household goods in the long run as well. If the household goods are exempt under applicable law, then bankruptcy permanently prevents their seizure to satisfy a court judgment. In some states, more generous exemptions apply when a person files bankruptcy.

Many non-purchase money security interests in household goods can also be canceled in bankruptcy if the goods are exempt under the bankruptcy law. Even if the creditor has a purchase money security interest, that interest may be eliminated in certain situations if the creditor has since refinanced the original loan used to purchase the goods.

Even if a security interest in certain household goods cannot be cancelled in bankruptcy, you may be able to keep the property after a bankruptcy filing by paying the creditor only what the property is worth. This is called "redemption." Used household goods may be worth far less than the outstanding debt. However, the 2005 amendments to the bankruptcy laws may limit your ability to pay only the current value of an item of personal property and keep it in a chapter 13 case. This limitation may apply if you incurred the debt to buy the property within one year of filing bankruptcy.

In an RTO transaction, if you want to keep the goods after filing bankruptcy, you have to pay any delinquent payments over time and keep current on future rent payments. In a few states you may be able to categorize the RTO transaction as a sale, and this will give you additional strategies in bankruptcy, including the possibility of redemption for the goods' real value.

In many of these situations, special papers have to be filed with the bankruptcy court to protect household goods. For more on bankruptcy, see Chapter Nineteen.

SPECIAL RIGHTS FOR ACTIVE DUTY SERVICEMEMBERS AND THEIR FAMILIES

If you are in the military and on active duty, you have special protections against creditors who want to seize your household goods. (These protections also apply to National Guard members who are called to active service authorized by the President or the Secretary of Defense for more than thirty consecutive days to respond to a national emergency.)

First, if you put up household goods (or any other personal property) as collateral for a debt before you entered active duty, the creditor cannot repossess the collateral without a court order. This is the case regardless of whether you incurred the debt to buy the household goods or for other purposes, regardless of whether there are cosigners on the debt, and regardless of whether the payments are up-to-date.

Second, if you entered into a rent-to-own contract before you entered active duty, the rent-to-own company cannot take back the rented items without a court order. This protection applies to you even if you or your family has fallen behind on the payments.

Third, you have many protections if a creditor sues you in court. The most important is that you can ask that any court proceeding against you be postponed, simply by sending a letter to the court. The letter must: (1) explain why your military duties interfere with your ability to defend the lawsuit; (2) state a date when you will be able to appear in court; and (3) include a statement from your commanding officer that your current military duty prevents you from appearing in court and that military leave is not authorized for you.

If you submit the letter, the court must postpone proceedings for at least ninety days. You can request additional postponements ("stays") by sending the court a similar letter and documentation when the initial stay expires. Your commanding officer or JAG Corps officer may be able to help you make this request. If you get a proceeding postponed, any co-signers can ask the court to make the postponement applicable to them, too.

18

Student Loan and Federal Income Tax Collections

TOPICS COVERED IN THIS CHAPTER

- Identifying the Type of Student Loan You Have
- What to Do If You Are Behind on Your Student Loans, Including Flexible Repayment Plans, Deferments, Forbearances, and Loan Consolidation
- What the Government Can Do to Collect Student Loans and How Borrowers Can Respond
- Getting Out of Default on Student Loans
- What to Do If You Owe Taxes to the IRS

WHY YOU SHOULD PAY PARTICULAR ATTENTION TO YOUR STUDENT LOANS

Because most student loans are government loans, it is the government who will come after you if you don't pay. The federal government has special powers to collect student loans if you default, including seizing your tax refunds, denying you new student loans and grants, garnishing a percentage of your wages without a court order, taking a portion of your Social Security benefits in some cases, and charging you very large collection fees.

To make matters worse, there is no time limit for collection on federal government student loans. The government can keep trying to collect twenty or even thirty years later. This makes it especially hard to hide from student loan debt.

On the other hand, the law provides a number of options for you to fend off these collection techniques. Unfortunately, you cannot sit back and wait.

You must know about and request these options on your own. Requesting one of these options may allow you to skip payments for a while, reduce your payments, stop collection efforts against you and, in certain cases, may even allow you to cancel the loan and receive a refund!

There is also a growing private student loan market. Banks and other financial institutions make these loans without any financial backing from the federal government. Many private lenders market their products very aggressively.

These loans can be very tempting given the soaring costs of higher education. However, you should be very careful if you are considering private loans to finance higher education. Among other problems, there are no interest rate limits on private student loans as there are for government loans. These loans can be very expensive, especially if you have problems with your credit history. In most cases, interest accrues from the time the loans are disbursed. Private loans also do not have the same range of flexible repayment and other borrower protections that government loans have. You should exhaust all federal grant and loan options (including PLUS loans) before considering a private student loan.

THE FIRST STEP IS TO IDENTIFY WHAT KIND OF LOAN YOU HAVE

There are many different types of student loans and many different lenders to whom you might owe repayment. Your rights and strategies will vary depending on what type of loan you have. This chapter focuses mainly on federal government student loans. If you have a private or state loan, you will need to check your loan documents to find out the name of the company and then contact that company for more information about assistance if you are having trouble paying the loans.

FFEL and Direct Loans. Most federal student loans are either Federal Family Education Loans (FFELs) or Direct Loans. FFELs are guaranteed by the government but given out by banks or other financial institutions. Direct Loans are loans directly from the federal government to borrowers with the assistance of the school. Lenders and guaranty agencies are cut out of the Direct Loan process.

Both FFELs and Direct Loans can be any of the following types:

- *Stafford Loans (formerly called Guaranteed Student Loans or GSLs)* can be either subsidized or unsubsidized. Subsidized loans are given out based on financial need and borrowers are not charged interest before repayment begins. Unsubsidized loans, on the other hand, are not based on financial need, but interest is charged from the time the loan is disbursed until it is paid off. Repayment on Stafford loans generally begins six months after a student leaves school or graduates.

- *PLUS Loans* are loans for parents to help finance their children's educations. As of 2006, graduate and professional students are also eligible for PLUS loans. Repayment on these loans generally begins within sixty days after the final loan disbursement. There are no loan limits on PLUS loans as there are for the other types of government student loans. Unlike the other federal loans, however, the government can deny a PLUS loan based on problems with your credit record.

- *Consolidation Loans.* There are both FFEL and Direct consolidation loans. These programs allow you to combine one or more loans into a new loan that has different, hopefully better, terms. Consolidation loans are discussed later in this chapter.

Perkins Loans. Perkins loans, formerly called National Direct Student Loans or NDSLs, are made directly from the school you attended. You repay the school. If you stop paying, the loan is eventually turned over to the U.S. Department of Education. Perkins loans have lower interest rates and are available only for borrowers with exceptional financial need.

How to Identify What Type of Loan You Have. The first place to look is the loan application and promissory note if you have it. You can also ask the lender or collector you are dealing with. Another way to figure out what type of loan you have is through the Department of Education's National Student Loan Data System. To use this system, you will need to get a Personal Identification Number on-line at www.nslds.ed.gov or by calling 800-4-FED-AID, TDD: 800-730-8913.

It is also important to understand how an FFEL loan works because it can be very complicated. Even if the school helped you fill out the loan papers, the loan was actually from a bank. That bank may have sold the loan to another lender, such as the Student Loan Marketing Association (Sallie Mae). Whoever is holding the loan might hire another company to "service" the loan. Loan servicers receive your payments and correspond with you. If you stopped making payments on that loan, the loan was then turned over to a guaranty agency. Most older loans are eventually passed on to the U.S. Department of Education. Both the guaranty agency and the Department of

Education may have hired a debt collection agency to go after you.

Direct Loans work differently. The school, not the bank, arranges for a loan between the United States Department of Education and the student. Payments are made directly to the United States Department of Education. If you are in default, just as with FFEL loans, the Department of Education is likely to hire a collection agency to come after you.

To make matters more complicated, many of the lenders that participate in the government student loan program also make private student loans. Below are a few tips to help you figure out whether you have a private or government loan:

1. The name of the federal loan program is written at the top of the loan document and also on the loan application and billing statements.

2. When you take out a private loan, you should be given a disclosure statement that looks like the statement you get when you take out a mortgage or car loan (see Chapter Six for sample mortgage loan documents). This is because most private loans are covered by the federal Truth in Lending Act, while federal loans are not. The federal student loan program has its own disclosure requirements.

3. Interest rates on federal loans are set by law. As of 2007, most federal student loans have fixed interest rates of 6.8%. Private loans do not have interest rate limits set by law. Most private loans have variable interest rates. If your loan has a very high interest rate, it is most likely a private loan.

4. With the exception of PLUS loans, the federal loan programs do not require borrowers to have minimum credit scores in order to qualify. For this reason, the federal programs do not require you to get a co-signer. Private lenders do require borrowers to meet certain credit standards and will often require co-signers.

5. There is a data base of information about federal student loans called the National Student Loan Data System (www.nslds.ed.gov). There is no similar information system for private loans.

WHAT TO DO IF YOU ARE BEHIND ON YOUR STUDENT LOAN

You have many more choices if you deal with student loan problems *before* going into default. And you have quite a bit of time—usually nine months for federal government loans—after you first get into trouble before your loan will go into default. But you must apply for this help, and you must do so quickly. This section lists some of your best options, both before and after default.

STUDENT LOAN CHECKLIST

To help you figure out how to handle student loan problems, ask yourself the following questions:

What type of student loans do you have? Your rights are different in many cases depending on the type of loan.

If you have a federal government loan, are you eligible for a full or partial loan cancellation?

— Was there a serious problem with the admissions process or did the school close while you were attending? If so, you might qualify for a closed school or false certification loan cancellation.

— Did you leave school early in the term? If so, did the school give you a refund? If not, you might qualify for an unpaid refund cancellation.

— Are you permanently and totally disabled? If so, you might qualify for a disability discharge.

— Is there a program that will allow you to cancel all or part of your loan because you are working in a public service job?

— Are you eligible for a cancellation because you have consistently made payments for ten years if you are working in a public service job or twenty-five years in other cases?

If you are not eligible for a loan cancellation and you are having trouble paying your loans, consider the following options:

Do you qualify for a deferment? These programs are available only if you are not yet in default.

Would a forbearance help? Whether you are in default or not, you might be able to get a loan forbearance and postpone payments.

Are you able to set up a more affordable or flexible repayment plan?

You should consider the following options:

— Flexible repayment plans if you are not yet in default;
— Loan Consolidation;
— Reasonable and Affordable Payment Plan;
— Loan Rehabilitation.

Can you discharge your loans in bankruptcy?

All of these options are discussed in this chapter.

Flexible Repayment Plans. If you are not yet in default, there are a number of repayment plans available that may help you stay out of default. The typical federal student loan repayment plan, called the standard plan, has the highest monthly payments. In general, you have up to ten years to repay your student loans under a standard plan.

You can change your repayment plan to one better suited to your present financial situation:

- *Extended Repayment Plans.* This option allows you to extend repayment over a longer period (usually no more than twenty-five years), thus lowering your monthly payment. These plans are generally available only if you have loans totaling more than $30,000.
- *Graduated Repayment Plans.* Payments start out low and increase every two years.
- *Income-Sensitive Plans for FFELs and Income-Contingent Plans for Direct Loans.* With these plans, the amount of your monthly payment is adjusted each year based on your total income. If you have an FFEL, you are currently required to pay enough to at least cover accruing interest each month. If you have a Direct Loan, including a consolidation loan, there is no minimum payment, so your payment can actually be zero, if your income is low enough.

ALERT: Beginning on July 1, 2009, there will be a new income-based repayment (IBR) program available in both the FFEL and Direct Loan programs. The formula to determine monthly payments is similar to the formula for the current Direct Loan income contingent plan (ICRP), although the IBR calculation may result in a lower monthly payment for many borrowers. As with the Direct Loan ICRP, the government will cancel the remaining balance after a borrower has made income-based payments or a combination of income-based and other payments for a certain period of time. This period is now twenty-five years for Direct Loan income contingent repayment. The Department of Education will set the time period for the new IBR program some time in 2008, but it will be no more than twenty-five years. For borrowers that are employed full-time in certain public service jobs, the time limit for cancellation will be only ten years.

Deferments. A loan deferment means that you delay repaying your loan, usually for a year, sometimes longer. You can renew the deferment for one or two or sometimes even three additional years. For subsidized loans, the government makes interest payments for you during the deferment period. Your loan principal will be no higher after the deferment period than before. When you defer an unsubsidized or PLUS loan, you will later have to pay back the interest that accrued during the deferment period.

You have a legal right to a loan deferment under specified conditions. For most loans that you got after July 1, 1993, the available deferments include:

- Student deferments for at least half-time study;
- Graduate fellowship deferments;
- Rehabilitation training program deferments;
- Unemployment deferments (for up to three years); and
- Economic hardship deferments (granted one year at a time for up to three years).

The rules are different for loans from before July 1993. Perkins loans also have different deferment rules.

Borrowers who are active military personnel or serving in the National Guard can defer certain loans. There is no maximum number of years for these deferments as long as borrowers continue to meet the eligibility requirements. In general, only relatively recent loans (loans taken out in 2001 or later) can be deferred through this program. The Perkins program also has deferments and other benefits for active members of the military. To get the latest information, check out the Department of Education website at www.ed.gov or call 800-433-3243.

It is essential to apply for a deferment as early as possible. If you wait too long to apply and get too far behind on your payments, you will no longer qualify for a deferment. Deferments are not available if you are already in default.

Forbearances. If you cannot qualify for a deferment, an alternative is to request loan "forbearance." Forbearance means that you do not have to pay for a while, and no adverse action will be taken against you during the forbearance period. Unlike a deferment on a subsidized loan, the government does not pay interest for you. You will eventually have to repay the full loan amount and all accrued interest. In many cases, you can get a forbearance even if you're already in default.

In some circumstances, you will have a legal right to a forbearance. For example, you have a right to forbear a FFEL or Direct Loan that exceeds 20% of your income even if you are many months delinquent. There are limits to how many times you can automatically get this and most other forbearances. Even if you don't have a right to a forbearance, lenders have the option to grant you one, especially if you are having health problems or other personal problems that affect your ability to make your monthly payments.

Consolidation. Another option is to consolidate, that is, exchange the type of student loans you have for a new loan. There are pros and cons to consolidation that you should carefully consider.

Pros and Cons of Consolidation

The "Pros"

1. Consolidation might help you if you want to extend the repayment term of your loan. But remember that extending the years of repayment increases the total amount you have to repay.

2. You may get an interest rate break, especially if you have variable rate loans.

3. Consolidation allows you to put all of your loans together and make just one monthly payment.

The "Cons"

1. The interest rate advantages for federal government consolidation loans are not as good as they used to be. This is because interest rates on most new government loans are fixed. The interest rates for consolidation loans are calculated based on the average interest rates of the loans that you are consolidating. Since most loans will now be fixed at 6.8%, the interest rates for the consolidation loan will also end up at around that rate.

2. You can no longer consolidate your loans while you are still in school.

3. You may lose rights by consolidating. This is most clearly a problem if you consolidate government loans into a private consolidation loan. You will lose the rights you get with government loans. You may also lose some of these protections if you consolidate government loans with one of the government programs.

4. If you are close to paying off your student loans, it may not be worth the effort to consolidate or extend your payments.

In general, you can consolidate your loans just once. There are some exceptions to this rule. An important exception is if you are in default on a FFEL loan and want to consolidate with the Direct Loan program. You should be able to get another consolidation loan in these circumstances if you agree to repay through the income contingent repayment plan.

Even if you do decide that you want to consolidate, keep in mind that not all loans are eligible. You may not have all of the same defenses to repayment after you consolidate. In addition, not all loans can be consolidated. Private loans, for example, cannot be consolidated through the FFEL or Direct Loan programs.

There are also a growing number of private loan consolidation products. It may be a good idea to look into one of these products if you have private loans and want to get lower interest rates. However, it is very dangerous to consolidate federal loans into a private consolidation loan. You will lose rights under the federal loan programs once you make this choice. Lenders may offer you other bonuses if you agree to consolidate with them. Be sure to read the fine print!

Congress is likely to make even more changes to this program. You should keep track of new developments and find out as much as you can before making a decision. For example, as of 2006, Congress eliminated the program that allowed married borrowers to jointly consolidate their student loans.

WHAT TO EXPECT IF YOU ARE IN DEFAULT ON YOUR FEDERAL GOVERNMENT STUDENT LOAN

The government has a number of actions it can take to come after student loan defaulters. This section lists these various actions and ways to deal with them. The next section discusses ways you can stop the student loan collectors entirely by getting out of default.

If you're in default, the government can deny you new student loans and grants. This may put you into a terrible trap. You want to go back to school to get the training you need but can't afford to pay for it. If your goal is to get new financial assistance to go back to school, you should carefully review the next section on getting out of default.

You can also assume that most student loan defaults will show up on your credit report. How long the information remains on your report depends on the type of loan. Most defaults will remain on your report for up to seven years. Perkins loans, however, may be reported indefinitely. For more information on credit reports, see Chapter Three.

Aggressive Collection Agency Contacts. The government hires debt collectors to do most student loan collection work. These government contractors are likely to act very aggressively in trying to collect from you. In many cases, the debt collectors will not know about (or will claim not to know about) your right to cancel your loan or get an affordable repayment plan. For more information about how to deal with debt collectors, see Chapter Eight. You should also complain to the Department of Education about debt collection harassment by student loan collectors.

Tax Refund Intercepts. If you are in default on your student loan, the government can take your tax refund, including any earned income tax credit you are owed. The only sure-fire way to avoid this collection method is not to have a tax refund due. You can accomplish this by decreasing your withholding or lowering any estimated tax payments you make.

There are several other steps you can take to deal with this seizure. If your joint tax refund is seized to pay for your student loan, your spouse can recover some of the amount seized by filling in a simple IRS form. IRS forms are available on-line at www.irs.gov.

The collector must notify you before any actual interception. This notice gives you the right to contest the intercept. Check whatever boxes are appropriate on the form (for example, the school closed or the school failed to give you a refund) and return it immediately, asking for a hearing. Send the form back with return receipt requested as proof that you sent it in. You will have to do this every year that you get a notice.

You should also be notified after any seizure. You should complain to the Department of Education if you did not have a chance to raise your defenses before your refund was seized.

Wage Garnishment. Student loan collectors have the right to garnish a certain amount of your wages *without first obtaining a court judgment.* The amount that can be garnished is the lesser of 15% of your disposable pay or the amount of disposable pay in excess of $175.50/week. Disposable pay is close to your take-home pay and includes your pay minus taxes and other amounts that are deducted by law.

For example:

Ms. D has weekly disposable pay of $300. The guaranty agency can take the lesser of 15% of $300 (= $45) and the amount Ms. D's income exceeds $175.50 ($200 - 175.50 = $24.50). Since $24.50 is less than $45, this is the amount the collector can take each week from Ms. D's wages.

ALERT: The amount protected each week (currently $175.50) is based on the minimum wage. The minimum wage in 2007 is $5.85/hour. It will go up to $6.55 on July 24, 2008 and to $7.25 on July 24, 2009. The amount of wages protected from garnishment will go up when these minimum wage increases occur.

There are a number of ways you can stop garnishments to repay your student loan, including:

1. You can ask for a repayment agreement instead of the garnishment.

2. You can stop a wage seizure if you lost your old job against your wishes and you have not been continuously employed in your new job for a full year.

3. The government is required to give you a notice about your right to a hearing. Request a hearing and explain any reason why you think you need not repay the loan. Among other reasons, you can stop the garnishment if you can show that it would result in extreme financial hardship.

Federal Benefit Offsets. Because Social Security is considered so essential for survival, it has traditionally been protected from attachment by creditors. A 1996 law took away some of this protection, but only when federal agencies are collecting debts owed to them. Examples include money owed to the Department of Education for student loans and money owed to the Department of Agriculture for food stamp overpayments.

This is an important change to the law, but it is not a reason to panic. It will not apply to everyone and not all benefits can be taken.

Certain amounts of other federal benefits may also be taken under this law, including:

- Certain Railroad Retirement Benefits;
- Black Lung Part B Benefits.

Supplemental Security Income (SSI) cannot be taken under this law. Veterans benefits also cannot be taken. You can find out more about which benefits are at risk on the Department of Treasury's website, www.fms.treas.gov.

Even if you receive benefits that the government can seize, you should not have to worry that the government will take your entire check. The government cannot touch the first $9,000 ($750/month) of your benefits. In addition, no matter how much money you get, the government cannot take more than 15% of your total benefits.

For example, Mr. A receives a monthly Social Security benefit of $850. The first $750 is completely protected from offset. The government can only take the lesser of: (1) 15% of the total benefit (= $127.50) or (2) the amount left above $750. In this case, the amount left is $100. Since this is less than $127.50, the amount of the offset would be $100.

You are also supposed to get a number of notices warning you that your benefits are going to be taken. The notices give you information about your right to request a hearing with the agency that is collecting the money. You should especially consider this strategy if you think you have defenses to re-payment or if you are facing financial hardships that may make you eligible for a reduction in the amount of offset.

In 2005, The Supreme Court rejected the argument that the government could not offset Social Security to collect student loans that were more than ten years old. Social Security offsets are now just like other types of student loan collection—the government can come after you forever! This is why learning about your rights is so important.

Collection Fees. Another consequence of default is that a large portion of anything you pay to a collection agency on the loan will go to collection agency fees and not to pay off your loan. These collection fees can be quite high, but should not be more than 25% of what you owe. Fees should be considerably less in some cases. For example, collection fees when you con-solidate or rehabilitate your loans can be no higher than 18.5% of principal and interest. Perkins loan collectors are allowed to charge up to 30% of the loan balance (including principal, interest, and late charges) for first collec-tion efforts and up to 40% for subsequent efforts.

Lawsuits. The government can also sue you to try to collect from you. There is no time limit for collection on federal loans. If you are sued, you most likely have a number of defenses to fight back. See Chapter Nine for more information about collection lawsuits.

Professional License Revocations. A number of states allow profes-sional and vocational boards to refuse to certify, certify with restrictions, sus-pend or revoke a member's professional or vocational license when the member defaults on a student loan. In some states, members can also be fined.

PRIVATE STUDENT LOAN COLLECTION

There is a time limit for collection of private student loans. These limits vary by state, but are usually about six years after default. You should contact an attorney in your state to find out more about time limits (also called statutes of limitations).

Private collectors do not have as many collection tools as the govern-ment. This does not mean that private student loans are better than govern-ment loans. In fact, federal government loans are usually more affordable and have a lot more borrower protections. Regardless of whether the loan is private or government, it is very difficult to discharge in bankruptcy.

Private lenders will often hire collection agencies. You have the same rights as with government loans to fight back against any harassment or abuse. The main collection tool private lenders have is to sue you in court (see Chapter Nine).

Any collection fees for private loans should be stated in the loan agreement. There may also be other laws in your state that place restrictions on the amount of collection fees that private creditors can charge. Private lenders may negotiate with you to set up a repayment plan or otherwise settle your debt.

GETTING OUT OF DEFAULT ON YOUR STUDENT LOANS

The previous section summarized the ways that the government can try to collect from you if you have defaulted on your student loan. If all of these tools seemed alarming, they are! You can avoid all of these problems by getting out of default, as described below.

The first question to ask is why you want to get out of default. One good reason is if you want to get financial assistance to go back to school, but be careful. The last thing you want to do is take on new debt that you may also have trouble repaying. You should first check into lower-cost alternatives, such as community college. Another reason to get out of default might be to avoid the government's aggressive collection tactics.

If the reason is because of the government's collection efforts, you should try to figure out whether you are truly in danger. It may be that you do not have sufficient wages to be garnished, no tax refunds to intercept, no special concern for your credit rating, and no interest in applying for new student loans and grants. In that case, you may decide to do nothing and instead use what income you have to pay your rent, mortgage, utility payments, or other priority debts. If you are not safe from collection or if you do want to go back to school, this section lists some strategies to help you get out of default. You may also want to consider discharging your loan in bankruptcy.

Loan Cancellation. You don't have to be in default to be eligible for a loan cancellation, but if you are in default, loan cancellations (also called discharges) are the best ways to get out of default. You not only completely wipe out the current loan but also get back any money you paid on the loan *and* any money that was taken from you through tax refund intercepts, wage garnishment, or other collection methods. In most cases, the government is also required to delete negative references on your credit report.

Cancellations for federal loans are only available in limited circumstances. If you have a private loan, you will need to contact your lender or current loan holder to discuss possible cancellation options.

The first three types of federal government loan cancellations apply mainly when there were serious problems with the school you attended. The fourth type, disability cancellation, is available regardless of what type of school you attended. A fifth type is available after a borrower's death. The next category provides for full or partial cancellations if you work for a certain period of time in a lower-wage profession such as teaching or nursing and other public service jobs. This category also includes cancellations for military service. There is also a loan cancellation program for victims of the September 11 terrorist attacks. The final category allows you to cancel the remaining balance of your loan if you have made consistent payments for a certain period of time.

More information about these programs is available from the Department of Education and, in the National Consumer Law Center's *Student Loan Law* manual and on NCLC's Student Loan Borrower Assistance website, www.studentloanborrowerassistance.org.

Canceling Your Loan Due to Serious Problems with the School You Attended. The three types of loan cancellations in this category are:

- *Closed School Cancellation.* You must show that your school closed while you were still enrolled or within ninety days of your leaving the school. (There are a few cases where the ninety days may be extended.)
- *Unpaid Refund Cancellation.* You are eligible to cancel all or a portion of a loan if you left school and the school failed to pay you a refund you were owed.
- *False Certification Cancellation.* The false certification cancellation is defined as any one of these types of fraud:
  1. You are eligible for a false certification cancellation if, at the time of enrollment, there was a state law that would have disqualified you from getting a job in the area for which you were being trained (for

example, the school enrolled you in a truck driving program even though you had a physical handicap that prevents you from obtaining a truck-driving license).

2. If you did not have a high school diploma when you went to the school, the school had the responsibility to make sure you could benefit from the educational program, usually by giving you an exam. You can receive a loan discharge if there were serious problems with the admissions process. For example, if a school employee took the test for you or gave you the answers, this means you did not go through the proper admission procedures and should be eligible for this cancellation.

3. The school forged your name on the loan papers or check endorsements, and you never went to school for the times covered by the forgery.

4. If you can show that your loan was falsely certified due to a crime of identity theft.

Only loans received after January 1, 1986 are eligible for these cancellations.

If you think you might qualify for one of these cancellations, you should ask whoever is holding your loan for the appropriate cancellation request form. These forms are also available on the Department of Education website at www.ed.gov. You should be prepared to meet resistance and delay. You will have to insist on your rights. Because it usually takes a long time to process cancellation applications, it is a good idea to request a forbearance so that collection activities will stop while your application is pending.

Disability Cancellation.   You can also cancel your loan if you are permanently and totally disabled. In general, this cancellation applies only if you became disabled or your disability worsened after you took out the loan. Pre-existing conditions qualify only if the condition has substantially deteriorated. To qualify for a disability cancellation, you must get a doctor to certify that you are disabled. You or your doctor will also likely be asked to provide supporting documents, such as medical records, to prove your disability.

Even if the government agrees that you are disabled, you will only be able to get a three year conditional cancellation at first. Until July 1, 2008, the three year period begins from the date the doctor says your disability began. This means that if you apply for a cancellation in 2006 and your disability

357

began in 2005, you will need to wait until 2008 to get a final cancellation. During this time, the Department of Education will keep track of you to make sure you are really disabled. They will mostly look to see whether you have earnings beyond a very minimal amount or whether you have taken out new federal student loans.

A number of important disability discharge rules will change beginning July 1, 2008. Starting on that date, doctors will no longer have to certify when your disability began. They will still have to state that you are totally and permanently disabled, but only as of the date that they fill out the application. Once the doctor fills out the form, you should submit it to your loan holder. The Department of Education will review the application. If the Department agrees that you are disabled, the conditional discharge period will begin from the date that the doctor signed the form, not from whenever you became totally disabled. Under the post-July 2008 rules, if you meet the requirements for a discharge at the end of the three-year period, you can get a refund of any payments made only back to the date that the doctor certified your disability on the application form.

Death Cancellation. Your government loans will not survive your death. This means that your estate will not have to pay back your student loans. Also, the death of both parents with a PLUS loan (assuming both took out the loan) is grounds for the "death discharge." The death of only one of the two obligated parents does not cancel a PLUS loan.

Discharge because of the borrower's death (or, in the case of PLUS loans, the death of the student for whom the parent borrowed) is based on an original or certified copy of the death certificate submitted to the school (for a federal Perkins loan) or to the holder of the loan (for a FFEL or Direct Stafford Loan).

There is no administrative discharge for private student loans when the borrower dies. Private loan debts will be handled the same way as other debts. That means that they will be part of the borrower's estate. This estate settlement process (also called probate) varies by state.

Cancellation for Certain Relatives of September 11 Victims.
This is a program for certain relatives of eligible public servants and other victims of the September 11 attacks. Eligible public servants include police officers, firefighters, other safety or rescue personnel, or members of the Armed Forces who died or became permanently and totally disabled due to

injuries suffered in the September 11 attacks. Survivors of eligible public servants include spouses only.

Eligible victims are individuals who died or became permanently and totally disabled due to injuries suffered in the September 11 attacks. Spouses and eligible parents of victims may be able to get discharges.

Borrowers must have owed the loan amounts as of September 11, 2001. Consolidation loans may also be cancelled if they include loans owed as of that date. Borrowers must still owe something on the loan at the time they apply for the cancellation. There are no refunds of payments already made.

JOB-RELATED AND MILITARY SERVICE CANCELLATIONS

There are programs that will fully or partially cancel student loans for borrowers who work for a certain amount of time in certain professions or in the military.

Teachers. Perkins loans may be fully cancelled for full-time teachers working at low-income schools or teaching certain subject areas. These programs are in addition to the public service forgiveness program discussed below.

If you received a Stafford loan on or after October 1, 1998, and teach full time for five consecutive years in a low-income school, you might be eligible to have a portion of your loan cancelled. This applies to FFEL Stafford loans, Direct Subsidized and Unsubsidized Loans, and in some cases, consolidation loans. Up to $5,000 may be cancelled. The limit is $17,500 for borrowers who teach five consecutive years as highly qualified math or science teachers in eligible secondary schools or as special education teaches in eligible elementary or secondary schools.

You should check the Department of Education website (www.ed.gov) for updates in this area. During 2008, the Department of Education will be establishing rules for a number of new teacher grant and loan forgiveness programs.

Child Care Providers. There is a loan forgiveness demonstration program for certain child care providers with FFEL or Direct Loans. Only loans made after October 7, 1998 qualify. The Department is not accepting new applicants into the program because no additional funding has been provided, but applications for renewal benefits are available for those borrowers who have previously been granted forgiveness.

Cancellation Programs for Perkins Loans Borrowers. Perkins loans may be completely canceled in certain circumstances, including:

- Full-time teacher in a designated elementary or secondary school serving students from low-income families;
- Full-time teacher of math, science, foreign languages, bilingual education, or other fields designated as teacher shortage areas;
- Full-time special education teacher (includes teaching children with disabilities in a public or other nonprofit elementary or secondary school);
- Full-time qualified professional provider of early intervention services for the disabled;
- Full-time employee of a public or nonprofit child- or family-services agency providing services to high-risk children and their families from low-income communities;
- Full-time nurse or medical technician;
- Full-time law enforcement or corrections officer;
- Full-time staff member in the education component of a Head Start Program;
- Vista or Peace Corps volunteer (up to 70%); or
- Service in the U.S. Armed Forces (up to 50% in areas of hostilities or imminent danger).

Military Service. The Perkins loan program has discharge programs for borrowers serving in the Armed Forces. The other loan programs do not have specific military cancellation programs. However, the new public service program, discussed below, includes relief for borrowers serving in the military. If you are serving in the military, you should also look into special programs to help you, including deferment and forbearance options.

Public Service Cancellation. This program is available to borrowers that work in public service jobs for ten years and repay their loans through an eligible repayment plan. The remaining balance is then cancelled after the ten years of service is completed.

The program applies only to Direct Loan borrowers, but it covers all types of Direct Loans, including Stafford, PLUS and consolidation loans.

Borrowers with other government loans can consolidate with Direct Loans in order to obtain this benefit, assuming they are eligible to consolidate.

In order to qualify, borrowers must not be in default and have made 120 monthly payments on their loans AFTER October 1, 2007. Payments can be made through any one or combination of eligible repayment plans, including the new income-based repayment system once it becomes available, income contingent repayment, ten-year standard plan payments, graduated or extended payments of not less than the monthly amount that would be due under a ten-year standard plan.

Because the IBR will not be available until July 1, 2009, borrowers that need income-based repayment can select a Direct Loan ICRP and then later switch to an IBR. The ICRP payments made after October 1, 2007 will count toward the ten-year cancellation period.

Borrowers must be employed in public service jobs at the time of the forgiveness and must have been employed in public service jobs during the period in which they made each of the 120 payments. The repayment period does not include time spent in deferment or forbearance.

The public service job must be "full-time." There is no requirement that the borrower must work in the same public service job for the entire ten-year period. There is also no requirement that the ten years of public service be consecutive. The Department will issue rules some time in 2008 to clarify these points.

Borrowers in other jobs making payments through the Direct Loan income contingent program or a combination of repayment plans are also eligible to cancel their remaining loan balances. However, these borrowers have to make payments for twenty-five years. The time limit for repayment through the new FFEL or Direct Loan IBR program (available in July 2009) will be established some time in 2008, but it will be no more than twenty-five years.

There may be tax consequences for borrowers that get loan cancellations.

GETTING OUT OF DEFAULT BY SETTING UP A NEW REPAYMENT PLAN

Loan Consolidation. Loan consolidation is another way to get out of default. It is also a strategy many borrowers use to try to get lower loan payments, as discussed earlier in this chapter. Both the FFEL and Direct Loan programs offer you the option of setting up a reasonable payment plan based on your annual budget. This is called an "Income Contingent Repayment Plan" if you get a Direct Loan and an "Income Sensitive Repayment Plan" if you get an FFEL loan.

The Direct Loan Income Contingent Repayment Plan will almost always be a better deal. This is because the FFEL's plan requires that you make payments that at least cover the interest that will accrue each month. On the other hand, there is no minimum payment with the Direct Loan Income Contingent Repayment Plan. This will change in July 2009 when the IBR program begins for FFEL and Direct Loans.

You are eligible to consolidate with the Direct Loan program as long as you have at least one FFEL or Direct Loan. In general, if you want to consolidate with the Direct Loan program but you have only FFEL loans, you will also have to certify that you were unable to obtain a FFEL consolidation loan with acceptable income-sensitive repayment terms. You may have to aggressively pursue this right with a FFEL lender that claims you are not eligible for Direct Loan consolidation. The law requires the Department of Education to offer Direct consolidation loans to borrowers with defaulted loans in order to resolve defaults.

There should be no efforts made to collect from you as long as you keep the new consolidation loan current. You will also be eligible for new loans and grants and for deferments as well. In addition, you will have a credit record showing a past delinquency but no current default, and what you owe for collection fees will be reduced.

There are a number of issues to consider before you decide to consolidate, as discussed earlier in this chapter. You should especially keep in mind that if you select a low monthly payment plan to help you get through a few years of financial difficulties, your payments will not make much of a dent in the total loan balance. You will be left with a sizable debt that eventually has to be repaid. However, if you have a Direct consolidation loan and are repaying through the Income Contingent Repayment Plan, the government will cancel the debt if you stay on the plan for twenty-five years. In general, you should choose consolidation as an option only if you are going to be able to make the required payments, even very low payments each month.

More information about consolidation loans can be found in NCLC's book *Student Loan Law* and on NCLC's Student Loan Borrower Assistance Project website, www.studentloanborrowerassistance.org. Another good resource is the Department of Education website at www.ed.gov. For more information about Direct Loan consolidation, call 800-557-7392 or check out the website at http://loanconsolidation.ed.gov. You can also obtain estimates of what your monthly payments would be under different repayment plans by using the calculator available on this website. The website, www.finaid.org, also has calculators.

Affordable Payment Plans and Loan Rehabilitation. An alternative to consolidation is to contact the party collecting on the loan and state that you want to renew your eligibility for a new loan and want a reasonable and affordable repayment plan. You have a legal right to a reasonable and affordable payment plan for this purpose. Payments in this type of plan can be as low as $5 a month, depending on your income. Generally, it is best to pay at least as much as your monthly accrued interest, if possible. But federal law states that you should not be required to pay more than you can afford.

Make sure you say words similar to "I want a reasonable and affordable payment plan so that I can renew my eligibility for new loans." These are the magic words collectors usually like to hear before they will offer you the plan. But you are not required to say these words in order to get a reasonable and affordable payment plan. You may have the right to sue collectors who tell you that there's no such thing as a "reasonable and affordable" payment plan or that you can't get this plan unless you use the right words to request it. (See Chapter Six.)

If you get a reasonable and affordable plan, it is important that you stay on it and make all payments on time. If you do not, you will not get another chance at a low payment plan.

The advantages of a reasonable and affordable payment plan are that you should not experience debt collection harassment, tax intercepts, or wage garnishment. Also, if you make six consecutive monthly payments, you will reestablish your eligibility for new student loans and grants.

Despite these advantages, your credit rating will still list the loan in default, a portion of what you pay may be going toward collection costs, interest charges will continue to grow, and you must continue to make monthly payments in order to remain eligible for new student loans and grants.

You will not automatically get out of default even if you make six consecutive payments. You can get out of default, however, if you can "rehabilitate" your loan. You have to make nine consecutive, timely payments in a ten month period. After making these payments and requesting rehabilitation, if you have a FFEL loan, the loan holder will attempt to sell your defaulted loan to a lender. If your loan is purchased, you are no longer in default, the default is removed from your credit record, and a ten-year repayment schedule is established. Usually, the schedule will require you to make larger payments than what you were paying under the reasonable and affordable payment plan. This does not have to be the case. You should be able to get an income-based repayment plan after you get out of default. After a successful rehabilitation, you will also be eligible once again for deferrals and forbearance.

BANKRUPTCY

It is generally difficult, but not impossible, to discharge a government student loan in bankruptcy. The only basis for doing this is to convince the bankruptcy judge that it will be a significant hardship for the foreseeable future to repay the loan. It is usually better to ask the bankruptcy court to make this determination at the time of the bankruptcy filing but, if you fail to do so, the bankruptcy court or a state court can later make that determination when collection attempts on the student loan are renewed. The type of hardship required usually involves serious economic problems which are likely to persist for reasons beyond your control.

MORE HELP WITH STUDENT LOAN PROBLEMS

There are a number of good resources to help you get more information about student loan problems. NCLC's book, *Student Loan Law*, has detailed information about collections, cancellations, repayment plans, and trade school abuses. NCLC's Student Loan Borrower Assistance Project has an extensive website with information to help you with all types of student loan problems (www.studentloanborrowerassistance.org).

The Department of Education also has information to help you deal with student loan problems. The Department's website, www.ed.gov, is extensive and contains a great deal of useful information. You can download from the website useful publications, including *Funding Education Beyond High School* and *Repaying Your Student Loans*. The publications are available in English and Spanish. Publications are also available by calling the Federal Student Aid Information Center at 800-4-FED-Aid and on the CD-Rom that accompanies NCLC's *Student Loan Law*.

The Department of Education has a student loan ombudsman office that is supposed to help borrowers needing assistance with federal loans. The ombudsman has a website and borrowers can submit problems on-line at www.fsahelp.ed.gov or by calling toll-free 877-557-2575. Many guaranty agencies and private lenders also have ombudsman or customer advocate units.

FEDERAL INCOME TAXES

When your debt burden is overwhelming, you may find yourself behind on your taxes. Most people have a variety of tax obligations. The three most common are property taxes and federal and state income taxes. Some advice on property taxes is found at Chapter Two. This section concentrates on back-due federal income taxes. Some of the information here also applies to state income taxes.

You must give special consideration to your federal income tax obligations for two reasons. First, the IRS has special powers to collect back taxes, making it important for you to pay these taxes ahead of many other types of debt. Second, the IRS sets out specific procedures and protections that you should know about if you are behind on your tax obligation.

File the Return on Time Even If You Do Not Pay the Taxes Owed. One of the worst things you can do if you cannot afford to pay your taxes is not file your tax return. You must file an income tax return, in general, if you are a U.S. citizen or resident alien, and your taxable income exceeds certain amounts. (For 2007 this amount is $8,450 for individuals, $10,850 for heads of households, and $16,900 for joint filers. Different amounts apply to those over 65. Self-employed taxpayers must file an income tax return if they earned over $400. These dollar amounts go up each year.)

April 15th is the deadline for most people to file individual income tax returns and pay any taxes owed. Filing extensions are available, but this does not extend your time to pay any taxes you are likely to owe.

If you fail to file your tax returns by April 15 and you owe taxes, you may be (although usually you will not be) prosecuted for a misdemeanor crime. More likely, the IRS will assess a penalty. If you owe taxes and are late sixty days or less in filing, the combined *late-filing* and *late-payment* penalty is 5% of the taxes owed for each month or part of a month that your return is late, up to 25%. If your return is over sixty days late, the minimum penalty is the smaller of $100 or 100% of the tax owed.

It is best to avoid these additional penalties because they increase your debt. Failure to pay is not, by itself, a crime. Instead you will merely be behind on a debt. The penalty for late payment is only a fraction of the larger penalty for not filing a return—it starts at only one half of 1% of the tax owed for each month late, up to a maximum of 25%. You will also be assessed interest.

Always file your tax return even if you
do not send in your tax payment—
the penalties will be much smaller.

Getting an extension to file is also not the solution it might seem to be. Although the IRS will automatically give you a four-month extension if you request it with payment of the taxes you are likely to owe, keep in mind that this is only an extension of time to *file*. It does not give you more time to *pay* the taxes you owe, and you will be charged both interest and probably a late-payment penalty during the time of the extension. As noted above, if you can't pay the taxes due, it is a better idea to file the return, pay as much as you can, if anything, and then consider negotiating with the IRS (discussed below).

Options for Paying Tax Debt. When you file a return but cannot afford to pay the taxes due, you will generally have four options:

1. Pay the taxes using a credit card or some other source of funds;

2. Enter into an installment plan with the IRS;

3. Negotiate with the IRS by seeking an "offer-in-compromise"; or

4. Request a temporary hardship determination.

All of these options except the first one require IRS approval. If IRS does not grant approval, you have the right to seek an appeal or ask for a review of your case.

The first option is to find another source of funds to pay the taxes. One way to do this is to put the tax obligation on your credit card (if you still have a card that works). A credit card payment will need to be processed by a private company that will charge you a "convenience" fee, generally about 2.5% of the payment. The credit card interest may be less than IRS interest and penalties, but this is not always true. However, charging the tax to your credit card allows you the time to develop a plan to pay down the credit card debt at a later time.

You should only put amounts on your credit card you believe you can repay. But, if your circumstances change and you cannot repay the debt as soon as you are required, it may be easier to deal with the credit card company than the IRS.

Another option is to ask the IRS to let you pay the amount due in monthly installments over a period of up to three years. The IRS will generally allow this but will impose interest, penalties, and a "user fee" of $105 (reduced to $52 if you agree to pay using direct debit from your bank account; $43 for low-income taxpayers). The interest rate will be the federal short-term rate plus 3%, which is lower than most rates for unsecured loans. If you have an installment plan, the penalty for late payment is only one-quarter of 1% for each month that the installment remains unpaid. Even with the penalties, an installment plan may cost you less than putting the taxes on your credit card. Sometimes you can even get the IRS to drop penalties. (The IRS will only drop interest if the IRS made an error that resulted in the tax liability.)

If you owe less than $25,000 and have already filed your return, you can request an installment agreement using an IRS website form called the "On-Line Payment Agreement." You can also use IRS Form 9465, "Installment Agreement Request," which you can attach to your return if you haven't filed it yet. You may also call the IRS at the phone number on your bill or notice, but always be sure that any installment plan is in writing. Note that, even if you pay your taxes under an installment plan, the IRS may still place a lien on your property until you make the final payment. However, the IRS cannot execute a levy while the installment plan is in effect. (See the next section on liens and levies.)

The third option is to seek an "offer-in-compromise." This is when the IRS settles with you and allows you to pay an amount less than what they claim you owe. An "offer-in-compromise" is generally granted only when you have a dispute as to what you owe, or when there is doubt that the past-due taxes could ever be collected in full. There are special IRS forms you must fill out to request an "offer-in-compromise" (Form 656 and 433-A or 433-B). You will also need to pay a $150 application or "user" fee plus 20% of your offer (or the first payment of a proposed payment plan), unless your income is below a certain amount and you fill in Form 656-A. Unless your offer is based on a dispute as to what you owe, the amount you will need to offer must equal or exceed your net equity in assets, your ability to make installment payments from future income, and other amounts at your disposal.

The fourth option is to seek a temporary hardship determination from the IRS, called "currently not collectible" status. The IRS will only grant you this status if you do not have any assets you could use to pay your taxes and you do not have any income left after "allowable expenses." An allowable expense is an amount determined by the IRS as what is necessary for living expenses. Be aware that what you may consider to be an undue hardship may be viewed by the IRS as a mere inconvenience.

"Currently not collectible" status is not permanent, and does not mean the tax is forgiven or reduced. This status can change if your financial circumstances improve, if you file another return with a balance due, or if you do not file a tax return. The IRS will monitor your tax returns and remove the hardship status if your returns suggest an improvement. Also, interest will continue to accumulate during this time, but penalties will not. To apply for "currently not collectible" status, you can fill out Form 433-F, "Collection Information Statement." In some cases, if you are dealing with IRS agents over the telephone, they can collect the information for Form 433-F and make the "currently not collectible" determination.

In certain limited cases, your responsibility to pay a tax may be cancelled when the tax is owed entirely by your spouse or ex-spouse. This is true even if you filed a joint return. Help from a tax professional is recommended.

Steps the IRS Can Take to Force Payment. If you do not set up a payment plan or obtain an agreement on an offer-in-compromise, the IRS will force payment. If you have not filed a return in which you calculate the amount due, the IRS will send you several letters asking for payment of the amount it claims is due. The last letter is called a "Notice of Tax Due and Demand for Payment."

If you do not respond to this notice, the IRS will send a notice saying that it is placing a tax lien on all your property, such as your house or car. This lien allows the IRS to claim your property as security for your tax debt. It makes your tax debt a secured debt.

The IRS may also send you a notice that it will seize or "levy" your property. The IRS can take any or all of your property, such as bank accounts, paychecks, and even homes, with the exception of certain exempt types of income and possessions.

Exempt from a levy are about $168 a week in wages for a single person (more for married filers and heads of household, with the amount depending on the number of exemptions), unemployment and workers' compensation, certain public assistance benefits, job training benefits, income needed to pay court-ordered child support, and certain pension benefits. Other exempt property will be certain amounts of clothing, furniture, personal effects, and job-related tools. A state homestead exemption will *not* protect your home from an IRS tax lien or seizure. See Chapter Nine for more information on exemptions.

The IRS can also recover past-due taxes by seizing certain federal wages, benefits, and other federal payments, including Social Security (but not Supplemental Security Income). This is a different levy from the federal benefits offset discussed earlier in the Student Loan section of this chapter. An IRS tax levy does not include an exemption for the first $750 of monthly benefits. The IRS can levy 15% of the entire Social Security benefit, regardless of whether or not the remaining benefit sent to you is less than $750. In some cases, the IRS has been known to levy even more than 15% of Social Security benefits; if this happens to you, you should contact the organizations listed in the section *Seeking Help* at the end of this chapter.

When you receive a notice that your property is being levied or a lien is being placed on it, you can request a review of your case called a "Collection Due Process" hearing on Form 12153. You have thirty days after receiving the notice to request a hearing. The hearing will result in a suspension of collection activities, including a levy, during the appeals process. During the hearing, you can dispute that you owe the tax or request one of the payment options discussed earlier in this chapter, such as an installment plan, an offer-in-compromise, or a hardship determination.

Unless most of your assets and all of your income are exempt from seizure, it makes sense to negotiate a payment schedule with the IRS to avoid seizure of personal property and income. Make sure any agreement is in writing. A good source for information about taxes is the IRS website at www.irs.gov.

The IRS has recently begun outsourcing some of its collections to private debt collectors. Private collectors can establish installment agreements—make sure to get any agreement in writing—but cannot agree to an offer-in-compromise or make a temporary hardship determination. Even though they are collecting federal income taxes, these private collectors still must comply with the Fair Debt Collection Practices Act (FDCPA), discussed in Chapter Eight.

Effect of Bankruptcy on Your Tax Debt. Bankruptcy is not as effective a remedy when dealing with taxes as with other debts. In general, most taxes cannot be discharged in a chapter 7 bankruptcy. Some exceptions apply when the taxes are more than three years delinquent if you properly filed the tax return for the year in question. Existing tax liens are likely to remain on your property even after the bankruptcy. In a chapter 13 reorganization, the full amount of the taxes owed can be paid in installments over a three- to five-year period. For more information about bankruptcy, see Chapter Nineteen.

Seeking Help. You may be able to get help with your tax problems from a Low-Income Taxpayer Clinic (LITC). These are legal clinics based at law schools and legal services offices that help low-income taxpayers who have disputes with the IRS. LITC locations are listed in "Low Income Taxpayer Clinic List," IRS Publication 4134.

In some cases, you can get assistance from the IRS Taxpayer Advocate Service, an independent system that helps taxpayers who have not been able to resolve tax problems through normal channels. You should fill out Form 911 or call 1-877-777-4778 to request Taxpayer Advocate Service assistance. IRS forms can be found at www.irs.gov.

19

Bankruptcy

TOPICS COVERED IN THIS CHAPTER

- Ten Factors to Consider in Deciding Whether to File Bankruptcy
- What Bankruptcy Can and Cannot Do for You
- How to Choose What Type of Bankruptcy, and When to File
- The Differences Between Chapter 7 and 13 Bankruptcies
- How to Satisfy the Bankruptcy Counseling and Education Requirements
- How to Get Help with Your Bankruptcy Filing

IS BANKRUPTCY THE RIGHT CHOICE FOR YOU? 10 IMPORTANT CONSIDERATIONS

1. Bankruptcy may be the easiest and fastest way to deal with all types of debt problems. Bankruptcy is a process under federal law designed to help people and businesses get protection from their creditors. Bankruptcy can be the right choice if you have no better way to deal with your debts. Although you may want to try other options first, you should not wait until the last minute to think about bankruptcy because some important bankruptcy rights may be lost by delay. For example, you must receive budget and credit counseling from an approved credit counseling agency within 180 days before your bankruptcy case is filed. The counseling will usually take less than an hour to complete, but it is important to get this done as soon as you think bankruptcy may be an option, especially if you may need to file to stop a foreclosure sale or repossession.

2. Most bankruptcy cases are complicated. You should consider getting professional help. Bankruptcy is a legal proceeding with complicated rules and paperwork. You may want to get professional legal help, especially if you hope to use bankruptcy to prevent foreclosure or repossession. Most bankruptcy attorneys will provide a free consultation to help you decide whether bankruptcy is the right choice.

3. Bankruptcy temporarily stops almost all creditors from taking any steps against you except through the bankruptcy process. This assistance is provided by the "automatic stay" that arises as soon as you file the necessary paperwork at the beginning of a bankruptcy case. Foreclosures, repossessions, utility shut-offs, lawsuits, and other creditor actions will be immediately (but perhaps only temporarily) stopped.

4. Bankruptcy can permanently wipe out your legal obligation to pay back many of your debts. This benefit arises because of the bankruptcy "discharge" that you get for successfully completing a bankruptcy case. But not all debts can be discharged. Certain debts, such as most student loans, liens associated with many secured debts, alimony, child support, and debts you incurred after the bankruptcy case was started, may not be discharged. After bankruptcy, you will continue to owe those debts. In the long term, you may have to fall back on strategies which are discussed in other parts of this book for those debts.

5. When bankruptcy does not wipe out a debt, a chapter 13 bankruptcy (a "reorganization") gives you an opportunity to catch up on that debt. For example, if you are behind on a home mortgage or car loan, bankruptcy will not usually allow you to cancel the mortgage or lien and still keep the property without repayment. If you want to deal with debts of that type in the bankruptcy process, you will need to propose a chapter 13 repayment plan. That requires affordable payments from your income over a period of three to five years.

6. In most cases, you will *not* lose property by filing for bankruptcy. Most of your property is likely to be protected from sale in the bankruptcy process by bankruptcy "exemptions." However, if you have certain types of very valuable property, the bankruptcy law may not allow you to keep it unless you pay its value to your creditors over a number of years in a chapter 13 plan.

7. The initial fee for bankruptcy is presently $274 under chapter 13 and $299 under chapter 7. The fee can be paid in up to four installments over a period of 120 days (or up to 180 days with court permission). If you cannot afford to pay the filing fee in installments in a chapter 7 case, and your household income is below a certain amount (150% of the official poverty line), you can ask the bankruptcy court to waive the filing fee.

8. If you file bankruptcy, you usually do *not* need to go to court. You will have to attend one meeting with the bankruptcy trustee (not with a judge). Creditors are invited to that meeting but rarely attend. You will not usually have to go to court for your bankruptcy case unless something out of the ordinary occurs. If you do receive a notice to go to court, it is important that you go. Before your case is closed, you must also take a course in personal finances, which will last for approximately two hours.

9. Bankruptcy will usually not make your credit report any worse. Most people filing bankruptcy already are behind on their bills and already have problems with their credit report. It is unlikely that bankruptcy will make a bad credit report worse. Some creditors may be *more* willing to lend you money than if you have a number of debts remaining in default. However, the fact that you filed bankruptcy can remain on your credit report for ten years, while your defaults may stay on your report for only seven years.

10. Watch out for bankruptcy related scams. There are many people and companies that advertise bankruptcy related services in order to take advantage of vulnerable, financially distressed consumers. Some advertise help with foreclosure when all they really do is put you into bankruptcy without providing any advice on how this will help or assistance in getting through the process. Many of these businesses charge enormous fees. Others make promises which they cannot possibly keep. Do not pay money for debt counseling, foreclosure assistance, or bankruptcy without being sure you are dealing with a reputable business.

GENERAL INFORMATION ABOUT BANKRUPTCY

The right to file bankruptcy is an important tool that society provides for people with debt problems. In the short term, bankruptcy prevents continued efforts by creditors to collect debts. In the long term, bankruptcy can completely eliminate repayment obligations so that you can get a fresh financial start.

It is often stated that bankruptcy should be considered as a "last resort" for financially troubled consumers. This advice is oversimplified. In some cases, legal rights can be lost by delay. You should be especially careful to get early advice about bankruptcy if you are hoping to use the bankruptcy process to help save your home or your car. (For example, bankruptcy cannot help you keep a home after it has been sold at a foreclosure sale.)

There have been many news reports suggesting that changes to the bankruptcy law passed by Congress in 2005 will prevent many consumers from filing bankruptcy. It is true that these changes have made the process more complicated. But the basic right to file bankruptcy and most of the benefits of bankruptcy remain the same for most consumers.

This chapter will provide you with an overview about bankruptcy. It is not a complete bankruptcy guide. If you are interested in filing bankruptcy, you should seek the services of a professional specializing in bankruptcy.

If you want a more detailed discussion about bankruptcy, there are several books that focus on bankruptcy exclusively. The National Consumer Law Center publishes *Consumer Bankruptcy Law and Practice* (8th ed. 2006 and Supp.), which is a detailed analysis of bankruptcy for lawyers and others specializing in bankruptcy. Another National Consumer Law Center publication, *Bankruptcy Basics* (2007) offers a step-by-step guide to current bankruptcy practice for pro bono attorneys, general practitioners, and legal services attorneys.

WHAT BANKRUPTCY CAN AND CANNOT DO FOR YOU

Bankruptcy may make it possible for you to:

- Eliminate legal responsibility for many of your debts and get a fresh start. This is called a "discharge." When a debt is discharged at the close of a successful bankruptcy case, you will have no further legal obligation to pay that debt.
- Stop foreclosure on your house or manufactured home and allow you an opportunity to catch up on missed payments.
- Prevent repossession of your car or other property, or force the creditor to return property even after it has been repossessed.
- Stop wage garnishment, debt collection harassment, and other similar collection activities and give you some breathing room.

- Prevent termination of utility service or restore service if it has already been terminated.
- Lower the monthly payments on some debts, including some secured debts such as car loans.
- Allow you an opportunity to challenge the claims of certain creditors who have committed fraud or who are otherwise seeking to collect more than they are legally entitled to.

Bankruptcy, however, cannot cure every financial problem, nor is it an appropriate step for every individual. In bankruptcy, it is usually *not* possible to:

- Eliminate certain rights of "secured" creditors. A "secured" creditor has taken some form of lien on your property as collateral for a debt. Common examples are car loans and home mortgages. Although you can force secured creditors to take payments over time in the bankruptcy process, you generally cannot keep the collateral unless you continue to pay the debt.
- Discharge types of debts singled out by the federal bankruptcy law for special treatment, such as child support, alimony, most student loans, court restitution orders, criminal fines, and some taxes.
- Protect all cosigners on their debts. When a relative or friend has cosigned a loan and you discharge the loan in bankruptcy, the cosigner may still have an obligation to repay all or part of the loan.
- Discharge debts that are incurred after bankruptcy has been filed.

POSSIBLE ADVANTAGES OF BANKRUPTCY

The Automatic Stay of Foreclosures, Evictions, Repossession, Utility Shut-Offs, and Other Creditor Actions. Your bankruptcy filing will automatically, without any further legal proceedings, stop most creditor actions against you and your property.

Your request for bankruptcy protection creates an "automatic stay," which will prevent the start or continuation of repossessions, garnishments, attachments, utility shut-offs, foreclosures, evictions, and debt collection harassment. The automatic stay will provide you with time to sort things out and solve your financial problems.

However, there are a few exceptions, usually based on prior bankruptcy filings, when the stay may not automatically go into effect or may later stop applying. For example, if you have filed another bankruptcy case that was dismissed within the previous year, the automatic stay may only last for the first thirty days of your bankruptcy case. If you had two prior cases dismissed within the year, the stay may not go into effect when your case is filed. Even when these exceptions apply, some creditor actions may still be stayed. Also, the bankruptcy court can extend or impose the stay if you file a written request (a "motion") with the court and the court finds that your bankruptcy case has been filed in good faith. It is important that you give your attorney information about all prior bankruptcy cases you may have been involved in so that your attorney can advise you on what to expect if a new case is filed.

Special Consideration for Eviction Cases

There is also a special set of procedures that apply to eviction cases. If your landlord has started an eviction case against you, the automatic stay will prevent the landlord from proceeding with the eviction if your bankruptcy case is filed before the state court has ordered that you should be evicted (this is known as a "judgment for possession"). If your bankruptcy case is filed after a judgment for possession against you, the full automatic stay will come into effect only for a period of thirty days, and then only if you file a document with the bankruptcy court certifying that (1) you have a right to cure the rent default under your state law or some other nonbankruptcy law, and (2) you have deposited with the bankruptcy court the rent that will come due during the first thirty days of your bankruptcy case (usually one month's rent). To get a stay for longer than thirty days, you will need to pay to the landlord all of the back rent owed as stated in the judgment for possession. If you do not get the full automatic stay when your case is filed or if it ends thirty days after you file, it is important to understand that the landlord is permitted only to take actions to get back possession of your apartment. The automatic stay still prevents your landlord from trying to collect any money judgment against you personally for back rent or damages. For example, any action by your landlord to coerce payment of back rent by preventing you from recovering your personal property would still violate the stay.

If you file bankruptcy and the automatic stay is in effect, a creditor cannot take any further action against you or your property without permission from the bankruptcy court. Sometimes creditors will seek such permission immediately, and sometimes they will never seek permission.

Permission to continue collection activity is rarely, if ever, granted to unsecured creditors. It is common for secured creditors to get relief from the stay in a *chapter 7* case to continue foreclosure or repossession of their collateral. (As described below, a chapter 7 bankruptcy has minimal impact on a secured creditor's collateral.) On the other hand, an automatic stay will almost always continue in effect to protect you in a *chapter 13* bankruptcy case as long as payments are being made on the secured debt.

If the creditor takes action against you despite the automatic stay, the creditor can be held in violation of the stay and may have to pay you money damages and attorney fees. If necessary, the creditor's actions against you can also be reversed. For example, a foreclosure sale which is held in violation of the automatic stay can be set aside.

Discharge of Most Debts.   The principal goal of most bankruptcies is to achieve a discharge. This will eliminate your obligation to repay many unsecured debts. Bankruptcy is a relatively easy way, though not the only way, to permanently end creditor harassment and the hardship, anxiety, and stress associated with excessive debt. (See Chapter Eight for other strategies to stop debt harassment.)

On the other hand, a creditor's collateral is not affected by your bankruptcy filing unless you pay off the debts that are secured by the collateral. A bankruptcy discharge does offer some protection for these secured debts. After you obtain a discharge, a secured creditor has no right to seek a deficiency judgment or to collect money from you in any way other than by selling the collateral.

This means that, after bankruptcy, the creditor can seize its collateral if you don't pay but cannot otherwise try to collect the debt. For example, if you do not pay a car loan, the creditor can seize your car and sell it. But it cannot sue you for the deficiency between what you owe and the amount for which the car was sold.

Protection Against Wage Garnishment and Enforcement of Judgment Liens.   After you file a bankruptcy petition, creditors are prohibited from garnishing your wages or other income. Bankruptcy even stops government agencies from recovering Social Security or other public benefit overpayments, so long as your receipt of the overpayment was not based on fraud.

Bankruptcy is also an effective tool to deal with some types of legal judgments against you. If a creditor's judgment for money against you does not create a lien against any of your property, that creditor is unsecured and the debt can be discharged in bankruptcy as if no judgment ever existed. If the judgment does create a lien on your property, you may ask the bankruptcy court to remove the lien if it affects exempt property.

Which items of property are exempt and protected from a court judgment is discussed in more detail later in this chapter and in Chapter Nine.

Bankruptcy offers two extra protections for this exempt property. First, bankruptcy can wipe out a lien entirely, while state exemption laws only prevent the creditor from seizing certain property. Without a bankruptcy filing, if your assets increase in the future, a lien may then allow the creditor to seize some of your property. A second extra protection offered by bankruptcy is that, in some states, you may use federal bankruptcy exemption amounts if they provide better protections for you than those offered by your state law. This depends upon whether your state has "opted out" of the federal exemptions.

Added Flexibility in Dealing with Secured Creditors.

Bankruptcy can be helpful in dealing with creditors who have taken items of your property as collateral for their loans. Usually, you still have to make payments on your secured debts if you want to keep the collateral. However, bankruptcy does provide added flexibility in dealing with these debts.

First, in some situations, bankruptcy can stop secured creditors from seizing collateral by "avoiding" (meaning removing or eliminating) the creditor's lien. This makes the debt unsecured.

For example, when you file bankruptcy, you can avoid liens on most household goods if you did not use money the creditor loaned to you to purchase those goods. To the extent that household goods are exempt—and most families' household goods will be completely exempt—you can request the bankruptcy court to "avoid" this kind of lien, which will eliminate the creditor's ability to seize that collateral. Some creditors may claim that a lien on certain types of household goods cannot be avoided based on a change in the law made in 2005. It is too early to know for sure but the change may not have any significant effect, and these liens should continue to be avoided. It is important to check with a bankruptcy attorney about any new developments regarding bankruptcy laws and the interpretation of these laws.

Second, a chapter 7 bankruptcy allows you to keep collateral by redeeming it, that is, paying the creditor not the amount you owe on the loan but the value of the collateral. For example, if a car is only worth $1,000, even though the car loan is $3,000, you can keep the car by paying the creditor only the $1,000. Even with this reduced amount, this option may not be helpful to consumers who are unable to come up with the cash to redeem before the chapter 7 case is concluded (approximately 3–5 months). Although some creditors may let you redeem in installments even after your chapter 7 case, the bankruptcy court cannot order installment payments if the creditor insists on a lump sum payment.

The greatest flexibility in dealing with secured creditors is available when a chapter 13 bankruptcy is filed. For example, if you are six months delinquent on a mortgage, filing a chapter 13 bankruptcy will stop a threatened foreclosure and allow you to gradually catch up on the back payments, perhaps over as long a period as several years. In some cases a chapter 13 filing may also allow you to make lower monthly payments by extending the repayment period or lowering the interest rate on the loan.

Utility Terminations. A bankruptcy filing will not only stop a threatened utility termination, but will also restore terminated utility service, at least for twenty days. To keep utility service beyond twenty days after the bankruptcy filing, you must provide a security deposit or other security for future payments and keep current on the new utility charges. Some utilities may not take a deposit, but you must offer to provide one. To keep service, you do not need to pay bills incurred *before* the bankruptcy was filed.

Driver Licenses. A driver's license can be critical to keep a job or to find a new job. In some states a driver's license can be taken away because you have not paid a court judgment arising from an automobile accident. In that situation, bankruptcy is sometimes the only possible way for you to keep or regain the license. Normally, bankruptcy can be used to discharge the obligation to pay the court judgment, and you then have a right to regain or retain the driver's license.

OTHER BANKRUPTCY CONSIDERATIONS, INCLUDING POSSIBLE DISADVANTAGES

In Most Cases You Will Lose Little or None of Your Property.

Some people believe that a bankruptcy filing results in the loss of most of their property. This belief is wrong. Everyone who files bankruptcy gets to keep some of their possessions. In fact, most people get to keep all of them.

Whether you get to keep *all* of your possessions depends on a number of factors. These factors include whether you file a chapter 7 or a chapter 13 bankruptcy, whether certain debts are secured or unsecured, and how much of your property is exempt.

Generally, you will keep all or almost all your property in a bankruptcy except property that is very valuable or that is subject to a lien you cannot avoid or afford to pay. All of your equity in property is divided into two categories—

exempt and non-exempt. Equity equals the value of your property minus what you owe on any debts secured by that property. State law or, in some cases, the federal bankruptcy law will specify which property is exempt. Usually, at least a certain amount of equity in your home, car, clothes, jewelry, appliances, and furniture will be exempt.

In valuing property for the purposes of bankruptcy, the question is not the property's original cost, but rather what the property in its present condition could be sold for at the time the bankruptcy is filed. It is often useful to imagine a hypothetical yard sale to try to estimate what the value of particular items will be. It is also important to understand how the concept of equity relates to exemption laws. If an exemption law protects a $2,000 motor vehicle, this applies to $2,000 of your equity in the car, not to the total value of the car. For example, if you have a $7,000 car with a $5,000 car loan balance, you have only $2,000 in equity. You can thus fully protect the $7,000 car with the $2,000 exemption. You will still have to repay the car loan, but you won't lose the car.

Remember also that exemption laws vary widely from state to state. It is important to check what exemptions are available in the state where you live. In some states, you are given a choice between using either the state exemptions or using the federal bankruptcy exemptions. If your state has "opted" out of the federal bankruptcy exemptions, you will be required to choose exemptions mostly under your state law. However, even in an "opt-out" state, you may use a special federal bankruptcy exemption that protects retirement funds in pension plans and IRAs.

Whether you have moved from a different state, and the timing of when your bankruptcy is filed, may also affect the exemptions you are entitled to claim. If you have moved to the state where your current home is located from a different state within two years of your bankruptcy filing, you may be required to use the exemptions from the state where you lived just before the two-year period. Also, if you bought a home within approximately 3.3 years (1215 days) of your bankruptcy filing, or if you sold a home located in a different state and used the proceeds to buy another home in your current state within this time period, there may be a limit on how much equity you can protect under a homestead exemption. This limit will not apply in most cases because it is set higher than most state homestead exemptions. Questions about whether property is exempt can be complicated and are best answered by a bankruptcy attorney.

In a chapter 7 case, you are permitted to keep all of your possessions that are exempt. Property which is not exempt may be sold, with the money distributed to pay your creditors.

If you have significant *non*-exempt assets, a chapter 13 bankruptcy may be a good way to keep all of your possessions. In a chapter 13 bankruptcy, the property you are allowed to exempt is the same as in a chapter 7 case. However, you can keep your possessions (unless you choose to sell them) in a chapter 13 case by paying their non-exempt value over time from future income under a plan approved by the bankruptcy court.

The Effect of Bankruptcy on Your Credit Report. A bankruptcy can remain part of your credit history for ten years. The effect of a bankruptcy on your credit report is unpredictable but of understandable concern.

For most people, this concern alone should not be considered a disadvantage of bankruptcy. If you are seriously delinquent on a number of debts, this information will already appear on your credit record. A bankruptcy is unlikely to make your credit worse. In fact, there is some evidence that the bankruptcy will make it *easier* to obtain future credit, because new creditors will see that old obligations have been discharged and that the new creditor will therefore be first in line for payment from your income. Also, once a discharge is received, many new creditors recognize that you cannot then receive a new chapter 7 discharge for the next eight years. More information about credit reports can be found in Chapter Three.

If you do not yet have problems with credit, the impact of a bankruptcy on your ability to obtain credit is more difficult to evaluate. The research on the effects of bankruptcy on future credit is inconclusive, but it seems fair to say that most credit decisions depend upon the judgment of individual lenders. Most lenders seem to look at a potential customer's income and income stability more than anything else.

The one area where bankruptcy is very likely to make it more difficult for you is in attempting to obtain a conventional mortgage to purchase a home. Even then, most lenders will not hold the bankruptcy against you if you have reestablished a good credit reputation for a period of two to four years after your discharge.

After bankruptcy, some lenders may demand collateral as security, ask for a cosigner, or want to know why bankruptcy was filed. Other creditors, such as some local retailers, do not check credit reports or inquire about bankruptcy on credit applications at all.

To improve your chance of getting credit after bankruptcy on reasonable terms, you should make sure that the information being reported about your bankruptcy is accurate. While the fact that you filed bankruptcy can be reported for ten years from the date your case was filed, information about individual debts may be reported separately under different rules. If your credit report states that a particular debt you listed in your bankruptcy case was discharged in bankruptcy (usually by noting "included in bankruptcy"), this information may stay on your report for seven years. It is very important that this same debt be listed on your report as having a zero balance, meaning that you do not owe anything on the debt. If the creditor does not update this information and continues to list the debt as having a balance owed, this will have a negative impact on your credit score and make it more difficult to get credit. You should check your credit report after your bankruptcy discharge and file a dispute with the credit reporting agencies if this information is not correct. (See Chapter Three.)

The Effect of Bankruptcy on Your Reputation in the Community. Most people find their reputations do not suffer any noticeable harm from filing bankruptcy. Bankruptcies are not generally announced publicly, although they are a matter of public record. It is unlikely that your friends and neighbors will know that you filed bankruptcy unless you choose to tell them.

However, especially in a small town, where debts are owed to local people, some difficulties connected with filing bankruptcy may still arise. You should weigh any possible embarrassment and damage to reputation against bankruptcy's potential advantages. If you believe that this is a problem, you may choose to voluntarily pay selected debts after bankruptcy. Voluntary payment of discharged debts is allowed by the bankruptcy law, but you cannot leave certain creditors out of the bankruptcy process entirely.

Feelings of Moral Obligation. Most people want to pay their debts and make every effort to do so if payment is possible. If bankruptcy is the right solution to your financial problems, you should balance these feelings of obligation with other considerations. Remember that a provision concerning bankruptcy is contained in the United States Constitution. Big corporations like Kmart, TWA, A.H. Robbins, Johns Manville, Macy's, and Penn Central, and famous people like Toni Braxton, Kim Basinger, Tammy Wynette, Larry King, Mickey Rooney, and Walt Disney have all chosen to file bankruptcy.

You may find comfort in the fact that the Bible mentions the need for a process which is like bankruptcy. The book of Deuteronomy states:

> At the end of every seven years thou shalt make a release. And this is the manner of the release: every creditor shall release that which he has lent unto his neighbor and his brother; because the Lord's release hath been proclaimed. (Deut. 15:1–2.)

Most importantly, bankruptcy should be considered in relation to the hardships it can avoid. During hard times, bankruptcy may be the only way to provide your family with food, clothing, and shelter. This book does explore alternatives to bankruptcy, and these should be considered carefully. But it may be that bankruptcy is your best or only realistic alternative.

There is no good reason to feel embarrassed about filing bankruptcy if it is the best solution to your financial problems.

Potential Discrimination After Bankruptcy. The bankruptcy law offers you some protection against discrimination by creditors and others. Government agencies, such as housing authorities and licensing departments, cannot deny you benefits because of a previous bankruptcy discharge of your debts, including debts owed to those agencies. Government agencies and private entities involved in student loan programs also cannot discriminate against you based upon a bankruptcy filing.

Employers are also not permitted to discriminate against you for filing bankruptcy. However, for some sensitive jobs which involve money or security, your bankruptcy may be considered evidence of financial problems which could be detrimental to your work. Also, the bankruptcy law does not prevent discrimination by others, including private creditors deciding whether to grant new loans.

Cost of Filing a Bankruptcy Petition. There are several expenses related to filing bankruptcy. First, there may be costs associated with hiring an attorney to handle the bankruptcy. Hiring an attorney and the advisability of alternatives are discussed later in this chapter.

In addition to an attorney fee, a bankruptcy petition presently requires a $274 filing fee under chapter 13 and a $299 filing fee for chapter 7. The fee can be paid in up to four installments over a period of 120 days (or up to 180 days with court permission). If you cannot afford to pay the filing fee in installments in a chapter 7 case, and your household income is less than 150% of the official poverty guidelines (for example, the figures for 2007 are $20,535 for a family of 2 and $30,975 for a family of 4), you can request that the bankruptcy court waive the filing fee. You will need to file a written application for waiver along with your bankruptcy petition. You may also file a waiver application after your case is filed for any remaining filing fee installments that you can no longer afford to pay.

The filing fee cannot be waived in a chapter 13 reorganization case but can be paid in installments. The chapter 13 trustee is usually entitled to a commission of about 10% of the payments made through the plan. These payments must be included with the amount that you pay the trustee under a plan.

In addition, utility companies may be entitled to collect a security deposit following a bankruptcy (usually equal to approximately twice the average monthly bill) just as if you were a new customer. Some, but not all, utility companies take advantage of this right. In most areas, you can request up to sixty days to make this payment.

Ability to File Another Bankruptcy If You Have More Financial Problems.
One consideration about filing bankruptcy is whether you will have the opportunity to file again if a new financial problem arises. The answer depends on what type of bankruptcy you file.

The different types of bankruptcy are discussed immediately below. You can think of a chapter 7 as an immediate discharge of many of your debts with the liquidation of any of your assets that are not exempt. A chapter 13 is a reorganization of your debt where you pay your creditors some or all of what they are owed over a period of years, but where you generally lose none of your property.

You can receive only one discharge under chapter 7 every eight years. For this reason, it is usually best to wait until other options have been explored before filing a chapter 7 case. Also, it may be best to wait if your creditors cannot take any of your income or property at this time and you are concerned about getting further into debt, especially if you do not have medical or auto insurance.

However, if you have filed under chapter 7, you may still be able to file again under chapter 13 before eight years have expired. For example, you can receive a discharge in a chapter 13 case if it is filed more than four years after a previous chapter 7 case, or more than two years after a previous chapter 13 case. Even if you are not permitted to get a discharge in a chapter 13 case if filed within the two or four year periods, you may still be able to file the case for other reasons, such as to cure a mortgage default, as long as you meet the requirements under chapter 13 when you file. Finally, you can receive a discharge in a chapter 7 case if six years have passed since you filed a chapter 13 case in which you received a discharge and your unsecured creditors were paid at least 70% of what they were owed.

Other issues can arise if your case is unsuccessful for some reason. It is rare to have an unsuccessful chapter 7 case, but chapter 13 cases frequently fail because the consumer cannot afford the necessary payments. If you voluntarily withdraw your case, the withdrawal may keep you from filing a new case for 180 days. As discussed earlier, a previous dismissal may also affect whether you will have an automatic stay when your case is filed.

WHEN BANKRUPTCY MAY BE THE WRONG SOLUTION

For some individuals, bankruptcy is the wrong solution. There are at least five situations in which bankruptcy may be a bad option:

1. You have only a few debts and strong defenses for each. Instead of filing for bankruptcy, you can raise these defenses aggressively. Usually the disputes can be settled out of court in an acceptable way. If they are not settled, you can use bankruptcy later. (You can also raise claims and defenses in the bankruptcy court if they have not been decided in other courts.)

2. The debts at issue are secured by your property—such as home mortgages or car loans—and you do not have sufficient income to keep up payments and also catch up on past due amounts. Bankruptcy may not help you when the long-term expense of keeping your home or car exceeds your long-term income.

3. You have valuable assets that are not exempt in the bankruptcy process and you do not want to lose these assets. (Note that a chapter 13 filing may still help if you can afford the necessary payments.)

4. Because of a prior bankruptcy, you cannot receive a discharge in a chapter 7 bankruptcy. However, in most cases, a chapter 13 petition can still be filed.

5. You can afford to pay all of your current debts without hardship.

There is also a situation in which bankruptcy is not the wrong choice, but in which it is not necessary or urgent. Where state exemption laws are generous, you may be totally "collection-proof" at the time you are thinking about bankruptcy. (See Chapter Nine for more information about exemptions and about what it means to be "collection proof.") If that is the case, creditors can do virtually nothing to harm you. There is no action they can take that will affect your property or your wages.

When there is no urgency for you to file for bankruptcy, it often makes sense not to file immediately. If you wait, additional debts may arise that can also be included and discharged in the bankruptcy case.

For a more detailed analysis of the advantages and disadvantages of a bankruptcy filing, see the National Consumer Law Center's *Consumer Bankruptcy Law and Practice* Ch. 6 (8th ed. 2006 and Supp.).

SATISFYING THE CREDIT COUNSELING REQUIREMENT

By the time you have given serious thought to filing bankruptcy, you have probably already considered other options and concluded that alternatives to bankruptcy are not going to work for you. Even though you may have reached this decision, the bankruptcy law requires that you must receive budget and credit counseling from an approved credit counseling agency within 180 days of the time your bankruptcy case is filed. If you decide to go ahead with bankruptcy, you will need to file a certificate from the credit counseling agency stating that you received counseling.

Finding an "Approved" Counseling Agency. You must receive the required counseling from an agency that has been approved by the United States Trustee Program for the jurisdiction where you are filing (consumers located in North Carolina or Alabama must use counseling agencies approved by the local Bankruptcy Administrator). You can check the United States Trustee Program's website for a list of approved agencies, at www.usdoj.gov/ust/. You can also ask the local bankruptcy court or your bankruptcy attorney for a list of approved agencies. Approved agencies are allowed to provide the counseling in-person, by telephone, or over the Internet.

This required credit counseling may be helpful for you and in any case, you have to do it if you want to file for bankruptcy. You should be very careful in choosing which of the approved agencies to contact. It is extremely difficult to sort out the good agencies from the bad. Many agencies are legitimate, but many are simply rip-offs. And being an "approved" agency for bankruptcy counseling is no guarantee that the agency is good. It is also important to understand that even good agencies won't be able to help you much if you're already too deep in financial trouble. Tips on finding a reputable counseling agency are discussed in Chapter Four.

Avoid For-Profit Debt Counseling. For-profit bankruptcy counseling is rarely a good idea. Unfortunately, there are many organizations that offer counseling and credit repair to people with debt problems in order to rip them off. If you are going to pay for debt counseling, you should be careful to avoid scams and offers of high-rate debt consolidation loans as a way out of debt. Most of these deals will only make your situation worse. If a deal seems too good to be true or if a solution to your problems seems too easy, it probably is. Also, for-profit counseling agencies cannot give you the certificate you need to file bankruptcy because only non-profit organizations can be approved agencies for the required bankruptcy counseling.

The Costs of Pre-Filing Counseling. You can expect that most agencies will charge between $30–$50 for the pre-filing counseling (some agencies charge the same amount for a married couple if both spouses are counseled at the same time). However, the law requires approved agencies to provide bankruptcy counseling and the necessary certificates without considering the consumer's ability to pay. If you cannot afford the fee, you should ask the agency to provide the counseling free of charge or at a reduced fee. If the agency refuses to consider your request for a fee waiver, or you believe your request has been wrongly denied, you should send a written complaint to the United States Trustee Program (or the local Bankruptcy Administrator in North Carolina or Alabama). Reputable counseling agencies will disclose their fee waiver policies up front, for example in a clear statement on their websites. You should demand clarification of the fee waiver policies before the session begins and stick to your position if the counselor later tries to persuade you to pay contrary to the agency's stated policy.

If you decide to sign up for a debt management plan and later change your mind, or find that you can no longer continue with the plan, you should ask the agency for a certificate before filing bankruptcy. As long as the initial counseling session was approximately six months (180 days) before you plan to file, you should not have to repeat the bankruptcy counseling and the agency should provide you with a certificate without charging any additional fees.

The Pre-Filing Credit Counseling Session. At the counseling session, which usually takes less than an hour, the agency will prepare and review with you a budget that looks at your income and expenses. It is important that you are realistic in describing your actual income and expenses. The session will go more quickly if you have written down your basic income and expense information in advance. It also helps to have a list of your debts handy, for example from a credit report. Some counseling agencies have their own worksheets and forms that you can use to prepare for the session. It can be worthwhile to spend the time to gather the data to complete these worksheets for the counseling session because you will need the same information later if you go on to fill out a set of bankruptcy schedules.

Based on your budget, the agency will review possible options available to you in credit counseling. In some cases, the only option that may be suggested is a debt management plan. As discussed in Chapter Four, before signing up for a debt management plan, you should carefully consider whether you can afford to make the suggested payments and whether such a plan will really solve your financial problems. If you sign up with the agency for a debt management plan, a copy of the plan must be filed in your bankruptcy case.

Is a Debt Management Plan (DMP) Right for You?

Below are a few questions to ask to help you figure out whether a DMP is right for you.

1. Are you having trouble mainly with secured debts? If you answered yes, a DMP is not likely to help you. There may be an exception to this general rule if you are only slightly behind on your secured debts. In that case, cutting your unsecured debts might free up extra money to help you pay your secured debts. Just remember that a DMP will not directly help you with your secured debt problems.

2. Do you have little or no money left over in your budget each month? If you answered yes, a debt management plan is not right for you.

3. Are you still current on your credit cards? If so, a DMP is probably not a good idea. You might be able to improve your situation by taking a budget counseling class and sticking to a tight budget, or by asking your creditors to reduce the interest rate on your cards.

4. Are you able to pay your priority debts and still have some money left over each month? If so, a DMP may be helpful. However, be sure to factor in any fees you will have to pay to the agency. Priority debts are discussed in Chapter One.

5. Can you make a long term commitment to making monthly payments? If you answered no, a DMP will not help you. The drop-out rates for these plans are very high and it is a particularly bad idea to start out thinking that you probably can't complete the plan. Ask the agency to explain to you how long it will take you to pay off your debts through a DMP. In some states, they are required to tell you this information.

6. Do you want to keep using all of your credit cards while on a DMP? If so, a DMP is not for you. Most agencies will require you to stop using any remaining credit cards. Some will allow you to keep one card for emergencies.

The bottom line is that a debt management plan is *never* a good idea if you do not have a significant amount of money left over each month to pay credit card debt.

Some agencies will also review with you the reasons that have caused you to consider filing bankruptcy. While it may help in avoiding problems in the future to review these factors, remember that the agency cannot refuse to provide you with a certificate because it believes your reasons for filing are inappropriate or not justified. Only the bankruptcy court can decide if you are entitled to bankruptcy relief under the law.

As part of the bankruptcy counseling session, the agency will also review with you a list of alternatives to filing bankruptcy. It is often hard to compare these alternatives with bankruptcy if you are not given legal advice about the advantages and disadvantages of bankruptcy in relation to your personal circumstances. This legal advice is critical, but should not be given to you by the credit counselors because they are not attorneys and are not permitted to give you legal advice. It is therefore usually a good idea for you to meet with an attorney before you receive the credit counseling. A reputable attorney will generally provide counseling on whether bankruptcy is the best option. If bankruptcy is not the right answer for you, a good attorney will offer a range of other suggestions.

ASKING THE COURT TO WAIVE THE COUNSELING REQUIREMENT

There are a few situations when you can request a permanent or temporary waiver of the counseling requirement. Your request for a waiver must be in the form of a signed statement ("certification") that sets forth your reasons for requesting a waiver and it is filed along with your initial bankruptcy papers.

You may request a waiver if you are disabled or incapacitated. However, the law sets out a rather strict standard on what it means to be disabled or incapacitated for purposes of the counseling waiver, so consumers may have difficulty convincing a court to grant a waiver on these grounds. You may also request a waiver if you are on active military duty in a combat zone. If the court grants you a waiver on one of these grounds (disability, incapacity, or active combat duty), you will not have to get counseling at any point during the bankruptcy process.

If you need to file bankruptcy in an emergency to stop a home foreclosure, car repossession, or wage attachment, or some other "exigent circumstances," you can request a temporary waiver of the counseling requirement. The court will grant this kind of waiver only if you file with your bankruptcy petition a signed statement that (1) describes the "exigent circumstances" that support your waiver request and (2) states that you requested counseling services before filing bankruptcy from an approved agency but were unable to get the services during the five-day period following your request. If your waiver request is approved by the court due to exigent circumstances, the counseling requirement is only postponed. You must still get counseling from an approved agency within thirty days after you file your bankruptcy. The court may, for cause, extend this period by giving you an additional fifteen days.

Since waivers are not easily approved, it is important to check carefully that you meet the requirements for a waiver before filing bankruptcy without a counseling certificate. Bankruptcy judges know that there are counseling services available on-line or by phone that will provide certificates on an emergency basis. For this reason it is rarely worth the risk to attempt to waive the counseling requirement with a motion claiming that "exigent circumstances" prevented you from obtaining the certificate to file with your petition. If your case is dismissed because the waiver is denied, you will incur additional costs if you need to refile, and you may lose certain protections when you refile, such as the full extent of the automatic stay.

CHOOSING THE TYPE OF BANKRUPTCY TO FILE

The Two Common Types of Bankruptcy for Consumers. The bankruptcy law provides for two main types of consumer cases: chapter 7 and chapter 13. If you file bankruptcy, you will need to decide which is the better chapter for you.

DESCRIPTION OF CHAPTER 7 (LIQUIDATION)

A case under chapter 7 of the bankruptcy laws is often called a "liquidation." In a liquidation case, your assets are examined by a court appointed trustee to determine if anything is available to be sold for the benefit of creditors. Property that cannot be sold and that you get to keep is called "exempt."

The trustee may sell only property that is either not exempt or has value exceeding the exemption limits. In most consumer bankruptcies, nearly all of the assets are exempt. This means that little or no property is taken away and sold. If property is partly exempt and partly non-exempt, the trustee may sell it and pay you the value of your exemption in cash. Or, if you have the money, you may pay the trustee the amount of the non-exempt value and keep the property.

Exemption laws vary from state to state and may be fairly complicated. You cannot make a final choice about bankruptcy without understanding the exemption laws for your particular state.

The best way to do this is to ask for a list of exemptions from a neighborhood legal services office, a private attorney, or pro bono bar organization. Another approach is to see if there is an accurate and up-to-date listing in a legal publication for your state. See Chapter Nine for more detail on state exemption laws. If you are not sure whether your property is exempt or whether you may benefit from choosing state or federal bankruptcy exemptions in states where that choice is available, you should consult with a bankruptcy attorney.

In deciding what can be sold, the trustee will only look to your *equity* in property. If you owe money on a mortgage or other lien on a home, that mortgage or lien reduces your equity in the home. The trustee will not sell property if your equity in the property is fully exempt.

In a chapter 7 bankruptcy, you get to keep all of your exempt assets, which usually include your home and your car.

For example, if the state exemption for your home is $50,000, the home's value is $150,000, and you have a $100,000 mortgage, all of your $50,000 equity in the home is exempt. The trustee will *not* sell the home in a chapter 7 liquidation. The trustee also is unlikely to sell your home if there is a small amount of non-exempt equity. This is because the equity would not cover the costs of sale, including realtor's fees and taxes. In the above example, the trustee is unlikely to sell the home even if it could be sold for $160,000.

At the end of a chapter 7 case, you obtain a discharge of most unsecured debts. This means that you will no longer have a legal obligation to pay those debts. Generally, the discharge will include credit card debts, medical bills, utility arrearages, and other similar debts for which the creditor does not have collateral.

Some unsecured debts, such as most student loans, debts based on fraud or malicious conduct, drunk driving debts, most tax debts, government fines, alimony, and child support are not likely to be discharged.

Chapter 7 bankruptcies rarely help with large secured debts, such as home mortgages, because the creditor keeps its rights in the collateral. While bankruptcy cancels your legal obligation to pay most personal debts, even secured debts, it does not prevent secured creditors from recovering their collateral if a debt is not repaid. This means that a chapter 7 case will not affect, except temporarily, the rights of a bank to foreclose on a home or repossess a car that is loan collateral. However, if you have received a chapter 7 discharge and a creditor later sells its collateral, the creditor may not sue you for any balance still owed.

ANSWERS TO SOME BASIC QUESTIONS ABOUT CHAPTER 7

Chapter 7 bankruptcy cases are usually straightforward. Occasionally, complications arise if creditors take aggressive action, if the trustee thinks you are hiding assets, or if you want to challenge creditors' claims. Those potential complications are not covered in detail here.

Who can file? Any individual who lives in the United States or has property or a business in the United States can file a chapter 7 bankruptcy. There are no preconditions to a bankruptcy filing, such as insolvency, although a judge can dismiss your chapter 7 case if you engage in an abuse of the bankruptcy system. This is rare but may occur if you are using bankruptcy for an improper purpose (such as to harass creditors) or if you have substantial income to pay your debts. If you received a chapter 7 bankruptcy discharge within the past eight years, you are disqualified from receiving a discharge in chapter 7. A similar disqualification may also apply if you received a discharge within the past six years in a chapter 13 case in which your unsecured creditors were paid less than 70% of what they were owed.

In 2005, a "means test" was added to the bankruptcy law to make it more difficult for wealthy consumers to file a chapter 7 bankruptcy. Most consumers who file bankruptcy are not affected by this change. If your income is below the median family income in your state (the national median family income for a family of 4 in 2006 was approximately $65,796—your state's figures may be higher or lower), you are protected by a "safe harbor" and not subject to the means test. The current median family income figures for your state are available on the website for the United States Trustee Program at: www.usdoj.gov/.

A consumer with income above the median must fill out a form that compares the consumer's monthly income with actual and assumed expenses in a variety of categories. If this form shows, based on standards in the law, that the consumer should have a certain amount left over to pay unsecured creditors, the bankruptcy court may decide that the consumer cannot file a chapter 7 case, unless there are special circumstances.

What are the first steps? The first step in a chapter 7 bankruptcy is completion of certain basic forms. These include a three-page initial "petition." You will also need to file a certificate from an approved credit counseling agency or a request for a waiver of the counseling requirement. A number of other forms must also be filed either at the same time as the petition or shortly afterwards. These include your statement of financial affairs, statement of intentions with respect to certain secured debts, statement of monthly income and means test calculations, copies of any pay stubs you received from an employer during the sixty days before filing your bankruptcy case, and a set of schedules listing all your debts, property, income, and expenses. It is important that all of these forms be filled out completely and accurately. Among other considerations, you should keep in mind that the Office of the United States Trustee now audits random bankruptcy cases. You could be called upon in an audit to explain any material inaccuracies in your schedules.

If requested by the bankruptcy court or trustee (or by a creditor in some situations), you may also need to provide or file with the court copies of certain tax returns, or a shorter version of the returns called "transcripts." This requirement does not apply if you did not need to file tax returns with the IRS, for example if your income was too low. Due to privacy concerns, no tax returns or other information filed with the bankruptcy court will be available to the public and cannot be viewed on the Internet through the court's website or the federal court's electronic document service called "PACER."
Also, you cannot be required to file tax returns or transcripts with the bankruptcy court unless the trustee or creditor has first filed a written motion with the court stating that there is a clear need for the tax information and that the information is not available from other sources.

At the beginning of the case you will also need to file a mailing list including all of your creditors. All of these forms must meet certain specifications required by the court. Bankruptcy courts often require that these forms be filed electronically, but most courts allow consumers without an attorney to file in paper form or provide scanning and other equipment at the court that consumers can use to convert the forms for electronic filing. You should check with a bankruptcy specialist or your local bankruptcy court for a full list of filing requirements.

What will happen after filing? Filing the petition triggers the automatic stay. With few exceptions, discussed earlier, this stops any creditor from taking collection action, pursuing a court case against you, or seizing your property based on debts that arose before you filed your bankruptcy petition. If you are worried about a creditor action like a foreclosure or repossession, you should make a special effort to notify that creditor so that the action is stopped before it occurs.

If a creditor does take action against you other than in the bankruptcy court, including making collection calls or sending letters, you should politely inform the creditor about the bankruptcy. The creditor action may violate the automatic stay. If you have an attorney, you should also tell your attorney about the contact. You may start a process to obtain damages for certain violations of the stay.

Within a few weeks after filing, the bankruptcy court or the trustee mails a notice of the stay and of the date and place for a "meeting of creditors." This notice will be mailed to all creditors, to you, and to your attorney, if you have one.

What is a bankruptcy trustee? After you file bankruptcy, a trustee is appointed to represent the interests of creditors. In a chapter 7 bankruptcy, the trustee collects any property that can be sold, handles the sale, distributes the property to creditors with valid claims, and makes a final accounting to the court.

What is the meeting of creditors? The meeting of creditors is conducted by the trustee. It is not usually held at the courthouse but rather at a separate government or office building. The meeting of creditors gives the trustee and others a chance to ask questions about your financial affairs.

Despite the name, few creditors appear at the meeting of creditors in a consumer bankruptcy. You, however, must attend. If you file jointly with your spouse, you must both attend. The meeting consists of a series of routine questions by the trustee and lasts from two minutes to half an hour. Usually, the best thing you can do to prepare for this meeting is review the papers you or your attorney have filed with the court. You may also be required to bring certain documents with you to the meeting, such as a copy of your most recent bank statement, a picture form of identification, proof of your current income such as your most recent pay stub, and some proof of your Social Security number (or a written statement that you do not have a Social Security number or that no proof is available).

What must I do after the meeting of creditors? After your bankruptcy has been filed, and usually soon after the meeting of creditors, you will need to complete an educational course on personal finances. As with the credit counseling requirement, you must take a course that has been approved by the United States Trustee Program, and you can get a list of approved courses from the Trustee Program's website, the local bankruptcy court, or your attorney.

The fee is usually $25–$50. However, the law requires approved agencies to provide education without considering the consumer's ability to pay. If you cannot afford the fee, you should ask the agency to provide the course free of charge or at a reduced fee. If the agency refuses to consider your request for a fee waiver, or you believe your request has been wrongly denied, you should send a written complaint to the United States Trustee Program (or the local Bankruptcy Administrator in North Carolina or Alabama).

In most cases, the course will take about two hours to complete. Many of the course providers give you a choice to take the course in-person at a designated location, over the Internet usually by watching a video, or over the telephone. The course generally includes written information and instruction on the following topics: budget development, money management, wise use of credit, and consumer information. If the course is well-designed and implemented effectively, it could help you avoid future financial problems.

After you have completed the course, the provider will give you a document certifying that you have satisfied the education requirement. This document must be attached to a form "certification of completion" that you will need to file with the bankruptcy court within forty-five days after the meeting of creditors. *If this form is not filed in your bankruptcy case, you will not receive a discharge of your debts.* You can request a waiver of the educational course requirement, but only if you can show that you are disabled or incapacitated, or if you are on active combat duty.

What happens after the meeting of creditors and after the education course is completed? Unless there is an objection to the exemptions you have claimed, after the meeting of creditors you keep the property listed as exempt in your schedules. Property that is mostly, but not totally, exempt is usually abandoned by the trustee, which means that you get to keep it.

If larger non-exempt assets remain, they are turned over to the trustee. You will usually be offered the option of paying the non-exempt value of the assets to the trustee in cash instead of turning over those assets. The trustee then sells any property collected, converts it to cash, and distributes it among the creditors.

The trustee must give notice of intent to sell the property. Any party, including you, can object within specified time limits to the proposed sale, which is either private or by public auction.

During a chapter 7 bankruptcy, you will have to take one of several steps to deal with your secured debts. You can surrender the collateral to the secured creditor if that is your intention, or you can keep the collateral by paying the creditor in a lump sum the value of the collateral. You also have the option of "reaffirming" the debt to protect the collateral. This option is discussed in more detail below.

Before the 2005 amendments many courts had said that in a chapter 7 case you had the option to keep personal property, such as a car, and continue making payments on the purchase loan without signing a reaffirmation agreement, paying off the car's value, or surrendering the car. The status of the option to keep your car and continue making loan payments is less clear under the current law. You should consult with a bankruptcy attorney about the availability of this option in your state. The law of your state may play an important role in whether you choose to exercise this option.

What is reaffirmation and when should I consider it? Reaffirmation is your agreement during bankruptcy to remain legally obligated on some or all of a debt which you could have otherwise eliminated. You should always approach reaffirmation agreements with a great deal of caution. By signing a reaffirmation agreement, you give back to the creditor rights to collect from you that it lost when you filed for bankruptcy.

You should never agree to reaffirm if:

- The debt is totally unsecured;
- The creditor cannot provide paperwork showing you that the debt is secured;
- The debt is secured and you have no interest in keeping the collateral;
- The debt is secured and you are hopelessly behind on payments, so that the property will be repossessed in any event; or
- The debt is secured and you are up to date on payments, but your bankruptcy court is one which allows you to keep up your payments

and keep the property without reaffirmation (check with a bankruptcy professional).

Reaffirmation is an agreement you make to repay debts despite your bankruptcy. It is unwise to reaffirm except in very limited situations.

You might consider reaffirmation if:

- The creditor gives you something valuable in return, such as an agreement to let you get caught up on a default in a manageable way or a reduction of a secured debt to the value of the property;
- You want to keep property used as collateral for a secured debt and your bankruptcy court will not allow you to keep it without reaffirming (and you cannot afford the better alternative of paying the creditor the value of the property in a lump sum); and
- You can easily afford the payments which will be required after bankruptcy.

What about reaffirming credit card debt? It is almost never a good idea to reaffirm a credit card debt, even store credit cards that may be secured. Some offers to reaffirm may seem attractive at first. For example, a card company may offer you a new $500 credit line on your card if you reaffirm $1,000 out of the $2,000 you owed before bankruptcy. The agreement might provide that you will only have to pay $27 per month on the reaffirmed amount. What the company might not tell you is that it will take five years to pay off the reaffirmation if they charge 21% interest and that you will pay a finance charge of approximately $620. This is a very high price to pay for $500 in new credit. And you can probably get a new credit card from another company (or even the same company) fairly soon after bankruptcy, one that won't come with a large unpaid balance.

Some credit cards, especially department store cards, may be secured. Though you may not be aware that the credit card is secured, the card agreement you signed may have stated that the items purchased with it are collateral. After you have filed bankruptcy, the credit card company may claim that they will repossess what you bought, such as a TV, computer, or sofa, if you do not reaffirm the debt.

Most of the time, store credit card companies will not repossess used merchandise. So, after a bankruptcy, it is much less likely that a store or creditor would repossess "collateral" than a car lender. However, it is possible. You have to decide just how important the item is. If you can live without it, or you can buy a replacement for less than it will cost to reaffirm the debt, then you should not reaffirm.

Three important points about reaffirmation:

1. If a creditor tries to pressure you to reaffirm, you can say no. Reaffirmation is always optional. It is not required by bankruptcy law or any other law.

2. Never reaffirm a debt just because a creditor offers to advance you some new credit or to keep your account in good standing. There are easier ways to obtain new credit than to agree to the expense of repaying a debt which bankruptcy can eliminate.

3. You can voluntarily pay any debts you want to pay after bankruptcy without signing a reaffirmation agreement. This is not the same as reaffirming a debt since you cannot be sued if you stop paying at some point.

If I reaffirm, does it have to be on the same terms? No. A reaffirmation is a new contract between you and the lender. The reaffirmation agreement you will be asked to sign includes a section (Part A) in which the creditor must disclose information about the credit terms of the original transaction, including the total of any fees and costs the creditor believes are owed at the time of the disclosure. It also includes a section (Part B) that describes any changes to the original transaction made as part of the reaffirmation. You should review this information closely and try to get the creditor to agree to better terms such as a lower monthly payment and interest rate. You can also try to negotiate a reduction in the amount you owe. The lender may refuse but it is always worth a try.

Must the reaffirmation be approved by the court? In some cases, yes. As part of the reaffirmation agreement, you must sign a section of the form (Part D) which states that, based on figures you list for your income and monthly expenses, you believe you have sufficient income left over after paying your expenses to make the payments required under the reaffirmation agreement. If the figures show that you do not have enough to make the reaffirmation payments, it will be presumed that the reaffirmation agreement is an "undue hardship," and you will need to explain on the form how you will be able to afford the payments and identify any additional sources of income you will use to make the payments. In this situation, the court is required to review the reaffirmation. If the court finds that your explanation is not sufficient, it may reject the agreement. There will not be any harmful consequences for you if the court rejects the reaffirmation agreement. The bankruptcy law requires only that under certain circumstances you may have to sign such an agreement. If you sign a reaffirmation agreement and the court does not approve it, the bankruptcy stay and the discharge order will continue to protect you and the car as long as you remain current in payments.

Can I change my mind after I reaffirm a debt? You can cancel any reaffirmation agreement for 60 days after it is filed with the court. You can also cancel at any time before your discharge order. To cancel a reaffirmation agreement, you must notify the creditor in writing. You do not have to give a reason. Once you have canceled, the creditor must return any payments you made on the agreement.

How do I get my bankruptcy discharge? The final step in most chapter 7 bankruptcy cases is the discharge. In most places, if no one objects to your discharge, the court enters the discharge without a hearing. You get the discharge order in the mail. However, you will not get a discharge unless you file with the court a certification that you completed an approved personal finance course.

What will my chapter 7 discharge cover? The discharge in chapter 7 covers all unsecured debts, including most credit card debt, medical bills, and back utility debts. Your discharge may *not* include:

- Certain taxes;
- Debts not listed in your schedules;
- Debts for alimony, child support, and family court property settlements;
- Most fines and penalties owed to government agencies;
- Student loans unless you can prove to the court that repaying them will be an "undue hardship";
- Debts incurred by driving while intoxicated;
- Debts incurred to pay taxes which cannot be discharged; and
- Debts you have formally agreed to repay despite the bankruptcy (by "reaffirming" your obligation to pay).

In addition, a court may find some other debts nondischargeable, but only if the particular creditor seeks a determination from the bankruptcy court within a strict time limit after the meeting of creditors and proves that the debt should not be discharged. These types of debts include:

- Debts incurred by certain types of fraud;
- Debts incurred while acting as a trustee for someone else's property; and
- Debts for purposely causing injuries to individuals or property.

If you incur a consumer debt for luxury goods or services of more than $500 to a single creditor within ninety days before filing bankruptcy, or cash advances of over $750 on an open-end credit account, such as a credit card account, within seventy days of filing, it may be presumed that the debt is nondischargeable if the creditor seeks a determination from the bankruptcy court. To challenge the presumption, you need to show that you had good reason to incur the debt and that you were not intending to obtain the debt by fraud.

A few creditors (mainly credit card companies) make accusations of fraud in nondischargeability proceedings even when consumers have done nothing wrong. Their goal is to scare honest consumers so that they agree to reaffirm the debt. You should never agree to reaffirm a debt if you have done nothing wrong. If the creditor files a nondischargeability fraud case and you win, the court may order the creditor to pay your lawyer's fees.

What should I do if a creditor tries to collect a debt which has been discharged? Collection of discharged debts is illegal. You should contact your lawyer if you have been subject to collection efforts. You may bring a legal action to have the discharge enforced and to recover any damages which the collection efforts caused you.

DESCRIPTION OF CHAPTER 13 (REORGANIZATION)

A case under chapter 13 of the bankruptcy laws is often called a "reorganization." Reorganization cases under chapter 13 work very differently from chapter 7 liquidations. In a chapter 13 case, you submit a plan to repay your creditors over time, usually from future income.

Most consumer reorganization cases take place under chapter 13 of the bankruptcy law. However, some debtors with large amounts of debt may be required (or may prefer) to proceed under chapter 11. Family farmers can also proceed under chapter 12.

In certain circumstances, there are advantages to filing a chapter 13 case rather than a chapter 7. Most importantly, in a chapter 13 case, you are allowed to get caught up on mortgages or car loans over a period of time.

For example, most mortgages and car loans allow the bank to call the whole loan due when you miss a payment or two. Although the bank may let you work out an agreement to catch up over time on back payments (and you should call to find out if this is possible), the bank usually is not legally required to let you catch up. Where the bank or any creditor is uncooperative, a chapter 13 bankruptcy may be the only way to force it to let you keep the property while you make the back payments over a period of years.

Chapter 13 cases also allow you to keep both exempt property, which would be protected in chapter 7, and non-exempt property, which would be sold in chapter 7. You can keep the property by paying its non-exempt value to creditors under a court approved plan, usually over a period from three to five years.

The heart of a chapter 13 case is your bankruptcy plan. This is a simple document outlining how you propose to make payments to various creditors while the plan is in effect.

The law places certain limits on what you may do under a plan. Nevertheless, there are substantial opportunities for reorganizing your debt payments and protecting your property from creditors, including mortgage and other lien holders, as long as appropriate payments are made.

A chapter 13 bankruptcy plan normally requires monthly payments to the bankruptcy trustee over a period of three years. However, plans can last for as long as five years with court approval. Consumers with higher incomes that are above the median family income in their state may be required to make payments that equal a five-year plan. In most jurisdictions, bankruptcy courts will routinely approve requests to have the monthly payments to the trustee paid automatically by wage deduction.

Once your payments are completed under the plan, you are entitled to a discharge just as in a chapter 7 bankruptcy. The discharge available in chapter 13 covers more debts than a discharge under chapter 7, though this benefit in chapter 13 has been scaled back considerably by recent changes in the law. If you have caught up on any mortgage debt or other secured loan, the loan will be reinstated and the law requires the creditor to treat you as if you never fell behind.

Reorganization cases can be quite complicated. Working out the best possible bankruptcy plan is frequently difficult. If you are considering a reorganization in bankruptcy, consult with an attorney specializing in bankruptcy as quickly as possible. Your delay may allow a foreclosure or repossession to proceed to the point where bankruptcy can no longer help.

In a chapter 13 bankruptcy, you may have as long as five years to catch up with overdue payments on secured debts, and you may be able to keep all of your property.

ANSWERS TO SOME BASIC QUESTIONS ABOUT CHAPTER 13

Most of the initial steps in a chapter 13 case are quite similar to those in chapter 7. The major difference is that in chapter 13, you must file a chapter 13 reorganization plan. You must begin making payments under that plan within thirty days after filing.

The following material is intended to point out some of the other significant differences in the procedure for chapter 13.

Who can file? Chapter 13 is available to "individuals with regular income" who live in the United States or have a place of business or property in the United States. An "individual with regular income" includes not only wage earners but also recipients of government benefits, alimony, or support payments, or any other type of regular income.

A chapter 13 discharge can even be obtained by a debtor who has received a chapter 7 discharge as long as the chapter 13 case is not filed within the first four years after the filing of the prior chapter 7 petition. Debtors who would not be granted a discharge because of some other provision in chapter 7 should also be able to get a chapter 13 discharge.

There are limits to the amount of debt that you may have as a chapter 13 filer. Since these limits are quite high (exceeding one million in total), they do not affect most consumer cases.

402

What are the initial forms and first steps? As with chapter 7, a chapter 13 bankruptcy begins with a three-page petition and a certificate from an approved credit counseling agency or a request for a temporary waiver of the counseling requirement. The additional forms and schedules must also be filed either with your petition or shortly thereafter. A chapter 13 plan must be filed with your schedules. This is your description of when creditors will be paid, how they will be paid, and how much they will be paid.

As with chapter 7, filing a petition sets the bankruptcy process in motion. The filing immediately establishes the automatic stay, which prevents any further creditor acts against you or your property. Unlike a chapter 7, the automatic stay in a chapter 13 case also prevents creditors from taking any action against any codebtors (cosigners) who have not filed bankruptcy, so long as the plan provides for payment of the debt.

A trustee is appointed and the meeting of creditors is held. At a meeting of creditors in chapter 13, the focus is usually on whether your plan meets the requirements of the law and whether you can afford to make the payments that are required in the chapter 13 process.

What will I have to pay? You must begin making plan payments within thirty days after filing your bankruptcy case, unless the court orders otherwise. These payments are held by the chapter 13 trustee and not paid out to creditors until your chapter 13 plan is approved by the court. If the court does not approve your chapter 13 plan, the payments are returned to you after deduction of administrative costs. Depending upon the terms of your proposed plan, or if required by the court, you may need to begin making payments directly to some secured creditors within thirty days after filing your bankruptcy case.

Your payments will be based on the debts you intend to pay, the rules of chapter 13, and your ability to pay based on your budget. This means that, after paying for necessary living expenses, you will need to pay the balance of your income to the trustee while your bankruptcy proceeds. If you choose, this can occur automatically by wage deduction.

Unsecured creditors may receive a share of the payments made under the plan. Depending upon the amount of your non-exempt property and income left over after paying necessary living expenses, your plan may pay unsecured creditors at less than the full amount they are owed, often as low as 5 to 10%. If your income is above the state median family income, the amount you are required to pay unsecured creditors is based on a formula that considers the actual amounts you spend for some expenses and fixed amounts for other expenses. In most cases, consumers are no longer required to pay unsecured creditors for any interest, late fees, and other penalty charges that would otherwise come due after the chapter 13 is filed.

Once your plan is in place, your case is likely to be dismissed if you fail to make payments. It is also very important that you keep up with alimony and child support payments you are required to make while your chapter 13 case is pending, otherwise your case may be dismissed and you will not be entitled to receive a discharge. Dismissal will put you back into the situation you were in before bankruptcy. In some cases you can avoid dismissal even if you cannot afford payments by converting your chapter 13 case to a chapter 7 case or by seeking a "hardship discharge" from the court.

What does a trustee do in chapter 13? The chapter 13 trustee has more to do than the chapter 7 trustee. The chapter 13 trustee may require that you provide additional documents, beyond those you must submit in a chapter 7 case. For example, under some local rules the chapter 13 trustee will require that you provide additional tax returns and documentation showing that homes and cars are insured. In addition to the duties of a chapter 7 trustee, the chapter 13 trustee must collect your payments and distribute that money to creditors. The trustee will ask the court to dismiss your case if you fail to make the plan payments.

The terms of your confirmed plan will determine how your plan payments are distributed and how much each creditor will receive. In order to get paid by the trustee, though, the creditor must file a proof of claim with the bankruptcy court by a specific deadline. Both you and the trustee can file a written objection to the claim if the creditor has overcharged you or if you have defenses to owing the money. The bankruptcy judge will then hold a hearing on the objection and decide how much the creditor should be paid.

Depending upon the type of case or the matter involved, and in some cases the trustee's personality, a chapter 13 trustee is either your friend or enemy. The trustee's opinion is not necessarily the last word on any matter. You have the right to raise any appropriate issue with the bankruptcy judge. Trustees are not judges and have no power to rule on disputes between creditors and debtors.

How does my plan get approved? The court will evaluate your plan at a "confirmation hearing." This occurs between twenty and forty-five days after the first meeting of creditors, unless the court orders that the hearing be held earlier or continues it to a later date. The court will inquire into whether the requirements of chapter 13 have been met and will hear any objections to approval of your chapter 13 plan raised by creditors or the trustee.

In many courts, there is no formal hearing at the time of confirmation unless there is an objection to your plan. Also, in many cases, if the plan is not challenged, you will be advised that you do not need to come to court.

For various reasons, you may want to change your original plan after it is filed. Before confirmation, a plan can be modified, so long as the modified plan meets the chapter 13 requirements. After confirmation, plans can still be modified, subject to court approval. Creditors or the trustee may object.

What if I fail to complete my plan? Some people are unable to complete their chapter 13 plans, usually because of loss of income. When this occurs, four options are normally available, each having somewhat different consequences:

- *Hardship Discharge.* Bankruptcy law provides for a hardship discharge of debts if problems are caused by circumstances for which you are not responsible, such as serious deterioration of your financial circumstances.
- *Modification.* It is possible to modify a plan to address new problems, but creditors have a right to object to the modification, and, if so, the court will decide whether to allow the modification.
- *Conversion.* You have the right to convert a chapter 13 case to a chapter 7 case. After the conversion, non-exempt property is liquidated and you receive a chapter 7 discharge.
- *Dismissal.* Occasionally, dismissal is preferable to any of the other options. You have the right to dismiss your chapter 13 case unless the case was previously converted from a chapter 7 case.

What debts are discharged in chapter 13? The final step in a successfully completed chapter 13 case is the discharge. As with chapter 7, you must complete an educational course on personal finances before you will be given a discharge. A certification that you have taken the course must be filed before your last chapter 13 payment as required by your plan.

The chapter 13 discharge includes all debts provided for by the plan, except for support and alimony payments and except for long-term debts with final payments due after the completion of the plan. Other exceptions to discharge in chapter 13 are most student loans (unless you can prove that repaying them will be an "undue hardship"), drunk driving debts, and criminal restitution debts. A chapter 13 discharge can eliminate legal responsibility on some debts that are not dischargeable in a chapter 7 case, such as claims for injuries to property purposely caused by you and debts from some property settlements in a divorce or separation proceeding.

The chapter 13 discharge can be enforced in the same way as the chapter 7 discharge discussed above. The fact that you filed a chapter 13 bankruptcy stays on your credit report for ten years from the date your case was filed.

CHOOSING THE RIGHT TYPE OF BANKRUPTCY

Advantages of a Chapter 7 Bankruptcy. If a chapter 7 bankruptcy will accomplish your goals, it is generally the best choice because it is simpler and quicker than a chapter 13 bankruptcy. Once the papers are filed, unless unusual issues are raised, you will receive a discharge within three to five months. A chapter 7 bankruptcy will generally meet your goals if it will discharge most of your debts and not result in the loss of any of your property.

Generally, chapter 7 is the best option when two factors are present:

- All or nearly all of your property is exempt; and
- The debts that are causing problems for you are unsecured and dischargeable in chapter 7.

Even if some of your property is not exempt, a chapter 7 bankruptcy may be the right choice for you because you can exchange small amounts of non-exempt property for exempt property.

Even where there are secured debts, a chapter 13 filing may not be necessary. This is particularly true if you are current on your mortgage, car loan, and other secured debt payments. If you can keep current on secured debt payments, you can keep your home or other collateral, if it is exempt, even while going through a chapter 7 bankruptcy. A chapter 13 filing is generally preferable if you are delinquent on a secured debt and want to cure this default over time.

Finally, the amount you will have to pay to your attorney will be considerably greater in chapter 13 than in chapter 7. However, the chapter 13 attorney fees can be paid over several years through the terms of a plan. Ultimately, the relative importance to you of the benefits you can obtain in a particular form of bankruptcy, not the amount you have to pay an attorney, should determine which type of bankruptcy you decide to file.

Some Considerations Favoring Chapter 13 Bankruptcies. Probably the most common reason for filing a chapter 13 petition is that one or more secured creditors cannot be dealt with satisfactorily in any other way. Few legal procedures create opportunities to deal with foreclosures and repossessions as quickly and effectively as a chapter 13 petition and plan.

Another reason to file a chapter 13 bankruptcy is to protect non-exempt assets, which would be sold in a chapter 7 case. However, the current value of the non-exempt property usually has to be paid over the course of the plan.

Other important reasons favoring a chapter 13 filing include:

- As discussed above, some debts that are not dischargeable in chapter 7 can be discharged in chapter 13.
- Some creditors consider a chapter 13 filing, compared to a chapter 7 filing, to be less harmful to your credit rating and reputation.
- If you obtained a chapter 7 discharge within the previous eight years, a new chapter 7 filing is not an option; only chapter 13 is available.

Even if you cannot afford payments to cure a default on your home mortgage, you can use the chapter 13 process to sell your home so that you can keep your equity and avoid the problems of a foreclosure sale. See Chapter Eleven.

You can change the type of bankruptcy you choose. Except in rare cases where the debtor engaged in some kind of fraudulent conduct in bankruptcy, it is easy to convert a case (at least once) from chapter 7 to chapter 13 or vice versa.

Should You File with Your Spouse? If you and your spouse are living together and have debts that you are both responsible for, it is usually preferable for you to file bankruptcy jointly. The filing fee is the same whether you file jointly or alone. If you file together, you will both get the advantages of a bankruptcy discharge. Since married couples often have joint debts, a spouse who does not file remains liable as a codebtor and may be pursued by creditors.

There is no requirement that you file together with your spouse. Therefore, if you want to file and your spouse does not (or vice versa), or if you and your spouse are separated, there is nothing to prevent a married individual from filing alone. However, the consequences of not filing jointly should be considered carefully.

Unmarried partners do not have the option of filing together. However, separate cases can be filed and administered by the court together.

THE TIMING OF YOUR
BANKRUPTCY FILING

The Emergency Bankruptcy. You may have no choice other than to file immediately to prevent a foreclosure, repossession, eviction, execution sale, or utility shut-off. Bankruptcies in an emergency can be filed with little preparation. A good discussion of how to do this is set out in the National Consumer Law Center's *Consumer Bankruptcy Law and Practice* § 7.2.2 (8th ed. 2006 and Supp.). But as discussed earlier, you must complete a credit counseling briefing before filing your bankruptcy, or have sufficient grounds to request a temporary waiver of the requirement based on "exigent circumstances," or a permanent waiver based on disability, incapacity, or active combat duty.

Delaying Bankruptcy in Anticipation of Further Debt. If you are not facing immediate loss of property and cannot avoid incurring further debt, such as new medical, utility, or unpaid rent bills, a bankruptcy filing should be delayed until after these debts occur. That way you will gain the maximum benefit from the discharge.

Debts incurred after the bankruptcy filing are *not* discharged in that bankruptcy case—you will still be obligated to repay them. As a general rule, bankruptcy should not be filed until your debts have peaked. If you do not have medical or automobile insurance, you should try to obtain insurance coverage before filing bankruptcy.

If you decide to wait to file bankruptcy, you must avoid the temptation to obtain goods or services on credit that you do not intend to pay for. In a chapter 7 bankruptcy, debts incurred in this way can be declared nondischargeable. Debts for prebankruptcy vacation trips and credit card shopping sprees have frequently been found to be nondischargeable. Expenses for medical bills and other essentials are rarely challenged.

Exemption Planning. You can legally take a number of steps to improve your legal position prior to filing bankruptcy. These steps are generally called exemption planning. Basically, exemption planning means arranging your affairs so that a maximum amount of property can be claimed under exemption provisions, and a minimum amount is lost to creditors.

It is similar to making arrangements to take maximum advantage of tax laws, and, if done reasonably, it is perfectly legal. However, an excessive transfer of property to create exempt assets can sometimes be found to be in bad faith. As discussed earlier, the timing of your bankruptcy filing in relation to when you may have moved from another state or when some of your property had been transferred or acquired can affect the amount of property you can claim as exempt. Exemption planning is also discussed in Chapter Nine.

Also, you **cannot** simply give away non-exempt property or sell it at nominal cost. Any transfer of property within two years of filing must be disclosed. Improper transfers of property to third parties can be recovered and may be grounds for denying a discharge.

HOW TO GET HELP WITH YOUR BANKRUPTCY FILING

Hiring a Bankruptcy Attorney. Generally, the best course of action if you are considering bankruptcy is to obtain the services of an attorney who is an expert in the field of bankruptcy. Hiring an attorney to handle any legal case is a difficult process. This is especially true in hiring a bankruptcy attorney.

As with any area of the law, it is important to carefully select an attorney who will be responsive to your personal situation. The attorney should not be too busy to meet with you individually and to answer your questions. Before hiring an attorney, you should meet the attorney personally and make sure that you are comfortable with the attorney's style. At all points in the case, your attorney should take time to answer questions either directly or through an office paralegal. If an attorney does not respond to your telephone calls, you should keep trying and demand an answer. If you have a dispute with your attorney, you can file a complaint with the court or the bar association.

The best way to find a trustworthy bankruptcy attorney is to seek recommendations from family, friends, or other members of the community. Retainers and other documents should be read carefully. An attorney retainer is a contract under which you hire the attorney. It governs what the attorney proposes to do for you and the fees for the proposed work. Make sure you understand the terms about what the attorney agrees to do if unusual issues come up during your case. Remember that the lawyer advertising the cheapest rate is not necessarily the best. More tips to help you find an attorney can be found in the Introduction to this book.

In most communities, there are *nonprofit* counselors who may be able to help you deal with your debts. However, they are not always easy to find. Try to get a referral, if possible, from local officials, from a friend or neighbor, or from a legal services office. If someone approaches you by mail or telephone because they read a foreclosure notice or announcement of a court proceeding against you, think twice before paying them for assistance. Chapter Four contains information about possible problems with both for-profit and non-profit credit counseling agencies and other "debt relief" companies.

Problems with Document Preparation Services. Document preparation services involve non-lawyers who offer to prepare the initial bankruptcy forms for a fee.

There are several reasons why these services have generated a lot of consumer complaints. Non-lawyers cannot offer legal advice on bankruptcy cases. Document preparation services also offer no services after a bankruptcy case is started. This means that, if issues arise after your forms are filed, you will have nowhere to turn for help. Often, the actual case will involve complications or even simple problems which you may not be prepared to meet. For these reasons, document preparation services are rarely a good place to get help with bankruptcy.

Preparing to Meet with a Bankruptcy Specialist. You should be prepared when first meeting a bankruptcy specialist to answer the following questions:

- What types of debt are causing you the most trouble?
- What are your significant assets?
- How were the debts incurred and are they secured by your property?
- Has any creditor started a process to collect any debt or to foreclose or repossess property? You should be prepared to report on the status of any pending lawsuits or foreclosures.

The answers to these general questions will reveal not only whether bankruptcy is likely to help you but also the dimensions of your financial problems—their cause, scope, and likelihood of recurring. Whenever possible, it is helpful to take written information about these issues to the bankruptcy specialist, particularly copies of your bills and any legal notices. Your bankruptcy specialist may ask that you get a copy of your credit report. This will help the specialist understand how much is owed and to whom. It will also provide necessary information such as account numbers and addresses of creditors.

Complete information is essential to an effective bankruptcy. If information is not complete, you may lose your rights in whole or in part. Expected tax refunds might be lost, major debts might turn out to be nondischargeable, and property might unexpectedly be considered non-exempt.

At the same time, you should try to find every possible debt so that you can use the opportunity to discharge your legal liability to its fullest. Debts not listed in the bankruptcy may not be discharged.

Try to review the full extent of your debts, including situations in which payments have not been recently demanded. Remember that any legal claim against you is a debt, if you are the one being sued. If you have recently obtained a credit report, a bankruptcy specialist can use that report to remind you about debts you may have forgotten.

In the worst case scenario, failure to provide complete and accurate information to your attorney or to the court can lead to big trouble. If a judge thinks that your failure to fulfill this obligation is significant and deliberate, you can be charged with criminal fraud. This happens rarely but is very painful when it does occur. More commonly (but still infrequently), you can be denied your bankruptcy discharge.

TAX CONSEQUENCES OF BANKRUPTCY

Unpaid debt usually has tax consequences. This is because the IRS views owing money in the same way it views borrowing money, with one important difference. Borrowed money is income. However, because you have to repay a loan, when you borrow money, the IRS does not tax the money you borrowed. When you cancel a debt, you do not repay the amount you "borrowed." Therefore, a canceled debt is not only income but taxable income. For example, debts wholly or partially written off through plans developed by debt settlement services may create new tax liabilities for you.

Bankruptcy is one exception to this rule. If debt is discharged in the bankruptcy process, you do not owe taxes on the unpaid amount of the debt.

You may receive a 1099C form from one or more creditors listing the amount you discharged in bankruptcy as canceled debt even though creditors are not required to file this form unless they have reason to think the loan was for business or investment purposes. Since this form also goes to the IRS, you should treat this amount as income which is exempt from taxes. You should attach an explanation to your tax form which includes your bankruptcy case number and the date of the discharge.

The tax laws are complicated. When in doubt, you should seek the advice of a qualified tax professional.

USING CREDIT WISELY AFTER BANKRUPTCY

Although bankruptcy can help with many financial problems, its effects are not permanent. If you choose bankruptcy, you should take advantage of the fresh start it offers and then make careful decisions about future borrowing and credit so you won't ever need to file bankruptcy again.

You should not assume that, because you filed bankruptcy, you will have to get credit on the worst terms. If you can't get credit on decent terms right after bankruptcy, it may be better to wait. Most lenders will not hold the bankruptcy against you if, after a few years, you can show that you have avoided problems and can manage your debts. As discussed earlier in this chapter, you should also make sure that information about your bankruptcy is accurately reported on your credit report.

Be wary of auto dealers, mortgage brokers, and lenders who advertise: "Bankruptcy? Bad Credit? No Credit? No Problem!" They may give you a loan after bankruptcy, but at a very high cost. The extra costs and fees on these loans can make it impossible for you to keep up the loan payments. Getting this kind of loan can ruin your chances to rebuild your credit.

You should also avoid credit offers that are aimed at recent bankruptcy filers. These may be an attempt to collect discharged debt in the form of a "disguised" reaffirmation agreement. For example, you should carefully read any credit card or other credit offer from a company that claims to own a debt you discharged or represent a lender you listed in your bankruptcy. This may be from a debt collection company that is trying to trick you into reaffirming a debt. The fine print of the credit offer or agreement will likely say that you will get new credit, but only if some or all of the balance from the discharged debt is added to the new account.

The next chapter contains a number of checklists to help you with your financial recovery.

20

Getting Back on Your Feet
A Checklist

This book has focused on the importance of making the best decisions possible during periods of financial distress. Many of the choices you must make to deal with urgent debt problems are temporary and can be reversed when your financial circumstances improve. Once you start resolving your financial problems, it is important to make choices for the future which will help you avoid getting into trouble again. This checklist is intended to be used as a guide for thinking about your financial life once your current debt problems are resolved.

I. YOUR BUDGET

You should not give up your new budget just because you are no longer facing a crisis. However, once your financial situation has changed, you should take another look to see if there is room to make some changes.

When faced with a financial crisis, you learned what your family can do without. In reexamining your budget keep in mind what your family's true needs are. Here are some suggestions about issues to consider:

- Can you start rebuilding your savings account? Savings is an important part of getting back on your feet. Your savings account can help to protect you against new financial problems if they arise.
- Did you postpone home maintenance or other necessities? These may

now be priorities.

- Did you cut back in areas, like auto maintenance, that require special attention in order to prevent future problems?
- Have you stopped paying any low-priority debts which you now wish to address?
- Did you reduce or eliminate contributions to a retirement plan or borrow against that plan? Do you need to resume contributions or repay a retirement plan loan in order to provide for a stable retirement?
- Did you reduce insurance or medical coverages to save money temporarily? Is it necessary to restore the original coverage?

II. YOUR CREDIT CARD CHOICES

You are likely to continue to get offers for credit cards despite your recent financial problems. While access to some credit can be necessary, you want to avoid getting back in over your head.

- Have you reduced your reliance on credit card spending? Can you start to pay your balance in full each month to avoid new problems?
- Do you have the cheapest available credit card? Do you understand all of its terms? (See Chapter Five.)
- Have you resolved any disputes about how much is due?
- Can you pay more than the minimum amount due so that you keep your balances manageable?
- Are you unnecessarily using a secured credit card, when an unsecured card at the same (or better) rate is available?
- Are you resisting "easy credit" offers that are too good to be true? These usually contain high fees and hidden costs.

III. PROTECTING YOUR HOME OR APARTMENT

To make sure that you can keep your home for the long term, here are some things to consider:

- If you have caught up on home mortgage or lease payments, have you reviewed your recent bills to make sure that your mortgage company or landlord thinks you are caught up as well? Has the lender or landlord properly credited all necessary payments? Have all court cases related to foreclosure or eviction been dropped?

- Is your current savings plan sufficient to protect you if urgent home repair needs arise in the future? Is your savings plan sufficient to help you get through any new period of financial difficulties?
- If you find that you are continuing to struggle financially, have you thought about moving to a cheaper residence? Would it relieve pressure for your family if you spent less on housing?
- Have you implemented utility conservation measures which will make your home less expensive to maintain in the long term?
- Have you shopped around for home insurance at the best possible rate?
- Have you applied for any real estate tax abatement you may be entitled to?
- Have you received a larger than expected escrow payment increase from your mortgage company? (If you are caught up on back-payments, this may be in error. Some mortgage companies are careless about escrow accounting. If you can't get the issue resolved quickly, you may want to see a lawyer.)

IV. IF YOU FILED FOR BANKRUPTCY

A bankruptcy case may have gone a long way toward helping you resolve financial problems. Some follow-up actions to consider that may be necessary include:

- Did you receive a copy of your bankruptcy discharge and have you put it in a safe place?
- Do you know what debts you still have to pay because they were not covered by your bankruptcy discharge? (If not, check with your lawyer or review Chapter Nineteen.)
- Have you checked your credit report to make sure that the debts discharged in your bankruptcy are being listed with an outstanding balance of $0? (If not, review your credit report and correct any errors as described in Chapter Three.)
- Are you still hearing from collection agencies or others about debts you

thought were eliminated in bankruptcy? (If so, check with your lawyer.)

- If you successfully completed a chapter 13 bankruptcy case, are you still getting correspondence which indicates that your home or auto lender thinks you are behind? (If so, see your lawyer.)
- Have you dealt with the problems which caused you to file bankruptcy in the first place? Will you be able to avoid filing again in the future?

V. REBUILDING CREDIT

As discussed in Chapter Three, if you have had financial problems, there are likely to be some things on your credit report which won't go away easily. However, there are some things you can do which may make things easier for you in the future.

- Have you checked your credit report to make sure it is accurate? (For more information including how to order a report, see Chapter Three.)
- Have you resolved any disputes about your credit report or sent the reporting agencies an explanatory statement to include when it distributes your report? (See Chapter Three.)
- Are you establishing better credit habits which will show new creditors that you are responsible? Have you tried borrowing a small amount of money and then repaying it immediately to show potential lenders that you can manage your debts?
- Have you canceled unnecessary credit cards and lines of credit which may make new creditors concerned about your potential to become overextended?
- Are you still getting credit card solicitations in the mail? Have you limited yourself to one unsecured credit card on the best terms offered?
- Have you opted out of pre-screening credit card offers? To do this, call 1-888-5-OPTOUT (1-888-567-8688). The three major credit bureaus use this same toll-free number to let you choose not to receive credit offers based on their lists.
- Are you shopping around for credit on fair terms? (If not, you may be making a mistake. Don't assume that, because one creditor tells you that you are a poor credit risk, others will tell you that as well.)

- When you apply for credit for big ticket items, like a home or car, are you providing a good explanation for your financial problems along with evidence showing that they have been resolved?
- Are you worrying about your credit report unnecessarily? Having resolved your financial problems, can you make a decision to reduce your reliance on credit for several years so that you don't have the pressure of new difficulties?

VI. AVOIDING SCAMS

Consumer scams are often targeted against people that have had recent financial problems. A company may get your name from bankruptcy court records, foreclosure records, or by purchasing lists from debt collectors. Some of these companies assume that you will be desperate enough to make bad decisions about credit. Here are some scams to avoid:

- **Paying for credit repair.** No credit repair agency can clean up your credit record if you have been behind on many debts. Promises to do so are lies designed to get you to pay for something that can't really help you. The self-help strategies discussed above and in Chapter Three are much more likely to help you get back on your feet.
- **Taking high-rate loans to tide you over.** Some lenders offer high-rate loans to help you get back into the market for credit. The worst of these are high-interest rate loans secured by your home. These lenders are counting on your belief that you cannot get credit on better terms elsewhere. They also may make false promises that the rate can be reduced if you establish a year or more of timely payments. Lenders offering high-rate credit in these circumstances are only trying to rip you off. See Chapters Six and Seven for more information about the choices that can cause the most problems.
- **Don't immediately accept a lender's statement that you are a "sub-prime" borrower who must pay very high interest rates to get credit.** You should always shop around rather than accept a higher than normal rate loan. You may have perfectly good credit in the eyes of another lender. Even if you are considered a high-risk, "sub-prime" borrower by every lender you contact, there are many types of sub-prime loans. You should shop among the different sub-prime loans until you find a reasonable rate and reasonable terms.

- **Beware of people or companies that market their services as "loan brokers."** Although some loan brokers are honest, there are others who will find a loan for you on the worst terms possible because high-rate lenders will pay them the biggest commissions. Brokers who advertise to people with a history of financial problems are among the most likely to be unscrupulous.
- **Beware of companies that advertise with claims such as "no credit check" or "bad credit no problem."** These companies are either loan brokers or lenders that are looking for borrowers who consider themselves too risky to pass a credit check. Companies that pretend they do not care about your credit record say so in order to find borrowers willing to sign up for high rates. You may discover that, when reputable lenders evaluate your credit record, they will find that you are a better credit risk than you might think.

SOME FINAL THOUGHTS

The first hurdle for many people coming out of a financial crisis is to get over feeling ashamed about past problems. The reality is that nearly everyone in this country experiences some type of financial difficulties at one time or another. It is nothing to be embarrassed about. It is important to be up-front with new creditors or lenders and not be afraid to acknowledge that you have had problems. Emphasize that you are back on your feet and financially stable.

Feelings of embarrassment might lead you to try to wipe the slate clean too quickly. This can be a mistake. It is important to realize that, even though not all past problems can be erased or covered up, most creditors and lenders understand that people fall on hard times and are usually willing to help you if you can prove that you are no longer facing financial problems.

Before you try to rebuild your credit, make sure that your past financial problems are fully fixed. Don't be too eager to take on substantial new debt. The most critical step in rebuilding is not necessarily the number of new credit cards that you have but, rather, evidence of your ongoing ability to repay loans or credit. Perhaps the worst thing you can do is to take on too much new credit too soon and fail a second time. It is best to rebuild your credit history by focusing on stabilizing your income and keeping your debt burden low.

Appendix

BUDGET CHARTS

MONTHLY INCOME BUDGET

	YOU	YOUR SPOUSE, PARTNER, OR OTHER CONTRIBUTING HOUSEHOLD MEMBER	TOTAL
Employment (1)	$	$	
Overtime			
Child Support/Alimony (2)			
Pension			
Interest			
Public Benefits (3)			
Dividends			
Trust Payments			
Royalties			
Rents Received			
Help from Friends or Relatives			
Other (List)			
TOTAL (MONTHLY)	$	$	$

We recommend that you make copies of this chart and use a new chart each month.

NOTES

(1) You can list either your take-home pay or your total employment income. If you use the total, remember to list all of your payroll deductions
as expenses in the expense budget chart. If you use your take-home pay, remember to check your pay stub to make sure that there are no unnecessary deductions.

(2) Include only the amounts you are actually expecting to receive if any.

(3) This should include all money received from public benefits each month including food stamps, welfare, Social Security, disability, unemployment compensation, worker's compensation, etc. If you are receiving more than one type of income, then you may want to use the box labeled as "other" at the bottom of the income budget chart.

MONTHLY EXPENSE BUDGET

TYPE OF EXPENSE (1)	TOTAL
Payroll Deductions (2)	
Income Tax Withheld	
Social Security	
FICA	
Wage Garnishments	
Credit Union	
Other	
Home Related Expenses	
Mortgage or Rent (3)	
Second Mortgage	
Third Mortgage	
Real Estate Taxes (4)	
Insurance (5)	
Condo Fees & Assessments	
Mobile Home Lot Rent	
Home Maintenance/Upkeep	
Other	
Utilities	
Gas	
Electric	
Oil	
Water/Sewer	
Telephone:	
Land Line	
Cell	
Cable TV	
Internet	
Other	
Food	
Eating Out	
Groceries	
Clothing	
Laundry and Cleaning	
SUBTOTAL PAGE 1	

MONTHLY EXPENSE BUDGET (cont.)

TYPE OF EXPENSE (1)	TOTAL
Medical (6)	
Current Needs	
Prescriptions	
Dental	
Insurance Co-Payments or Premiums	
Other	
Transportation	
Auto Payments	
Car Insurance	
Gas and Maintenance	
Public Transportation	
Life Insurance	
Alimony or Support Paid	
Student Loan Payments	
Entertainment	
Newspapers/Magazines	
Pet Expenses	
Amounts Owed on Debts (7)	
Credit Card	
Credit Card	
Credit Card	
Medical Bill (8)	
Medical Bill	
Other Back-Bills (List) (9)	
Cosigned Debts	
Business Debts (List)	
Other Expenses (List) (10)	
Miscellaneous (11)	
TOTAL	

We recommend that you make copies of this chart and use a new chart each month.

INCOME AND EXPENSE TOTALS

A. Total Projected Monthly Income		_____
B. Total Projected Monthly Expenses	–	_____
Excess Income or Shortfall (A minus B)	=	_____

NOTES

(1) Include the total expenses of everyone in your household who shares expenses.

(2) Do *not* fill out this section if you have used your take-home pay in your income budget. However, you should check your pay stub to make sure that there are no unnecessary deductions from your pay. *Do fill out this section if you used your gross employment income budget or if you are self employed.*

(3) Include amounts here only for your primary home. If you have a vacation home or a time share, include that below under "other expenses." This will help you determine whether you can make ends meet by giving up your second home or time share.

(4) Include your real estate taxes only if these amounts are not included with your escrow payment on your mortgage.

(5) Include your home insurance payments if these amounts are for renter's insurance or if they are not included with your escrow payment on your mortgage.

(6) This should not include your back bills. Back medical bills are unsecured debts which should be handled differently in your budget and listed below under "Amounts Owed on Debts."

(7) List here the monthly payments you plan to make on your unsecured debts like credit cards and medical bills.

(8) List your back bills here. Current anticipated medical expenses should be listed separately above as a higher priority expense. Old bills can generally be dealt with like other low priority unsecured debts.

(9) Some examples might include other debts owed to professionals such as lawyers or accountants, personal loans, bills owed to prior landlords, deficiency claims on prior foreclosures or repossessions and any other debt for which the creditor has no collateral.

(10) Everyone has a different situation. You should think about any other source of regular household expenses and list them here. Some frequently overlooked items include cigarettes, diapers, children's allowances, lay-away payments, rent-to-own, etc. Some of these items can be quite costly and will throw your budget out of whack if they are not accounted for.

(11) You may want to include a small sum here for the miscellaneous small expenses or for the emergencies which are unaccounted for elsewhere.

Visit SurvivingDebt.org

Go to www.survivingdebt.org to find more information on how to get legal assistance. The website also has free consumer information, including consumer brochures on credit reports and credit scores, loans, banking, tax refunds, mortgages, home improvement scams, utility service, bankruptcy, and more. Check the website for future updates.

CONSUMER EDUCATION BROCHURES:

- The Truth About Credit Reports & Credit Repair Companies (Available in English, Chinese, Korean, Russian, Spanish, and Vietnamese)
- Don't Pay to Borrow Your Own Money: The Risks and Costs of Tax Refund Anticipation Loans (Available in English, Chinese, Spanish, Korean, Russian, and Vietnamese)
- High-Cost Home Loans: Don't Be a Target (Available in English, Chinese, and Spanish)
- Cashing Checks and Opening Bank Accounts: How to Save Money and Avoid Theft (Available in English, Chinese, Korean, Russian, Spanish, and Vietnamese)
- Beware of Dishonest Immigrant Consultants (Available in Chinese, English, Korean, Russian, Spanish, and Vietnamese)
- Shopping for Money Wire Transfer Services (Available in English, Chinese, Korean, Russian, Spanish, and Vietnamese)
- Borrower Beware: The High Cost of Small Loans, Pawn Brokers and Rent-to-Own Stores (Available in English, Chinese, Korean, Russian, Spanish, and Vietnamese)

EDUCATION BROCHURES FOR SENIORS (AND OTHER CONSUMERS)

- What You Should Know About Your Credit Report
- Tips for Consumers on Avoiding Foreclosure "Rescue" Scams
- Your Credit Card Rights

- Tips on Choosing a Reputable Credit Counseling Agency
- Dealing with Utility Companies Regarding Disputed Bills and Utility Deposits
- Protect Yourself from Identity Theft
- What You Should Know About Refinancing
- Tips for Seniors on Living Trusts
- Tips for Consumers on Reverse Mortgages
- What To Do If You've Become the Victim of Telemarketing Fraud
- When Your Social Security Benefits are Taken to Pay Back Money to the Federal Government
- Answers to Common Bankruptcy Questions
- Using Credit Wisely After Bankruptcy
- Your Legal Rights During and After Bankruptcy

INFORMATION FOR ADVOCATES AND SERVICE PROVIDERS WORKING WITH SENIORS AND OTHER CONSUMERS

- Dreams Foreclosed: Saving Older Americans from Foreclosure Rescue Scams
- Understanding Credit Scores
- Credit Card Debt and Credit Counseling
- Avoiding Living Trust Scams: A Quick Guide for Advocates
- Medical Debt and Seniors: How Consumer Law Can Help
- When You Can't Go Home Again: Using Consumer Law to Protect Nursing Facility Residents
- Dealing with Utility Companies Regarding Disputed Bills and Utility Deposits
- Advice for Seniors About Credit Cards
- How to Help Older Americans Avoid Loss of Utility Services
- INTERNET RESOURCES: Helpful Consumer and Elder Law Web Sites
- Spending the House: A Quick Guide for Advocates on Reverse Mortgages
- What to Do When Utility Service Has Been Disconnected
- Protecting Older Americans from Telemarketing Scams: A Quick Guide for Advocates

Bibliography

OTHER NCLC PUBLICATIONS

All National Consumer Law Publications can be ordered from Publications, National Consumer Law Center, 77 Summer Street, 10th Floor, Boston, MA 02110, 617-542-9595, FAX 617-542-8028, publications@nclc.org. To order by mail, please use the order form at the back of this volume. Visit **www.consumerlaw.org** to order securely on-line or for more information on all NCLC publications.

NCLC BOOKS FOR A GENERAL AUDIENCE

NCLC Guide to Surviving Debt: provides a great overview of consumer law. Everything a consumer, paralegal or new attorney needs to know about debt collectors, managing credit card debt, whether to refinance, credit card problems, home foreclosures, evictions, repossessions, credit reporting, utility terminations, student loans, budgeting, and bankruptcy.

NCLC Guide to The Rights of Utility Consumers: details the rights consumers have to obtain electric, gas, and other utility services, and the protections they have to prevent shut-offs or restore already-terminated service. The book also includes straightforward advice on bill payment options and tips on how to lower monthly bills. It explains how utilities set deposit amounts, the effect of outstanding bills owed by others or from prior addresses, how to apply for heating assistance, and how to dispute bills.

NCLC Surviving Credit Card Debt Workbook: provides strategies for consumers overwhelmed by credit card bills. It contains easy-to-use checklists of warning signs of credit card trouble and step-by-step advice on how to get out of credit card debt. The special advocate's section lists legal remedies and explains legal protections for consumers with credit card problems. The CD-Rom contains sample letters and forms, consumer education brochures, and more. (Bulk orders of 10 or more copies for this title only.)

NCLC Guide to Consumer Rights for Domestic Violence Survivors: provides practical advice to help survivors get back on their feet financially, and safely establish their economic independence addressing the effect of the abuser's credit history, joint debts and credit cards, identity theft by the abuser, economic redress, victim compensation funds, child support, divorce scams, and much more.

NCLC Guide to Mobile Homes: explains what consumers need to know about mobile home dealer practices, and what to look for in-depth about mobile home quality and defects, when not to buy a home, what to look for about delivery and installation, how to obtain warranty service, and tips on maintaining a home. Over 30 photographs graphically demonstrate construction details.

Return to Sender: Getting a Refund or Replacement for Your Lemon Car: describes how lemon laws work, what consumers and their lawyers should know to evaluate each other, how to develop the facts, legal rights, and how to handle both informal dispute resolution proceedings, and more.

National Consumer Law Center Consumer Education Brochures: NCLC has a wide array of brochures, some translated into other languages, that are available at www.survivingdebt.org.

INTRODUCTORY LEGAL BOOKS FOR COUNSELORS AND LAWYERS

Foreclosure Prevention Counseling: Preserving the American Dream with CD-Rom: Loaded with practical advice on stopping a threatened foreclosure, including how to obtain workout, tailored for six different types of mortgages: Fannie Mae and Freddie Mac, subprime, FHA-insured, VA, and Rural Housing Service. Also includes homeowner strategies for reducing and prioritizing debt, dealing with loan over-charges and servicing errors, legal protections against foreclosure, answering questions about bankruptcy, and homeowner options after the foreclosure sale.

STOP Predatory Lending: A Guide for Legal Advocates: provides a roadmap and practical legal strategy for litigating predatory lending abuses, from small loans to mortgage loans. The CD-Rom contains a credit math program, pleadings, legislative and administrative materials, and underwriting guidelines.

Bankruptcy Basics with Companion Website: a nuts and bolts guide for attorneys new to bankruptcy practice, that makes filings practical even after the 2005 amendments. Provides step-by-step instructions, from the client interview and completing the initial forms to the final discharge. Subscribers gain access to a dedicated website with bankruptcy forms software, a date calculator, sample pleadings, and other practice aids—all continuously updated.

LEGAL PRACTICE MANUALS FOR LAWYERS

The Consumer Credit and Sales Legal Practice Series contains 17 titles, each with a CD-Rom that allows users to copy information directly onto a word processor. Each manual is designed to be an attorney's primary practice guide and legal resource when representing clients in all fifty states on that consumer law topic, and is updated annually. The 17 titles are arranged into four "libraries":

DEBTOR RIGHTS LIBRARY

Consumer Bankruptcy Law and Practice: the definitive personal bankruptcy manual, with step-by-step instructions from initial interview to final discharge, and including consumers' rights as creditors when a merchant or landlord files for bankruptcy. Appendices and CD-Rom contain over 130 annotated pleadings, bankruptcy statutes, rules and fee schedules, an interview questionnaire, a client handout, and software to complete the latest versions of petitions and schedules.

Fair Debt Collection: the basic reference in the field, covering the Fair Debt Collection Practices Act and common law, state statutory and other federal debt collection protections. Appendices and companion CD-Rom contain sample pleadings and discovery, the FTC's Official Staff Commentary, all FTC staff opinion letters, and summaries of reported and unreported cases.

Repossessions: covers every aspect of motor vehicle, manufactured home and household goods repossessions and deficiency claims, and is the only treatise to go well beyond UCC Article 9 to also examine hundreds of other state and federal protections. The CD-Rom reprints numerous pleadings, statutes, and regulations.

Foreclosures: details what you need to protect a home from foreclosure, including how to negotiate workouts, foreclosure defenses, special protections for FHA, VA and RHS mortgages, servicer obligations, tax liens, and even steps to take after a foreclosure. The CD-Rom reprints sample pleadings, HUD, VA, and RHS handbooks, and other key materials.

Student Loan Law: student loan debt collection and collection fees; discharges based on closed school, false certification, failure to refund, disability, and bankruptcy; tax intercepts, wage garnishment, and offset of social security benefits; repayment plans, consolidation loans, deferments, and non-payment of loan based on school fraud. CD-Rom and appendices contain numerous forms, pleadings, interpretation letters and regulations.

Access to Utility Service: the only examination of consumer rights when dealing with regulated, de-regulated, and unregulated utilities, including telecommunications, terminations, billing errors, low-income payment plans, utility allowances in subsidized housing, LIHEAP, and weatherization. Includes summaries of state utility regulations.

CREDIT AND BANKING LIBRARY

Truth in Lending: detailed analysis of all aspects of TILA, the Consumer Leasing Act, and the Home Ownership and Equity Protection Act (HOEPA). Appendices and the CD-Rom contain the Acts, Reg. Z, Reg. M, and their Official Staff Commentaries, numerous sample pleadings, rescission notices, and two programs to compute APRs.

Fair Credit Reporting: the key resource for handling any type of credit reporting issue, from cleaning up blemished credit records to suing reporting agencies and creditors for inaccurate reports. Covers credit scoring, privacy issues, identity theft, the FCRA, the new FACTA provisions, the Credit Repair Organizations Act, state credit reporting and repair statutes, and common law claims.

Consumer Banking and Payments Law: unique analysis of consumer law (and NACHA rules) as to checks, money orders, credit, debit, and stored value cards, and banker's right of setoff. Also extensive treatment of electronic records and signatures, electronic transfer of food stamps, and direct deposits of federal payments. The CD-Rom and appendices reprint relevant agency interpretations and pleadings.

The Cost of Credit: a one-of-a-kind resource detailing state and federal regulation of consumer credit in all fifty states, federal usury preemption, explaining credit math, and how to challenge excessive credit charges and credit insurance. The CD-Rom includes a credit math program and hard-to-find agency interpretations.

Credit Discrimination: analysis of the Equal Credit Opportunity Act, Fair Housing Act, Civil Rights Acts, and state credit discrimination statutes, including reprints of all relevant federal interpretations, government enforcement actions, and numerous sample pleadings.

CONSUMER LITIGATION LIBRARY

Consumer Arbitration Agreements: numerous successful approaches to challenge the enforceability of a binding arbitration agreement, the interrelation of the Federal Arbitration Act and state law, class actions in arbitration, collections via arbitration, the right to discovery, and other topics. Appendices and CD-Rom include sample discovery, numerous briefs, arbitration service provider rules and affidavits as to arbitrator costs.

Consumer Class Actions: makes class action litigation manageable even for small offices, including numerous sample pleadings, class certification memoranda, discovery, class notices, settlement materials, and much more. Includes contributions from seven of the most experienced consumer class action litigators around the country.

Consumer Law Pleadings on CD-Rom: Over 1,000 notable recent pleadings from all types of consumer cases, including predatory lending, foreclosures, automobile fraud, lemon laws, debt collection, fair credit reporting, home improvement fraud, rent to own, student loans, and lender liability. Finding aids pinpoint the desired pleading in seconds, ready to paste into a word processing program.

DECEPTION AND WARRANTIES LIBRARY

Unfair and Deceptive Acts and Practices: the only practice manual covering all aspects of a deceptive practices case in every state. Special sections on automobile sales, the federal racketeering (RICO) statute, unfair insurance practices, and the FTC Holder Rule.

Automobile Fraud: examination of title law, odometer tampering, lemon laundering, sale of salvage and wrecked cars, undisclosed prior use, prior damage to new cars, numerous sample pleadings, and title search techniques.

Consumer Warranty Law: comprehensive treatment of new and used car lemon laws, the Magnuson-Moss Warranty Act, UCC Articles 2 and 2A, manufactured home, new home, and assistive device warranty laws, FTC Used Car Rule, tort theories, car repair and home improvement statutes, service contract and lease laws, with numerous sample pleadings.

 Consumer Law in a Box: combines all documents and software from the companion CD-Roms of the 17 NCLC titles listed above. Quickly pinpoint a document from thousands found on the CD-Rom through keyword searches and Internet-style navigation, links, bookmarks, and other finding aids.

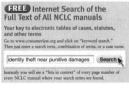 **Internet search of full text of NCLC's 17 legal manuals.** Visit www.consumerlaw.org and click on "keyword search" to find a list of all book titles and pages numbers from all NCLC legal manuals that satisfy your search terms.

OTHER NCLC PUBLICATIONS
FOR LAWYERS

 The Practice of Consumer Law: Seeking Economic Justice: contains an essential overview to consumer law and explains how to get started in a private or legal services consumer practice. Packed with practice pointers for even experienced consumer attorneys and invaluable sample pleadings on the CD-Rom.

NCLC REPORTS is a newsletter that covers the latest developments and ideas in the practice of consumer law, issued 24 times a year. Practice areas covered include: Bankruptcy and Foreclosures; Consumer Credit and Usury; Debt Collection and Repossessions; and Deceptive Practices and Warranties.

BOOKS BY OTHER PUBLISHERS

Center on Budget and Policy Priorities, *EITC Community Outreach Kit* is a particularly helpful resource on the earned income tax credit. It is designed for organizations and counselors to help them inform low-income families about their potential eligibility for tax refunds. The kit contains a fact sheet, eligibility guidelines, campaign posters, flyers printed in English and Spanish, and a summary of effective outreach strategies. To receive the kit, write to the EITC Campaign, Center on Budget and Policy Priorities, 820 1st Street, NE, #510, Washington, D.C. 20002, (202) 408-1080 or download the PDF files at the Center's website www.cbpp.org.

Draut, Tamara, *Strapped: Why America's 20- and 30-Somethings Can't Get Ahead* (2005) analyzes the economic and financial problems of younger Americans and possible solutions.

Elias, Leonard, & Renauer, *How to File for Chapter Seven Bankruptcy* (2007) is a guide for those attempting to file bankruptcy on their own. Available from Nolo, 950 Parker Street, Berkeley, California 94710, 800-728-3555. www.nolo.com.

Federal Home Mortgage Association, *Sellers' and Servicers' Guide* contains the guidelines all Freddie Mac lenders must utilize in foreclosing on a home and negotiating repayment schedules. For more information visit the website at www.freddiemac.com/singlefamily/getguide.htm or call AllRegs (800) 848-4904.

Federal National Mortgage Association, *Servicing Guide* contains the guidelines all Fannie Mae lenders must utilize in foreclosing on a home and negotiating repayment schedules. The guide can be viewed on-line at www.allregs.com/efnma.

Food Research Action Center, *Guide to the Food Stamp Program* (11th ed. 2006) is available for $40 directly from the Food Research Action Center, 1875 Connecticut Ave. NW, Suite 540, Washington. D.C. 20009-5728, 202-986-2200, or online at www.frac.org/pdf/flyerfsp.pdf.

Hendricks, Evan, *Credit Scores and Credit Reports: How the System Works, What You Can Do* (2004) includes practical information about credit scores, credit reports, privacy issues and identity theft.

Leonard, Robin, *Credit Repair* provides consumer-friendly information on credit reporting issues. Available from Nolo, 950 Parker Street, Berkeley, CA 94710, 800-728-3555. www.nolo.com.

Leonard, Robin, *Solve Your Money Troubles: Get Debt Collectors Off Your Back and Regain Financial Freedom* is a consumer self-help manual for certain types of consumer debt problems, such as straightening out a credit report or dealing with billing errors. Available from Nolo, 950 Parker Street, Berkeley, CA 94710, 800-728-3555. www.nolo.com.

Lord, Richard, *American Nightmare: Predatory Lending and the Foreclosure of the American Dream* (2004) explores the spread of predatory lending practices.

National Health Law Program, *Advocates' Guide to the Medicaid Program* (2001 ed.) is available for $135 for non-profit organizations and $235 for for-profit entities, educational institutions and government agencies from NHELP, 2639 S. La Cienega Blvd., Los Angeles, California 90034, 310-204-6010. www.healthlaw.org.

Scurlock, James D., *Maxed Out: Hard Times, Easy Credit and the Era of Predatory Lenders* (2007) is a companion book to a documentary exploring Americans' use and misuse of credit.

Singletary, Michelle, *Seven Money Mantras for a Richer Life* (2004) provides advice and personal stories about money management.

Sommer, Henry J., *Consumer Bankruptcy: The Complete Guide to Chapter 7 and Chapter 13 Personal Bankruptcy* (1994) provides information about bankruptcy from a national bankruptcy expert. Although published in 1994, it is a useful resource that should be supplemented with more current materials.

Strong, Howard, *What Every Credit Card User Needs to Know* (1999) includes almost everything you want to know about selecting and using credit cards. Includes numerous sample complaint letters as well as an in-depth look at the ins and outs of the credit card industry.

Warren, Elizabeth and Amelia Warren Tyagi, *The Two-Income Trap: Why Middle Class Parents Are Going Broke* (2003) contains startling facts on bankruptcy with a proposed set of innovative solutions for a growing number of families caught in financial distress.

PERIODICALS BY OTHER PUBLISHERS

Clearinghouse Review: Journal of Poverty Law and Policy (Sargent Shriver National Center on Poverty Law) covers recent developments in all areas of poverty law, including government assistance, rights of consumer debtors, housing issues, health law, and special issues relating to the elderly, migrant workers, immigrants, and veterans. Annual subscription is available from the Sargent Shriver National Center on Poverty Law, 50 E. Washington St., Suite 500, Chicago, Illinois 60602, 312-263-3830. www.povertylaw.org.

The Health Advocate (National Health Law Program), a quarterly publication concentrating on Medicaid benefits and other low income health law issues. It is available from NHELP, 2639 S. La Cienega Blvd., Los Angeles, CA 90034, 310-204-6010.

www.healthlaw.org. Information about cost is available on the website or by calling NHELP.

Washington Weekly (National Senior Citizens Law Center), a weekly publication focusing on issues of interest to seniors including Social Security, Medicare and other health issues. It is available from NSCLC, 1101 14th St., NW Suite 400, Washington, D.C. 20005, 202-289-6976. www.nsclc.org. Information about cost is available on the website or by calling NSCLC.

HELPFUL WEBSITES

Car Information
www.autosite.com
Good collection of resources regarding cars, including fact sheets, reports on used and new cars, and information on repairs and financing.

www.carwizard.com
Car pricing and safety information for used and new cars.

Kelly Blue Book: www.kbb.com
Information on new and used automobile prices and other automobile information.

Credit Bureaus (and to order credit reports):
Equifax: www.equifax.com

Experian (formerly TRW): www.experian.com

TransUnion: www.transunion.com

To order free reports: www.annualcreditreport.com.

Loan Information
Bankrate.com: www.bankrate.com
This website includes information about the cost of loans as well as a number of helpful calculators to understand the cost of car and mortgage loans as well as credit cards.

Coalition of Community Development Financial Institutions: www.cdfi.org

National Federation of Community Development Credit Unions: www.natfed.org.

Reverse Mortgages
U.S. Department of Housing and Urban Development: www.hud.gov

National Reverse Mortgage Counseling Network (as of 2006):
   National Foundation for Credit Counseling (NFCC): www.nfcc.org
   Money Management International (MMI): www.moneymanagement.org
   American Association of Retired Persons (AARP): www.aarp.org

General Consumer and Legal Sites
AARP: www.aarp.org
This website provides information about elder-related issues, including many consumer issues such as reverse mortgages and predatory lending.

American Bankruptcy Institute: www.abiworld.org
This website provides bankruptcy information for consumers and lawyers.

Americans for Fairness in Lending: www.affil.org
AFFIL is an organization that raises awareness of abusive credit and lending practices and works for re-regulation of the industry.

America Saves: www.americasaves.org
America Saves is a nationwide campaign in which a broad coalition of nonprofit, corporate, and government groups helps individuals and families save and build wealth.

Better Business Bureau: www.bbb.org
You can check on a businesses' complaint record or file a complaint on-line.

Center for Law and Social Policy: www.clasp.org
This website contains research and other information about economic security issues.

Center for Medicare Advocacy: www.medicareadvocacy.org
This non-profit center can tell you just about everything you need to know about Medicare.

Center for Responsible Lending: www.responsiblelending.org
The Center for Responsible Lending (CRL) is a unit of the Center for Community Self-Help (Self-Help), based in Durham, NC. The website provides a wealth of information for opponents of predatory lending.

Center on Budget and Policy Priorities: www.cbpp.org
Non-partisan research organization and policy institute that analyzes government policies and programs, particularly those affecting low- and moderate-income people. The Center is also an excellent resource for information about TANF (Temporary Aid to Needy Families) benefits and the Earned Income Tax Credit (EITC).

Consumer Action: www.consumer-action.org
A California-based consumer advocacy group that works on behalf of consumers nationwide. Consumer education information translated into a number of different languages is available on the website.

Consumer Federation of America: www.consumerfed.org
A membership organization that advocates for consumers. The website also has educational information for consumers.

Consumers Union: www.consumersunion.org
Consumers Union, publisher of *Consumer Reports*, is an independent, nonprofit testing and information organization serving consumers. The website includes information on a wide range of consumer topics.

Credit Scoring: www.creditscoring.com
This is a private site that has news and information regarding credit scoring.

Demos: www.demos.org
A non-profit organization that publishes reports and other information about social and economic issues. The organization combines analysis with advocacy work.

National Association of Consumer Advocates: www.naca.net
Provides a listing of consumer attorney members throughout the country, divided by practice area. Also includes updated information on hot consumer topics and other events.

National Association of Consumer Bankruptcy Attorneys: www.nacba.org
Contains general information about consumer bankruptcy issues as well as referrals to bankruptcy attorneys nationwide.

National Consumer Law Center: www.consumerlaw.org
Updated to include information on key developments in consumer law. Also includes information on how to order NCLC publications, including books, periodicals and consumer education materials.

National Employment Law Project: www.nelp.org
NELP offers a wealth of resources dealing with work and employment issues. Various publications can be downloaded or ordered from the website or by contacting NELP at (212) 285-3025.

National Housing Law Project: www.nhlp.org
Provides information, resources and publications related to fair and affordable public and private housing for low-income renters and homeowners.

National Senior Citizens Law Center: www.nsclc.org
A very helpful website for the latest information on issues of particular interest to seniors. The focus is on Social Security, Medicare and other health issues.

Nolo Press: www.nolo.com
Well-known and respected national publisher of self-help legal manuals. The website contains information about how to order Nolo publications as well as helpful legal tips.

Penn State Dickinson School of Law Bankruptcy Pro Bono Directory:
www.dsl.psu.edu.
The "publications" section of this website contains a directory of national bankruptcy *pro bono* programs sorted by state.

Privacy Rights Clearinghouse: www.privacyrights.org
Privacy Rights Clearinghouse is a nonprofit consumer education, research and advocacy program. Their publications provide practical tips on privacy protection.

Project on Student Debt: www.projectonstudentdebt.org
The Project on Student Debt works to increase public understanding of student loan borrowing and the implications for America's families, economy, and society.

Student Loan Borrower Assistance Project (SLBAP): www.studentloanborrower assistance.org
The Student Loan Borrower Assistance Project is a National Consumer Law Center program that provides information about student loan rights and responsibilities for borrowers and advocates.

U.S. PIRG: www.uspirg.org
U.S. PIRG is the national advocacy office of the state public interest research groups.

Government Sites

Federal Emergency Management Agency: www.fema.gov
Information about disaster relief programs.

Federal Trade Commission: www.ftc.gov
Information from the FTC, including consumer education publications.

Housing and Urban Development: www.hud.gov
Includes information about HUD-approved housing and reverse mortgage counselors.

Internal Revenue Service: www.irs.gov
An IRS site that is helpful in answering basic tax filing and other questions.

Government Services Agency: www.pueblo.gsa.gov
The government's consumer information center. Contains direct links to federal indexes and agencies, consumer-help organizations, community nets and free nets and other sites providing helpful consumer information.

National Do Not Call Registry: www.donotcall.gov
Gives consumers the choice to reject telemarketing calls at home.

National Highway Traffic Safety Administration:
www.nhtsa.dot.gov/cars/problems.
Information about vehicle recalls, service bulletins, consumer complaints and safety investigations.

U.S. Department of Education: www.ed.gov
Offers a number of very helpful free publications, including Student Guide, a guidebook for understanding student loans and grants. The publications are also available through ED Pubs, P.O. Box 1398, Jessup, MD, 27094-1398; (877) 4ED-PUBS (433-7827).

Glossary

[Words in italics are separately defined in this glossary.]

Acceleration. When a *creditor* claims the total balance of a loan is due immediately. This cannot usually occur unless you have fallen behind on payments. In the case of a home mortgage, receipt of a letter stating that a loan has been "accelerated" is normally an important warning sign of foreclosure. See Chapter Twelve.

Accord and Satisfaction. This is the legal term which applies when you make clear that you consider your payment the full and final resolution of a disputed debt. If the creditor accepts the payment, the law treats that acceptance as the final payment of the debt.

Adjustable Rate Mortgage (ARM). A mortgage in which the interest rate can be adjusted at specified intervals by a given formula using an *index* and *margin*.

Amount Financed. The amount of money you are getting in a loan, calculated under rules required by federal law. This is the amount of money you are borrowing after deduction of certain loan charges that the *Truth in Lending Act* defines as *finance charges*. You should think of the amount financed as the real amount you are borrowing. You will find the amount financed for a loan on the *disclosure statement* that is given to you when the loan papers are signed. See Chapter Six.

Annual Percentage Rate. The interest rate on a loan expressed under rules required by federal law. It is more accurate to look at the annual percentage rate (as opposed to the stated interest rate) to determine the true cost of a loan, because it tells you the full cost of the loan including many of the lender's fees. You will find the annual percentage rate for a loan on the *disclosure statement* that is given to you when the loan papers are signed. See Chapter Six.

Answer. In a lawsuit, this is a legal document that the *defendant* must file to respond to the claims being raised. There are often short time deadlines to file an answer. Failure to file an answer can result in a *default judgment*. See Chapter Nine.

Appraisal. An estimate of the value of property made by a qualified professional called an "appraiser."

Arrears. The total amount you are behind on a debt. Usually the amount of all back payments plus any collection costs.

Assignment. The transfer of a *mortgage* or *deed of trust* to another party usually evidenced by a document showing that the current mortgage holder (assignor) assigned its rights to the new holder (assignee).

Attachment. A legal process that allows a creditor to "attach" a *lien* to property that you own. Depending on state law, almost any kind of property may be subject to attachment, including your home, automobile, bank accounts, and wages. Once a *lien* is attached to the property, you may face further collection action on that property, including *execution, garnishment* or *foreclosure*. See Chapters Nine and Seventeen.

Automatic Stay. An automatic end to credit collection activity. Filing bankruptcy is the only way to get this protection. See Chapter Nineteen.

Auto/Car Title Loan. A short-term loan secured by a borrower's car title. See Chapter Seven.

Balloon Payment. A large lump-sum *payment* that is due as the last payment on a loan. Often used by lenders as a way to make monthly payments artificially low.

Bankruptcy. A legal process available in all states that allows you to address your debt problems according to a set of special rules while getting protection from continued collection activity. See Chapter Nineteen.

Bond. Amounts required by a court order to protect a party to a lawsuit while the case proceeds. A bond may be required in some circumstances to pursue an appeal. See Chapter Nine.

Bounce Loans. A short-term loan granted by a bank to cover an overdraft incurred by using either paper checks or debit cards. Banks charge high penalty fees for each overdraft, ranging from $20 to $35 per overdraft plus a per-day fee of $2 to $5 at some banks until the account is brought to a positive balance. With "bounce loan" programs, banks pay themselves back the amount of the overdraft and fees out of the next deposit. See Chapter Seven.

Capitalization. Capitalization occurs when items owed on a loan are treated as part of a new principal balance. When *arrears* are "capitalized," the amount of the arrears is included in the principal before the interest rate is applied. Often, capitalization and *reamortization* go hand in hand. If the arrears are "capitalized" and the loan is "reamortized," your lender will recalculate your payment using the existing interest rate and the new principal balance.

Chapter 7 Bankruptcy. See *liquidation*.

Chapter 13 Bankruptcy. See *reorganization*.

Closed-End Loan. A loan with a fixed term.

Closing. The process of signing loan papers which obligate the borrower to repay a loan. This term is associated with the signing of a mortgage loan. It is also called the *settlement*.

Collateral. Property put up to secure a loan. If you have given a creditor collateral, that creditor can normally take and sell the collateral if you are not able to repay the loan. A creditor with collateral is normally known as a *"secured creditor."* See Chapter One.

Collection-Proof. Also known as "judgment proof," this term is applied to people or businesses with property of minimal value, which can be entirely protected by *exemptions*. If you are collection-proof, it is difficult or sometimes impossible for any creditor to force you to pay a debt. See Chapters One and Nine.

Complaint. A document beginning a lawsuit. A complaint normally includes a statement of all of the claims being raised by the person bringing the lawsuit. See Chapter Nine.

Conventional Loan. A loan issued to a borrower with an excellent or very good *credit report or score*. Conventional loans do not include those insured by the federal government, such as the Federal Housing or Veterans Administration, or subprime loans.

Cosigner. A person who agrees to be responsible for someone else's debt. A cosigner is normally responsible for paying back a debt just as if he or she had received the money.

Counterclaim. A response to a lawsuit in which the person being sued raises legal claims against the person (or business) which started the case. For example, if you are sued by an automobile seller who claims you did not pay for a car, you might counterclaim that the car was a "lemon." See Chapter Nine.

Credit Bureau, also called consumer reporting agency or credit reporting agency. This is a company that receives information about a consumer's credit history and keeps records that are available to those seeking data about that consumer. See Chapter Three.

Credit Insurance. Insurance designed to pay off a borrower's mortgage debt if the borrower dies or is otherwise incapable of meeting the loan obligation.

Credit Report, also called a consumer report or a credit record, is the information about a consumer that a credit bureau has on file that it can report to others. The report includes the credit history and current status of a consumer's monthly payment obligations and public information such as bankruptcies, court *judgments*, and tax liens. See Chapter Three.

Credit Score. A credit score (sometimes called a "FICO" score), is a number that summarizes your credit history. The purpose of the score is to help lenders evaluate whether you are a risky borrower. See Chapter Three.

Creditor. Any person or business to whom you owe money.

Cure a Default. If you have defaulted on a debt, this is a process for correcting the *default*. Most often, a "cure" refers to getting caught up on missed payments (paying the *arrears*). A cure may also be called *reinstatement.*

Debt Collector. The most common use of this term applies to anyone who collects debts. However, under the federal *Fair Debt Collection Practices Act* "FDCPA," the term "debt collector" only applies to collection agencies and lawyers (or their employees) that are collecting debts for others. State laws may cover other types of collectors. See Chapter Eight.

Debt Consolidation. Refinancing debt into a new loan. In the mortgage lending context, relatively short-term, unsecured debt is often rolled into long-term mortgage loans, putting the home at greater risk. See Chapter Six.

Debt Management Plan. Debt management plans are offered by many credit counseling agencies. Through debt management plans (DMPs), consumers send the credit counseling agency a monthly payment, which the agency then distributes to the consumer's creditors. In return, the consumer is supposed to get a break, usually in the form of creditor agreements to waive fees and to lower interest rates. See Chapter Four.

Debt Settlement. Negotiation and settlement services are different from debt management services (see *Debt Management Plan*) mainly because the debt settlement agencies do not send regular monthly payments to creditors. Instead, these agencies generally maintain a consumer's funds in separate accounts, holding the money until the agency believes it can settle a consumer's debts for less than the full amount owed. See Chapter Four.

Debtor. Any person who owes money to another. In *bankruptcy,* the term "debtor" refers to the person who begins a bankruptcy case.

Debtor's Examination, also known as "post-judgment process," "asset examination," and "supplementary process." This is normally a court ordered proceeding in which a debtor must appear in court or in an attorney's office to answer questions about current income and assets from which a *judgment* may be collected. In many states, failure to appear at a debtor's examination can result in an arrest warrant. See Chapter Nine.

Deed. An instrument that transfers ownership from the seller to the buyer upon the closing of the sale.

Deed in Lieu. An agreement to turn real estate over to a lender as an alternative to *foreclosure.* See Chapter Eleven.

Deed of Trust. In some states, this is the term used for a pledge of real estate as *collateral.* It is similar to a *mortgage.*

Default. Failing to meet the requirements of an agreement. Most defaults involve failure to make required payments. However, other types of defaults are possible, including failure to maintain necessary insurance and failure to keep *collateral* in proper condition.

Default Judgment. A *judgment* in a lawsuit against a party who did not meet legal requirements in connection with the case. The most common reason for a default judgment is failing to file an *answer* or other necessary papers before deadlines specified by law. See Chapter Nine.

Default Rate. The interest rate the creditor will charge once the borrower defaults on the loan. If a default interest rate is listed in a loan contract, is will always be higher than the contract interest rate.

Defendant. In a lawsuit, this is the person or business that is being sued. See Chapter Nine.

Defense. A legal reason why a court should not award any or all of what is requested in a lawsuit. For example, a statement that the money is not owed is a defense to a collection lawsuit. See Chapter Nine.

Deficiency. The amount a debtor owes a creditor on a debt after the creditor seizes and sells the *collateral.* A deficiency arises when the collateral is sold for less than the amount of the debt. Normally, a creditor must bring a lawsuit to collect a deficiency. See Chapters Nine, Ten, and Sixteen.

Deposition. A proceeding in a legal case in which a person is asked questions about relevant facts (usually in a lawyer's office) and gives sworn answers under oath. Your deposition may be required if you start a lawsuit or if one is filed against you. Your lawyer may require depositions of others. Depositions are a normal part of the *discovery* process used to prepare for a court trial. See Chapter Nine.

Discharge. A document that ends a debtor's legally enforceable obligation to pay a debt. It is common to get a discharge of a mortgage debt after the mortgage is fully paid off. In addition, most bankruptcies result in a discharge at the end of the case that applies to many debts. See Chapters Ten and Nineteen.

Disclosure Statement. This term is commonly used to refer to the document that explains loan terms according to the *Truth in Lending Act.*

Discount Fees. See *points.*

Discovery. This term covers a variety of legal processes by which the parties to a lawsuit obtain information from each other and documents related to the case.

Equity. Your equity in property is the amount of cash you would keep if you sold property and paid off all of the liens on that property. For example, if you own a house worth $100,000, but you owe $60,000 on your original mortgage and $10,000 on a second mortgage, you have $30,000 in equity. The same principle applies to cars and other types of property.

Escrow. Amounts set aside for a particular purpose. A formal escrow usually requires a legal agreement that covers permissible usage of the escrow and how and where the money is to be kept. One type of escrow is money you pay to your mortgage company to cover taxes and insurance. Escrow is also used when you have a dispute with a creditor. You may choose to set up an escrow to pay the debt in the event you lose the dispute.

Eviction. A legal process terminating the right to occupy a home, apartment or business property. State law eviction proceedings are required before putting someone out. See Chapter Fourteen.

Execution. The process of enforcing a court judgment by taking property from the *defendant*. Execution of a judgment of *eviction*, for example, involves the sheriff or a public official putting the tenants out. Execution of a *judgment lien* involves seizing and selling the property subject to the lien. See Chapter Nine.

Exempt Property. Property that the law allows you to keep when you are being faced with collection on an *unsecured debt*. In *bankruptcy*, exempt property is protected from sale to satisfy the claims of creditors. Your exemption applies to your *equity* in the property after deduction for the amounts you owe to pay *liens* on that property. See Chapters Nine, Seventeen and Nineteen.

Exemptions. These are laws that give you the right to keep your *exempt property*.

Fair Credit Reporting Act. A federal (national) law that regulates *credit bureaus* and the use of credit reports. See Chapter Three.

Fair Debt Collection Practices Act. A federal (national) law that governs the conduct of debt collectors and that prevents many abusive collection tactics. See Chapter Eight.

Federal Law. A law of the United states that applies throughout the country. The *bankruptcy* law is an example of a federal law.

Finance Charge. The amount of money a loan will cost you expressed as a dollar figure. The finance charge includes the interest together with certain other loan charges specified by the *Truth in Lending Act*. You will find the loan's finance charge on the *disclosure statement* given to you when you sign the loan papers. See Chapters Six and Thirteen.

Finance Company. A company engaged in making loans to individuals or businesses. Unlike a bank, it does not receive deposits from the public.

Fixed-Rate Mortgage. A mortgage on which the interest rate is set for the term of the loan.

Force Placed Insurance. The insurance policy your lender will "force" you to purchase if your insurance is cancelled or if your lender does not have proof of your insurance coverage. Force placed insurance is *very* expensive.

Foreclosure. A legal process to terminate your ownership of real estate that is *collateral* for a debt, based on a *mortgage* or *deed of trust*. In some states, foreclosure involves a court proceeding ("judicial foreclosure"), while in others foreclosure occurs by creditor action alone ("non-judicial foreclosure"). See Chapters Ten through Thirteen.

Fraudulent Transfer. Giving away property to keep it out of the hands of creditors. The law allows *creditors* to sue to get the property back. See Chapter Seven.

Garnishment. A *creditor's* seizure, to satisfy a debt, of property belonging to the *debtor* that is in the possession of a third party. Usually a court has to authorize the seizure in advance. An example would be seizure of money in your bank account to repay a court judgment. Wages owed to you can also be garnished in many states. See Chapter Nine.

Guarantor. A person who agrees to pay another person's debt in the event that he or she does not pay. The term guarantor is often used interchangeably with *cosigner,* even though there are some minor legal distinctions in the collection process.

Hazard Insurance. Insurance that covers property loss or damage, usually paid for by borrowers and required when obtaining a mortgage.

Home Equity Loan. This term is generally used to describe any mortgage loan that is not used to finance the purchase of the home.

Home Ownership and Equity Protection Act (HOEPA). This is a federal (national) law that provides special protection to homeowners when they obtain home mortgage loans at high interest rates or with high fees.

Homestead Exemption. The right, available in most states and in the *bankruptcy* process, to treat your residence as *exempt property* that cannot be sold to satisfy the claims of *unsecured creditors.* In most states, the homestead exemption covers a certain dollar amount of your equity in your residence. A home cannot normally be sold to pay claims of your creditors unless your equity in the home exceeds the amount of the exemption. A homestead exemption will not normally protect you from *foreclosure* when you have voluntarily pledged your home as *collateral.* See Chapters Nine and Thirteen.

Index. A published rate often used to establish the interest rate charged on adjustable rate mortgages or to compare investment returns. Examples of commonly used indexes include Treasury bill rates, the prime rate, and LIBOR (the London Interbank Offered Rate).

Insolvent. A person or business that does not have sufficient assets to pay its debts.

Interest. The cost of borrowing money over time. Interest rates are expressed as a percentage.

Judgment. A determination by a court as to the outcome of a lawsuit, including any amounts owed.

Judgment Lien. A *lien* that attaches to property as the result of a *judgment.* For example, if you lose a collection lawsuit, the creditor normally has the right to an *attachment* on any real estate that you own.

Judgment-Proof. See *collection-proof.*

Lemon Law. This is a state law that gives you protection if you purchase an automobile that does not work properly and cannot easily be fixed. Most lemon laws only apply to new cars, but some also apply to used cars.

Levy. A process, in some states, for *attachment* of a *judgment lien* and/or *execution* of that *lien.*

Lien. Also called a "security interest," it is a legal interest taken by creditors in your property to secure repayment of a debt. A lien can be created voluntarily in connection with a loan, such as when you pledge real estate by giving a creditor a *mortgage* or *deed of trust.* A lien can also be created without your consent by *attachment* based on a court order. A creditor with a lien is called a *secured creditor.*

Liquidation. Sale of property to pay creditors. The term is also used as a shorthand name for the chapter 7 bankruptcy process, even though property is not always sold in that bankruptcy process. See Chapter Nineteen.

Margin. The number added to the *index* to determine the interest rate on an adjustable rate mortgage. For example, if the index rate is 6%, and the current note rate is 8.75%, the margin is 2.75%.

Mortgage. An agreement in which a property owner grants a *creditor* the right to satisfy a debt by selling the property in the event of a *default.* See Chapters Ten through Thirteen.

Mortgage Broker. An individual who offers to arrange financing for a consumer. Brokers are supposed to operate as agents for consumers, seeking the best products. States vary as to whether or not the brokers are regulated.

Mortgage Insurance. See *private mortgage insurance.*

Mortgage Servicer. A bank, mortgage company, or a similar business that communicates with property owners concerning their *mortgage* loans. The servicer usually works for another company that owns the mortgage. It may accept and record payments, negotiate *workouts,* and supervise the *foreclosure* process in the event of a *default.* See Chapters Ten and Eleven.

Negative Amortization. Negative amortization occurs when your payments do not cover the amount of interest due for that payment period. For example, if you have a $50,000 loan at 10% interest for fifteen years and make monthly payments of $400 a month, that loan will negatively amortize. At the end of the fifteen years, even if you make all of your payments, you will still owe more than $50,000. Negative amortization is usually associated with a large *balloon payment* due in the last month of the loan.

Negative Equity. Negative *equity* arises when the value of an item of property you own is less than the total you owe on all the liens on that property. For example, if you own a home worth $100,000 and borrow $125,000 to consolidate debts, you have negative equity of $25,000.

Non-Purchase Money Security Interest. A non-purchase money security interest arises when you agree to give a lender collateral that was not purchased with money from that loan. For example, a finance company may insist that you give a lawn-mower or living room set as collateral for a loan you take out to pay for car repairs. See Chapter Seventeen.

Non-Sufficient Funds (NSF). Fees are charged for non-sufficient funds (NSF) when a checking account is overdrawn. NSF fees are different than overdraft fees, which are charged for the extension of a loan using bank funds to cover the amount you would have overdrawn.

Note. This term is commonly used as a name for a contract involving the loan of money.

Notice of Right to Cancel. This document explains your right to cancel a loan in some circumstances. You should receive such a notice in connection with most door-to-door sales and for *mortgage* loans that are not used to buy your residence. Cancellation rights are discussed in Chapters Six and Thirteen.

Notice to Quit. In most states, this is a notice given by an owner of property (usually a landlord) demanding that a tenant leave within a specified period of time or face eviction proceedings. See Chapter Fourteen.

Open-Ended Loan. A loan without a definite term or end date.

Origination Fee. A fee paid to a lender for processing a loan application. It is stated as a percentage of the mortgage amount, or "*points*."

Overdraft Loans. Also called "bounce-check protection" or "courtesy overdraft protection," these are a form of high-cost, short-term credit. With these products, financial institutions cover their customers' overdrafts when they have a negative balance, and then charge them a fee. See Chapter Seven.

Payday Loan. (Also called "cash advances," "deferred presentment," "deferred deposits" or "check loans.") Payday loan customers write the lender a post-dated check or sign an authorization for the lender to take money out of an account electronically for a certain amount. The amount on the check equals the amount borrowed plus a fee that is either a percentage of the full amount of the check or a flat dollar amount. The check (or debit agreement) is then held for up to a month, usually until the customer's next payday or receipt of a government check. At the end of the agreed time period, the customer must either pay back the full amount of the check (more than what the lender gave out), allow the check to be cashed, or pay another fee to extend the loan. See Chapter Seven.

Personal Property. Property other than real estate.

Plaintiff. This is a person or business that begins a lawsuit.

Points/Loan Discount Points. A cost of the credit imposed by the lender. Points are prepaid in cash or financed as part of the loan principal. Each point is equal to 1% of the loan amount (for example, two points on a $100,000 mortgage would cost $2,000). Generally in the conventional market and sometimes in the subprime market, points are paid to lower the loan's interest rate. In that event, the points are called discount points.

Predatory Lending. A term for a variety of lending practices that strip wealth or income from borrowers. Predatory loans are typically much more expensive than justified by the risk associated with the loan. Characteristics of these loans may include, but are not limited to, excessive or hidden fees, charges for unnecessary products, high interest rates, terms designed to trap borrowers in debt, fraud, and refinances that do not provide any net benefit to the borrower.

Prepayment. Paying off all or part of the loan balance before it is due.

Prepayment Penalty. A fee charged by a lender if the borrower pays the loan off early. The lender's rationale for imposing prepayment penalties is to cover the loss of costs advanced by the lender at the time the loan is made. Mortgage loans with prepayment penalties often include a *yield spread premium payment* by the lender to the broker.

Pre-Sale. Sale of property in anticipation of *foreclosure* or *repossession,* usually with the lender's consent. A pre-sale is likely to lead to a higher sale price than foreclosure or repossession. See Chapter Eleven.

Principal. The amount borrowed.

Private Mortgage Insurance (PMI). Insurance provided by non-government insurers that protects lenders against loss if a borrower defaults. This insurance is usually required when a borrower makes less than a 20% down payment. When the borrower's equity in the property equals 20%, she may request that the insurance be cancelled.

Pro Se (also called pro per). Representing yourself (without an attorney) in a legal case or bankruptcy proceeding.

Punitive Damages. Special damages that are sometimes awarded in court to punish a party which is responsible for serious misconduct.

Purchase Money Mortgage. The mortgage loan obtained to purchase a home.

Purchase Money Security Interest. A lien on property that arises when you agree to allow a lender to take as collateral the property you are purchasing with the loan. See Chapter Seventeen.

Reaffirmation. An agreement in the *bankruptcy* process to pay back a debt that would otherwise be *discharged* in bankruptcy. Most reaffirmation agreements are a bad idea. See Chapter Nineteen.

Real Estate Settlement Procedures Act (RESPA). The purpose of this *federal law* is to protect consumers from unnecessarily high settlement charges and certain abusive practices that have developed in the residential real estate market. The law requires disclosures before and at the *closing* as well as periodically throughout the term of the mortgage loan. See Chapter Ten.

Reamortization. When a loan is reamortized, your payment is recalculated based on loan terms that are different from the original terms. For example, if you have paid for five years on a ten-year loan, your lender might consider starting the ten-year period again and recalculating your payments. This will lower your payments as discussed in Chapter Eleven. Similarly, your *arrears* may be *capitalized* (included in the principal) and your loan reamortized to reflect the higher principal balance on which interest is accruing.

Redeem. Recovering *collateral* from a *creditor* by paying the entire amount you owe whether past due or not.

Refinancing. The process of paying back old debts by borrowing new money either from an existing *creditor* or a new creditor. See Chapter Six.

Refund Anticipation Loan. See *tax refund anticipation loans.*

Reinstatement. The process of remedying a *default* so that the lender will treat you as if you had never fallen behind. See *curing a default.*

Rent to Own. Rent-to-own companies "rent" merchandise to a consumer for a stated period, after which the consumer owns the merchandise. A consumer pays over four times the value of the merchandise under a typical contract. See Chapter Two.

Reorganization (Chapter 13 Bankruptcy). This is a bankruptcy process to get relief from debts by making court-supervised payments over a period of time. The alternative is usually *liquidation* under chapter 7. See Chapter Nineteen.

Replevin. The legal process in which a creditor seeks to recover *personal property* on which it claims a *lien.* Replevin is often threatened, but rarely occurs. See Chapter Seventeen.

Repossession (often called "self-help repossession"). Seizure by the creditor of *collateral* after the debtor's *default,* usually without court supervision or permission. Repossession is most common in connection with car loans. See Chapters Sixteen and Seventeen.

Rescission. A right under some laws to cancel a contract or loan. The most common example of rescission arises in home equity loan transactions. You have the right to rescind that loan within the first three business days after the loan is signed. In some cases, if the *creditor* has violated the law, your right to rescind may continue after the three-day period is up.

Retaliatory Eviction. An *eviction* where a landlord seeks to punish a tenant for exercising his or her legal rights (such as complaining to the building inspector or forming a tenant's organization). See Chapter Fourteen.

Reverse Mortgage. A *refinancing* option usually available only to older homeowners who have built up substantial equity in their property. In a reverse mortgage, money is drawn based on the value of the property without an immediate repayment obligation, because the lender expects repayment by sale of the property at some point in the future. See Chapter Six.

Satisfaction. This is a legal document that states that a debt has been fully paid or that partial payment has been accepted as payment in full. A satisfaction is a type of *discharge*.

Secured Credit Cards. A credit card for which the card issuer requires that the card holder place a certain amount of money in a bank account with the card issuer. If the debtor does not repay the credit card, the card issuer can seize the money in the bank account. See Chapter Five.

Secured Creditor. Any *creditor* that has *collateral* for a debt.

Secured Debt. A debt for which the *creditor* has *collateral* in the form of a *mortgage, lien,* or *security interest* in certain items of property. The creditor can seize the property (*collateral*) if the *debtor defaults* in repayment of the debt.

Securitization. The process of investing in and providing capital for the creation of mortgage and other loans. See Chapter Eleven.

Security Interest. See "*Lien,*" above.

Self-help Repossession. This is a process by which a *creditor* that has taken property as *collateral* can *repossess* the property without first getting court permission. See Chapters Sixteen and Seventeen.

Servicer. See "*Mortgage Servicer,*" above.

Settlement. The *closing* of a mortgage loan. Also, the delivery of a loan or security to the buyer.

Settlement Statement (the "HUD-1"). *The Real Estate Settlement Procedures Act* requires lenders to give this disclosure at *closing* or one day in advance of closing if the consumer requests it. It should be the final statement of settlement costs. See Chapter Six.

Short Sale. A type of *pre-sale* in which the *creditor* agrees to let you sell property (usually real estate) for less than the full amount owed and to accept the proceeds of the sale as full *satisfaction* of the debt. See Chapter Eleven.

State Law. A law passed by an individual state that only applies to transactions in that state.

Statute. Another word for a law passed by a state or federal legislative body. Laws enacted by local entities, such as city councils, usually are called ordinances.

Subpoena. A document that is normally issued by a court in connection with a lawsuit, and that directs your attendance in a court or law office at a particular time. A subpoena may require production of documents related to the case.

Subprime Loan. A loan that is more expensive than a comparable prime loan. Subprime lending is generally defined as less than prime lending. This type of lending is designed to provide credit to borrowers with no credit history or past credit problems at a higher cost than *conventional loans*. Most of the *predatory loans* occur in the subprime market.

Summons (also called "original notice" or "notice of suit"). This is a document that is provided at the beginning of the lawsuit to tell the *defendant* what is being requested and what must be done to respond to the *complaint*. The term "summons" is also sometimes used interchangeably with *subpoena* for other legal papers that direct a person to be at a particular place at a particular time. See Chapter Nine.

Tax Refund Anticipation Loan. A loan to the *debtor* to be repaid out of the debtor's tax refund. The refund is often then sent directly to the lender. These loans can be very expensive. See Chapter Seven.

Trustee. A trustee is a person or business that is responsible for managing assets for others. In *bankruptcy*, the trustee is a person appointed to administer the bankruptcy case and its assets to maximize the recovery for unsecured creditors.

Truth in Lending Act. A federal (national) law that requires that most lenders, when they make a loan, provide standard form disclosures of the cost and payment terms of the loan.

Underwriting. The process of applying established lending criteria to the qualifications of a particular loan applicant.

Universal Default. Under a "universal default" policy, some credit card companies automatically hike their customer's interest rate for missing a payment, even if they missed a payment on a different card issued by a different company. See Chapter Five.

Unsecured Creditor. A *creditor* that has no *collateral* for the debt owed. See Chapter One.

Unsecured Debt. A debt that does not involve *collateral*.

Usury. The practice of lending and charging the borrower interest, especially at an exorbitant or illegally high rate.

Variable Rate. Interest rate that changes periodically in relation to an *index*.

Variable-Rate Mortgage. This is a mortgage loan on which the interest rate can change over time. The changes can affect the amount of your monthly payments. See Chapter Six.

Wage Assignment. An agreement to have wages paid to a person other than yourself. For example, some people assign a portion of their wages to be paid directly to cover a credit union bill.

Wage Garnishment. *Garnishment* of the *debtor's* wages from the debtor's employer. See Chapter Nine.

Warranty. Goods or services you purchase contain explicit and/or implicit promises (called warranties) that the goods or services sold will meet certain standards. A seller's failure to live up to warranties often can be a *defense* to repayment of the debt. See Chapter Nine.

Workout. This term covers a variety of negotiated agreements you might arrange with *creditors* to address a debt you are having trouble paying. Most commonly, the term is used with respect to agreements with a *mortgage* lender to restructure a loan to avoid *foreclosure.* See Chapter Eleven.

Yield Spread Premiums (YSP). A fee from a lender to a loan broker paid when the broker arranges a loan where the interest rate on the loan is inflated to an amount higher than the "par" rate. The "par rate" is the base rate at which the lender will make a loan to a particular borrower.

Index

ORDER FORM

- [ ] The NCLC Guide to Surviving Debt (2008 ed.) .... $20 ppd.
  (SAVE! $14 each for 5 or more, $12 for 20 or more, $8 for 100 or more.)
- [ ] Foreclosure Prevention Counseling with CD-Rom (2007) .... $50 ppd.
- [ ] STOP Predatory Lending with CD-Rom (2d ed. 2007) .... $60 ppd.
- [ ] The NCLC Guide to the Rights of Utility Consumers (2006 ed.) .... $15 ppd.
  (SAVE! $10 each for 5 or more. $7 each for 100 or more.)
- [ ] The NCLC Guide to Consumer Rights for Domestic Violence Survivors
  (2006 ed.) .... $60 ppd.
  (SAVE! $10 each for 5 or more. $7 each for 100 or more.)
- [ ] **10 copies** Surviving Credit Card Debt Workbooks with CD-Roms
  (2005 ed.) .... $40 ppd.
  (Minimum order of 10 copies; $4 for each additional copy over 10)
- [ ] The NCLC Guide to Mobile Homes (2002 ed.) .... $12 ppd.
- [ ] Return to Sender: Getting a Refund or Replacement for Your Lemon Car
  (2000 ed.) .... $16 ppd.

- [ ] **Please send me more information about NCLC books for counselors and lawyers.**

  Name _____

  Organization _____

  Street Address _____

  City _____ State _____ Zip _____

  Telephone _____

  E-mail _____

Mail to: National Consumer Law Center, Inc.
Publications Department

BEFORE   77 Summer Street, 10th Floor
Aug. 1, 2008   Boston, MA 02110

AFTER   7 Winthrop Square
Aug. 1, 2008   Boston, MA 02110

> **Telephone orders**
> 617-542-9595
> or FAX 617-542-8028
> for credit card orders

- [ ] Check or money order enclosed, payable
  to the National Consumer Law Center
  - [ ] MasterCard - [ ] DISCOVER - [ ] VISA - [ ] AMERICAN EXPRESS Cards

Card# ☐☐☐☐☐☐☐☐☐☐☐☐☐☐☐☐

Exp. date ☐☐☐☐   Signature _____

(card number, expiration date, and signature must accompany charge orders)

NATIONAL CONSUMER LAW CENTER
Tel. (617) 542-9595 • FAX (617) 542-8028 • publications@nclc.org

Order securely online at
www.consumerlaw.org

RECEIVED MAR 1 6 2